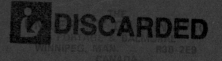

W. EDMUND CLARK is Director of the Long-Range and Structural Analysis Division of the federal Department of Finance.

With its emphasis on rural development as opposed to urban development. Tanzania has pursued an individual path in socialist development. This work is the first empirical analysis of public investment in matters of agriculture, education, rural health, manufacturing, and commerce, comparing the actual program of investment to the strategy outlined in the Arusha Declaration of 1967.

In *Socialist Development and Public Investment in Tanzania 1964-1973,* Dr Clark finds that Tanzania has been more successful in reorienting its program of social investment than its program of economic development. This failure stems from real differences within Tanzania, and among socialists generally, about appropriate investment strategies for a country at Tanzania's stage of development. In fact, no clear specification of an economic strategy exists and, as a result, policy has been heavily determined by the interests of the dominant political groups. It also reflects the fact that, in its initial stages, Tanzanian socialism was not a mass movement. It was imposed from the top and consequently, the bureaucracy remains relatively immune from the pressures of the people and the poverty in which they live.

Dr Clark argues that Nyerere's basic strategy is appropriate to Tanzania at a stage when it lacks the resources to pursue the traditional socialist goal of an integrated industrial economy, but that the implementation of this strategy should and must be improved. Skilfully blending political and social with economic analysis, he provides a provocative interpretation of socialist investment strategy in Tanzania and provides an illuminating perspective on the economics of developing countries.

W. EDMUND CLARK

Socialist Development and Public Investment in Tanzania, 1964-73

UNIVERSITY OF TORONTO PRESS

Toronto / Buffalo / London

© University of Toronto Press 1978
Toronto Buffalo London
Printed in Canada

Library of Congress Cataloging in Publication Data

Clark, W.Edmund, 1947-
Socialist development and public investment
in Tanzania, 1964-73.

Bibliography: p.
Includes index.
1. Government spending policy – Tanzania.
2. Tanzania – Public works. 3. Socialism in
Tanzania. I. Title. II. Title: Public
investment in Tanzania.
HC557.T3C56   332.6'725   77-8180
ISBN 0-8020-5376-9

TO MY MOTHER AND FATHER

Preface

I have always been annoyed when reading studies which were obviously published long after they were written. One is usually critical of the author for not going back to update his data and conclusions. It is particularly galling when he attempts to solve the problem by writing a new introduction, or a preface to the old introduction, which supposedly gives the impression of bringing the study up to date.

This study was written three years ago. Being partly guilty on the first count, I will not fall guilty on the second and claim that this preface can adequately serve as a replacement for such a revision.

The reader does have a right to know, however, whether or not the author feels that subsequent events have surprised him. This author does not. However, I will not claim perfect foresight. I have in fact been 'lucky' in that subsequent developments have supported my main theoretical conclusions to an unusual extent. Tanzania has not been so lucky.

Tanzania continues today to ignore its rural sector. It has suffered enormously in recent years because of this failure. The appeal of the large transformation project remains. While not accepting the basic goods industrial strategy in its entirety, the thrust is in that direction. Rural development continues to suffer as management skills and other economic resources are drained off in another direction.

There is a tendency in Tanzania, as in most countries, to look hard for exogenous factors to blame for its recent economic problems (in particular, shortage of foreign exchange and food crop failures). While such factors clearly were present, the main message should not be ignored. Nor should despair over the difficulty involved in achieving growth and the length of time required for such development lead one to believe that it can come quickly through the rapid transformation of any one sector. If economic development means in reality the development of people, which I believe it does, it is inevitably a slow process.

Tanzania, however, is a remarkable country. It has already achieved more than many countries with better resources. Let us all hope it can rise once more to the challenge of development and avoid the pitfalls into which so many countries have fallen.

W.E.C.

Acknowledgments

Most of the empirical work presented here was based upon data collected while I was in Tanzania on the University of Toronto Tanzania Project. I would like to thank the Director of the Project, David Nowlan, for the opportunity of going to Tanzania, and for the valuable intellectual insights with which he has provided me on the problems of development.

I wish also to thank the Harvard Development Service of Harvard University and the Canada Council for providing me with support for a year at Harvard while I wrote the thesis. In particular I would like to thank Ellen Delaney for her patience in providing me with secretarial help.

Professors Albert Hirschman and Arthur MacEwan both devoted considerable energy and time to reviewing the manuscript. Their efforts made a considerable difference in the quality of the work. As well, I should take this opportunity to thank them for the considerable amount which they managed to teach me about economics and development.

Rik Davidson of the University of Toronto Press and Alison Adair both made extremely valuable editorial comments.

I would like to thank the Tanzanians, and especially the workers at Devplan for allowing me the chance to experience their country and their attempt to build socialism. In particular I would like to thank Mr Charles Nyirabu who provided me with a much greater understanding of what socialism means in Tanzania.

The book has been published with the help of a grant from the Social Science Federation of Canada, using funds provided by the Canada Council, and a grant to the University of Toronto Press from the Andrew W. Mellon Foundation.

W.E.C.

Contents

Introduction

Tanzania is, in many ways, similar to most Third World countries. It has suffered under colonialism and had its social and economic structure distorted by international capitalism. It is very poor. Indeed, it is one of the poorest countries in the world. Yet it differs from most Third World countries, and from almost all African countries, in its strategy for development. Tanzania has rejected the traditional path of reliance on foreign private investment and its accompanying elite-oriented growth. Instead it has adopted a socialist strategy emphasizing equality. Moreover, Tanzania is attempting to build socialism without a revolution. Large parts of the economy remain in private hands, and the economy as a whole remains integrated into international capitalism. For socialist scholars in particular, but indeed for all scholars interested in the process of development, Tanzania presents an interesting attempt to develop an alternative strategy for development, and one worthy of serious study.

This study will attempt to make two contributions. The first is an empirical one. The writing on Tanzania has been largely dominated by political scientists and is often theoretical in nature. Most of the empirical work consists in duplicating tables presented in the development plans or in the economic surveys published by the government. There has been little work done by economists in re-working the official statistics, or in presenting published statistics not presented in the plans or surveys. The author spent a year revising the data on both parastatal and ministerial expenditure. As well, new data were collected and brought together. The result presented here is the first comprehensive analysis of what has actually happened to the pattern of public investment in Tanzania over the periods covered by the First and Second Five Year Plans. In particular, the study will seek to answer the question of whether or not the shift in ideology which occurred in Tanzania, and which was embodied in the Arusha

Declaration[1] of 1967, actually made a significant difference in the pattern of public investment.

The second type of contribution which the study attempts to make is theoretical. The analysis of the pattern of investment is made from the perspective of trying to determine why it occurred, and the implications of the Tanzanian experience for developing a strategy for socialist development. The study will examine the issue as to what is an appropriate investment strategy for socialist development in Tanzania. In doing so, it will also focus on the institutional/ bureaucratic structures and social/political developments which are necessary if such an investment strategy is to be successful. It will argue forcibly that the rural-oriented strategy developed by Nyerere is indeed the only one which will bring socialism to Tanzania.

The study is seen as part of the larger effort by scholars everywhere to turn their attention to the issue of how to build socialist societies. It is my belief that socialist scholars in particular should devote more of their energy to analysing the problems of socialist societies and the problems of transition to socialism, and somewhat less to criticizing capitalist societies. While anti-capitalist critiques can take us part way towards understanding how to build a socialist reality, they are not sufficient.[2] I will argue later that one cannot go from such critiques directly to a strategy of socialist development, for socialism is not simply the negation of capitalism.

I should pause here, and make some of my biases clear. In presenting the empirical side of the study I do so in a way which contrasts what has occurred with what was espoused in the Arusha Declaration. I take, therefore, the goal of rural-oriented socialism as a given.

I have chosen this method of presentation for two reasons. First, the goals were unusually well spelled out (although there were, as I will argue later on, important gaps), and therefore it is interesting in and of itself to examine the extent to which such goal enunciation influenced actual events.

Secondly, I have presented the data in this fashion because I believe that the thrust in the Arusha Declaration was essentially correct. I therefore implicitly reject the notion that the differences between what actually occurred, and what

1 This declaration will be discussed more fully in chapter 2. It set out in the clearest terms to date the strategy of development which Tanzania hoped to follow. In fact, Tanzania is also rare in the sense that it has a document which sets out a strategy sufficiently explicit that one can test whether or not it is being followed.

2 To be fair, one of the real problems confronting socialist scholars from capitalist societies is the very great difficulty in studying socialist societies. The societies they know best are capitalist. Access to many socialist countries is difficult, and most socialist scholars find the alienation which is inherent in living temporarily in a socialist country very difficult to take in personal terms.

one might have expected to occur given the position taken by the Tanzanian leadership, reflected only a realization on the part of the bureaucracy of errors in those positions, and an adjustment of the policies to a more pragmatic and sensible viewpoint.

To the uninitiated (i.e., uninitiated in the debates over socialist development strategies), it may seem unnecessary to stress my agreement with the thrust of Nyerere's ideas. To those familiar, however, with such debates, and particularly with these debates in Tanzania, it will be clear that there is no universal agreement on the basic soundness of Nyerere's approach. In fact, much of the writing on Tanzania by socialist scholars has been highly critical of his approach.

It may be helpful to the reader who is about to work his way through the maze of empirical results which makes up the central chapters of this study to anticipate a little the discussion in the final two chapters, so that he is aware of the contrasting viewpoints from which one can approach an examination of what has actually occurred in Tanzania. In these chapters I present two views of what ought to occur in Tanzania. One view, critical of Nyerere, stresses the need to develop a more self-sufficient economy, with an ability to produce self-generating growth. Essential to this strategy is a stress on the construction of an industrial base oriented toward the production of intermediate and basic goods. The advocates of this approach are sincere in their belief that it is the only strategy which will ensure socialist development in Tanzania. They are critical of what has gone on in Tanzania, but from a perspective quite different from my own.

The other view on a strategy for socialist development presented is my own. I say it is my own only to accept fully any criticism of it which others may have. Clearly it draws heavily on what Nyerere has said, and indeed on what has been written by many others on the development of countries other than Tanzania. I criticize what has occurred in Tanzania from the perspective of a comparison between reality and rhetoric, because I believe that the thrust of the rhetoric is correct. The opponents of Nyerere's views criticize what has occurred by contrasting it to another, quite different path of development.

In my view this other path (i.e., one involving the rapid development of an industrial base producing intermediate and basic goods) is as potentially damaging to the long-run socialist development of Tanzania as the deviations which have occurred from the original policy set out in the Arusha Declaration. The adoption of such a strategy will create an urban-oriented elite, and a class structure almost as exploitative and unacceptable as one produced by capitalist development. Moreover, there is a question of whether or not such a strategy is economically viable. There is a very real danger that Tanzania will partially embark on such a strategy only to find itself soon trapped in a quagmire of economic stagnation.

I do not intend in this introduction to engage the debate, but rather only to make the reader aware of the contrasting views concerning what type of development is desirable which one can bring to a study of empirical reality.

OUTLINE OF THE STUDY

In the first chapter I try to set out some of the background needed for this study. The concept of a socialist strategy of investment is defined. It involves two aspects: first, it is directed towards a multiplicity of goals, and not just towards an increase in material production, and second, its ultimate success depends very much on its being part of a much more comprehensive political strategy for the society as a whole. The key issues around which the investment strategy debate will focus are isolated. These issues are: equality and growth, roles of agriculture and industry, choice of technology, trade and integration, and urban/rural dichotomy. An attempt is made to outline briefly the main arguments which have been presented by both neo-classical and socialist economists on these issues.

In the next chapter I try to complete this background. Because a socialist strategy of investment must be embedded in a good understanding of the particular social, political, and economic structure of the society, an attempt is made in the first half of the chapter to provide the reader with this background. The second half of the chapter is devoted to outlining the official Tanzanian response to their situation. In particular, the development of an African brand of socialism by the President, Julius Nyerere, is traced from his early commitment to equality, to his most recent statements on decentralization. Nyerere's writings are examined in order to discern his position on each of the five issues isolated as being central to the debate on investment strategy.

The next four chapters are devoted to a review of the developments in Tanzania in the period 1964 to 1973 in relation to the pattern of public investment. The question of the extent to which the government has followed its declared ideology is closely studied. Chapter three is devoted to government ministerial expenditure. Chapters four and five deal with the investment by publicly-owned corporations, called parastatals in Tanzania. Chapter six looks at the financing of public investment and its effect on the pattern of spending, and analyses the issue of self-reliance.

The last three chapters of the study are analytical. In chapter seven I try to trace out some of the factors which account for the pattern of investment shown in chapters three to five. Such factors as the continued existence of class conflict, the force of exogenous constraints, the lack of an explicit strategy, and nationalism are discussed. In chapter eight I look at the response of several writers on Tanzania to events over the last ten years. Although this study is the first comprehensive empirical look at the pattern of investment, many writers have an intuitive feel for what has gone on, and many are quite critical. Much of this criticism is directed towards the inadequacies of Nyerere's strategy, and there has been some attempt to begin to define an alternative strategy. I will look closely at these alternative strategies.

Finally, in the last chapter, I attempt to bring the study together by proposing my own investment strategy for Tanzania. Essentially I argue that Nyerere has correctly assessed the present stage of development in which Tanzania finds itself. Although one might wish that Tanzania could advance at a faster pace towards a more highly industrialized and economically integrated society, it could do so at only a very high cost in terms of abandoning its non-economic goals, particularly the goal of equality. Nyerere's strategy has been inadequate because he has not committed himself, in explicit terms, to the issues which are crucial to an investment strategy. The time has come for him to do so, and to prevent the continued drift in policy. Nevertheless, his strategy is not inadequate in its basic understanding of Tanzanian society and its potential, and therefore should not be abandoned, but built upon.

One final aspect of the study should be mentioned at this point. In many ways it is critical of what has gone on in Tanzania, and of much of the intellectual work of socialists in Tanzania. This criticism should not be misinterpreted. One is critical of Tanzania only because its prospects for developing socialism are so much better than those anywhere else in Africa. Socialists feel frustrated if Tanzania is not wholly successful in building socialism. But one need only travel the world to see that Tanzania has, by any standard other than its own goals, achieved a great deal. The commitment to equality, criticized by so many as being naïve, stands in stark contrast to most of the rest of the world's, both capitalist and many socialist countries', willingness to allow the few to enjoy so much, while the many enjoy so little. The basic non-hierarchical relationships, the informality which characterizes Tanzania, is immediately apparent to any visitor to the country. The possibility of a truly socialist pattern of development does exist in Tanzania despite its awful colonial past. It is that possibility which calls forth the criticism, made by many writers, and also by this writer. It is hopeful and sympathetic criticism.

Similarly, in certain places, the study is critical of the ideas advanced by other writers, all socialists. This criticism as well should not be misconstrued. Anyone involved in radical politics cannot help but be dismayed at the way leftists devote so much of their energies to needless internal fights. I do not regard this study as falling into this category of dispute. The issue addressed by this study is a critical one, and goes to the heart of much that is important in socialism. Yet the very nature of the issue makes it difficult to know who is correct. Only history will tell, and even then it will not be clear whether or not another strategy would have been better. Thus I make no claim that I am right nor that I know the best strategy for Tanzania. I offer this study as only a small contribution to the debate in the hope, shared by most writers, that the more issues are discussed, and the more that is known about them, the better will be the ultimate decision.

SOCIALIST DEVELOPMENT AND

PUBLIC INVESTMENT IN TANZANIA 1964-73

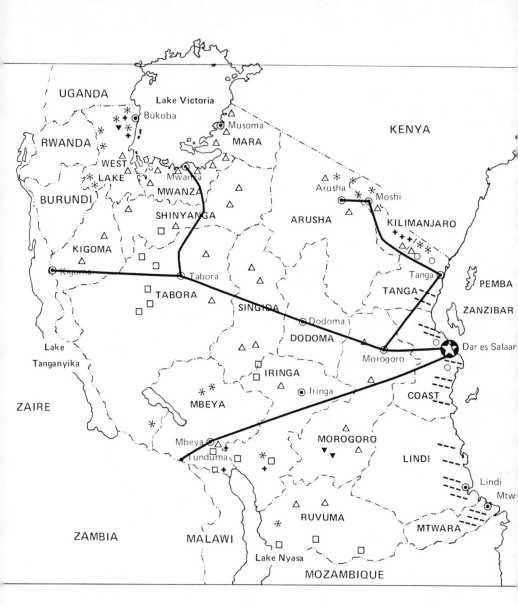

Sisal - ○ Coffee - ✳ Tobacco - ☐ Railways - ▬

Cotton - △ Tea - + Cashewnuts - ➳➳ Sugar - ▼

1

Issues and themes

Purpose of chapter
The focus of this study is the pattern of public investment in Tanzania over the ten-year period, 1964 to 1973. The orientation will be to examine this investment in order to explore its relation to the goal and reality of socialist development in Tanzania. In order to do so it is probably worthwhile to step back a little from Tanzania, and review briefly some of the more fundamental questions which must be asked about socialist development, and the answers which have been given in contexts other than Tanzania.

This chapter, then, will attempt to present some of the theoretical foundations behind the types of questions which I tried to answer from my data. As well, it will provide a broader perspective to the discussion, in the latter chapters of the study, on what strategy appears appropriate for Tanzania at this stage.

What is socialism?
To analyse a socialist investment strategy one must have a notion of what socialism is, for it is only with a firm idea of where one wants to go, that one can know how to get there.[1] Most socialists would agree that a socialist society is a democratic one, in which the benefits of increased production go to the mass of the population. By democratic, I mean a society in which people control their environment, both defined broadly in terms of the society as a whole and narrowly in terms of the work place and local

---

1 This does not imply, as we shall see, that knowing where one wants to go necessarily means knowing how to get there. Indeed, this study is partially devoted to examining the debate on this issue.

community.[2] While socialists probably disagree as to the level of material welfare which is desirable, there seems to be little debate on the view that a country as poor as Tanzania must significantly increase the level of production of the economy.

Socialist investment strategy

This study will be concerned with the issue of a socialist strategy of investment. What is such a strategy? A priori, there is no such thing as a socialist strategy of investment, although many writers, of both the left and the right, act as if there were. A socialist strategy of investment is that strategy which is most effective in encouraging the development of socialism. The particular strategy suitable for a specific country depends upon the historical situation in which that country finds itself. If there is one lesson which scholars can learn from Marx, and economists need to learn this more than most, it is that one must develop an economic strategy for a country by studying the reality of its current and historical political, social and class structure, as well as its economic position. A socialist strategy is one which moves a country towards socialism given this reality.

Thus, one must be suspicious of socialist scholars who cart around the same intellectual baggage to every country, proposing the same path to socialism for all. Surely, it is as absurd as the broken record of neo-classical economics ('emphasize primary exports, build a good climate for foreign investment, keep your tariffs low') which the international capitalist agencies have air-lifted for so long, record player and all, to every Third World country. To label anyone who argues that Tanzania must worry about primary product exports a bourgeois lackey, is as silly as accusing Cuba of selling out by abandoning its excessive industrialization drive to concentrate on sugar exports. What matters is the over-all strategy involved.

It is also clear that a correct investment strategy does not ensure socialist transformation. One chooses a strategy which encourages political, social, and economic developments which are conducive to socialist development. But the investment strategy is only one, and probably not the most important, factor among many. Socialism consists of many elements, and progress must be made on all fronts if socialism is to be built. Sweezy (1972) sets out six key elements of socialism. A socialist strategy must involve significant progress towards all these elements. They are: (i) equality, both materially and in terms of status; (ii) workers' participation in management *and* management's participation in work;

---

2 There is of course disagreement among socialists as to what is meant by control by the people, and what are the best methods of obtaining it. I will not get into that issue here.

(iii) complete freedom of discussion and criticism; (iv) agriculture and industry must be combined, urban conglomerations must be broken down; (v) work to be treated as life's most creative activity; (vi) an end to the system whereby earning and spending of incomes is the key mechanism for the distribution of goods.

Any socialist investment strategy must have implicit in it a programme which will ensure progress towards achieving all of Sweezy's goals. It necessarily runs the risks of encouraging the wrong type of social or political concomitant developments. One interesting throw-off of the present ecology movement in western societies is an increased awareness by all that it is very difficult to predict all the effects of any change. Nevertheless, any change involves risks, and these risks can be minimized only by developing a parallel political programme to accompany an economic programme. In chapter nine I call for a renewed commitment to Nyerere's basic emphasis on rural development, and a turning away from what I consider strategies which are based more on a sense of nationalism than on an understanding of the requirements for socialist development. These other strategies centre on the development of basic intermediate and capital goods industries. The danger in my strategy is that it leads to the development of the one sector which is still firmly in private hands. Thus a rapid development of the rural areas, at this stage, may well strengthen the tendency to develop a rural capitalist class. This result can be avoided only by a multi-sectoral approach. A rural investment strategy in the absence of any other programme would indeed have that effect. But, it is possible to devise a rural strategy which tries to direct the growth along co-operative lines – Ujamaa farming, Ujamaa factories, District Development Corporations, co-operatives, etc. If these institutions become the focus of the effort, the result will be a strengthening of socialism in Tanzania.

Thus a socialist investment strategy is distinguished from one that is purely economic by a number of things. First, its aim is socialism and this implies the acceptance of goals besides growth. Secondly, it is a strategy whose formulation depends heavily on an understanding of the political and social context of the situation, since the resulting political and social repercussions of the pattern of investment are considered as important as the economic effects. Thirdly, a socialist strategy of investment must be part of a much larger political strategy, involving the use of many different policy tools. A 'correct' investment strategy will not by itself lead to socialism.

There are, then, many elements in socialism and many tools or instruments which can be used to encourage its development. I have chosen to look at only one tool – investment. I have done so because it is the area with which I am most familiar. From 1971 to 1973 I worked in the Programming and Reporting Division of the central planning ministry. This division was chiefly responsible for monitoring the development programmes of the different central government ministries and government-controlled enterprises (called parastatals), and for co-ordinating the annual budget exercise at which time all investment decisions of these agencies were scrutinized and approved. In this position I was able to have an overview of the Tanzanian development effort. As well, I was forced to come to grips with some of the very difficult problems of developing a socialist invest-ment programme.

ISSUES IN CHOICE OF STRATEGY

There are a number of issues which lie at the heart of the debate over the best socialist investment strategy. Some of these centre on the question of how to maximize economic growth. As such, they draw on and are part of similar debates in neo-classical economics. Others are based on the differential emphasis placed by scholars on the key elements in socialism, or in the transition to socialism. This differential emphasis leads some writers to worry more about the impact of an investment strategy on a certain variable, equality for example, than do other writers. We shall look at each of these issues in turn.

Equality and growth
Perhaps no issue in either neo-classical economics or socialist debates engenders so much controversy or overlaps with so many other issues as the question of equality and economic growth. Neo-classical economists have traditionally phrased the issue as equality *versus* growth. Around this issue has grown up a whole set of literature devoted to estimating the cost, in terms of material output, of emphasizing equality.[3] The position usually held by neo-classical economists is that an equal distribution of income, by lowering the average savings ratio for the society, lowers the growth rate. Leibenstein (1963)[4] and Galenson have formed an investment selection criterion on the basis of this model: the most capital-intensive projects should be selected, because such pro-jects will increase the share of profits in the distribution of income, and thus raise the investment ratio.

   Neo-classical economists choose here, as they do in most issues, to separate the issues of growth and equity. They see the problems of inequality as being solved at some future date when the society has achieved a much higher level of output. Proponents of the growth before equity view point to work of people

---

3 See for example Cline (1972).
4 The view that unequal distribution of income increases savings has been challenged by a number of writers, and is not valid for situations where a Friedman-type consumption function is thought to apply.

like Kuznets (1966, 218-19) which show income differentials narrowing over time, as western nations developed.

Recently, this whole view has come under attack from within western economics. People like Seers[5] at the Sussex school reject it because of the social implications of ignoring equity considerations: the resulting social and political costs of uneven growth are seen as too great. These costs include increasing urban unemployment, political repression (as in Brazil), and the massive personal hardships the majority must endure. Others reject the notion that there is any long-run tendency for the benefits of development to trickle down and the distribution of income to become more even over time. They point out that a pattern apparent in the first countries to experience rapid industrial growth, especially when such growth involved massive movements of the population from one continent to another, will not necessarily be duplicated by countries developing at present.

One person who has made a significant switch in position is Mahbul ul Haq. Haq was one of the chief architects of the Pakistan strategy for development in the late 1950s and 1960s. The bankruptcy of the uneven growth model was nowhere more apparent than in Pakistan.[6] Haq now argues that the focus of a development strategy must be the elimination of poverty, not growth: '... the concerns for more production and better distribution should be brought together in defining the pattern of development, the present divorce between the two concerns must end ... the problem of development must be defined as a selective attack on the worse forms of poverty. Development goals must be defined in terms of progressive reduction and eventual elimination of malnutrition, disease, illiteracy, squalor, unemployment and inequalities' (1971, 12).

The notion that a trade-off exists between equity and growth has also been attacked. Such a trade-off implies that the critical variable in growth is investment. It implicitly assumes a simple Domar-like model of growth. But much of the literature in development economics has centred on showing that other variables, such as entrepreneurship, level of skills of the population, and technology are important. Since equity considerations can substantially influence

5 Seers has headed several studies on particular countries which set forth an employment-oriented approach to development. See ILO (1970, 1971, 1972), also Seers (1969).

6 Papanek (1967, 242) describes the inequality which was inherent in Pakistan's strategy of development in these words: 'The problem of inequality exists, but its importance must be put into perspective. First of all, the inequalities in incomes contribute to the growth of the economy which makes possible a real improvement for the lower-income groups. The concentration of income facilitates the high savings which finance development.'

these variables,[7] no simple relation between equity, savings, investment, and economic growth can be posited.

The issue of growth and equity has also been the focus of much debate among socialist scholars, especially when the experience of the Soviet Union is discussed. The Soviet model of development parallels, in many respects, that advanced by many neo-classical economists. Stalin, as we know, rejected equity considerations as important.[8] This lack of concern for equality implied an approach to such issues as the use of incentives, the capital intensity of investment, or the role of agriculture. The Chinese have rejected this view. To them, equality is the heart of socialism, and this opinion is shared by such western socialists as Sweezy (1972, 10): 'It is necessary to proclaim that egalitarianism is the most fundamental principle of a socialist society organized on Marxian lines.'

The Soviet approach places primacy on economic growth; the Chinese view this as unacceptable. To them, socialist development involves the over-all development of a society in which all will be equally well off, and equally powerful. As important to the Chinese as the issue of equal distribution of goods is that of breaking down the barriers that separate different groups of people. From this simple commitment flows a whole series of policy implications for patterns of investment. We shall look at these in more detail later. At this point, suffice it to say that the Chinese view the decision about investments as being concerned as much with equality as with growth.

MacEwan argues that concern over equality is essential if one wants to build democratic socialism. He also relates the issue of equality and the concern about growth:

Equality is another factor which, although usually viewed as a goal of socialist development, is an instrument for the establishment of democratic control. In a society characterized by widespread equality of income, social status, education and so forth − as is generally the case in both Cuba and China − there is no way to develop an ideology that would rationalize control being in the hands of an elite group. In other words, social and material equality are incompatible with inequality of power, and accordingly establishment of social and material equality provides a foundation for democratic control ... When production is put

7 There is much evidence to suggest that investment in the health and education of workers produces dividends in terms of increased output. Moreover, the more subtle but no less significant aspect of training a labour force is ignored in any analysis which accepts uneven growth.

8 The ideal of equality was, in Stalin's view, a 'reactionary, petty bourgeois absurdity worthy of a primitive sect of ascetics but not a socialist society organized on Marxian lines.' Quoted from Deutscher, (1960, 338)

forth as the overriding goal of social organization, there is a firm basis for the rise of experts, bureaucrats and administrators, because these people can make an immediate contribution to the dominant goal. But when a revolutionary society stresses from the outset such goals as equality and mass participation, and when socialist development is seen as a *simultaneous* transformation of productive forces and social relations, the special importance of experts *et al.* is reduced. Consequently, there is an inhibition on the rise to power of such elite segments (1974, 55).

The issue of equality and growth is also sometimes seen as a question of the use of personal incentives. Neo-classical economists (see Riskin, 1973) have a theory of behaviour which postulates that people will work only if directly and immediately rewarded in proportion to their output. Again, the Soviet Union has accepted much of this argument. The Chinese (see Gurley, 1970) and Cubans (see Silverman, ed., 1971) as well as many western socialists[9] reject this view. It is not important for this study to review the arguments of this debate in detail. However, there are two major points which are important to an analysis of investment strategy. First, the discussion on the use of incentives brings to the fore the question of whether or not socialist society must strive for *simultaneous* or *sequential*[10] development. Those who argue for simultaneous development fear that if the other goals of socialist development are temporarily abandoned, they will be lost forever. As a result they insist that one must strive toward all the goals of socialist development at once. In particular they reject the view that there should be an attempt to raise the level of material welfare of the society through the use of incentives, and the suppression of democratic control before implementing equality and workers' control.[11]

Secondly, the debate on incentives is important because it points to the necessity of the multi-sectoral approach. Collective incentives are influential in bringing about equality, but they are only one aspect. If the pattern of

9 Carl Riskin (1973) summarizes the case against the neo-classical view of incentives.
10 I am indebted to Arthur MacEwan for this term.
11 Ché Guevara was a strong proponent of simultaneous development. He attacked the sequential view in the following way. 'The contrary [sequential view] would be to assume that the task of building socialism in a backward society is in the nature of an historical accident and that its leaders, in order to excuse the *mistake* should strive to consolidate all the categories inherent in the intermediate society [capitalist society]. All that would remain as foundations of the new society would be the distribution of income according to labor and the tendency to eliminate man's exploitation of man. These things alone seem inadequate as the means to bring about the enormous change in conscience needed to face the transition.' (See Ernesto Che Guevara, 'On the Budgetary Finance System,' Silverman, ed., 1971, emphasis in original).

investment is such that differences between groups are reinforced, then real equality will not be achieved.[12] It is easy to imagine a situation of collective incentives where the pattern of investment was such as to produce great differences in the welfare of the different collective groups. Even if taxes ameliorated the differences in material welfare, they would not reduce the differences in status, differences which people like Mao have stressed as being at least as important as material ones. Similarly, an investment policy which creates greater equality in the society will be ineffective if collective incentives are not introduced in the production units.

Thus the issue of equality and growth can be seen as essential in any discussion of investment strategy. If one accepts the notion that socialist development involves the simultaneous progress towards several goals, then the investment strategy must be one which achieves growth with equality. It is, however, clear that many socialists reject the need for simultaneous development, or are at least willing to place primacy on one goal, usually growth, at an early stage. Finally, there is the view held by many socialists that these two goals are not contradictory. Long-term economic transformation of underdeveloped areas can best be achieved by involving the people, and this strategy necessarily implies an emphasis on equality.

Roles of agriculture and industry

Neo-classical economists have had a long-standing debate over the relative roles which should be assigned to agriculture and industry in the development of an economy. The importance of agriculture has gone up and down as economists despair, then feel confident about the ability of agriculture to be transformed. The early view, presented by Lewis (1954), clearly marked agriculture as playing a secondary role in development. Agriculture's role was to provide foreign exchange, through the production of primary goods for export, and labour for the developing industrial sector. The early economists all saw industrialization as critical to the problem of development.

The logic behind the emphasis of industrial development was simple. The process of development in western countries had clearly involved the increasing importance of the industrial sector. In fact, a significant source of growth has been the transfer of workers from low-productivity jobs to high ones. In Third World countries this path seems even more inviting. One of the so-called

---

12 Sweezy (1972, 9) describes the failure of Yugoslavia in these words: 'If the system as a whole is dominated by value relations, the effect of workers' control is simply to transform the workers (or rather an inner core of privileged workers) in each enterprise into a sort of collective capitalist.'

'advantages' of being a late-comer is the availability of advanced technology, which is much more transferable in the case of industry than in agriculture. If only enough investment funds could be obtained, then growth could be secured by the development of industry.

This emphasis on industrialization led to the Big Push approach advocated by people like Nurkse (1961) and Rosenstein-Rodan (1948, 1962). They saw the obstacles to industrialization as being lumpiness of needed infrastructural investment, complementarity of demand, lack of savings, and the lack of the proper psychology needed for development. All these obstacles could be removed by a Big Push, by undertaking a massive set of investments at one time. Such a bunching together of investments would improve the economics of infrastructure investment, create demand, increase the savings available by rapidly raising the incomes of the population, and break the psychological barriers to growth. The Big Push was really a call for a Marshall Plan for the Third World countries where the developed nations would finance the initial drive which would put these countries over the hill, and on the road to self-sustaining growth.

On the other hand, the argument was increasingly being made, beginning with Schultz (1964), that traditional agriculture was not resistant to change. Numerous studies indicated that farmers were responsive to changes in price (see Falcon, 1964), or the availability of new technologies or capital. Moreover, the enormous payoffs in terms of over-all production[13] of new techniques indicated that it was not only industry in which growth through research could be obtained.

Others began to question the whole basis of the Lewis-type model. It would be impossible for agriculture to play the role as supplier of foreign exchange and labour if it was allowed to stagnate. It was important to look after agriculture. As economic growth proceeded, the role played by agriculture would increase. Increased incomes would generate increased demand for food which must be supplied by either imports (using scarce foreign exchange earned by agricultural exports) or through domestic production. Finally, the Lewis model ignores demand. Given the difficulties of penetrating markets for industrial goods, it is important that countries develop their internal market. If the agricultural sector is allowed to stagnate, internal demand will be severely restricted, putting a limit on growth.[14]

13 The distributional effects of changes in technology have been enormous. This fact points to the need to look at the whole social/political context in which change takes place. See, for example, Gotsch, n.d.
14 The importance of agriculture has been stressed by a number of writers. See Mellor and Johnston (1961) or for a view on Africa by a member of the World Bank see Kamarck (1971).

The experience of the countries which have undergone periods of rapid industrialization since World War II has also served to disillusion some of the advocates of industrialization. The effect of such industrialization has not been as positive as originally hoped. Often, it only exacerbated the dualism in the society, creating a small group of highly-paid workers in very inefficient industries subsidized by the agricultural sector.[15] Because the value added in these industries is low, the growth effects have been small.

It would be wrong to gain the impression from the discussion so far that neo-classical economists now reject industrialization as the route to development. Rather, the role of agriculture which was almost completely ignored has now been raised to a level of equality with industry, and the need for selective industrialization is stressed. In many ways, neo-classical economists have returned to their basic inclination to lay heavy stress on comparative advantage, although most economists in the field now recognize that no simple interpretation of that concept can be taken.[16]

It would also be wrong to leave the impression that there does not remain a large body of economists who feel that industrialization is ultimately the key to growth, and that the diseconomies of the present pattern of industrialization among Third World countries can be exaggerated. Hirschman (1968) argues that import-substituting industrialization can create a situation where backward linkages can be exploited, despite the existence of strong political/economic forces working against such backward linkages.[17] As well, the development of certain industries, especially certain quite capital-intensive industries, can be an important dynamic in the society encouraging the development of other industries, and producing a more productive work force.[18]

15 There has been a whole host of studies of effective protection which make this argument. See Little, Scitovsky, and Scott, (1970), or Balassa (1971).

16 See Chenery (1961) for the best summary of neo-classical literature on this subject.

17 Hirschman sets out the economic and political forces shaping this type of industrialization. He recognizes that such late-stage industrialization produces a class of industrialists who have a real interest in preventing backward integration because it will reduce their effective protection. Nevertheless, the fact is that many countries have undergone such integration despite this resistance. In general, Hirschman is an optimist who sees societies responding to challenges, and developing in different ways. He therefore rejects the approach of many traditional economists who want all countries to replicate past patterns.

18 Hirschman (1970) argues that many basic industries such as steel, chemicals, etc. have the greatest linkage effects. As well, capital-intensive projects often demand greater accuracy and efficiency on the part of workers, and thus produce a better work force. See also the section on choice of technology in this chapter for a discussion of Hirschman.

As in the case of the issue of equality and growth, a parallel debate has gone on in the socialist camp. The Soviet Union clearly assigned a secondary role to agriculture. It was willing to tax the rural population in order to finance a programme of rapid industrialization. In general, western leftists, until recently, have regarded this basic economic strategy[19] as correct. This agreement stems from the widespread view held by socialist scholars that an emphasis on agricultural exports has been a trap for most Third World countries, which can be escaped only by opting out of the world capitalist economy. As well, socialists inherit an intellectual framework from Marx which lays heavy stress on the process of industrialization as an essential stage in the development of socialism, and which assigns the peasantry to a passive role.

The debate on the role of agriculture has been a prominent part of post-revolutionary Cuban political and economic history. Cuba initially adopted a policy of rapid industrialization. Revolutionary thought in Cuba associated the country's stagnation under capitalism with its over-dependence on sugar.[20] The initial response was to try to restructure completely the orientation of the economy. Fidel Castro (quoted in Barkin and Manitzas, 1973, PR 261-1) summarized the orientation of the economic programme in a speech given in 1953:

With the exception of a few food, lumber, and textile industries, Cuba continues to be a producer of raw materials. We export sugar to import candy, we export hides to import shoes, we export iron to import plows. Everybody agrees that the need to industrialize the country is urgent, that we need steel industries, paper and chemical industries, that we must improve cattle and grain production, the techniques and the processing in our food industry, in order to balance the ruinous competition of the Europeans in cheese products, condensed milk, liquors and oil, and that of the United States in canned goods; that we need merchant ships; that tourism should be an enormous source of revenue. But the capitalists insist that the workers remain under a Claudian yoke; the State folds its arms, and industrialization can wait for the Greek calends.

It was not long after the programme of industrial and agricultural diversification had begun that problems with the approach became apparent. Like many capitalist countries, Cuba found that import-substituting industrialization did

---

19 Many, of course, reject the severity of the programme, or the political repression which accompanied it.
20 See Huberman and Sweezy (1961) for a discussion of the stagnation of pre-revolutionary Cuba, and the relation of this stagnation to sugar.

not solve the balance of payments problems. Moreover the difficulties of establishing industries quickly, even in a country as advanced as Cuba, were profound. The programme had to be quickly abandoned.

By this time (1962) it was already clear that import substitution, through industrialization, from which so much had initially been expected, would provide no solution to the balance-of-payments problem and in fact might even contribute to making it worse for a long time to come. The reason was not only that starting the industries in question required large imports of machinery and equipment but also that in most cases operation of the newly established industries depended on imported raw materials, fuel, replacement parts, etc. The net result was little or no gain in substituting national production for imports.

There were other reasons, too, why the early enthusiasm for industrialization cooled off with experience. Technicians, administrators, skilled workers – all kinds of qualified manpower – were scarce or nonexistent. Much of the plant and equipment acquired from the socialist countries turned out to be of poor quality. But above all it became increasingly obvious that Cuba's demand for industrial products was not and under no conceivable circumstances could become large enough to justify the establishment of a wide variety of modern, technologically efficient industries. By committing herself to a program of industrial diversification, Cuba would in effect be condemning herself to industrial backwardness. Clearly, the situation called for a new strategy of economic development (Huberman and Sweezy, 1969).

The response was a return to a stress on agriculture. Agriculture was to be the 'pivot on the road to development' (Barkin and Manitzas, 1973, PR 261-2). Cubans call this strategy, the 'key sector strategy' (*ibid.*, PR 261-21). In effect it is a return to stressing Cuba's comparative advantage, and using the surpluses generated by the most productive sector to diversify the economy gradually and selectively.[21]

21 Barkin (Barkin and Manitzas, 1973, PR 261-4) describes the Cuban approach as a type of turnpike strategy. 'In practice, the Cubans modified the so-called theoretical 'turnpike' model to take account of a growing population and their inability to produce a broad range of machinery and consumer goods. They decided to concentrate on agricultural products and to develop trade relationships with other nations, so that needed capital equipment could be purchased from the proceeds of agricultural sales. From their perspective, agriculture was the least expensive sector to develop and represented the most expedient way of increasing their limited export base. They explained that it not only offered the possibility of exporting a large proportion of the expanded production and reducing present imports of foodstuffs, but it also could make use of unexploited reserves of fertile land. Both land and labor productivity could be raised without demanding the numbers of trained personnel and imports of capital goods which other sectors would require.

The Chinese have adopted a strategy of 'walking on two legs,' which emphasizes the need simultaneously to develop both agriculture and industry. The Chinese policy is summarized in the slogan 'Agriculture as the foundation of the economy and industry as the leading sector' (quoted in Wheelwright and McFarlane, 1970, 54). While agriculture will continue to be the basis of the economy, the development of an industrial sector is important for two reasons. First, certain industrial products are necessary as inputs into the agriculture sector. These industries must be developed first. Secondly, a socialist investment strategy must seek to transform the economy. Given the very large resource base of China, and its wide internal market, it would be economically irrational not to develop a strong industrial base.

The different responses on this issue by the Chinese and Cubans reflect the differences in resources and historical development of the two countries. The Chinese, because of their large country, do not have the option of depending on trade for industrial inputs for their agricultural sector. Transportation difficulties make this need for domestic production of such goods even greater. Moreover, the size of China makes a two-leg policy economically sound. In contrast, Cuba is both able to and from an economic point of view is probably forced to continue to rely on imports for many goods. It is therefore essential for it to develop a strategy which will ensure its ability to import these goods, while, at the same time, allow it to develop over the long-run. Such a strategy involves a short-run emphasis on agriculture, and a selective use of the surpluses generated in that sector to develop selective industries.

Choice of technology

The choice of technology for Third World countries has been the centre of considerable debate. The initial argument for labour-intensive industries is simple and straightforward. Countries like Tanzania are terribly poor, have little surplus to invest in both relative and absolute terms, and yet generally have large amounts of labour whose opportunity costs are relatively low (whether zero or not is irrelevant). Thus to maximize growth, one should maximize the use of the surplus factor (labour), and minimize the use of the scarce resource (capital).

Paralleling this general economic argument, the Sussex school has taken a position which involves looking at the wider social and political implications of a strategy. They regard any strategy of development which increases inequalities or even leaves them the same, and which fails to confront the issue of rapidly rising urban unemployment, as unacceptable. Capital-intensive strategies lock the society into a vicious circle. They create a small group of highly-paid workers who tend to demand luxury imported goods, or goods which if locally produced are based on foreign, capital-intensive technologies. 'The kind of technology that is used, particularly when effective protection is high, is related to the kind of products that are in demand, the demand in turn being determined by the distribution of income' (ILO 1973, 133). And of course the distribution of income is partly determined by the kind of technology that is used.

The Sussex school is not categorical about the purely economic effects of a labour-intensive strategy. Its members are unwilling to declare that it will increase growth, but are also unwilling to accept that it will necessarily decrease it. Undoubtedly their bias is that its economic effects will be positive. Nevertheless, these effects are largely irrelevant since they could not be so strong in the negative direction as to outweigh the negative social effects of an alternative strategy.

The choice of technique argument, then, becomes intimately involved with the equality and growth debate. Labour-intensive strategies are seen as integral to any strategy which hopes to reduce poverty.[22] We will see later in this chapter that some see labour-intensive strategies as an answer to the problems of rapid urban growth, and rising urban unemployment.

Stress on labour intensity has been attacked in two ways. Some have stressed the undesirability of such a stress, others the impossibility. Leibenstein, as I pointed out earlier, has argued that capital-intensive investments maximize profits, and therefore the investible surplus. He also argues that capital-intensive sectors are the areas of the greatest innovation, and thus of rapid growth.[23] Hirschman also has two arguments favouring capital intensity. Capital-intensive processes tend to be self-pacing, thus raising the productivity of the sector.[24] Moreover, the linkage effects of capital-intensive sectors tend to be greatest. Thus the over-all growth effects will be maximized. Finally, Baer and Herve (1966) argue that the real shortage in less-developed countries is not capital, but skilled labour. In many cases capital is being substituted for this skilled labour.

Other writers have concentrated on the lack of possibilities of substitution. The capital goods industry is concentrated in the developed countries where processes are developed to meet their factor proportions. Although a number of

22 There is a growing literature which defines the problems of Third World countries as revolving around the issue of employment rather than low income. This concern stems from the growing awareness of the difficulties which arise when distributional aspects are ignored. For a discussion of this approach see Turnham (1971).

23 Liebenstein also suggests that in some circumstances modern techniques may be more efficient in their use of *both* capital and labour. This argument has recently been revived by Streeten and Stewart (see Streeten, 1972).

24 Roemer (1972) has written a paper giving a variant of this argument. He found in Ghana that in many processes, capital-intensive systems were more accurate, and saved on materials costs, often the most significant cost factor. Thus it was rational to use a capital-intensive device. Since many of the processes used imported inputs, shadow pricing did not alter this conclusion.

large less-developed countries now have capital goods industries, e.g., India and China, the amounts they have to export are small relative to the demand. Moreover, attempts by countries to buy second-hand machinery have had only mixed success. Every poor country is filled with stories of the government being taken by a foreign supplier who sold second-hand equipment at far above its value. Often the problem is that the equipment has such an indeterminable value. Its value to the seller, because it is obsolete, is quite low, but to the buyer, because it is as good or better than more sophisticated equipment, is quite high. This is a classic bargaining position, and if the last twenty years has taught us anything, it is that such situations usually end in the favour of the supplier and not the poor country.

C.R. Frank Jr. (1968) makes the point that the ability of countries to switch from capital- to labour-intensive technologies does not match the magnitude of the employment problem. He points out that the major area where substitution is possible is manufacturing, and yet this sector is only a small part of the whole economy. His conclusion is that the focus must be shifted to the development of the rural sector, rather than the development of labour-intensive urban industries. I will return to this argument later.

Because socialist countries have been less concerned with the issue of the proper pricing of scarce factors, the choice of technique debate has not been so explicit in socialist literature. It has, instead, been submerged in other debates over growth and equality, or urban versus rural divisions, or trade versus autarchy. In general, socialists have not been shy of advanced technologies, and there are few advocates of importing second-hand equipment.[25] Even the Chinese who, for other reasons, oppose the excessive development of capital-intensive industries, have a firm policy of buying only the most modern equipment when they buy from abroad (Wheelwright and McFarlane 1970, 163). Socialists who argue for a capital-intensive strategy do so often because of trade/ dependency considerations. It is probably better, then, to deal with their arguments under that heading, than under choice of technology.

Trade and integration

Neo-classical trade theory,[26] in its original form had really two messages for Third World countries. The first was that trade was beneficial because it allowed a country to import goods which it was relatively inefficient at producing by

---

25 In theory, of course, socialism offers the opportunity of really separating the technique choice from the question of income distribution. In fact, however, the two are difficult to separate.

26 For a good summary of trade theory see Caves (1960).

exporting goods which it was efficient at producing with a net increase in its available consumption. Secondly, trade theory argued that Third World countries ought to concentrate their resources on the production of the goods in which they had a relative comparative advantage. In general this meant that the Third World nations would produce primary products or labour-intensive manufactured goods, and the developed nations would produce capital- or technology-intensive goods.

The notion of comparative advantage has been under significant attack in the last two decades by neo-classical economists (see Chenery, 1961). In general it is argued that the concept must be broadened to include a host of longer-term economic factors summarized by Scitovsky's (1954) term 'dynamic external economies' as well as the non-economic considerations introduced by people like Hirschman.

The advantages of trade continue to be a matter of dispute. The original attack on trade was started by the continued assertion that poor countries ought to rely upon exports of primary products. Both Prebisch (1964) and Singer (1950) argued that because of the inability of Third World countries to control output, all gains in productivity passed to the developed nations. They pointed out that declining terms of trade for primary products which result from their low income and price elasticities[27] implied that Third World countries had to run faster and faster just to stay even.

Myrdal (1957) and Hirschman (1970) added to the attack by showing how trade can often exacerbate[28] rather than narrow inequalities. Myrdal (1970, 143) showed how both capital and skilled labour would be drawn from poor to rich regions. 'If left unregulated, international trade and capital movements would thus often be the media through which the economic progress in the advanced countries would have backsetting effects in the underdeveloped world, and their mode of operation would be very much the same as it is in the circular cumulation of causes in the development process within a single country.' While neither Myrdal nor Hirschman proposed an autarchic strategy of development, both argued that considerable intervention in the free flow of resources was justified in some cases if poor countries or regions were to develop.

Socialist scholars have always been critical of arguments favouring trade. The notion that trade and exploitation are integrally related has a long history in

27 There has been a large dispute over the assertion that these elasticities are necessarily low. Obviously for some products they are not, and it may well pay a country to specialize in them. Nevertheless, in general terms of trade seem to have worsened for Third World countries.

28 This theory directly challenged the notion advanced by neo-classical economists that undisturbed trade would lead to an equalization of factor prices. For this point of view see Heckscher (1950), Ohlin (1933), Samuelson (1949), and Mundell (1957).

Socialist thought, dating at least from Lenin's (1939) writings on imperialism (see also Magdoff, 1969). Since World War II socialist scholars have turned their attention on the role of trade in maintaining colonial-like relations between the former colonies and the original colonial power (or a new power like the United States). Writers like Andre Gunder Frank (1970, 1973) showed how periods of interruption of trade were associated with periods of growth in Latin America. The emphasis on primary exports in Third World countries had led to a transfer of their investible surpluses into the hands of people with little incentive to invest in non-exporting enterprises, i.e., foreign investors or local dependent bourgeoisie. These people control the state, and thus measures to transform the economy are resisted.[29]

As well, Marxist scholars have always deplored the emphasis on primary product exports because of the instability of the markets involved. While traditional western economists were largely unconcerned about income distribution, this has always been a centre of focus for the left. Since it is the poor who suffer when incomes drop sharply, a strategy which involves continuing fluctuations in income is unacceptable.

Industrialization came to many poor countries in the 1950s and 1960s, but when it came it was not the nirvana expected. The real value added in many industries was often quite low, and the numbers employed few. Moreover, the dependency relation with the developed world remained. The technological basis of the industry remained abroad. The balance of payments were still critical. The new industries rarely increased exports. Often they only marginally reduced imports, because of their low value added, and the high-dividend and -interest, and patent rights payments involved in their establishment were a heavy drain on the balance of payments. In fact, politically the balance of payments became more important. As Little, Scitovsky, and Scott (1970)[30] point out, before industrialization a poor country could alleviate short-run balance of payments by stopping non-essential imports. Now many of these goods are partially manufactured in the country. Stopping the intermediate good imports used in the manufacture of them produces large unemployment, and thus serious political problems.

In part, the difficulties which accompanied this process of industrialization can be traced to the original dependence on primary product exports. Industrialization came after a long state of deprivation, and was a hothouse programme. There was not a large enough indigenous industrial class to lead the transformation, and thus the industrialization process involved a continued heavy reliance on foreign firms. As well, the failure to have a more gradual

29 For these arguments see Baran (1957), and Weisskopf, 'Capitalism and Underdevelopment in the Modern World' in Edwards, Reich, and Weisskopf (1972).
30 This argument was originally made by ECLA in the mid-1950s.

process of industrialization meant that when industrialization came, the measures used to promote it (e.g., tariffs) were not selective, but widespread, encouraging almost every type of industry, and encouraging a multiplicity of inefficient firms in every sector.

Marxists and other writers in response to the problems of industrialization widened their scope of criticism to include all forms of relationships with developed countries. It is impossible, they argued, to develop industries which do not have these characteristics — high external dependency, low value added, low export potential, high capital intensity — while continuing one's economic integration in the developed world. Technologies which reflect the indigenous environment must be developed indigenously. Moreover, independent and rapid growth will only be assured when the capacity to develop new technologies is transferred to the less-developed countries. This will not occur if the country is integrated into international capitalism.[31]

This belief in the need for seclusion was strengthened by the success which countries like the Soviet Union, China and Korea had in transforming their economies (largely without external aid). The particular model chosen depends upon the ideology of the writer, and the country under study. In Tanzania, Korea often is taken as the symbol of what can be done.

Almost all radical theories which discuss the detrimental effects of international capitalism also centre on the role played by foreign aid (see Hayter, 1971). This role can be a very overt one of supporting regimes which agree to integration into the capitalist world, or a more subtle one of distorting the country's choices. Agencies such as the World Bank or the United Nations tend to put a strong emphasis on good export performance and thereby encourage the country's continued integration into international capitalism. Aid, in general, makes capital-intensive technology artificially cheap. It tends to bias the government towards large rather than small projects. It leads, through the influx of western technical personnel, and through the use of scholarships, to a socialization of the elite in a style of life which requires quite high incomes, and a set of values emphasizing personal achievement and acquisition.

It should be noted that one socialist country, Cuba, has taken a positive view of both aid and trade. The switch in policy in 1963 was very much an acceptance of the need to emphasize exports, and a willingness to accept aid. This policy differs from the typical Third World position because Cuba negotiated a long-term agreement with the Soviet Union on sugar. In this way it removed one of the problems with emphasizing primary products — the inability to plan ahead because of fluctuating prices. Nevertheless, Cuba has continued to

31 For this argument see Weisskopf, 'Capitalism and Underdevelopment in the Modern World'.

trade extensively with capitalist nations, and even accepts selective amounts of aid from them.

In general neo-classical economists, while aware of some of the problems of aid, have tended to regard its net effects as favourable. The debate has been restricted to assessing the over-all contribution of aid to capital formation. Weisskopf (1972) has argued that it reduces savings in the country, while others, like Papanek (1972, 1973), argue that by alleviating the foreign exchange constraint, it can increase savings while raising the rate of growth.

Self-reliance is an important emphasis in Nyerere's writings.[32] Essentially there are two themes in his stress on self-reliance. One was that Tanzania must develop a strategy which was not dependent for its success on large inflows of foreign capital. The second which followed from the first, was that the strategy must involve the use of local resources – labour, land, and natural resources rather than foreign resources. In the empirical section on Tanzania I will try to look at the degree to which it has followed a policy of self-reliance in a number of the senses in which the term has been used – lack of dependency on foreign capital, use of local resources, technological independence, and reduced stress on trade. I will, nevertheless, tend to concentrate on one version of self-reliance, the use of local resources, because a theme which I hope to develop is the thesis that, at this stage in Tanzania's development, a few simple indicators are all that are necessary to decide whether or not a project is consistent with the strategy. The two main indicators are capital/labour ratio and import intensity. Moreover I will argue that, in general, characteristics of investments tend to be highly correlated. Thus import-intensive industries tend to be capital-intensive, urban-located, and dependent on foreign technology. In contrast, local resource-based industries are generally less capital-intensive, can be located in rural areas, and have much simpler technologies. This correlation is, of course, the result of both Tanzania's particular resource base, and its current level of development. At a later stage in development much of this correlation may disappear,[33] or may cease to be relevant.[34] Thus one must be very careful about generalizing from the methodology.

---

32 The next chapter will present his writings more fully.

33 As the country develops, and backward linkages are exploited, industries switch from being import-intensive to local resource-based. In fact Hirschman, as was pointed out earlier, sees this as one pattern of development. Moreover, development alters the resource base of the country. It is difficult at this stage to know what is Tanzania's resource base because so few resources have gone into discovering and exploiting it. Over time, new resources will undoubtedly be found and used.

34 At a subsequent stage of development, I will argue later, Tanzania will have to adopt a strategy less simplistic than rural socialism. At this stage, however, such a strategy is appropriate.

Urban/rural dichotomy

In chapter two I will show that urban/rural conflict is an essential aspect of Nyerere's view of development. Until recently neo-classical economists have not thought in these terms at all. In general they like to avoid thinking of society as divided into groups. While development economists are less guilty of this fault than the rest of the profession, they too generally fail to see development as a political process whereby some groups dominate others. Nor do they want to make any *a priori* judgements that certain types of economic development are bad. To do so runs directly counter to the ideology of neo-classical welfare economics.

Just as it has become impossible to continue to ignore distributional considerations, so too has it become difficult to ignore the problems inherent in the very rapid growth of urban centres in the Third World. It is clear that Third World countries define rapidly-growing urban centres as a problem. They are an economic problem because they strain a government's ability to supply infrastructure and a political problem because they breed discontent as the rise in urban population surpasses the increase in urban employment possibilities.

Neo-classical economists have defined the urban/rural dichotomy as a problem of (a) excessively fast-growing urban centres, and (b) urban unemployment. A large number of studies have been undertaken to determine the factors which account for rural/urban migration. Originally economists tended to view the problems as simply one of wide income differentials. Gradually, however, they have come to realize that the factors which cause people to move to an urban area are very complicated. What causes them to move is their sense of the *probability* of improving their *own life style*.

The nature of the cause of the first problem, excessively fast growing urban centres, makes solving the second problem, urban unemployment, very difficult. Harbison (1967) describes how Kenya tried to solve the problem of urban unemployment by initiating an agreement among employers and workers that wages would be held constant in return for employers hiring twenty per cent more workers. The result was not lower, but higher urban unemployment. The increase in jobs altered the perception of workers in the rural areas about the probability of their obtaining urban employment, and thereby induced them to migrate.

Increasingly, then, neo-classical economists have come to the conclusion that the urban problem, as defined above, can be solved only by developing the rural areas. Todaro (1969) makes just this point:

Perhaps the most significant policy implication emerging from the model is the great difficulty of substantially reducing the size of the urban traditional sector without a concentrated effort at making rural life more attractive. For example, instead of allocating scarce capital funds to urban low cost housing projects which would effectively raise urban real incomes, and might therefore lead to a worsening of the housing problem, governments in less developed countries might do better if they devoted these funds to the improvement of rural amenities.

Socialists have not spent a lot of time discussing the relation of urban centres to rural areas. Marxist literature deplored the social conditions which existed in urban areas, but regarded them as part of the over-all process of industrialization. When socialism came, these problems would disappear.[35] Recently, however, socialists have come to realize that a socialist strategy on the growth of urban areas is essential.

The Chinese have been the most explicit in developing an urban strategy. They have developed policies designed to thwart the continued growth of urban centres for two reasons. First, they have many of the same feelings which all Third World countries have about the economic and political costs of excessive urban growth.[36] Secondly, and perhaps more importantly, they realize that the rapid development of urban centres will increase the very divisions in the society they are trying to avoid.

I talked earlier, in the section on equality and growth, about the two notions of equality advanced by the Chinese. It is the second notion, equality of position and outlook, which lies at the heart of their strategy on urban growth. Elites will be created if technologically advanced industries are developed at a rapid rate in

35 Marxists thus inherited a rather romantic anti-urban feeling, but not a sense that policies must be designed now to prevent the growth of an urban/rural dichotomy. Marx viewed the barriers between urban and rural areas as being broken down under communism: 'In communist society, where nobody has one exclusive field of activity but each can become accomplished in any branch he wishes, society regulates the general production and thus makes it possible for me to do one thing today and another tomorrow, to hunt in the morning, fish in the afternoon, rear cattle in the evening, criticise after dinner, just as I have a mind, without ever becoming hunter, fisherman, shepherd or critic' (Marx and Engels, 1939, 22).

36 Wheelwright and McFarlane (1970, 199) summarize the Chinese view: 'One aspect of economic development that the Marxist strategy seems to have understood well is that one of the foremost tasks of development planning is to bring about a stable pattern of life in the hinterland, outside the main cities, and to ensure that people are not driven to the urban areas by need or frustration. The labor power and productive effort of millions of ordinary people can be successfully mobilized only if new jobs and new work places are created close to where they already live, and not simply in a few big towns. This, naturally, presupposes a decentralized approach supported by a great deal of local initiative, and a feeling of self-reliance inside enterprises and communes.'

the urban areas. It is important, instead, to encourage industries in the rural areas where the barriers between peasants and urban workers will be broken down.

The Chinese seem willing to accept some loss in productivity to create firms which are located in rural areas. Moreover, it is also clear that the Chinese, especially the followers of Mao, are willing to accept that such an emphasis on rural development means adopting a programme that puts less stress on rapid development of high technology industries. 'Mao is certainly in sympathy with resistance to *all-out* or *crash industrialization*; he sees its imperatives as being in conflict with many noneconomic aims he feels China should be pursuing ... Such rationings of industrial society into the rural areas have a twofold objective: to bring material benefits to the peasant, and to prevent the dictatorship of the city over the countryside' (Wheelwright and McFarlane 1970, 219; emphasis in original).

It is clear that the issue of urban/rural dichotomy cannot be treated in isolation from the other issues. Concern over this problem will affect one's approach to the issue of the roles of agriculture and industry, or to the issue of the choice of technique. Indeed, in developing an investment strategy one will necessarily have to make decisions about all these issues, and will find that in doing so the issues are highly interrelated. Nevertheless, this type of classification of the issues can be helpful in understanding the positions taken by different individuals or groups on investment strategy.

2

Background to Tanzania

HISTORICAL BACKGROUND

Political
There is not a great deal of knowledge about the pre-colonial history of what is now called Tanzania. Little has been written about early African society in this area. It is clear that the level of productivity was not very high and that, relative to most societies, there was a low degree of social and economic differentiation among the population. Arabs first came to the territory around 975 AD (see Coupland, 1939; Moffet, 1958, 27-8). The Portuguese first arrived in 1500 (Moffet, 1958, 29). Arabs and Portuguese competed (largely without interruption from other world powers) for control of the coastal area until the nineteenth century.

Although this study is concerned with mainland Tanzania, some mention should be made of Zanzibar[1] since it dominated this region in this early period. In 1828, Said bin Sultan, Sultan of Oman, set up his second home in Zanzibar. From this position Seyyid Said established Zanzibar as a commercial and financial centre. The clove industry was begun on the island, and the slave and ivory trade became centred there. Seyyid Said brought in a number of Indians[2] to act as government clerks, and thus began the process of establishing Indians as the middle class of East Africa.

Throughout the period of the Sultan's rule European explorers were penetrating different parts of East Africa. The drive to seize parts of Africa had

1 In 1964 Zanzibar and Tanganyika joined to form the United Republic of Tanganyika and Zanzibar later called Tanzania. Zanzibar is made up of two islands off the coast of Tanganyika, one called Zanzibar and other called Pemba. The total population of the islands was 354,000 in 1967, compared with 11,568,339 for the mainland.
2 In general the term Asian is now used in East Africa to denote Pakistanis and Indians. In the period before partition, however, the term Indian was used.

begun, and there was intense rivalry between European powers to colonize the continent. In September 1884, H.H. Johnston[3] obtained the right to several parcels of land from the chief of the Chagga (Ingham, 1967, 135). In 1885, the Germans formed the German East Africa Company to colonize the area. The British responded by forming in 1887 the British East Africa Association (Morris, 1968, 7).

Britain was, at this time, heavily involved in the affairs of Egypt. It was anxious to maintain its supremacy in East Africa, while at the same time avoiding open conflict with Germany. It succeeded in reaching this goal by signing a number of treaties with European powers which delimited the territories (in central and East Africa) to be controlled by each country. In 1885 the Congo Basin Treaties were signed by a number of countries, outlining their sphere of influence in central Africa. In 1886 Britain and Germany signed a separate agreement. This limited the Sultan's control to Zanzibar and Pemba, and a strip of land ten miles deep along the coast. The area which is now called Kenya became a British sphere of influence, and what is now called mainland Tanzania fell to German control. Uganda remained in dispute (Ingham, 1967, 137-8).

In 1887 the Sultan granted Britain the right to develop the coastal strip in the area under its control. A similar right was granted to Germany the following year. Another agreement was signed by Britain and Germany in 1890 specifying in more detail the boundaries between their two areas, and granting control of Uganda to Britain.

Germany retained control of its territory up until the end of World War I. By the Versailles Treaty, Germany had to renounce all its overseas territories. In 1920 Britain assumed control of what was then called Tanganyika Territory.[4] Tanganyika was transferred to Britain as a League of Nations Mandate Territory. In the early 1920s there was some consideration of establishing a federation of Kenya, Uganda, Tanganyika, and Rhodesia, but the idea was dropped because of strong opposition by non-Kenyan settlers who feared Kenyan domination. A common market was, however, established for the three East African territories in 1923. In 1946, Tanganyika became a United Nations Trust Territory under Britain.

The struggle for independence was neither very long nor bitter. In 1953 Juluis Nyerere returned from Edinburgh University and became the President of the Tanganyika African Association, an association of civil servants. In

3 Travelled under the auspices of the Royal Geographical Society.
4 Up to World War I it was German East Africa. From 1919 until 1948 it was called Tanganyika Territory, named after Lake Tanganyika, and in 1948 it became simply Tanganyika. I shall try to use the name appropriate to the time period under discussion, i.e., German East Africa (1886-1920), Tanganyika (1920-64), Tanzania (1964-   ).

1954 this association changed its name to the Tanganyika African National Union (TANU) and became a more political organization. Nyerere was appointed to the Legislative Council in 1954. In this year, the United Nations also began to pressure Britain to grant more self-government, and a United Nations commission called for a political timetable which would give Tanganyika independence in twenty or twenty-five years. At the time, this seemed an optimistic goal.

British opposition to independence was not long-lasting. British officials attempted to thwart TANU by aiding the development of the United Tanganyika Party, an inter-racial party which wanted Europeans and Africans to be given political parity. In 1958, however, TANU-supported candidates won all the seats. In 1960 under an expanded suffrage TANU candidates won 70 out of 71 legislative seats. Thus the UTP was completely unsuccessful. On 1 May 1961 internal self-government was granted, and Nyerere became the prime minister. On 9 December 1961 Tanganyika became independent.

The independence struggle stands in stark contrast to the battles fought by revolutionary movements as a basis of socialism. The Tanganyikan struggle differed from many other African movements in the degree to which TANU was a rural- rather than an urban-based party. Tanganyika, as I shall show later, was characterized by a very small African urban working class, and an almost non-existent African middle class. Thus its independence struggle did aid in the development of a party which had the potential to build rural socialism. Nevertheless, the ease of the independence struggle, which was the result of the general indifference of Britain to Tanganyika, meant that the party was weak, and did not develop either the discipline or the depth of support to really organize the people for a transformation to socialism. This lack of a party which is able effectively to mobilize the resources[5] of the peasants remains a critical weakness in Tanzania's efforts to build socialism.

In 1962 Tanganyika became a republic, and Nyerere was elected president. The continuing dominance of TANU posed a serious problem in terms of allowing people a choice in their political representatives, since TANU candidates won virtually every election. People were forced to vote against the party of their choice if they did not like the particular candidate. Some means of giving them a choice of representatives was needed. The solution to this difficulty was the establishment of a one-party state in which two TANU candidates would run for

5 It is important to recognize that one of the chief attributes of socialist movements is their ability to release the latent potential of people. For this reason, one must always be suspicious of top-down socialism, for it does not represent this type of mobilization of the people.

each seat. Thus in 1965 TANU became the only legal party on mainland Tanzania.[6]

Zanzibar became a British Protectorate in 1890. The Sultan continued to control the internal affairs of the island, and little was done to improve the position of the African majority. In 1957 the Afro-Shirazi Party was formed under the leadership of Sheikh Abeid Karume to represent the interests of the Africans. The Nationalist Party represented the Arabs. A small party led by Abdul-brahman M. Babu was the only really multi-racial party. Independence was granted to Zanzibar on 10 December 1963. The Nationalist Party continued in power despite the fact that a majority of the population voted for the Afro-Shirazi Party, because of the unrepresentative nature of the distribution of seats. On 11 January 1964 a coup against the Sultan was begun, and the Afro-Shirazi Party assumed control. Karume was named head of the Revolutionary Council, and the government dedicated itself to implementing socialism. Three months later, Zanzibar joined with Tanganyika to form a union, and the country became known as Tanzania. In fact, the two areas continue to operate quite auto-nomously. The mainland government has little control over the internal affairs of Zanzibar. I will look at only mainland Tanzania in this study, and exclude Zanzibar data from the analysis wherever possible.

Economic

The economy of Tanzania has been heavily shaped by external forces. Prior to colonization the economy was one of subsistence peasants working at a very low level of productivity. Trade initially was based on ivory, then slaves. New crops were brought by both the Arabs and the Portuguese. The development of clove plantations on Zanzibar created a demand for food, as well as labour (Iliffe, 1970, 4), and thus provided a stimulus for increased production.

The German period

The Germans accelerated the change in agriculture. Because of their lack of colonies, they were anxious to develop German East Africa as quickly as possible, and in a way which would allow the colony to provide for some of Germany's need for raw materials, especially non-food crops. These two factors influenced the pattern of development.

Rubber, partly collected wild and partly estate grown, was the most important export in the pre-World War I period. After World War I the market for

---

6 The more democratic nature of a one-party state in the circumstances in which Tanzania found itself is argued in Cliffe (1967), and Nyerere (1966, 1968).

the crop collapsed and it had no further significance in Tanzanian history. The Germans introduced a number of export crops, of which sisal, cotton, and coffee were the most important. Sisal was an estate crop, whose introduction involved alienation of land to European settlers. The estates were clustered around the two rail lines (see Map 1), one from Tanga to Moshi which was started in 1893 and completed in 1911, and one from Dar es Salaam to Kigoma on Lake Tanganyika, which was completed in 1914 (Fuggles-Couchman, 1964, 16-17). The sisal estates went only as far as Kilosa, about half-way to Morogòro. Sisal was introduced primarily because of its importance in providing Germany with an independent supply of rope for its navy.

Cotton was introduced for similar strategic reasons. American cotton was cheaper than that grown in German East Africa, but Germany did not want to remain dependent upon the United States for its supply. Unlike sisal, cotton became chiefly a smallholder crop grown by Africans in the area around Lake Victoria.

Coffee was introduced by German settlers in the 1890s in the East Usambaras, mountains just west of Tanga. The most important coffee area was later established at the foot of Mt Kilimanjaro and Mt Meru, and again this involved pushing the native population off the land. In this case, the population moved further up the mountain, and began to grow its own coffee. Soon African production of coffee in this area was equal to European production. As well, coffee production was also started by Africans in the Lake Victoria area.

Other crops introduced were tea, which was grown largely in estates around the Southern Highland, hills about half-way between Dar es Salaam and the Zambia border, and in the Usambara Mountains; tobacco, grown mainly by Africans in the Southern Highland; and sugar grown in estates in the Lake area, and near Arusha.

It is possible to summarize the economic developments in the period of German rule as follows. The Germans introduced a number of export crops, which were only partially grown by Europeans. In fact, a major part of the output was from African smallholders. German anxiety to develop the colony meant that German officials were willing to encourage African production. Their desire for certain strategic materials meant that they centred on non-food export crops. Production of these crops was centred in two areas, the most important of which was a strip running along the northern border of German East Africa and Kenya. A railway followed this border and provided transportation to the ocean, at least as far into the interior as Moshi where the European estates ended. The second area was west from Dar es Salaam out a short distance along the railway to Kigoma, and in the Southern Highlands on the way to Zambia.

British rule

The British did not significantly alter the basis of the economy. The trends begun under German rule were merely intensified, not changed. As mentioned, rubber ceased to be an important export, while cotton and coffee grew in importance. Economic development continued to be concentrated in a few regions. In fact the process of development in Tanzania can be described, in the manner of John Iliffe (1970, 20-21), as one in which a hierarchy of regions was formed. The hierarchy consisted of metropoles – cash crop areas and major towns; dependencies – areas surrounding metropoles and supplying them with food; and peripheries – areas without cash crops which supplied labour to the metropoles and/or stagnated economically. Thus the severe problems of regional disparities, and the wide dispersal of economic activity,[7] problems which have been the focus of much government attention, have their roots in the early colonial type of development, and in the geography.

There is no need to detail the development of the economy over the period of British rule. The inter-war periods saw the expansion of output of export crops despite poor prices. This expansion was largely based upon African production. New settlers came but their total number was never large and their efforts centred on a few commodities – sisal, tea, and coffee.[8] Pyretheum[9] and cashew nuts, both peasant crops, were introduced, setting the basis for later diversification of exports. The world wide rise in prices for commodities which resulted from the Korean War encouraged even further expansion of export crops (see Table 1).

The growth in export crops did involve an increase in the total productivity of the society. Increased incomes were not, as was pointed out, equally

---

7 The rich areas are not concentrated, but spread in a circle around Tanzania. Thus, as Hawkins (1965, 7) points out: 'From the port of Dar es Salaam to the Lake Region, the largest single market in Tanganyika, it is over 750 miles by rail; from Dar es Salaam to the next largest market, the Moshi-Arusha area, is 400 miles by road ... The main centres of population, and therefore of purchasing power are not grouped conveniently together as they are in Kenya and Uganda.' This dispersal has forced Tanzania to spend large amounts of money on developing its communication system, and poses severe problems for large-scale central production units.

8 In 1947 native production of coffee was equal to 92 per cent of total coffee production. By 1957, it had fallen to 75 per cent. Nevertheless, estate agriculture as a share of total agriculture fell significantly. If we classify sisal, coffee (weighted with the above shares), and tea estate crops, then estate crops were 64 per cent of non-diamond exports in 1948, and 35 per cent in 1958.

9 Again this crop was introduced for strategic reasons. It was important in the war. As a result, production rose from 244 tons in 1940 to 697 tons in 1945. After the war, production fell again to 170 tons in 1948 (Moffet, 123, and Tanzania, *Statistical Abstracts*, 1938-58, 26).

TABLE 1

Exports from Tanganyika (shs million)

	1938	1948	1958	1962	1972
Sisal	28.5	178.6	207.0	314.7	145.0
Coffee	7.7	17.9	151.5	131.5	383.0
Cotton	7.6	26.6	145.0	147.9	336.0
Diamonds	–	20.8	88.3	108.5	124.0
Tobacco	0.3	5.0	0.9	10.6	49.0
Tea	0.09	13.2	12.6	32.2	54.0
Meat and meat preparations	–	–	18.1	46.4	42.0
Hides and skins	4.2	9.3	24.0	29.8	42.0
Pyretheum	–	0.4	N.A.	N.A.	N.A.
Cashewnuts	–	–	21.7	46.7	150.0
Others	25.9	52.8	165.5	156.5	498.0[2]
Total	74.2	324.6	834.6	1024.8	1823.0[1]

SOURCE: Tanzania, *Statistical Abstract*, 1938-52, 22, 26; *Budget Survey*, 1961-2, 10; *Hali Ya Uchumi*, 1972-3, 20.

1 Cloves have been excluded from these figures to eliminate the main effect of Zanzibar.
2 The increase in this figure is largely the result of the rise in petroleum exports. These exports, almost exclusively to Zambia, are matched by imports from Kenya. They do not represent any increase in foreign exchange earnings. If petroleum exports were excluded, 'other exports' would total shs 283.0 in 1972, and total exports would be shs 1608.0.

distributed. They were concentrated in certain regions (because these regions had the best soils and climates for the crops and were close to transport routes), and resulted in increasing differentiation between peasants within areas. Moreover the gains in production were as much a result of increases in the area under cultivation as in improvements in methods of cultivation. As a result, land shortage, a problem unknown in earlier times, became an increasingly important difficulty in certain areas. The basis for further rapid expansion in output was gradually exhausted in these areas. Further expansion would come much more slowly, and would involve more significant changes in the methods of cultivation. In the areas where cash crops were not cultivated, agricultural production remained much the same. Shifting cultivation dominated these regions,[10] and there was little improvement in the techniques employed.

10 The problem posed by shifting cultivation is that it was not particularly conducive to technological change (Kamarck, 1971, 135).

Infrastructure development
The protectorate status of Tanganyika, and the lack of a strong British community to lobby with the mother country resulted in a much lower development of infrastructure, both social and economic, in Tanganyika than in Kenya. British official aid to Kenya was higher than to Tanganyika, despite Tanganyika's larger population. In 1962 Kenya received shs 182 million in grants and loans from the United Kingdom (shs 21 per capita) (Kenya, *Statistical Abstract 1964*, 23). Tanganyika in the same year received only shs 94 million (shs 9 per capita) (Tanzania, 1966, 65). As well, the presence of a larger European population in Kenya meant a greater inflow of unofficial aid.

In 1962, Kenya had 840,677 African students or 10 per cent of the population in primary school, versus only 518,663 students in Tanganyika, 5.5 per cent of the population. There were 86,201 motor vehicles licensed in Kenya in 1961 compared to 42,256 in Tanganyika. In 1964 there were 1125 miles of bituminized roads in Kenya, whereas much larger Tanganyika had only 782 miles (Kenya, *Statistical Abstract 1964*; Tanzania, *Statistical Abstract*, 1964).

Development of mining and manufacturing
In 1940 diamonds were discovered by Dr W. Williamson. Diamond exports rose quickly, as we can see from Table 1. As well as providing an important and steady source of foreign exchange, the diamond industry was a significant source of government revenue[11]. The mining sector, as a whole, was not particularly large, and was greatly dominated by diamond mining. By 1961, diamonds were 72 per cent of mining output, and mining was 4 per cent of GDP at factor cost.

Tanganyika did not develop any significant manufacturing sector. To the extent that there was industrialization in East Africa, this industrialization was concentrated in Kenya. As mentioned earlier, Tanganyika joined the common market which existed between Uganda and Kenya in 1923. It is now generally agreed that this common market worked to the disadvantage of Tanganyika, and to the advantage of Kenya.[12] This was the result of a number of factors. First, Tanganyika's legal position as a protectorate rather than a colony meant that

11 In 1958-9 the government, through royalities, taxation and dividends received shs 320 million from Williamson Diamonds. This was 8 per cent of its current revenue (i.e., excluding development assistance grants). See IBRD, 1961, 12, 143).
12 See Ghai (1964). His conclusion: 'From our analysis of the territorial distribution of benefits and costs of the EACM, it appears that Kenya has been the greatest net beneficiary, that Uganda has on balance gained rather than lost, and that Tanganyika has suffered a substantial net loss' (*ibid.*, 39).

there was always some uncertainty about its future. British investors, accordingly, preferred to serve the East African market from Kenya rather than from Tanganyika. Secondly, the European and Asian populations were larger and more concentrated in Kenya than in Tanganyika. It was these populations which formed the basis of the market for import-substituting industries. Thirdly, the European population in Tanganyika was not exclusively British, but rather a mixture of a number of nationalities.[13] There was, therefore, no strong, coherent group to lobby with Britain for Tanganyika's position.

Kenya, then, developed an industrial base, first in the 1920s, and then to a much greater extent in the post World War II period that was based on the East African market. By 1961, Kenyan exports to Tanganyika were 10 per cent of its GDP, and of these exports, only 13.6 per cent were non-protected items. In contrast, Tanganyika's exports to Kenya were only 2 per cent of its GDP, and 46 per cent were non-protected items (Ghai, 1964). Kenya was also the centre of all common East African services, and thus enjoyed the substantial multiplier effects of their expenditure. Trade also tended to pass through Kenya. Almost 25 per cent of Tanganyika's imports came in through Mombasa rather than through Tanga or Dar es Salaam (Hawkins, 1965, 27).

Dependence on Kenya

Tanganyika's dependence on Kenya has been important for several reasons. First, it has meant that Tanganyika was unusually undeveloped. In 1961, manufacturing was only 3 per cent of Tanganyika's GDP, whereas it was 10 per cent of Kenya's GDP. While Kenya consumed 426 million kilowatts in electricity in 1961, Tanganyika consumed only 143 million kilowatts. Secondly, the relationship with Kenya has influenced the Tanzanian perception of the world, and, in particular, of international capitalism. Tanganyika did not do well with international capitalism, and the Tanzanians have inherited a feeling of suspicion and distrust.[14] It is this feeling which helped to form the basis of their shift in policy. Thirdly, the lack of development in Tanganyika had an effect on the country's class formation. Tanganyika did not develop an African class which was as firmly committed to the development of the urban sector as Kenya did and this in turn

---

13 Of the 1666 people holding long-term leases on land as of 31 December 1960, only 470
    (28 per cent) were British, and 107 (6 per cent) South African. Other major groups
    were Greeks – 279 (17 per cent), Asians – 287 (17 per cent), and Germans – 45 (3 per
    cent) (Ruthenberg, 1964, 15).
14 Nyerere (1968, 240) speaks of 'our historically induced suspicion of national foreign
    investment.'

allowed a different political option to be taken.[15] In order to clarify this point, it is important to understand the whole class and tribal development of Tanganyika.

Class and tribal development

In order to fully understand political and economic developments in Tanzania, one must have a grasp of the social structure which evolved under colonialism. In basic terms, Tanganyika had what is called a three-tier structure with Europeans at the top, Asians in the middle, and Africans at the bottom. There was little development of an African entrepreneurial class, and only a small development of an African urban working class. When independence came, the overwhelming share of Africans had only a peripheral relation to the urban economy. To understand how this came about, one must understand the history of the Asians in East Africa.[16]

The arrival of Asians

Indian involvement in East Africa extends back many hundreds of years. Trade carried on through Arab caravans and Indian traders had tied the two areas together. Direct Indian migration in large numbers did not begin until Seyyid Said moved his kingdom to Zanzibar. There became established in Zanzibar a large and prosperous Indian population. In 1844 this population numbered 1000, and by 1860 it had risen to 6000 (Mangat, 1969, 4-5). By this time the Indians completely dominated the trade of the area, and also played a crucial role on the island as financial intermediaries. Indian credit was essential to Arab traders. The Indians themselves did not penetrate the interior of East Africa; rather, this was done by Arab caravans. The role of the Indians was strictly one of middle-men, buying from European firms, or from India, and selling ivory, rubber, and slaves bought by the Arabs. The Indian rupee became the currency of Zanzibar.

15 Comparisons with Kenya figure prominently in any discussion of Tanganyika or Tanzania. They do so for several reasons. The two countries are of relatively comparable size. Kenya's population in 1972 was estimated at 12.0 million, Tanzania's at 14.1 million. They both had British administrations for most of their colonial life. On the other hand, Kenya has clearly opted for a capitalist pattern of growth with heavy reliance on foreign investment, and an acceptance of highly unequal incomes. Tanzania has opted for a type of socialism. In both countries there is a sense of rivalry, and a strong belief among the elite that the other country's strategy is wrong. Moreover, for Tanzanians, the dominance of Kenya for so long has left its mark in a slight feeling of inferiority towards Kenya, and a sense that doing well means doing better than Kenya.
16 For more detailed works on the Asians in East Africa, see Morris (1968); Mangat (1969); Ghai (1965).

TABLE 2

Population of Kenya and Tanganyika

	Kenya			Tanganyika		
	African	European	Asian	African	European	Asian
1911		3175	12,000	4,145,000	5336	10,000
1921		9651	25,253	4,107,000	2447	14,991
1928					5778	14,900
1931		16,812	43,623			
1948	5,251,120	29,660	97,687	7,400,000	11,300	47,500
1962	8,365,942	55,759	176,613	9,467,000	22,000	88,700
1967	9,651,000	42,000	192,000	11,476,506	16,861	74,972

SOURCES: Pankhurst (1954, 46); *Handbook of Tanganyika*, 1930, 32-3; Kenya, *Statistical Abstract 1964, 1972;* Tanzania, *Statistical Abstract*, 1970.

Large-scale Indian immigration to the interior began with the German and British administrations. Britain consciously tied the development of East Africa to India. East Africa was to be a source of trade for India, buying her textiles and selling her raw materials. It was Indian troops who were used to conquer the territories (Mangat, 1969, 29). Indian administration was copied directly, and many old British colonial officers who had served in India were brought over to East Africa.

The extensive trade with India brought a flow of immigrants from India to both German and British East Africa. Its size was, however, greatly increased by the building of the railways in both countries. Both Germany and Britain relied upon Indian labour to build the railways. In the British case it was largely indentured labourers; in the case of Germany, it was free immigrants. Indian immigration to British East Africa was 24,000 in the period 1897 to 1901, reaching a peak inflow of over 8000 in 1898-9 (Mangat, 1969, 38).

While many of these immigrants returned to India, many remained and the Indian population became an important community in both colonies (German and British East Africa). By 1911, there were 12,000 Indians in Kenya, and 10,000 in German East Africa (see Table 2).

Role of Asians

The role played by the Indians as merchants was critical to the development pattern followed by Tanganyika. There were two types of traders. The first was the petty trader. He established small bazaars in the villages in the interior. By bringing trade goods into previously unpenetrated areas, he accelerated the process of bringing these areas into the external world. These petty traders played the crucial role in persuading Africans to grow cash crops. It was they who brought in the trading goods which provided an incentive for the Africans to switch crops. It was the Indian who bought these crops, and carried them back to the larger centres, and it was often the Indian who took a direct role in distributing seed and in persuading the farmers to grow cash crops.

The petty trader was an arm of colonial policy. It was he who could go where no European trader would. Many writers of the period recognized this, as did the governments themselves. 'The commercial enterprise of the German and British Indians ... added largely to our revenues, and did a great deal to encourage the natives to embark in trade in the products of their country. To the British Indians I can only wish unlimited success, since they trade under the British flag, and create trade, just in a small, and then in a large way, where no trade had hitherto existed' (Mangat, 1969, 58).

The second type of trader was the large merchant who was centred in the major towns. He typically fulfilled several roles. First, he completed the link in the chain between the African producer and the firms of the mother country or of India. It was he who bought from the large, foreign firms the goods to be traded in the interior, and sold to them the primary products he obtained from the petty traders. He also became a source of credit to the government, and more importantly, to the many petty traders. This was an important role because many of the traders could not survive without credit. Finally, he also played the role of the industrial entrepreneur. To the extent that forward and final demand linkages were exploited, it was often the Indian that exploited them.

Indians were also an important source of skilled and semi-skilled labour. They were important to both private industry and the government, and filled both white-collar and skilled blue-collar jobs. In 1952, 61 per cent of Asian males were employees, while 10 per cent were employers, and 29 per cent own-account workers.[17] Almost half (48 per cent) of those Asian males whose occupation was known were professionals or managers, 28 per cent were white-collar workers, and the rest skilled craftsmen or manual workers (24 per cent) (Tanzania, *Statistical Abstract*, 1938-52, 48).

Lack of African entrepreneurs
The emergence of an Asian entrepreneurial and skilled working class was aided by the lack of a developed African class to fill these two roles. More importantly, the rise of the Asians tended to discourage the development of this

17 Tanzania, *Statistical Abstract* (1938-52, 48). Those with no occupation were excluded.

African class. Both colonial policy and economic forces worked against successful competition by the African with the Asian. Africans found it difficult to gain
credit to develop businesses. Even if wholesalers would lend them money, they
were limited by law to lending them only shs 600, hardly sufficient to start a
major enterprise. The British trusted the Asian more, and tended to use him
instead of an African wherever possible. The Asian enjoyed all the benefits of
having close connections with a successful business community. The African
who tried to start a business had few contacts, and no larger community to fall
back upon.

As independence approached, there was some development of an African
business class, and Africans increasingly filled the role of skilled workmen, but it
is nevertheless true to say that the African was significantly excluded from the
middle class. In 1957, no Africans were listed in the category of professionals,
managers, or executives in the occupational census. There were 4571 African
teachers, the only real avenue of upper mobility for Africans. About 15,000
Africans, out of a total wage-earning work force of 330,000 earned over shs 200
a month (Tanzania, *Statistical Abstract*, 1958, 66). Of this group, over 8000
were in the public service. Africans did hold the majority of trading licences
(Hawkins, 1965, 34-5), but most of the trade was conducted by Asians or
Europeans.

As stated earlier, the linkages which were developed in the economy were
developed either by Asians or Europeans. There was almost no indigenous manufacturing. The World Bank Report of 1960 summarized the situation: 'Except
for the brewing of beer (pombe) by Africans, there is little "cottage" industry
engaged in the production of traditional handicrafts for the African market. In
the towns and villages, however, in numerous small establishments, the production of footwear, clothing, simple furniture and other household items is carried
on mainly by Asians' (IBRD, 1961, 129).

African work force
The lack of industrialization in Tanganyika meant that the numbers of Africans
employed in the urban economy were small. In 1957, there were 71,101
Africans working in the private non-agricultural sector. This represented 21 per
cent of the African wage-earning work force. The majority of African employees
(167,425 or 51 per cent), worked in agriculture, and the remainder worked in
the public service (92,686 or 28 per cent). In contrast, there were 156,800 Africans in the private non-agricultural sector in Kenya, which was twice the number
in Tanganyika (despite the fact that the African population was more than 10 per
cent smaller) (Tanzania, *Statistical Abstract*, 1958, 66). This was about 28 per
cent of the Kenyan African work force (Kenya, *Statistical Abstract 1964*, 111).

The Tanganyikan agricultural work force was, as well, less a fully proletariat working class than that in Kenya. The estates in Tanganyika produced, as I have said, non-food crops. This meant that they had to rely upon the surrounding areas for their food, and as a result did not draw their labour force from these areas as much as from regions farther away. The working force created by the estates was largely a migrant force. The worker left his family in his home region, and returned there when he could. This contrasted with the pattern in Kenya where the estates grew their own food, and drew the labour force from the tribe (largely the Kukuyu) that they displaced. The labour force created in Kenya was clearly a permanent working class, and depended for its livelihood on the monetary economy to a much greater extent than did its counterpart in Tanganyika.[18]

Role of the Europeans
At the top of this three-tier system were the Europeans. They were the owners of the very large estates, the managers of the foreign firms, and the executives of the government. Most Europeans (89 per cent in 1957) were employees of the government or foreign-owned firms, rather than employers (Tanzania, *Statistical Abstract*, 1958, 64). While Asian firms were vital to the retail trade, important in the wholesale trade, and significant in small-scale processing and manufacturing, foreign firms dominated the import trade and all large-scale manufacturing. The financial system was exclusively foreign.

Tanganyika stands in contrast to Kenya in respect to the size and importance of its European population. In Kenya, the European population was more than twice as large (see Table 2). Europeans in Kenya owned more of their own businesses, and were more important to the whole economy. In 1963 large farms contributed 78 per cent of cash revenue to farm producers in Kenya (Kenya, *Economic Survey 1967-8*, 16). In contrast, only 21 per cent of the value added in the monetary sector in agriculture and livestock in Tanganyika came from estates. Thus in terms of understanding the role of Europeans in Tanganyika, it is important to note that although they were very important, they were also very vulnerable. They were less deeply embedded in the economy and social structure than in Kenya. They were of mixed nationalities, and thus were not a cohesive community. Their ability to resist independence, and to influence the policies of the independent government, was not great.

Tribal situation
A brief note of the tribal situation in Tanzania should be given in order to provide a proper background for the discussion. In contrast to most African

18 For a discussion of class formation in Tanganyika, see Iliffe, (1970).

countries, tribal considerations have not been a paramount issue in politics. The pattern of strong rivalry for control by two or three tribes, with one tribe gaining and exploiting positions of power is not present in Tanzania. This is the result of the fact that the tribes which received the best education, and which were located in the regions of most rapid economic growth, are not the largest tribes. The two tribes which tend to dominate the elite are the Wahaya and the Wachagga. Both had about 420,000 members in 1967, and together they made up only 7.5 per cent of the population (Tanzania, *Statistical Abstract*, 1970, 54). It is difficult, then, for them to dominate the political system without going outside the democratic system. So far they have not done so.

The lack of tribal influences in politics is accentuated by the general fragmentation of tribes. Only one tribe, the Wasukuma, has a significant proportion of the population, and their share was only 12.5 per cent in 1967 (Tanzania, *Statistical Abstract*, 1970). The rest of the tribes have individually 5 per cent of the population or less. About a quarter of the population live in tribes of under 100,000 persons (less than 1 per cent of the population), and 71 per cent live in tribes with less than 400,000 people (about 4 per cent of the population).

Importance of class development

The particular class development which occurred in Tanganyika under colonialism partially explains the government behaviour after independence. Tanganyika was, at independence, an essentially rural society with very little class differentiation within its indigenous population. Much of the class development which normally accompanies entry into international capitalism had been thwarted by the arrival of the Asians, who, rather than the Africans, played the role of the dependent bourgeoisie. Thus the Tanganyikan bourgeoisie had little basis in the society. It was essentially a foreign bourgeoisie sitting on top of a largely undifferentiated rural[19] African population[20]. It was, therefore, very vulnerable to attack.

19 The terms rural and urban will play an important role in this study. It is worth taking some time, then, to give a more precise definition of what constitutes the urban population. In Tanzania, the definition has varied over time. Up until 1967 the population criterion for a settlement to be considered urban was over 5000 people. In 1967 the level was raised by the Central Statistical Bureau to 10,000. I will define the urban population as including all those living in towns which in 1971 had a population of 10,000 or more. Thus towns will be included as urban centres in 1948 even if their population was then below 5000. I do this because it is my belief that the list of fifteen towns so formed constitutes the urban population as perceived by most Tanzanians. Places like Mbeya, which had less than 5000 people in 1948, were important urban centres, and probably should be classed as such. Table 3 gives the population of those towns for four years, 1948, 1957, 1967, and 1971-72. Where a division between Africans and non-Africans was available, this is given. Total urban population in Tanzania

TABLE 3

Urban population growth in Tanzania

	1948		1957		1967	1971/72
	African	Total	African	Total	Total	Total
Dar es Salaam	50,765	69,227	93,363	128,742	272,821	395,000
Tanga	16,671	22,317	27,973	38,053	61,058	71,480
Mwanza	8885	11,296	15,241	19,877	34,861	46,300
Tabora	10,755	12,768	12,005	15,361	21,012	23,000
Morogoro	7308	8173	12,440	14,507	25,262	31,500
Moshi	5533	8048	9399	13,726	26,864	36,500
Dodoma	7499	9414	10,386	13,435	23,559	30,000
Kigoma/Ujiji	7000[1]	7200[1]	15,887[1]	16,255	21,369	24,700
Mtwara	5000[1]	5300[1]	9617	10,459	20,413	21,500
Lindi	7425	8577	8370	10,315	13,352	15,500
Arusha	2946	5320	5161	10,038	32,452	50,000
Iringa	5500[1]	5702	9300[1]	9587	21,746	32,000
Mbeya	3000[1]	3179	6700[1]	6932	12,479	16,900
Bukoba	3200[1]	3247	5200[1]	5297	8141	13,600
Musoma	6800[1]	7000[1]	15,800	16,000	20,000	21,800
Total	148,287	186,668	256,842	328,584	615,389	835,100
Percent of population	2.0	2.5	2.9	3.8	5.1	6.1

SOURCES: Tanzania, *Statistical Abstracts*, 1964, 16; 1970, 46; *Economic Survey*, 1971-2, 106.

1 Estimate

has grown at a rate of about 7 per cent per year since 1948. Most of this increase is accounted for by the growth of the African urban population since the Asian and European populations in the country as a whole have stagnated in growth. In 1948, 2 per cent of the African population lived in urban centres. This rose to 2.9 per cent in 1957. We can estimate, by assuming that the urban Asian population was only slightly greater in 1967 than in 1957, that 4.7 per cent of the African population lived in urban centres in 1967 and 5.5 per cent in 1971-2. Thus it seems fair to say that Tanzania still is today a very rural society.

20 Some will object to this statement as being a simplification, and one that ignores the beginnings of class differentiation within the rural sector, and the very real disparities in incomes between regions. While this is true, it is nevertheless clear that compared to most societies, the African population was less differentiated.

The lack of an indigeneous African middle class posed a real problem to the independent government in terms of developing the economy. Encouraging private enterprise meant encouraging Asian or foreign enterprise. In explaining the nationalizations which occurred in Tanzania in 1967, Nyerere put this view succinctly: 'Private investment in Africa means overwhelming foreign private investment. A capitalist economy means a foreign dominated economy. These are the facts of Africa's situation. The only way in which national control of the economy can be achieved is through the economic institutions of socialism' (1968, 264). While nationalizations of foreign firms helped to solve this problem, it did not resolve the issue of Asian enterprise. In later chapters, I will talk in more detail about the need to fill the role played by Asian, as well as foreign firms. In the next section however, I will examine in more detail the response of people like Nyerere to Tanganyika's position at independence.

POLITICAL RESPONSE SINCE INDEPENDENCE

In this section I will try to trace out the response of the government to Tanzania's position at independence. Here I will present what might be called the 'official ideology' of the country, which is essentially the response of one man, President Nyerere, to the difficulties of developing socialism in a small, poor country in the middle of Africa. Nyerere's views have heretofore been the views of the government, and indeed the country. While it is clear that there has been disagreement within the government about policies, and while it is also clear that among politically articulate Tanzanians there is significant criticism of many of Nyerere's positions, it is nonetheless true that Nyerere's views have generally prevailed, and that his political and intellectual dominance of the country is overwhelming.[21] I will, in chapter eight, look at some of the criticisms of his ideas. At this point, however, it is best to study his views on over-all strategy, and on investment strategy in particular.

The ideological response of the government since independence can be seen as involving a gradual evolution both in understanding what is involved in the notion of socialism, and in understanding the need to institutionalize socialism

21 The reasons why the elite in Tanzania was able to propell the country towards socialism, and why one man could, in the period immediately after independence, so dominate the elite are not clear. My view is that a political vacuum existed in Tanzania as a result of the lack of class development in the African population. This created the unusual situation where certain individuals had extraordinary influence. This period is coming to an end, and the politics of the country will be increasingly determined by the political strength of the different social and economic groups which have developed in the post-independence period. This argument is pursued more fully in chapter seven.

and the forms that institutionalization must take. These parallel processes of defining what one wants socialism to mean, and in discovering the social institutions necessary to create socialism continue today in Tanzania. In fact, I will argue in later chapters that some of the failure to implement the goals of socialism result from a failure to develop the proper institutions to implement them.

Early view

TANU was committed to building 'socialism' in Tanzania (then Tanganyika) as early as 1962. This commitment to socialism was not unusual. Most newly independent African governments adopted the rhetoric of socialism, but in almost all cases there was little content to the commitment. Initially this was true in Tanzania as well. In a pamphlet issued by the Party in April of that year called *Ujamaa – The Basis of African Socialism* (reprinted in Nyerere, 1968b), Nyerere sets out what he regards as socialism. 'Socialism – like democracy – is an attitude of mind. In a socialist society it is the socialist attitude of mind, and not the rigid adherence to a standard political pattern, which is needed to ensure that the people care for each other's welfare' (*ibid.*, 1). A socialist, to Nyerere, is one who does not desire to exploit or dominate his fellow man. At this stage, then, Nyerere held what many would regard as a rather naïve view of socialism, since it was devoid of almost any institutional framework for achieving the desired attitude of mind or mode of behaviour.

If there is a basic theme to Nyerere's writings it is his stress on equality. 'The basic difference between a socialist society and a capitalist society does not lie in their methods of producing wealth, but in the way that wealth is distributed' (*ibid.*, 2). The foundation of Nyerere's commitment to socialism has never altered. He says he is a socialist because he is committed to helping create a society where all men will be equal. This basic theme recurs again and again in all his writings.

Nyerere also introduces at this stage his rather controversial view that African society prior to European colonisation was essentially socialistic. It was colonialism which introduced the desire to accumulate, and thus to exploit. 'Our first step, therefore, must be to re-educate ourselves; to regain our former attitude of mind. In our traditional African society we were individuals within a community. We took care of the community, and the community took care of us. We neither needed nor wanted to exploit our fellow men' (*ibid.*, 6-7).

The government's programme of development corresponded to this naïve view of socialism. It differed hardly at all from the development plans of other African countries less committed to socialism. Private investment, both local and foreign, was to be a major engine of growth.[22] The government development corporation (National Development Corporation) was seen as a vehicle for attracting private capital[23] rather than for extending the control of the government over the economy.

Change in views
Several forces worked together to gradually change Nyerere's ideas on the viability of a traditional strategy. The belief that Tanzania could move towards increasing equality, and the development (or restoration?) of a socialist state of mind without at the same time altering the basis of the economy or the society could not be held for long. Nyerere soon realized that socialism required some form of institutionalization. In the preface (written in July 1968) to his book *Ujamaa: Essays on Socialism* (1968b) Nyerere describes his change in view.

It gradually became clear that the absence of a generally accepted and easily understood statement of philosophy and policy was allowing some Government and Party actions which were not consistent with the building of socialism, and which even encouraged the growth of non-socialist values and attitudes. Thus, for example, the Africanization for which TANU had campaigned during the independence struggle was being interpreted to mean replacement of non-African landlords, employers, and capitalists by African ones. Also, the increasing number of Africans driving large cars or living in luxurious houses was being advanced as a sign of national progress. Meanwhile the masses of the people were continuing to live in poverty, because their conditions of life were not affected by such transfer of privilege from non-citizen to citizen (*ibid.*).

The economic viability of the strategy also appeared in doubt. Independence did not alter the position of Tanzania relative to Kenya, or to international capitalism. Tanzania was not particularly attractive to foreign investors. It had a small market, and had less advantages then Kenya for the investor interested in the East African market. Thus foreign investment did not flow in as expected. Rather, it came only when coaxed by the government.

22 In the First Five Year Plan, private investment was to contribute 47 per cent of total fixed capital formation. This contrasts to 27 per cent in the Second Five Year Plan.
23 Nyerere said on 8 June 1965: 'This does not mean that the NDC is, or should be, sole owner of what it participates in. Its job is to promote maximum development, and to use its own resource to achieve the greatest possible growth in the economy ... this will mean that by investing less than £2 million the NDC will have promoted investment in Tanzania worth £8 million ...' (1968a, 42).

The original strategy also assumed that foreign aid would play a major role in developing the economy. Here too the government was disappointed. Tanzania was soon involved in a number of political disputes with its major aid donors.[24] The reaction of the donors showed the Tanzanians that aid often involved political obligations. If they were to pursue a policy of non-alignment, a policy which they had accepted, then a strategy which depended upon aid inflows was not very secure.

The Arusha Declaration

The result of this increasing disillusionment with a traditional strategy was the Arusha Declaration (printed in Nyerere, 1968b), passed by TANU in February 1967. The Arusha Declaration represents both an attempt to define further the meaning of African socialism, and to institutionalize some of that meaning. The document set forth the principles of socialism to which TANU was dedicated. It called for the government to '[exercise] effective control over the principle means of production and [pursue] policies which facilitate the way to collective ownership of the resources of this country' (*ibid.*) Secondly, it made public what had already been accepted privately by the government, that the policy of relying on foreign assistance, both private and public, for development was a failure. It therefore, called for self-reliance in development. 'We should not lessen our efforts to get the money we really need, but it would be more appropriate for us to spend time in the villages showing the people how to bring about development through their own efforts rather than going on so many long and expensive journeys abroad in search of development money. This is the real way to bring development to everybody in the country' (*ibid.*, 32).

Thirdly, the declaration called for an emphasis on agriculture. It argued that the only way the lives of the majority could be improved was by improving agriculture, and that this could be done only by mobilizing the people. 'From now on we shall stand upright and walk forward on our feet rather than look at the problem upside down. Industries will come and money will come but their foundation is *the people* and their *hard work*, especially in AGRICULTURE. This is the meaning of self-reliance' (*ibid.*, 33; emphasis in original).

Finally, the declaration called for a shift in the party away from a broad-based one containing people of many views and backgrounds to one consisting solely of committed socialists. All leaders (defined as members of the TANU

24 In 1964, the United States was accused of attempting to overthrow the government. In the same year, West Germany withdrew its recognition of Tanzania because it allowed an East German consul to continue to remain in Zanzibar after union. In 1965 Tanzania broke relations with Great Britain, and Britain stopped all aid after it refused to crush the illegal declaration of independence by Rhodesia.

executive, senior government or parastatal officials, or elected officials) would have to abide by a leadership code. The code proscribed any capitalist behaviour on the part of leaders. One could not earn more than one salary, hold director-ships in private companies, rent houses to others, or hold shares in any company.[25]

The Arusha Declaration was followed by a series of acts[26] which ensured government control over the major sectors of the monetary economy. All private banks were nationalized and merged into the National Bank of Commerce. The government acquired complete control of the National Insurance Corporation (it had previously owned 51 per cent, the remaining shares were held by private insurance companies) and NIC became the sole insurer in Tanzania. Seven major milling operations were nationalized, and later formed into the National Milling Corporation.[27] Under the Industrial Acquisition Act majority ownership was acquired in seven firms, the largest industrial concerns in the country. A few months later about half the sisal estates were nationalized.[28] Altogether, the government acquired shs 362 million[29] in assets (see chapter five for break-down). Almost all large-scale enterprises were now government controlled. The only major exceptions were in estate agriculture where large numbers of private firms remained.

The Arusha Declaration was followed by two policy statements 'Education for Self-Reliance' and 'Socialism and Rural Development' (reprinted in Nyerere, 1968b), setting out in more detail the implications of Arusha. These papers were part of the process of refining the meaning of Tanzanian socialism. The first paper dealt with the education system.

'Education for Self-Reliance'
In 'Education for Self-Reliance,' Nyerere argues that Tanzania inherited a system of education which was designed for a colonial state.[30] This system was entirely

25 In 1973 this code was strengthened when an act of parliament was passed which gave the leadership code legal status. Leaders who violated the code now risked criminal punishments.
26 The acts were: (1) Industrial (Acquisition) Act – passed 15 February 1967; (2) National Bank of Commerce Act – passed 14 February 1967; (3) State Trading Corporation Act – passed 14 February 1967; (4) National Agricultural Products Board Act – passed 15 February 1967; (5) National Insurance Corporation Act – passed 15 February 1967.
27 National Milling Corporation Act 1968
28 Tanzania Sisal Corporation Act – passed 27 October 1967 – originally nationalized 39 estates, later amended to 40 estates.
29 Taken as difference between parastatal assets at end of 1967 and parastatal investments in 1967 and parastatal assets at the end of 1966.
30 For a fuller discussion of the topic, see Resnick (1968).

oriented to producing the needed clerks and junior officials for the colonial bureaucracy. Primary education was centred around the 13 per cent who would get a place in a secondary school, not the 87 per cent who would not. Both the economic and social costs of such waste are great.[31]

In other words, the education now provided is designed for the few who are intellectually stronger than their fellows; it induces among those who succeed a feeling of superiority, and leaves the majority of the others hankering after something they will never obtain. It induces a feeling of inferiority among the majority, and can thus not produce either the egalitarian society we should build, nor the attitudes of mind which are conducive to an egalitarian society. On the contrary, it induces the growth of a class structure in our country (Nyerere, 1968b, 55).

The curriculum of the schools was to be completely revamped. Primary education should prepare a student to return to agriculture. It should be an education complete in itself, and not oriented solely to preparing and selecting students for further education. As much as possible, primary schools should be self-reliant, producing their own food, doing their own repairs. Students should be taught modern techniques in agriculture both in the classroom and through practical work. The techniques should not be capital-intensive, but ones applicable to the average farmer.

The same applied to the secondary schools, but with more force. Here the problem was the need to break down class elitist attitudes. This would be done only by developing a school which taught admiration for manual labour, rather than disdain. Students at the secondary school level should be old enough to make their schools almost totally self-reliant. The great emphasis in the society on education and degrees should be played down.

'Socialism and Rural Development'

In September of 1967, Nyerere (1968b) set out, in the paper 'Socialism and Rural Development,' a more detailed view of the type of development he envisaged for the rural areas. He began by arguing again the need to develop them if equality is to be maintained. The urban areas are centres of attraction, which create unrealistic desires among the people.

In fact only about 4 per cent of our people live in towns ... Unfortunately, the life of these tiny minorities has become a matter of great envy for the majority. Life in the towns has come to represent opportunities for advancement, a chance

31 See Bowles (1971a, b) for this same argument applied more generally.

of excitement, and the provision of social services, none of which is easily available in the rural areas. Most of all, there is an almost universal belief that life in the towns is more comfortable and more secure — that the rewards of work are better in the urban areas and that people in the rural parts of the country are condemned to poverty and insecurity for their whole lives (*ibid.*, 111).

The other development which distressed Nyerere was the beginnings of class development in the rural areas. There was developing in Tanzania a number of 'progressive farmers' to use Dumont's (1967) term who were beginning to expand their land holdings and use paid labour. To Nyerere, this development threatened the whole socialist future of Tanzania.

If this kind of capitalist development takes place widely over the country, we may get a good statistical increase in the national wealth of Tanzania, but the masses of the people will not necessarily be better off. On the contrary, as land becomes more scarce we shall find ourselves with a farmers' class and a laborers' class, with the latter being unable either to work for themselves or to receive a full return for the contribution they are making to the total output. They will become a 'rural proletariat' depending on the decisions of other men for their existence, and subject in consequence to all the subservience, social and economic inequality, and insecurity, which such a position involves (Nyerere, 1968b, 115).

A socialist strategy for the rural areas was essential, for: 'The land is the only basis for Tanzania's development; we have no other. Therefore, if our rural life is not based on the principles of socialism our country will not be socialist, regardless of how we organize our commercial and political arrangements. Tanzanian socialism must be firmly based on the land and its workers' (*ibid.*, 118). This can be done only by the development of Ujamaa villages, 'economic and social communities where people live together and work together for the good of all' (*ibid.*, 120). 'In a socialist Tanzania then, our agricultural organization would be predominately that of co-operative living and working for the good of all. This means that most of our farming would be done by groups of people who live as a community and work as a community. They would live together in a village; they would farm together; market together; and undertake the provision of local services and small local requirements as a community ... The land this community farmed would be called "our land" by all the members; the crops they produced on that land would be "our crops"...' (*ibid.*, 124).

The Ujamaa village was to be based on traditional agriculture and involve gradual improvement in the productivity of the peasant farmer. 'The important thing is that there should be no reliance on great outside capital injection (*ibid.*,

142).[32] The government's role was 'to help the people organize themselves, to advise them on how they can become eligible for advances for seed, or for small loans for farm equipment' (*ibid.*, 143), and to 'ensure the necessary agricultural advice' (*ibid.*, 142). The development of Ujamaa villages was another attempt, as we will see in chapter three, at villagization[33] of peasants who were often scattered widely. It therefore offered the possibility of providing social services to people (at a reasonable cost), which is an essential ingredient of any rural-oriented strategy, by bringing the people together. If this scheme was to be successful, it would have to be part of a larger programme which would provide services to all the rural areas, not just to a few showpiece rural communities. The services provided to Ujamaa villages had to be at a level which could be provided economically to all the rural sector, although it was clear that Ujamaa villages were to be given priority in receiving these services.

What of the role of state farms or estates? 'Thus, indeed in the rural and agricultural organization of a socialist Tanzania, there must be some state or other public enterprises, operated under the control of appointed managers and employing labor just as the nationalized food mills do. But this should only be a small part of the agricultural sector in Tanzania. It should not be our purpose to convert our peasants into wage-earners, even on government farms' (*ibid.*, 124).

TANU Guidelines

In 1971, the Party issued the TANU *Guidelines*. These reemphasized the party's commitment to building socialism and liberating Africa. In particular they stressed the need for equality between leaders and the people. Article 15, which sets out the qualifications of a leader, has become a major instrument for workers to use against management of both government- and non-government-controlled firms. 'There must be a deliberate effort to build equality between the leaders and those they lead. For a Tanzanian leader it must be forbidden to be arrogant, extravagant, contemptuous and oppressive. The Tanzanian leader has to be a person who respects people, scorns ostentation and who is not a tyrant' (TANU, 1971, 5).

The *Guidelines* also stressed the need to bring the people into the decision-making apparatus. This was the beginning of attempts to bring workers control into the factories, and lay the basis for the later decentralization. '... we have

32 In arguing for a non-capital-intensive approach, Nyerere was reacting to the settlement schemes developed by the colonial, and immediate post-independence administrations which sought dramatically to raise the living standards of a few peasants. See chapter three for more discussion of these schemes, and the Ujamaa programme.

33 The need to bring peasants together has always been, and continues to be today an important goal of the government.

inherited in the government, industries and other institutions the habit in which one man gives the orders and the rest just obey him. If you do not involve the people in work plans, the result is to make them feel a national institution is not theirs, and consequently workers adopt the habits of hired employees' (*ibid.*, 4). 'If development is to benefit the people, the people must participate in considering planning and implementing their development plans' (*ibid.*, 9).

Decentralization

The *Guidelines* had stressed the need for the people to be involved in the planning process. In 1972, the government responded to this call by decentralizing much of its administration. While some government departments (called ministries in Tanzania) had always been partially decentralized, this decentralization shifted a large part of the work of nine key ministries[34] to the regions. In the process of doing so, the government created regional administrations which were to be as important as central ministries.[35] (See Map 1 for location of regions.)

The decentralization can be seen as having had two goals. First, it was to create a strong bureaucratic lobby for rural development. The areas which were decentralized were those of most concern to rural development. Thus, primary education became a regional concern, but not secondary education. Rural water and water for small towns fell under regional jurisdiction, but water for the large cities did not. Rural health centres and regional hospitals were decentralized, but consultant hospitals were not. The young Tanzanian official who was sent to the regions could not make a name for himself by proposing grandiose schemes to build steel mills, or hydro dams. The areas under his control, and therefore in which he had to succeed, were those of most immediate concern to the rural peasant. His energies had to be directed towards rural development, even if he felt more comfortable working out schemes for urban development.

A second goal of decentralization was to bring some measure of participation into the planning process. Initiation and development of projects was to begin at the ward level and work its way up, not start at the top and work down. 'The purpose of both the Arusha Declaration and of Mwongozo [TANU *Guidelines*] was to give the people power over their own lives and their own development. 'We have made great progress in seizing power from the hands of capitalists and traditionalists, but we must face the fact that, to the mass of the people power is

34 These ministries were: Regional Administration, Agriculture, Lands and Urban Planning, Health, Water, Labor and Social Welfare, Natural Resources, Education, and Commerce and Industries.
35 For a description of the decentralization, see Mulokozi (n.d.).

still something wielded by others — even if on their behalf' (Nyerere, 1972a, 1). 'One of the major purposes of this reorganization is to ensure that future econo- mic planning stems from the people and serves the people directly' (*ibid.*, 5).[36]

Thus, over a period of about ten years much progress was made in defining the concept of socialism, and in building the institutions to help achieve the goals. Socialism was originally only a 'state of mind.' By 1972, it implied state ownership of the means of production, an emphasis on rural development, or- ganization of agriculture along the lines of co-operative villages, a leadership code for the elite, and decentralization of much of government administration. The process is not finished, but will continue as long as Tanzania's commitment to socialism remains.

Investment strategy

While Nyerere was developing the implications of his commitment to equality for over-all development strategy, he was also specifying in greater detail his ideas on an investment strategy. Nyerere has never written a paper on a socialist investment strategy for Tanzania. Indeed, in many cases, his views remain vague, and sometimes contradictory. There is, nevertheless, a consistent general approach which makes it possible to interpret his position on most issues. More- over, Nyerere has made a surprisingly large number of statements explicitly on investment decisions. It is possible, as a result, to know Nyerere's views on each of the strategic issues outlined in chapter one.

Nyerere's position on the equality and growth issue is clear enough. He is quite prepared to trade off growth for equality. He is prepared to accept this trade-off for investments both within, and between sectors. Nyerere finds unacceptable an agricultural programme designed to promote rural development through investing in the most progressive farmers. Such a programme would produce in his view a kulak class.[37]

The stress on equality also implies an approach to inter-sectoral investment allocations. Public investment had to be concentrated on improving agriculture, because it was only in this way that the lives of the vast majority of the popula- tion could be improved. Moreover at this stage in Tanzania's development, a Big

36 By moving the bureaucracy closer to the people, and attempting to set up a decision- making structure which allowed local organizations to have some voice in the planning procedure, the government hoped that mass participation would be increased.
37 'Firstly, what are the social objectives of change? For example, we in Tanganyika would reject the creation of a rural class system even if it could be proved that this gives the largest overall production increase. We would reject this method of securing national economic improvement because it would defeat the total purpose of change, which is the well-being of all our people' (Nyerere, 1966, 237).

Push approach to industry is simply not viable. There are not in Nyerere's view the resources available to establish a large industrial sector.[38] Agriculture, on the other hand, is a sector where a small investment can make a large difference.[39] It should be the priority sector,[40] therefore, on both social and economic grounds.

The sense of poverty of the country and the belief that foreign capital was not readily available for Tanzania both led to a lack of emphasis on industries and implied that labour-intensive industries should, in general, be favoured, although Nyerere's position on this issue has never been clear cut.[41]

The emphasis on rural development also implied an attitude to urban development. Urban development as a whole was to be deemphasized so that towns would not develop as centres of attraction for the rural areas. This could be

38 In the Arusha Declaration, Nyerere said: 'Because of our emphasis on money, we have made another big mistake. We have put too much emphasis on industries. Just as we have said, without money there can be no development, we also seem to say, "Industries are the basis of development, without industries there is no development" ... The mistake we are making is to think that development begins with industries. It is a mistake because we do not have the means to establish many modern industries in our country. We do not have either the necessary finances or the technical know-how' (1968b, 25-6).

39 In a speech to the University of Dar es Salaam on 5 April 1967, Nyerere said: 'The one thing we certainly do not have is money searching for investment opportunities. The *per capita* income, in terms of 1966 prices, was almost shs 525 last year. That does not allow very much to be withdrawn from current consumption and invested in development. Indeed we did very well last year to find shs 125 million (that is, about shs 14 per person) from internal resources for development. But to provide one job in a highly mechanized industry can cost shs 40,000 or more. To build the oil refinery cost more than shs 110 million. To build a modern steel mill would cost rather more than that. On the other hand, it is possible to double the output of cotton in a particular area by spending shs 130 on fertilizer and insecticide; it is possible to double a farmer's acreage under crops by the provision of an ox plough at a cost of shs 250 or less and so on. In other words, whereas, it is possible to find the sort of investment capital which can bring great increases in agricultural output from our present resources, it is not possible for us to envisage establishing heavy industries, or even very much in the way of light industries, in the near future' (1968b, 95-6).

40 In a speech at the opening of the Morogoro Agricultural College on 18 November 1965 Nyerere began: 'Agricultural progress is the basis of Tanzanian development. This truth is said so often that people forget it. They almost don't listen, the words become part of the atmosphere and have no impact any more. To talk of the importance of agriculture is like playing a record which has been heard too often. Yet it remains true. Agricultural progress is indeed the basis of Tanzanian development – and thus of a better standard of living for the people of Tanzania' (1968a, 104).

41 In an address to Cairo University in April 1967, called 'The Varied Paths to Socialism' Nyerere said: 'But even when we are building factories which serve the whole nation, we have to consider whether it is necessary for us to use the most modern machinery

accomplished only by investing in the rural areas to make life there more enjoyable.[42] The emphasis on primary education, and the change in the curriculum (designed to maintain students' interest in remaining in the agricultural sector) are part of the policy of emphasis on the rural areas. Nyerere was very much aware of the tendency in many Third World countries for the government to follow policies which in effect taxed the rural areas to develop the urban areas. He regarded such policies as potentially a new form of exploitation.[43]

Nyerere has never been explicit on an urban strategy, but it is clear that he wants to see urban development integrated into rural development. The Second Five Year Plan put a major priority on a more equitable regional allocation of

---

which exists in the world. We have to consider whether some older equipment which demands more labor, but labor which is less highly skilled, is not better suited to our needs, as well as being more within our capacity to build and use' (1968b, 98-9). Later, in introducing the Second Five Year Plan, he said 'Although mass production is the best and cheapest way of meeting the needs of our people for certain types of goods, there are many others where the needs can be best met by labor intensive, small scale industries and craft workshops' (Tanzania, 1969, vol. I, xiii).

Nevertheless, Nyerere does not envisage solely concentrating on labour-intensive processing and consumer goods industries. He recognizes the need to begin to develop industries which reflect the future structure of the economy. 'We shall continue to expand simple manufacturing, the processing of primary commodities, and the provision of basic construction materials ... it is comparatively easy to produce your own textiles, cement and similar goods, beginning to produce your own capital goods, and goods which are used only in the production of other things, is a more complex operation and demands a more sophisticated degree of economic planning. Yet such a move is essential for long term growth ...' *ibid.*).

42 The Second Five Year Plan states: 'The nature of urban growth cannot be divorced from the problem of rural development. Funds allocated to the development of towns are not available for rural development; the pursuit of rural development implies restraint in the provisions or urban services' (*ibid.*, 7).

43 In the Arusha Declaration Nyerere said, 'our emphasis on money and industries has made us concentrate on urban development ... Yet the greater part of this money that we spend in the towns comes from loans. Whether it is used to build schools, hospitals, houses or factories, etc. it still has to be repaid ... To repay the loans we have to use foreign currency which is obtained from the sale of our exports ... What does this mean? It means that the people who benefit directly from development which is brought about by borrowed money are not the ones who will repay the loans. The largest proportion of the loans will be spent in, or, for, the urban areas, but the largest proportion of the repayment will be made through the efforts of the farmers. There are two possible ways of dividing the people in our country. We can put the capitalists and feudalists on one side, and the farmers and workers on the other. But we can also divide the people into urban dwellers on one side and those who live in the rural areas on the other. If we are not careful we might get to the position where the real exploitation in Tanzania is that of the town dwellers exploiting the peasants' (1968b, 26-8).

investment, and stressed a policy of locating industry in towns other than Dar es Salaam.[44] Nyerere had made the point as early as 1965 that industry should be decentralized as much as possible.[45]

Nyerere's emphasis on self-reliance does not flow from the traditional leftist view that aid and trade are detrimental to growth. Self-reliance was initially a strategy of necessity rather than choice. It originated in the view that large amounts of foreign capital inflow were simply not available, and when they were available, it was not on a secure long-term basis. Self-reliance was therefore mandatory. If aid was available on acceptable political terms, Tanzania was ready, and anxious to receive it. Nyerere has also frequently criticized Tanzanians who complain about the use of expatriates. The government has pushed to 'localize' positions as fast as possible, but Nyerere continually reasserts the need for foreign expertise.

Nor did self-reliance imply a lack of emphasis on exports. Quite the contrary; Nyerere has repeatedly stated the need to raise exports to earn foreign exchange. Thus Nyerere's view of self-reliance does not correspond to the typical socialist's interpretation of the meaning of the term. He is not unaware of the real benefits of true self-reliance, especially the benefits derived from unlocking the potential of the people. Yet, Nyerere remains convinced that both aid and trade[46] are essential to Tanzania.

44 The Second Five Year Plan states: 'Also urban growth must be planned so as to increase rural development possibilities; the tendency to concentrate most urban development in Dar es Salaam must be checked and a number of alternative urban centres encouraged, to spread the secondary effects of urban growth amongst the major centres of rural population' (Tanzania, 1969, n. II, 7).

45 Nyerere said, in opening a printing shop in Arusha on 29 November 1965: 'From a social and economic point of view it is better if our industrial development is scattered throughout the United Republic. In so far as there is a choice, we in Tanzania would infinitely prefer to see many small factories started in different towns in our country rather than one big factory started in any one of them. Such a dispersal means that we are saved very many social problems of too rapid growth in any one city, and from the consequent break-up of all our traditional social organization; it promotes agriculture in the different regions of our country by providing local markets of wage earners, and a communications centre; and it spreads an understanding and familiarity with the possibilities and requirements of modern living and modern working. But although I have no ambition to see our capital city – or any other town – become a great soul-less mass, in which people live in isolation while crowded among their fellow citizens, there is only one way in which this can be avoided. That is by having new industrial enterprises scattered throughout our nation' (1968a, 107).

46 In a speech given to the University of Dar es Salaam on 5 August 1967, Nyerere said: 'There are, however, two respects in which our call for self-reliance has been widely misunderstood or deliberately misinterpreted. The doctrine of self-reliance does not imply

In chapters three to six I will be looking in detail at the extent to which public investment has been consistent with Nyerere's strategy. Before doing this, I must present one more piece of background data. To understand the role and pattern of public investment, one must have a grasp of the development of the economy in the period since independence. As well, one should know the pattern of total investment. The purpose of the next section is to provide this background.

THE ECONOMY SINCE INDEPENDENCE

General performance

The Tanzanian economy has been characterized by steady, if unspectacular growth in the period since independence. Given some of the severe challenges which the country has had to face, both from falling international prices for its major export, sisal, and from the inherent difficulties involved in switching an economy from reliance on capitalist entrepreneurs to a socialist government as the main source of investment, the economy has done remarkably well. From 1964 to 1972,[47] GDP in 1966 prices grew at an annual average of 5.4 per cent, while monetary GDP grew at an average of 6.4 per cent per year. Per capita growth of real GDP was 2.6 per cent per year, and of monetary GDP, 3.6 per cent per year (see Appendix I).

There has been rapidly growing investment. Total capital formation more than tripled in size in the period 1964 to 1972 and rose from 13.7 per cent of GDP in 1964 to 24.3 per cent in 1972. Part of this increase reflects the construction of the railway (called Tazara) by the Chinese to Zambia. The peak period of construction was in 1971 when investment was 29.2 per cent of GDP. If Tazara is excluded from our figures, investment would still have increased 2.5 times since 1964, and equalled 19.7 per cent of GDP in 1971.

---

isolationism, either politically or economically. It means that we shall depend on ourselves, not on others. But this is not the same thing as saying we shall not trade with other people or co-operate with them when it is to mutual benefit. Obviously we shall do so. We shall have to continue to sell enough of our goods abroad to pay for the things we have to acquire ... The other thing which is necessary to understand about self-reliance is that Tanzania has not said it does not want international assistance in its development. We shall continue to seek capital from abroad for particular projects or as a contribution to general development' (1968b, 99-100).

47 I shall use the years 1964 to 1972 as the base of comparison, because national accounts data before 1964 have not been revised, and are regarded by CSB as somewhat unreliable.

This increased investment has been financed to only a very limited extent by an increase in internal capital accumulation. A very rapid rise in foreign capital inflows, of private capital in the early years, and of foreign aid recently, largely accounts for the good investment performance. Figures on capital inflows are not complete, but the revised National Accounts (Tanzania, 1972b) indicates that foreign capital's net contribution to investment was only 4 per cent of total investment in 1966 and 25 per cent in 1970 (*ibid.*, 16). Thus, the movement of the government to a policy of socialism and self-reliance did not decrease the inflow of foreign capital. I will pursue this point in further detail in chapter six which centres on the financing of public investment. There I will argue that the shift in policy caused the increased inflow of foreign capital.

Economic growth in Tanzania has not been characterized by the rapid inflation typical of many poor countries. Over the period 1964-72 the GDP deflator rose at an annual average rate of 1.9 per cent per year, 1.4 per cent for monetary GDP. If we take the period 1964-72, the minimum wage earners price index rose at an average annual rate of 4.4 per cent, while the middle grade civil servants index rose 3.7 per cent. The rate of inflation has increased in recent years (the GDP deflator rose 5.9 per cent in 1972) and has hit the low-income urban worker more than the middle-grade civil servant. The item whose price has risen quickest in recent years is food, an item which absorbs more of the low-income worker's than the high-income worker's income. Food price increases have resulted from shortages of several important commodities, and these shortages reflect both supply and distributional problems.[48]

Wage employment has grown quite slowly. Total wage employment grew, on the average, at 2.1 per cent per year in the period 1964 to 1971 (see Table 4). As a share of total population, wage employment has remained constant. The slow growth in employment reflects the difficulties of estate agriculture, particularly sisal estates.[49] Total employment in estate agriculture has fallen about 30 per cent in the period. Non-agricultural employment has grown about 6.4 per cent a year,[50] somewhat less than the growth rate of the non-agricultural monetary GDP.

48 There have been many problems associated wth the gradual elimination of Asian middle-men. Attempts to replace them with socialist institutions have faced extreme difficulties, and have often failed. As well, total agricultural output has grown slowly. Food could become a constraint on growth if a very urban-oriented strategy was adopted, since little has been done to improve the productivity of the rural sector.

49 Employment in sisal estates fell from 76,493 in 1965 to 43,213 in 1969, a drop of 33,280 or 44 per cent over the period. Total estate agriculture in this period dropped only 26,000. See Tanzania (1969, 27).

50 Urban population has been growing at about 6.6 per cent per year indicating only a small problem of urban unemployment.

TABLE 4

Wage employment 1964-71 ('000 persons)

Sector	64	65	66	67	68	69	70	71	Average annual growth (%)
Estate agric.	164	139	126	124	109	113	107	110	−7.0
Mining	8	8	7	6	6	6	6	6	−4.7
Manufacturing	24	26	30	31	35	40	44	55	18.4
Public utilities	5	5	5	7	10	10	11	11	17.1
Construction	34	31	37	42	47	53	55	53	8.0
Commerce	17	18	21	20	21	19	21	23	5.0
Transport	26	26	28	30	32	32	34	40	7.7
Finance	−				−	4	5	6	
Services	75	81	83	86	91	91	93	101	5.0
Total	351	334	336	347	352	368	376	402	2.1
As % of population	3.0	2.8	2.9	2.9	2.9	2.9	2.9	3.0	

Exports have grown at only a moderate rate. Over the period 1964-72, the value of commodity exports grew 5.5 per cent annually, on average, equivalent to the rate of growth of total GDP, but below that of monetary GDP. They have ceased, then, to be the leading sector. A blow to exports was the dramatic decline in the price of sisal, from shs 1467 per ton in 1960 to a low of shs 832 per ton in 1971. In 1972, it recovered somewhat to shs 946 per ton. As the leading producer of sisal, Tanzania restrained output in an effort to maintain the price. Tanzania was very successful in phasing out its emphasis on sisal, and developing new export crops. Sisal exports dropped from shs 424 million in 1964 to shs 145 million in 1972. If this drop had not occurred, exports would have been 10 per cent higher than they were in 1972 (see Appendix I).

The collapse in the price of sisal has made its mark on the political scene by bringing home to Tanzanians the vulnerability of Third World countries to the vagaries of international commodity markets, markets which are dominated by the wealthy capitalist nations. Tanzania has suffered a fairly steady deterioration in its terms of trade since independence.[51] Export prices have fluctuated significantly, and have evidenced no long-term upward trend. The commodity boom of the early 1970's plus the devaluation of the Tanzanian shilling has, however,

51 I have taken the indices given in the *Statistical Abstracts* for 1964 and 1970, and updated them using price data from *Hali Ya Uchumi* 1972-3 for exports. For imports, I was forced to use Kenyan data, obtained from the *Economic Survey 1973*.

raised prices in the last two years. Over-all, export prices have risen 41 per cent since independence, all gained in the last two years. Import prices, on the other hand, have risen in a more steady manner, and also more sharply. They have risen 63 per cent since independence. As a result, the terms of trade have declined on the average of about 1.4 per cent per year.

Imports, financed by the inflow of foreign aid, and often connected to foreign aid projects have risen quickly. They have increased from shs 1252 million in 1964 to shs 2991 million in 1972, a rise of about 140 per cent. Again, however, it may be more meaningful to exclude Tazara.[52] The increase in imports was 96 per cent, or about 8.8 per cent per year if Tazara non-consumer good imports are omitted.

The composition of imports, has altered significantly. In the period 1966-72, the only period for which we have consistent data, imports of consumer goods have risen at an annual rate of only 1.5 per cent per year, or 10 per cent over the period. In fact, the total increase in imports occurred in 1972. Up to that point, imports of consumer goods remained below their 1966 levels of shs 800 million. Intermediate goods rose 130 per cent in the period 1966-72, and capital goods 60 per cent. If Tazara is excluded, intermediate goods imports rose 77 per cent and capital goods 60 per cent.[53] In 1966 consumer goods were 47 per cent of imports. By 1972 they had fallen to 39 per cent of imports, if Tazara non-consumer goods are excluded, and to 30 per cent if they are included. The source of Tanzania's imports has also changed since independence. Here, the influence of foreign aid is very apparent. China supplied none of Tanzania's imports in 1962. In 1972, it supplied shs 508 millions worth, or 17 per cent of external imports. The European Economic Community supplied 14 per cent of the imports in 1962. Now it supplies 21 per cent. In contrast, Britain's share has dropped from 33 per cent to 16 per cent.

52 Tazara is the railway being built by the Chinese to Zambia — see chapters three and four for history. If Tazara is excluded, one should exclude only non-consumer goods which Tazara imports. Tazara local costs are paid for by the Chinese loan. In order to reduce the foreign exchange drain on China, Tanzania has agreed to try to divert some of its consumer goods imports to China. When these goods are imported, the revenue from their sale goes into a special account to pay for the local costs of the railway. Because most of these goods would have been imported anyway, they should be counted in any estimate of the growth of imports which tries to exclude the effect of Tazara.

53 In order to make these calculations, we have had to assume that 60 per cent of Tazara non-consumer good imports are intermediate goods. If so, then Tazara's imports in 1972 were shs 150 million in consumer goods, shs 316 million in intermediate goods, and shs 210 million in capital goods.

The trade gap which Tanzania has suffered with its East African partners has remained, but has declined in relative importance because of the stagnation of trade[54] in the Community (see Appendix I). The deficit with Kenya and Uganda combined was shs 199 million in 1972, up from shs 177 million in 1962. In relative terms, however, the 1972 deficit represented only 8.6 per cent of trade export earnings versus 16.3 per cent in 1962. Trade with Kenya has grown at an annual average rate of 5.2 per cent, with exports growing at 7.7 per cent and imports at 4.7 per cent. In contrast, trade with Uganda, never very large, has almost disappeared, equalling only shs 21 million in 1972.

Structural changes in the economy
An important issue in any discussion of investment strategy is the degree to which and the speed with which structural change can be effected in the economy. For those who would like to see a rapid transformation of the Tanzanian economy, the ten years since independence have been disappointing. The basis of the economy remains much as it was at independence. Exports are still 30 per cent of the GDP. This is a drop from the 37 per cent share they held in 1964, but still represents a significant proportion of the value added generated in the economy. Moreover, exports continue to be externally oriented, and not based on domestic demand.[55]

The agriculture sector has grown slowly, about 3 per cent a year, but continues to dominate the economy. Almost 40 per cent of the GDP in 1972 (39.6 per cent) originated in agriculture. While this represents a drop from 46.7 per cent in 1964 (see Table 5), much of this drop was accounted for by the decline in production of sisal. Some of the industrialization which has occurred in Tanzania since independence has involved the exploitation of linkages with agriculture. Thus, the importance of agriculture to the economy is probably greater than the figure of 40 per cent of the GDP would indicate.

54 The stagnation of trade with the community raises some important questions about strategies based upon exploiting the larger African market through co-operation between independent states. There has been little success in achieving such co-operation within the EAC. There is still intense competition for and much duplication of industries. Often the members of the Community act as if the only way they can increase growth in their own country is by stopping the exports of the other members. As long as there is little political integration, and all the countries remain peripheries, then these attitudes will probably continue.
55 In chapter eight I present the views of Clive Thomas who advocates a strategy which would integrate the economy. Under this strategy exports would be promoted only if they are goods consumed domestically. Products such as sisal, tobacco, diamonds, cashew nuts would be de-emphasized.

While the manufacturing sector has grown fairly rapidly (about 9.8 per cent per year in terms of value added), it still represents less than 10 per cent of the GDP (9.8 per cent in 1972 at constant 1966 prices). Industrialization has largely been concentrated in import-substituting industries, and mainly in consumer goods. While public enterprises have been initiated in a few intermediate goods sectors, the capital goods sector remains almost completely undeveloped. Thus the industrial sector remains quite small, and undiversified.

Two other sectors have grown quite rapidly. The transport sector has grown about 10.2 per cent per year. Much of this growth represents the development of trade links with Zambia. These links were developed in response to the unilateral declaration of independence by Rhodesia (UDI) in 1964. Zambia did not want to remain dependent on transportation routes through Rhodesia. As a result a pipeline (Tazama) was built to supply oil, and a trucking firm developed (Zam-Tam Road Service) to haul goods. The Americans agreed to reconstruct the road from Dar es Salaam to Tunduma (on the border of Zambia) and the Chinese are building the railway (Tazara). While this sector is important (its share of GDP has risen from 6.9 per cent to 9.9 per cent, and it is a major foreign exchange earner), it is the result of a very particular set of political circumstances, and does not represent the over-all development of the transport sector, but simply the development of an importing-exporting service for Zambia.

The other sector which has grown rapidly is utilities. It has grown at a rate of about 10.3 per cent per year. This growth reflects the decision on the part of the government to invest fairly heavily in electricity. Nevertheless, the sector remains only a small part of the economy. In 1972, utilities generated 1.3 per cent of the GDP.

The lack of significant structural change in the economy should, however, be put in the context of Tanzania's position at independence, and its stage of development. While it is true that exports are still important, their importance has fallen. Moreover there has been some diversification, not away from externally-oriented products but to a broader range of these crops.[56] Efforts are

---

56 This diversification appears larger than it actually is. In 1962, four commodities, sisal, coffee, cotton and diamonds made up 65 per cent of the total domestic exports. By 1972, these four commodities were only 48 per cent of domestic exports. These figures exaggerate the diversification because they include cloves and petroleum products. Since cloves are grown only on Zanzibar they should be excluded. Petroleum exports are matched by imports so there is no foreign exchange gain. With these two items excluded, the share of these four commodities dropped from 68 per cent to 61 per cent over the period. Real diversification will take more time. For data see Tanzanian *Hali Ya Uchumi* (1972-3, 20) or Appendix II.

TABLE 5

Gross domestic product at factor cost by industrial origin (at 1966 prices): percentages

	1964	1965	1966	1967	1968	1969	1970	1971	1972
Agriculture, hunting, fishing and forestry	46.7	44.6	45.3	43.3	42.7	42.0	41.0	39.1	39.6
Mining and quarrying	2.5	2.8	2.9	2.7	1.9	2.0	1.8	1.9	1.6
Manufacturing and handicrafts	7.1	7.7	8.1	8.6	8.7	9.4	9.4	9.7	9.8
Electricity and water supply	0.9	0.9	0.9	0.9	1.0	1.1	1.2	1.2	1.3
Construction	3.4	3.4	3.4	4.4	4.4	4.0	4.1	4.6	4.3
Wholesale and retail trade	11.9	12.3	12.7	12.5	13.2	13.3	13.5	12.9	13.1
Transport and communications	6.9	6.9	7.4	7.9	8.6	8.7	9.4	10.1	9.9
Finance, real estate	10.2	10.8	9.5	10.3	9.9	10.2	9.8	9.9	9.8
Public admin. and services	11.0	11.4	10.6	10.8	10.7	10.5	11.1	11.8	11.9
Less imputed bank services, service charges	0.7	0.8	0.8	1.4	1.1	1.2	1.3	1.4	1.4
GDP at factor cost	100.0	100.0	100.0	100.0	100.0	100.0	100.0	100.0	100.0

TABLE 5 cont'd

	1964	1965	1966	1967	1968	1969	1970	1971	1972
Subsistence sector									
Agriculture hunting, forestry and fishing	24.5	23.9	23.6	23.1	21.6	20.8	20.8	20.5	20.5
Construction	0.9	0.9	0.8	0.8	0.7	0.8	0.7	0.7	0.7
Owner-occupied dwellings	7.6	7.6	6.9	6.8	6.7	6.7	6.5	6.4	6.3
Total subsistence production	33.0	32.4	31.5	31.2	30.5	29.1	28.0	27.6	27.5
Total production in the monetary economy	67.0	67.6	68.5	68.8	69.5	70.9	72.0	72.4	72.5
Total production	100.0	100.0	100.0	100.0	100.0	100.0	100.0	100.0	100.0

SOURCE: Tanzania, *Hali Ya Uchumi*, 1972-3, 8

being made to increase the output of crops like cotton, cashewnuts, and meat, whose long-run price performance can be expected to be better than such items as coffee or sisal.

While Tanzania has not developed a diversified industrial structure, the industrial sector has grown rapidly. Its small share reflects the very small base from which Tanzania started. Much of this study is devoted to studying the issue of an appropriate industrial strategy, so I will not elaborate on it in detail here. Suffice it to say that it does not seem to me necessarily inappropriate to exploit some of the many obvious industrial linkages from the agricultural base of the economy before embarking on an industrialization programme committed to producing an integrated industrial sector.

Role of the public institutions in the economy

This study is devoted to a detailed analysis of public investment. Before undertaking this analysis I should like to present the reader with an overview of the role of public institutions in the economy so that the reader will understand the context in which public institutions operate. I will not look at all public investment in this study, but mainly that carried out by the government and the corporations in which it holds equity. I will therefore try in this section to discuss briefly the other types of public institutions which exist in Tanzania. I will argue that their exclusion from the analysis does not affect any of the conclusions.

Public institutions monopolize a few sectors, and are important in several others, but by no means dominate the whole economy. In a very real sense the Tanzanian economy is a mixed one, with the private sector still fulfilling some very critical roles. Public institutions are, however, significantly more important in the monetary economy, particularly in its most modern sectors. They also dominate new investment in the economy. Thus, they represent the economy's most dynamic factor, and their role will continue to grow.

There are a number of institutions which can be called public. There is the government itself, and the corporations it owns. This study, as I have said, is largely concerned with the investment carried out by these institutions, for they clearly form the most important vehicle for the extension of public control, and for implementation of the government's development strategy. The other institutions which could be called public are the East African Community and its enterprises, the co-operatives, Ujamaa villages, and District Development Corporations. Before one can really understand the pattern of investment of the government and its corporations, one must understand the role played by these other public institutions. As well, one should have a knowledge of the area still controlled by the private sector. Let us, then, look at the economy as a whole, and the part played by each of the public institutions, and by the private sector.

Government departments, called ministries, are concerned with the provision of social and economic infrastructure and the supply of public services. The share of government administration in GDP has grown, but not quickly. It rose from 8.2 per cent in 1964 to 9.0 per cent in 1970 (Tanzania, *National Account 1964-70*, 23). One can estimate the share in 1972 at 9.7 per cent.[57] Recurrent government expenditure has risen fairly fast (about 13 per cent per annum in the period 1964-72), but government employment has risen somewhat slower. Central government investment has risen fairly quickly, increasing 240 per cent in the period 1964 to 1970. It was equivalent to 21 per cent of total investment in 1972 excluding Tazara and 17 per cent including it. Since then it has stabilized. This higher investment reflects the rise in development expenditure, although the two items are not strictly the same thing.[58]

The development of the parastatal sector represents the most important change in the role of public institutions in the economy. In chapter four I will trace out the development of the parastatal sector Here I simply want to summarize that development. Value added by parastatals[59] has risen from about 2 per cent of total GDP in 1964[60] to 6.9 per cent in 1967 (Tanzania, *National Accounts 1964-70*, 23) to 9.1 per cent (Tanzania, *Hali Ya Uchumi*, 1972-3, 5, 48) in 1972. In terms of monetary GDP, the rise has been from about 2.5 per cent in 1964 to 12.0 per cent in 1972. Employment by parastatals has risen from about 5000 or 1.4 per cent of wage[61] employment in 1964 to 26,292 or 7.5 per cent in 1967 (Tanzania, 1972) to 75,924 or 18.3 per cent in 1972 (Tanzania, *Hali Ya Uchumi*, 1972-3, 8).

57 The private sector's share in 'Public Administration and Other Services' has been gradually declining as Asian doctors leave, and private hospitals and schools are taken over by the government. In 1964, the private share of this sector was 23 per cent. In 1970 it was 19 per cent. There are no data on the breakdown of this sector after 1970, so I have assumed that the 1970 share remained constant. See Tanzania, *National Accounts 1964-70*, 22, 26.

58 Development expenditure includes all non-recurring government expenditure items, and thus includes items which are not strictly investments – e.g., experimental projects. Virtually all foreign aid is included in the development budget. Some recurrent items, such as replacement of vehicles, are investments. In general, however, government investment falls under the development budget.

59 The Central Statistical Bureau defines a parastatal as a corporation in which at least 50 per cent of the equity is government owned. This ignores some important corporations in which the government has a minority interest, and in chapters five and six I include these corporations. For this analysis, I will, unless stated otherwise, use the CSB definition and figures.

60 This is an estimate based upon data for the mining, electricity, and construction sectors, the main parastatal activities in 1964.

61 Again an estimate based upon mining and electricity data.

Parastatals are not equally important in all sectors. They dominate the mining sector and utilities.[62] They monopolize the finance and insurance sub-sectors, and dominate real estate in the monetary economy. They are also important in manufacturing. Parastatals which are 50 per cent or more government owned[63] contributed 33 per cent of value added in the manufacturing and cottage indus- try sector in 1972. If cottage industry is ignored, the share of parastatals was 47 per cent. If non-majority parastatals are included, the share would be closer to 57 per cent. Parastatals are not significant in agriculture, and construction, and are a minor part of the commerce and transport sectors (see Table 6).

Parastatal investment has been the most dynamic part of total investment. It has risen from shs 57 million in 1964[64] (7 per cent of total investment) to shs 293 million in 1967 (22 per cent of total investment) to shs 460 million in 1972 (27 per cent of total investment excluding Tazara, and 19 per cent including it). If Tazara is treated as a parastatal, then parastatal investment in 1972 was shs 1122 million of 47 per cent of total investment.

The East African Community represents an important force in the economy, but one which is restricted largely to one sector, transport and communications. The most important harbours are developed and maintained by the Community, as are the telephone and postal systems. The railway system is Community-run except for Tazara. The railway company also provides road transport to com- munities not served by rail, and owns a number of hotels. The East African Airways is a Community enterprise.

Data on employment and investment by the Community in Tanzania are not comprehensive, but a general picture can be pieced together from the data available. The Community's role in Tanzania has grown, but only marginally. Employment rose from 16,878 or 5.0 per cent of the wage force in 1966 to 20,033 or 5.4 per cent in 1969 (see Table 7). Investment by the Community and its enterprises rose from shs 36 million in 1964, or 4.7 per cent of total invest- ment to shs 106 million or 5.4 per cent of total investment excluding Tazara in 1972 (Tanzania, *Hali Ya Uchumi*, 1972-3, 12) (4.4 per cent including Tazara). The Community is a significant part of the transport sector, employing 57 per cent of the workers in 1966 and 56 per cent in 1969. Nevertheless its role has decreased in importance as parastatals have played a more active investment role.

62 The non-electrical part of utilities is water, which is provided by the government. Thus this sector is 100 per cent government controlled.
63 See note 59 and chapter five.
64 These figures are taken from chapter five, and include my adjustments to the data, but exclude non-majority parastatals. If these parastatals were included, then the figures for 1964 would be shs 59 million or 7.7 per cent and for 1967 shs 332 million or 26 per cent.

TABLE 6

Role of parastatals in the economy

	Value added parastatals 1972	Monetary GDP in economy 1972	Share parastatals (%)
Agriculture	42.7	1834.0	2.3
Mining	88.5	124.0	71.4
Manufacturing	324.1	973.0	33.4
Utilities	70.1	107.0	65.5
Construction	19.5	501.0	3.9
Commerce	191.3	1280.0	15.0
Transport	101.9	868.0	11.8
Finance, services	176.7	374.0	47.2
Public admin.	–	1142.0	–
Less imputed bank charges		152.0	–
Total	899.6	6975.0	12.9

TABLE 7

Employment by community enterprises

	1966	1967	1968	1969
Harbours and railway	13,682	13,263	15,745	14,671
Post and telecommunications	2081	2080	2378	3551
Community administration	1115	1229	1609	1811
Total	16,878	16,572	19,732	20,033
Share of total wage employment (%)	5.0	4.8	5.6	5.4

SOURCE: Tanzania, *Survey of Employment and Earnings*, 1969

In 1966 Community investment constituted 24 per cent of transport investment. By 1970, it was only 16 per cent excluding Tazara, and 10 per cent including it.

The co-operatives have been significant in Tanzania for a long time. They were the first commercial institution dominated by Africans. Initially they were only marketing co-operatives, but today they have expanded into processing as well. Co-operatives are also important in transport and commerce. Data on co-operatives are poor. They cover only a few years, and are not complete. We do know that in both 1968 and 1969 marketing co-operatives had 2 per cent of the wage employment of the enterprise sector, and about 1 per cent of total

TABLE 8

Ujamaa village programme

	No. of villages	Population ('000)	Share of rural population (%)
1969	1100	500	4
1970	1628	531	4
1971	4484	1599	13
1972	5556	1981	16

SOURCE: Tanzania, *Annual Economic Surveys*, 1969-72

employment.[65] Their investment has never been large, and although it has been rising, its rate of increase has been less than that of total investment in the economy. As a result their share of total investment has fallen from about 2.5 per cent in 1964 to 2 per cent in 1970 to an expected 1 per cent for the past two years of the Second Five Year Plan.[66]

Co-operatives are, as I have said, concentrated in the transport and commerce sectors. They probably account for about 8 per cent of the employment and value added in these sectors, and should not be overlooked. Inclusion of co-operatives with the parastatals and East African Community enterprises would make the public share of transport GDP probably well above 40 per cent. The addition of the co-operatives to the parastatals in the commerce sector would still leave this sector as essentially private with under 20 per cent of the GDP being generated by public institutions.

The Ujamaa village programme represents the core of the government's attempt to bring socialism to the rural areas. As we have seen, parastatal activity in the rural sector is small, contributing only 2.3 per cent of the monetary GDP and only 1.1 per cent of total GDP in agriculture, forestry, hunting, and fishing. Figures are available on the number and size of Ujamaa villages beginning in 1969 (see Table 8). The number of villages has increased more than five times since 1969, and the number of villagers has almost quadrupled. By 1972 16 per cent of the population lived in Ujamaa villages.

It is difficult to know precisely what this growth means. It is clear that villages differ greatly in the extent to which they are truly socialist. The government has tried to categorize villages by stages. Stage I can be as little as issuing

65 See Tanzania, *Survey of Employment and Earnings* (1969, 5), and *Statistical Abstract* (1970, 174). The latest figures published for co-operatives showing a breakdown of type are for 1964. In that year 91 per cent were marketing co-operatives, 3 per cent banking, 3 per cent consumer, 2 per cent industrial and 1 per cent transport co-operatives (Tanzania, *Statistical Abstract*, 1970, 181).

66 Based upon an analysis done using data from Tanzania (1972).

TABLE 9

Distribution of Ujamaa village population by region

	Ujamaa pop. Dec. 1971	Total pop. Dec. 1971 ('000)	Ujamaa pop. as share of total pop. (%)	Per capita farm output 1967
Kilimanjaro	2616	742	0.4	277
Tanga	35,907	854	4.2	212
Arusha	14,018	696	2.0	167
Morogoro	10,513	739	1.4	158
Iringa	216,200	754	28.7	105
Mwanza	18,641	1169	1.6	101
Shinyanga	12,205	992	1.2	97
Coast	93,503	543	17.2	86
Tabora	81,408	609	13.4	84
West Lake	9491	710	1.3	75
Mbeya	64,390	1081	6.0	70
Mtwara	371,560	479	77.6	67
Lindi	203,128	802	25.3	
Mara	127,371	623	20.4	64
Ruvuma	20,500	437	4.7	57
Kigoma	27,200	501	5.4	35
Dodoma	239,366	774	30.9	34
Singida	51,230	483	10.6	28

SOURCE: Tanzania, *Annual Economic Survey*, 1971-2, 61

'an expression of intent' (Tanzania, *Annual Economic Survey*, 1971-2, 61) to live communally. Stage II involves some degree of economic co-operation, and a much higher level of organization. Stage III villages are true co-operatives, and can be formally registered as such. At the end of 1971, 92 per cent of the villages were in stage I, and 6 per cent in stage II. Only 2 per cent of the villages were in stage III (*ibid.*, 6). Thus only a very small proportion of the rural population is living co-operatively.

The Ujamaa village programme has been successful in only a few regions, generally the poorest ones. Five regions contain 70 per cent of the Ujamaa population. Only one of these regions had above average per capita income. The regions which are the centres of the cash crops – Arusha, Kilimanjaro, Morogoro, Mwanza, Shinyanya, Tanga, and West Lake – and the regions with the largest land pressure have very small Ujamaa programmes. These seven regions contain 5.9 million people or 44 per cent of the mainland population. Their Ujamaa population totalled only 103,451 in 1971, or 6.5 per cent of the Ujamaa population. Less than 2 per cent of the population in these regions lived in Ujamaa villages at the end of 1971 (see Table 9). Unless Ujamaa can make some headway in these regions it could easily become a programme essentially for poor regions. Such a development would threaten the over-all Tanzanian strategy.

District Development Corporations are relatively new phenomena and have little impact on the over-all economy. They are important, however, because they represent a different type of public enterprise from those previously mentioned. DDC's are corporations originally set by the town councils. They now fall under the control of the district offices, which are part of the regional administration. So far as possible, I will include them in my detailed analysis.

The enterprises established by DDC's are generally small. They have tended to be centred on the retail trade (butcheries, petrol stations, bars) but there have been a number of small manufacturing operations, and some transport firms. The DDC's represent an attempt to find an alternative to the small Asian entrepreneur. They contrast with the parastatals which can be seen as replacing the foreign firm or the large Asian capitalist. So far, the DDC's have performed badly. They have been staffed generally with bureaucrats left over from the town councils, and these people have proved incapable of running a business. Many have gone bankrupt, or have been heavily subsidized. Their impact in extending the area of public control has been minimal so far. Nevertheless they are a critical instrument in a strategy of socialist development. They are a type of socialist institution which could fill some of the important roles currently filled by Asian capitalists. To understand these roles, let us look at what part of the economy remains in private hands.

Public institutions are dominant in mining, utilities, finance, and insurance. They are very important in manufacturing and transport, but on the other hand about half these sectors remain in private hands. The commerce, service, construction and agriculture sectors remain essentially private. If we look at the whole economy, the importance of public institutions is still relatively small. About 26 per cent of total GDP, or about 36 per cent of monetary GDP, in 1972 was derived from public institutions.[67] The importance of the private agricultural sector becomes clear if we exclude it from the analysis. Public institutions contributed 49 per cent of the non-agricultural monetary GDP. Public institutions are more important in terms of employment. In 1971 they provided over 64 per cent of wage employment (see Table 10).

---

67 Estimate based upon following: government administration shs 1142 million or 11.6 per cent; parastatals, shs 900 million or 9.1 per cent; EAC, shs 250 million or 2.5 per cent; Tazara, shs 160 million or 1.6 per cent; the co-operatives, shs 90 million or 1 per cent.

TABLE 10

Distribution of employment by sectors[1]

	1968		1969		1970		1971	
	A	B	A	B	A	B	A	B
1 Private enterprise	142,468	40.5	143,986	39.1	141,438	37.6	143,332	35.7
2 Co-operatives and non-profit-making institutions	42,101	6.9	20,523	5.6	14,648	3.9	12,089	3.0
3 Parastatal sector[2]	45,712	13.0	52,438	14.3	64,461	17.2	82,041	20.4
4 Government and EA and its allied services	139,430	39.6	150,979	41.0	155,088	41.3	164,450	40.9
5 Public sector (2 + 3 + 4)	209,243	59.5	223,940	60.9	234,197	62.4	258,580	64.3
Total	351,711	100.0	367,926	100.0	375,635	100.0	401,912	100.0

SOURCE: Tanzania, *Annual Economic Survey*, 1971-2, 41

A = wage employment in sector

B = employment in sector as a percentage of total recorded wage employment

1 Provisional figures and excluding figures for Tazara and Kilimanjaro International Airport

2 This includes all institutions which receive parastatal directives from the Standing Committee on Parastatal Organization

The move towards socialism meant a significant increase in the role of public institutions in the economy. Nevertheless, large sections of the economy remain in private hands. The sectors left to the private sector are those characterized by small enterprises. The government has found it easiest to move into the most modern parts of the economy. I shall argue later that this emphasis has important implications for the possibility of successfully implementing a strategy of rural socialism. Let us now turn to look in more detail at the extent to which the government actually seemed to follow its investment strategy. This analysis of investment by the government and its institutions will form the next four chapters.

the urban areas. It is important, instead, to encourage industries in the rural areas where the barriers between peasants and urban workers will be broken down.

The Chinese seem willing to accept some loss in productivity to create firms which are located in rural areas. Moreover, it is also clear that the Chinese, especially the followers of Mao, are willing to accept that such an emphasis on rural development means adopting a programme that puts less stress on rapid development of high technology industries. 'Mao is certainly in sympathy with resistance to *all-out* or *crash industrialization*; he sees its imperatives as being in conflict with many noneconomic aims he feels China should be pursuing ... Such rationings of industrial society into the rural areas have a twofold objective: to bring material benefits to the peasant, and to prevent the dictatorship of the city over the countryside' (Wheelwright and McFarlane 1970, 219; emphasis in original).

It is clear that the issue of urban/rural dichotomy cannot be treated in isolation from the other issues. Concern over this problem will affect one's approach to the issue of the roles of agriculture and industry, or to the issue of the choice of technique. Indeed, in developing an investment strategy one will necessarily have to make decisions about all these issues, and will find that in doing so the issues are highly interrelated. Nevertheless, this type of classification of the issues can be helpful in understanding the positions taken by different individuals or groups on investment strategy.

3

Allocation of ministerial spending

INTRODUCTION

This chapter is devoted to an analysis of ministerial spending. In it I will look at the overall sectoral distribution of government development expenditure, showing that the distribution has remained surprisingly constant over time. During the Second Five Year Plan the ministries concerned with rural economic development will not have received any more proportionately than they did during the First Five Year Plan. In fact, they will have received less. Social service ministries are also receiving about the same share as in the First Five Year Plan, but their programmes have been altered to provide increased emphasis on rural areas. Transportation development has absorbed a large share of the resources available to ministries under both Plans. Major trunk road development has dominated the programme under both plans, and feeder roads have been neglected.

Over-all, there has not been a marked change in the emphasis on rural areas in ministerial spending. The most significant area of change has been in social services, but even here the constraints of an unchanged economic strategy have prevented too great a shift from occurring. There are signs that there will be more emphasis on the rural areas in the future. The decentralization exercise has helped by creating bureaucratic units devoted almost exclusively to rural development. Much needs to be done, however, before the goals of the Arusha Declaration are reflected in ministerial spending.

Data base

In the central planning ministry (Devplan), a planning information system has been established. This system (for a complete description see Appendix II) holds data on all development projects by ministries, regions, DDC's, and parastatals. Each project is classified in a number of different ways in order to facilitate analysis of expenditure patterns. The data on the system for ministerial and regional projects come largely from the Auditor-General's Reports and the spending estimates published by the Treasury. Published documents have, however, failed to reflect accurately the inflow of foreign aid. As a result, official figures on ministerial expenditure often understate the true value of the expenditure. I have revised the data to include all aid given directly to projects which was missed in the published documents. This revision is explained more fully in chapter six and in Appendix V.

The system contains data on all projects in the First and Second Five Year Plans. Data were available for earlier years, but was not included because it was felt that the earlier expenditure reflected the colonial administration much more than the independent government. Throughout this study the basic comparison will be between the First FYP and the Second FYP. This is the most convenient way of analyzing the shift in expenditure. Although the Arusha Declaration occurred in the middle of the First FYP, its effects on policy and behaviour took some time to be felt. The Second FYP was the first major document to incorporate the new ideology, and as such can be regarded as the first real test of whether any shift in actual performance has occurred.

At the time of writing (June 1974), accurate data on actual expenditure by ministries in 1972-3 and 1973-4 were not yet available. I have had to use estimates for these years rather than figures on actual expenditures. For all other years the figures are actuals. There are some biases involved in using estimates for these last two years, and where these appear important I have noted them. In general, estimated spending is more rural-oriented than actual spending. Since this bias only strengthens my conclusions it is not a serious problem.

ALLOCATION BETWEEN MINISTRIES

In order to obtain a consistent, long-run view of ministerial spending, I have classified all projects according to the agency which would have implemented them if they had been undertaken in 1972-3 prior to the decentralization. Table II shows the spending by each of the ministries in each year from 1964-5 to 1973-4, and also shows the over-all share in each of the plan periods.

The most obvious conclusion which can be drawn from this table is that no significant change in emphasis has occurred at this level. There has been a remarkable constancy in the allocation of funds. The relative share of each ministry in total ministerial expenditure differs by only a few percentage points from one Plan to the other. The ministry which gained the most was Health.

TABLE 11

Allocation of ministerial spending (shs million)

	1964-5	1965-6	1966-7	1967-8	1968-9	First FYP	per-cent	1969-70	1970-71	1971-2	1972-3¹	1973-4¹	Second FYP	per-cent
Regional Adminis-														
tration and Rural														
Development	18	24	11	30	42	125	9	31	38	36	41	52	198	6
Agriculture	12	12	31	22	44	121	9	34	38	24	64	95	255	8
Natural Resources	5	5	11	16	18	55	4	23	22	20	21	48	134	4
Education	43	45	30	26	13	157	11	37	47	43	74	77	278	9
Health	1	3	1	8	7	20	1	39	43	22	14	50	168	5
Transport	26	31	86	83	185	411	29	183	227	179	156	177	922	28
Urban Develop-														
ment and Lands														
Survey	3	4	10	21	8	46	3	15	21	8	13	25	82	3
Water	40	34	33	45	57	209	15	59	66	48	79	170	422	13
Defence	6	8	59	56	44	173	12	46	75	124	106	140	491	15
Other	14	15	25	27	16	97	7	36	56	45	68	77	282	9
Total	168	181	297	334	434	1414	100	503	633	549	636	911	3232	100

1 Estimate. Figures for these years in all subsequent tables are also estimated.

Defence also had a noticeable increase in its share. Regional Administration and Education were the largest losers.

More importantly, the table shows no significant change in the share of government expenditure going to economic programmes to develop the rural areas. If the expenditure by the ministries of Regional Administration and Rural Development, Agriculture, and Natural Resources, the three ministries designed to encourage rural economic development, are combined, the total share of these ministries in the Second FYP is actually less than in the First FYP (18 per cent versus 22 per cent).

Before concluding that the Arusha Declaration had little impact on ministerial spending, it is necessary to look more closely at the type of expenditure of each of these ministries. Changes within ministerial programmes have occurred, and these changes do, in part, reflect the shift in policy which occurred.

AGRICULTURE

I tried to show in chapter two that the fundamental economic challenge facing Tanzania was to eliminate the backward character of its agriculture. Agricultural policy can be understood only in terms of agricultural planners coming to grips with the primitiveness of the agriculture, and with the need to improve the rural sector because so vast a majority of the population live there. Just before independence, the World Bank was invited to undertake a study of the economy. This study set the basis for the economic development programmes of the first five to six years after independence, and in particular set the basis of the approach to agriculture.

The key to long-range agricultural development was the transformation approach.[1] The 'transformation' approach was not so new as the Bank made it appear. Essentially it was one of abandoning the current situation, and attempting to develop a new one, quite different, by transferring the population from one place to another, and from one level of technology to another. It was an agricultural Big Push. Its forerunner was the Groundnut Scheme (Ward, 1950), a scheme to transform the southern Tanganyika undertaken by the British which ended in total failure.

1 ' ... with these considerations in mind, the Mission recommends, side by side with the continuation of the "improvement" approach, the adoption on an increasing scale of the "transformation" programs aimed at the creation of markedly more efficient agricultural systems' (IBRD 1961, 6). The transformation approach essentially involved the use of large amounts of capital to raise dramatically the productivity of rural peasants. Since the country could not afford to do this for all peasants, the approach meant concentrating the development effort on a small minority of the people in the rural areas.

There were, in fact, two transformation approaches. The first involved actual re-settlement of people. A special agency was created for this work, which later fell under the Ministry of Lands and Settlement. The settlement approach was a response to an on-going problem in Tanzania, the scattered nature of its population. In only a few regions do the people live in villages. The schemes, then, were villagization schemes designed to bring people together[2] so that social services could be provided at an economic cost. They also allowed a transformation in agricultural technology. Settlements were provided with many inputs, tractors, ploughs, fertilizers, unavailable to the average peasant.[3]

The second type of transformation approach was irrigation schemes. These were often formed around places where some irrigation had already begun. Again, the nation was to introduce a much more advanced level of technology by heavy infusions of capital.

The transformation approach was stopped in 1966. The capital-intensive nature of the projects, and their failure to produce any major increase in output forced its abandonment. In April 1966 R.M. Kawawa announced the new policy. 'In the future, it has been decided that, instead of establishing highly capitalized schemes and moving people to them, emphasis should be on modernizing

2 In his Inaugural Address, Nyerere said: 'Before we can bring any of the benefits of modern development to the farmers of Tanganyika, the very first step is to make it possible for them to start living in village communities' (1966).

3 Lionel Cliffe and Griffiths Cunningham (in Cliffe and Saul, 1972, vol. 1, 134) describe the settlement schemes in this way: 'Settlement ideology was also backed by a number of assumptions about the economic rationality of this form of development. It was seen as a means of improving the provisions of rural services – with people grouped in clusters it would be much cheaper to provide school, water supplies, medical facilities and other services. It was also expected to make mechanisation possible, and this was seen as the critical means of making peasant farming productive. This argument was associated with the assumption that the schemes would enable other innovations to be introduced, including especially the introduction of new crops. In some cases settlements were expected to bring other new factors into production, especially new land and unemployed labour either from the towns or overcrowded rural areas. In some instances the justification was the sharing of equipment, tasks or services, as in the case of the sisal decorticator. There was thus an (often implicit) assumption that economies of scale would provide the basis for some form of group farming leading to a division of labour, better organisation of labour, or people just working harder. However, the actual programmes paid little attention to the possible gains from such organised, collaborative effort.

In short it is clear that there was little explicitly socialist ideology behind the various supervised settlement programmes. Both expatriate planners and nationalist politicians and bureaucrats wanted a vehicle for "modernisation." Each, for different reasons, believed that a complete break with the past was necessary for real agricultural advance.'

existing traditional villages by injecting capital in order to raise the standard of the villagers.'[4]

In 1967, Nyerere presented his paper on rural socialism (which I described in chapter two). The paper is best understood in the context of the policy just described. Nyerere now argued against capital-intensive, transformation projects. Rural development must transform the country evenly. In the Second FYP the issue of the degree of selectivity of the Ujamaa programme was faced. 'There is a choice which must be made between two alternative strategies: (i) Selective: To concentrate attention on limited areas which are capable of making movement to complete Ujamaa living over a short period of time ... (ii) Frontal: The alternative approach is to move towards Ujamaa on all possible fronts, mobilizing the full range of governmental and political institutions behind the principles of Ujamaa ... The frontal, or broad-based, approach has been chosen because of the desire to mobilize the widest possible participation in socialist activity throughout the rural society,' (Tanzania, 1969, vol. I, 27).

On the surface, the Ujamaa strategy contrasts sharply with the previous programmes. It is broadly based, and non-capital-intensive. It has sought to use existing institutions to transform the rural areas. Thus the water ministry is supposed to give priority to Ujamaa, rather than there being a special Ujamaa water division. Nevertheless, many of the same elements remain. Much of the programme has, in fact, involved re-settlement,[5] and the use of offers of better social services as inducements. There is still a special division for Ujamaa villages, and a feeling of separateness to their development. Lionel Cliffe argues that the Ujamaa programme does not differ significantly enough:

It is worth summarizing the deficiencies of the whole planning method that emerged during this period of Settlement and the two separate 'Approaches', for even though the new Ujamaa programme is very different in basic intent, the continuity in the thinking of agricultural planners, at the drawing board stage as it were, is often marked. Basically, this planning approach was one that could not come to terms with peasant societies and their ongoing patterns of farming; instead, it reached the conclusion that administratively it was easier to start from

---

4 Address by Second-Vice President R.M. Kawawa quoted in *From Village to State in Tanzania,* Ingle (1972, 51). Kawawa does not confront the issue of what to do about peasants not living in villages. The ultimate response of the government is a non-capital-intensive scheme to collect people into near villages – the Ujamaa programme.

5 Some type of re-settlement programme is probably necessary in Tanzania. It is important, however, that such programmes have the support of the people, and that they are integrated into an over-all plan of improving the productivity and welfare of rural peasants.

scratch elsewhere. The dual strategy, (and the designation of separate institutions to plan the two Approaches) also precluded any possibility of comprehensive planning for the rural sector as a whole. A compartmentalized pattern of thinking developed, which has its parallel today in the planners' view that there is an Ujamaa programme on the one hand, and that there is an agricultural development policy on the other; missing therefore, is a more meaningful and integrated alternative approach which sees Ujamaa, socialist production relations, as a principle which underlies all rural planning (Uchumi Editorial Board, 1972, 98).

The early approach to the backwardness of the rural areas was to ignore it, and try to build isolated pockets of modernity. The Ujamaa programme involves a fundamental rejection of this approach and as such represents a move towards solving the real economic challenge in Tanzania. Nevertheless, problems with the Ujamaa programme remain, and more importantly, emphasis on the rural areas, despite the Arusha Declaration and subsequent documents, has not increased in terms of spending on the economic programmes. Because this spending is more widespread and less capital-intensive, its benefits are probably greater. Nevertheless, as yet, large resources have not been put into economic programmes to develop the rural areas. In part, I will argue later, this reflects a continuing desire to ignore the problem, and to put resources into areas, like manufacturing, which offer a hope, even if false, for a quick transformation of the economy. In part, it reflects simply a lack of knowledge as to how to transform the rural areas. Agricultural programmes which work are much harder to develop than plans to build industries. Finally, it reflects a lack of an effective lobby group for rural development. The increasing power of TANU and the decentralization of government administration should help to solve this. I will return to these points in later chapters.

If we look at the data on ministerial expenditure, we can see this tendency to opt out of solving the agricultural programme. The settlement schemes have been classified as part of the Ministry of Regional Administration and Rural Development. In the early years these schemes dominated the spending of this ministry, which is above the level of the agricultural ministry (see Table 11). In the first two years of the First FYP Regional Administration spent shs 42 million while Agriculture spent only shs 24 million. After 1966, expenditure on settlement schemes continued, but no longer dominated total ministerial expenditure on agriculture. It was not until the middle of the Second FYP that all expenditure on settlement schemes was finally halted.

With the decline in the favour of the settlement programme, agriculture's budget climbed, but a significant part of that rise reflected increased spending on state farms and other directly productive projects, which was the new form of opting out. This emphasis on state farms continued into the early years of the Second FYP, in which, according to the Plan, they were to play a prominent part.[6] By 1970-71 doubts were already being expressed about the state farm programme[7] and by 1971-2 state farms were no longer in favour.[8] Development expenditure on them fell.

Now, however, the government has turned to Ujamaa villages, especially in livestock, parastatal ranches, and the state dairy farms under the new regional administrations, as part of the answer to the agricultural problem. This could easily be another way of opting out.

The Ministry of Regional Administration did alter its activities in a way which should promote local initiative and rural development. Two funds were started – Nation-Building Self Help and Regional Development Fund – which made funds available for local, small-scale projects. The money was allocated by the Area Commissioner. These funds have grown rapidly, and now dominate the ministry's programme (see Table 12).

It is possible to summarize the discussion of ministerial spending on agricultural development in this way. Emphasis on this sector has, contrary to one's expectations, decreased rather than increased. The share of the two ministries involved has fallen from 18 per cent in the First FYP to 14 per cent in the Second FYP. Throughout the period under study, and indeed for much of the colonial period, there has been a strong tendency on the part of the government to seek programmes which will provide a quick answer to the low level of agricultural productivity. Settlement schemes, state farms, and parastatal ranches all can be thought of as ways in which the government has tried to create islands of modernity in the rural areas. Table 13 summarizes ministerial expenditure on

6 The Second FYP stated: 'The extension of the principles of Ujamaa vijijini will bring many Tanzanians into collective production activities; it will not, however, provide the answer to all the problems of agricultural organization. Certain agricultural products for which fast output growth is required and which benefit from mechanization and/or a large scale irrigation, from organized innovation, and from centralized management of a large scale operation will be produced effectively on state farms. To meet this need over 250,000 acres of new state farms are planned for the Second Plan period' (Tanzania, 1969, vol. II, 30).

7 In the *Annual Economic Survey* (1970-71, 63) the government declared: 'For various reasons their [state farms] performance during the year under review has not been up to expectations. Weather conditions coupled with inexperienced management and inadequate planning were responsible for the low yields obtained.'

8 In the *Annual Economic Survey* 1971-2, the change in position became clearer: 'The performance of the majority of these farms has not been too satisfactory. Most of the state farms have not attained commercial viability.'

TABLE 12

Allocation of funds to Self-Help and RDF

	1964-5	65-6	66-7	67-8	68-9	69-70	70-71	71-2	72-3	73-4
Allocation (shs million)	–	2	1	9	21	21	25	31	31	46
Share of reg. admin. budget (%)	–	9	9	30	51	68	65	85	85	88

TABLE 13

Ministerial spending on directly productive activities and transformation schemes (shs million)

	1964-5	65-6	66-7	67-8	68-9	FFYP	69-70	70-71	71-2	72-3	73-4	SFYP
Settlement schemes	11	20	4	12	16	63	2	1	–	–	–	3
Directly productive ministerial activities	2	2	13	9	10	36	11	11	3	9	21	55
Total	13	22	17	21	26	99	13	12	3	9	21	58
Total as share of Reg. Admin. and Agriculture spending (%)	43	61	40	40	30	40	20	16	5	9	14	13

directly productive activities and settlement schemes. These approaches have been important in both plans.

The real problem in Tanzania will not be solved by such approaches. Its solution rests with transforming the life and methods of production of all rural peasants, not a select group. The Ujamaa village programme has been designed for this purpose. This programme does, then, represent an important shift in the direction of government policy. An increasing proportion of funds spent on the rural areas has been directed towards this programme. As Table 13 below shows, 40 per cent of the expenditure by Regional Administration and Agriculture in the First FYP went either to directly productive activities or settlement schemes, while only 13 per cent will go to these areas in the Second FYP. Nevertheless, the emphasis on agricultural development remains small, given its priority in terms of the development strategy of the country. There is, as well, the very real danger, as pointed out by L. Cliffe, that the Ujamaa villages will become settlement schemes. Already there are signs that some villages become models heavily endowed with inputs while others receive nothing at all.

NON-AGRICULTURAL RURAL DEVELOPMENT

A consistent tendency in Tanzania has been to neglect non-agricultural rural development. The president often speaks as if rural development and agricultural development were synonymous. While it is certainly true that agriculture dominates the rural area (about 90 per cent of the value added by agriculture, forestry, fishing, and hunting is agriculture) (Tanzania, *National Accounts 1764-70,* 11) there are other important sources of primary production such as forestry and fishing, and of secondary production, such as small scale manufacturing, which could be developed.

Up to this point the government has remained relatively uninterested in these activities. The development of rural manufacturing, other than that based on forestry and fishing, has been left entirely to the parastatal sector, which in turn has practically ignored it. (See section on manufacturing in chapter five). Ministerial expenditure on forestry and fishing has stagnated in relative terms as shown in Table 14. The rise in spending in 1973-4 is the result of the decentralization. The regions have put a much greater emphasis on these two areas, especially fishing, than did the central government. Decentralization may, then, mean that this long neglected sector will receive a higher priority. At present, however, it remains an area of untapped potential.[9]

SOCIAL SERVICES

Total expenditure on social services has not varied over the last ten years, but there has been significant change in the type of services provided. There has been a relative decline in expenditure on education, a small decline in water, and a rise in health. These shifts in over-all spending are related to the types of programmes undertaken in each area. Expenditure on social services is an important part of any rural strategy, as there are important economic benefits to be derived from such expenditure. Moreover, any over-all development strategy which depends upon developing the rural areas must involve provision of services to the rural areas if they are to remain attractive places in which to live. Thus, it is not only the over-all level of expenditure on social services which is important, but

9 The sector does not lack resources. Tanzania has excellent fishing waters for both salt and fresh water fish. In fact, in places like Lake Tanganyika a large proportion of the fish is spoilt because of lack of drying facilities. The Canadians have recently completed an inventory of Tanzania's forests which has indicated huge reserves of wood. The problem is that few resources have been devoted to exploiting these forests.

TABLE 14

Ministerial and regional spending on forestry and fishing

	1964-5	65-6	66-7	67-8	68-9	FFYP	69-70	70-71	71-2	72-3	73-4	SFYP
Fishing	–	0.4	4.5	3.0	5.2	13.1	3.3	2.5	1.4	7.5	19.0	33.7
Forestry	3.8	3.3	5.6	9.2	9.0	30.9	14.0	12.0	14.8	12.6	21.2	74.6
Total	3.8	3.7	10.1	12.2	14.2	44.0	17.3	14.5	16.2	20.1	40.2	108.3
Share of ministerial spending (%)	2.3	2.0	3.4	3.7	3.3	3.1	3.4	2.3	3.0	3.1	4.4	3.4

also the orientation of such services. The crucial question is whether or not they support a strategy of rural development.

Education

In education one can see a clear change in policy over time. In the First FYP the emphasis was on secondary and post-secondary education. This reflected the very grave shortage of skilled manpower of the country at the time of independence. If the country was to gain control over its own institutions, it had to replace expatriates with Tanzanians, and this meant that the production of skilled personnel had to be accelerated. This policy was largely successful. In 1962, only 39 per cent of senior- and middle-grade civil servant posts were held by citizens. By 1971, 91 per cent were held by Tanzanians. The number of non-citizens in these posts fell to almost one-third, while the number of citizens increased more than five-fold (Tanzania, *Annual Economic Survey*, 1971-2, 133). In 1962, there were only 1950 Form IV graduates, only 199 Form VI graduates and in 1963 only 23 Tanzanian graduates from the universities in East Africa. By 1972, Form IV graduates were more than three-and-one-half times in number: 7300. Form VI graduates had increased eight-fold to 1600, and there were 650 University of East Africa graduates (Tanzania, *Annual Economic Survey*, 1968-9, 36; 1971-2, 130).

This early emphasis on secondary and post-secondary education was abruptly stopped in 1967 with the publication of the President's paper on education. A continued emphasis on higher forms of education was seen as reinforcing the urban-oriented pattern already developing in Tanzania. In the introduction to the Second FYP, Nyerere clearly stated the new emphasis: 'At the beginning of the last Plan we took a very definite decision to give priority to the expansion of secondary education, teacher training, and the University. Because to plan is to

TABLE 15

Allocation of education budget (shs million)

	1964-5	65-6	66-7	67-8	68-9	FFYP	69-70	70-71	71-2	72-3	73-4	SFYP
Primary	2.5	4.5	2.2	1.9	2.2	13.3	15.1	20.0	9.3	15.0	22.3	81.7
Non-primary	40.7	40.1	27.9	23.7	10.4	142.8	21.6	26.9	34.1	58.8	55.0	196.4
Total	43.2	44.6	30.1	25.6	12.6	156.1	36.7	46.9	43.4	73.8	77.3	278.1
Share of primary (%)	6	10	7	7	17	9	41	42	21	20	29	34

choose, that meant that we had very little money available to devote to expanding the primary school system ... This state of affairs must be unacceptable to a country which claims to be building socialism. Obviously the emphasis in the new Plan must be shifted to primary education' (Tanzania, 1969, vol. I, xi).

In Table 15, I show the share of educational expenditure devoted to primary education. The shift is dramatic. In the First FYP 8.8 per cent of the education budget went to primary education. In the Second FYP 34.0 per cent was allocated to primary education. The shift was lessened by the impact of foreign aid which went entirely to secondary and post-secondary education. Thus the share of primary education fell in 1971 and stabilized at a level well above the First FYP level, but below the level of 1969-70 and 1970-71, because of the very rapid growth in aid to non-primary education. In 1973-4, non-primary education will receive only shs 12.5 million in local funds; yet total spending on non-primary education will be shs 55.0 million, more than twice the shs 22.3 million spent on primary education, which is all local funds.[10]

A tension will always exist between the country's obvious need for high-level manpower, and the need to develop the skills of the mass of the population. This tension will be heightened or reduced by the over-all economic strategy adopted. A strategy which calls for the rapid development of a modern urban sector will place heavy demands on post-primary education. It will be impossible to continue to stress primary education if such a strategy is adopted. Moreover, an emphasis on primary education is politically viable only if the economic strategy is one that provides employment for vast numbers of low-skill level rural workers. If a labour-intensive industrialization strategy, and particularly one based on rural areas, is not adopted, the result will be the production of large numbers of unemployable primary school graduates[11]. This is the problem in most African countries today.

10 For a discussion of the effect of foreign aid on the allocation of investment see chapter six.
11 Sam Bowles (1971) analyses this contradiction.

Health

I showed in chapter two that a desire for equality was basic to the Tanzanian ideology as expounded by Nyerere. In almost all capitalist less-developed countries, the provision of medical services is highly unequal. The rich receive a qualitatively different type of care from the poor; urban medical facilities are much superior to rural facilities. Merely changing the ownership of the means of production does not alter this tendency. The bureaucratic elite residing in urban areas has a real interest in ensuring that the best possible medical care exists in urban areas. This care, however, can only be attained by robbing the rural areas of basic medical facilities. Traditional medical wisdom has always stressed the need for a well-developed referral system. This system involves the provision of a hierarchy of medical institutions, at the top of which stand a few, high-quality consultant hospitals. Such a system not only provides poorer health care for the nation as a whole,[12] but also represents a fundamental rejection of the principle of equality. In a country as poor as Tanzania, a decision to build a referral system, because of the enormous capital and operating costs of consultant hospitals, is a decision to deny even minimum care to the rural areas. Like all investment choices, the choice of the best medical system to develop is not an academic one. It involves a political choice, and provides a real test of a country's commitment to socialism.[13]

In Tanzania the issue has been faced only recently. Unlike the case of education, the President has issued no explicit document outlining the implications of

12 Oscar Gish (1973a, 402), the head of the health planning unit in Tanzania in 1971, puts the case this way: 'In fact, it is axiomatic to health care planning in virtually all poor countries that the "thinner" the spread of any given volume of resources, the greater the return in terms of better health; that is, the lessening of morbidity and mortality ... Of course there is a minimum level of "thinness" below which it is not possible to go if coherence is to be retained within a given health care delivery system. The appropriate level of "thinness" to be aimed for in any specific country is a matter of experience and research. However, the question remains essentially academic for virtually all Third World countries in that, probably without exception, the present pattern of health sector expenditure is far too intensive and can with complete safety be very extensively "thinned" before problems of the other extreme are likely to occur.'

13 M. Segall (in Uchumni Editorial Board, 1972, 159), a professor at the University of Dar es Salaam, summarized the issue in this way: 'Neo-colonialism would not be so successful if it did not benefit someone. Sophisticated medical facilities are concentrated in the towns and they benefit the urban dwellers. In particular, the higher income urban groups have major expectations in medical care and they create the pressures to have their demand fulfilled. This is a class interest, which is in conflict with the interests of the peasants. The competitive demands of these two groups on the health budget is an example of class struggle. (cont'd on p. 84)

the Arusha Declaration for health policy. The Second FYP did announce a shift in policy: 'During the First Plan effort was directed towards the development of physical medical facilities, mainly located in urban centres ... The Second Plan will increase emphasis on the development of preventive and rural health services, mainly through the agency of rural health centres' (Tanzania, 1969, vol. I, 162). In the First FYP, the capital cost of rural health centres was shared between the central government and local governments, and the recurrent costs were borne by the local governments. The result was that few centres were built, and many operated at less than full capacity. In the Second FYP the government took over the full cost of the rural health centre programme. This represented a major increase in the priority accorded to rural health.

Despite this increased priority, actual policy has been erratic. As Table 16 shows, expenditure on rural health programmes has fluctuated significantly. Only in the last two years has there been any clear indication that the government has committed itself to a more rural-oriented programme. As well, large sums are now being spent on training, most of it devoted to rural medical personnel (Gish, 1973b). While the old policy was supported and reinforced by foreign aid (two consultant hospitals were built by foreign aid at the beginning of the Second FYP), it has also been foreign aid, led by the Nordic countries but also including USAID, which has encouraged and supported through significant financial contributions the shift in policy. Over 75 per cent of the health programme in 1973-4 is expected to be financed by foreign aid. Almost all this aid will be for rural health personnel.[14]

Water

Expenditure on water programmes, like many government programmes, helps to determine other government programmes, but is also determined by them. As with health expenditure, the provision of rural water supplies is an effective tool

---

The urban elite also want to feel on a par with the bourgeoisie of the capitalist world, with whom they identify. They reasonably want to demonstrate national "achievements," but these are seen in terms of prestige buildings and other material accoutrements of modern medicine; such interpretation of achievements is truly "bourgeois." A socialist achievement in health would be the maximum well-being of the mass of the people; this would be something to show the world. The demands of the urban elite, their bourgeois nationalism, and neo-colonialism are the main determinants of the current health policy of the country.'

14 Again, see chapter six for a further discussion of the effect of foreign aid on the pattern of investment.

TABLE 16

Allocation of health budget (shs million)

	1964-5	65-6	66-7	67-8	68-9	FFYP	69-70	70-71	71-2	72-3	73-4	SFYP
Rural programmes	–	0.1	–	4.1	1.9	6.1	0.4	3.5	1.5	8.3	24.6	38.6
Training	–	–	–	0.6	2.9	3.5	1.5	5.2	–	2.8	22.2	31.7
Other	1.3	2.4	1.3	3.6	2.4	11.0	37.0	41.3	2.9	2.7	3.2	87.1
Total	1.3	2.5	1.3	8.3	7.2	20.6	38.2	50.0	4.4	13.8	50.0	157.4
Rural as share (%)	–	4	–	49	26	30	2	7	34	60	49	25

for making living in rural areas an attractive alternative to urban centres. Moreover, the economic benefits of providing water within close walking distance should not be underestimated. For most rural dwellers several man-hours (usually, in fact, woman-hours) are lost every day in getting water.

Expenditure on water has been affected by four forces: demands made by the industrialization drive, the character of the agriculture programme, an ideological commitment to providing better rural water supplies, and foreign aid. The First FYP saw a need to transform the economy by developing industries which had been neglected under the colonial administration. This involved the development of good urban water supplies, and as a result expenditure on urban water was generally high, usually over 40 per cent of the water budget, averaging 45 per cent of the budget in the First FYP (see Table 17). Agriculture development, as I showed earlier, was characterized in this period by a heavy emphasis on the transformation approach. Irrigation and river development programmes dominated the rural water programme. These programmes took up 23 per cent of the water development budget in the First FYP, falling from 38 per cent in 1964-5, when the transformation approach was at its peak, to 11 per cent in 1968-9 when the programme was being phased out.

The Arusha Declaration, with its commitment to developing the rural areas, and to a type of rural development which emphasized a frontal, non-capital-intensive approach, brought about some change in the water programme, but not a total one. The type of expenditure on the provision of rural water altered. The trend towards de-emphasizing large scale schemes, and towards providing local water to small Ujamaa villages, which began in the last part of the First FYP, increased in the Second FYP. Irrigation schemes took only 3 per cent of expenditure in the Second FYP; in contrast, other forms of rural water supplies rose from 19 per cent in the First FYP to 45 per cent in the Second FYP.

TABLE 17

Allocation of water spending

	1964-5	65-6	66-7	67-8	68-9	FFYP	69-70	70-71	71-2	72-3	73-4	SFYP
Urban water	18.4	15.8	12.1	21.3	26.0	93.6	24.8	23.1	6.1	11.8	84.7	150.5
Rural water	3.6	3.0	7.2	11.3	14.0	39.1	19.8	31.5	34.5	44.3	61.5	191.6
Irrigation and river development	15.0	10.6	10.3	5.0	6.1	47.0	9.7	3.1	0.5	0.3	0.2	13.8
Surveys	3.0	5.0	3.7	7.2	10.2	29.1	5.0	7.9	7.4	22.5	23.5	66.3
Total	40.0	34.4	33.3	44.8	56.9	208.8	59.3	65.6	48.5	78.9	169.9	422.2
Urban as share (%)	46	46	36	48	46	45	42	35	13	15	50	36
Irrigation as share (%)	38	31	31	11	11	23	16	5	1	–	–	3

There has been some decline in the expenditure on urban water in the Second FYP, but no clear-cut trend. Expenditure or urban water should be about 36 per cent of the water budget in the Second FYP. (versus 45 per cent in the First FYP). In 1973-4, however, expenditure, having fallen steadily in relative terms, will rise to 50 per cent of the budget. Two factors explain this behaviour. There has been a divergence in the policies followed by different sectors of the economy. While the government was formally committed to developing the rural economy, many parts of the government have continued to follow policies which encourage rapid development of the urban areas. I will show, in chapters four and five that parastatal expenditure has tended to reinforce the old urban-oriented pattern. The Arusha Declaration is only beginning to have an effect on parastatal investment. The bulk of parastatal investment continued to be centred in a few urban areas. For a while, the water ministry, in effect, simply ignored this contradiction. Expenditure on urban water decreased, even in absolute terms. Now, however, the shortage of water in the urban areas is reaching crisis proportions. The water ministry is forced to allocate a large part of its budget to develop better urban water supplies, especially in Dar es Salaam. Thus water policy must follow other policies, and if these other policies continue to promote the growth of urban areas, then water policy will be urban oriented.

Mention should also be made of the effect of foreign aid. Foreign aid donors, especially the Nordic countries, have been attracted by Tanzania's commitment to rural development. They have allocated a large part of their aid budgets to supporting the rural water programme, and have been relatively uninterested in urban water development. Foreign aid has contributed shs 144 million out of shs 192 million spent on rural water in the Second FYP, 75 per cent of the total. In contrast, it is only in 1972-3 that foreign aid again started to flow to urban water,[15] first from W. Germany, and now from Canada. Canada is undertaking a major programme of water supply to Dar es Salaam. In 1973-4, foreign aid will contribute some shs 76 million of the shs 85 million being spent on urban water, 89 per cent of the total. Aid, then, has tended to make shifts in policy more dramatic. It helped to reinforce the rural water programme, and now, when it is felt that the urban centres need better water supplies, it accelerates the shift back to emphasizing urban water. (See chapter six for a discussion of foreign finance.)

ECONOMIC INFRASTRUCTURE – TRANSPORT

Transport policy can be an effective tool for restructuring the economy, but it is one which takes a long time before its impact is felt, and one which must work

15 It had financed the early emphasis on urban water.

with the constraints posed by the past and current development of other sectors. Tanzania inherited, as was mentioned in chapter two, a transport system designed for colonial exploitation of the country. Transport routes were developed solely to pull the export crops out of certain regions, and the other regions were neglected. They were relegated to the role of exporters of labour to exporting regions. Transport links which would encourage inter-regional trade were poorly developed. As a result, many regions remain isolated from much of the country for many months of the year. Even where there are trunk routes, feeder roads do not exist in many regions. Poor transport facilities became a major block to rural economic development.

The importance, then, of developing a better transport system in the country has combined with a number of other factors in making transport the most important sector in terms of government spendings. In both plans, as I showed earlier, it took about one-third of ministerial development expenditure. This tendency has been reinforced by the attraction of transport projects to foreign aid donors, especially to the more traditional donors, like Britain, the United States, Canada and West Germany. In general, 60 per cent of the transport budget has come from foreign aid.

The second factor is the ease of development of transport projects. It is difficult to develop good programmes to stimulate growth, particularly programmes in the rural areas. Road projects, especially with the availability of foreign donors and contractors, are easily started. They are thus very attractive to governments anxious to show that they are doing something. Moreover, transport projects are less obvious failures, and therefore are not stopped when they fail to stimulate growth.[16]

It is difficult to decide *a priori* what a socialist transport policy would be.[17] The development of new trunk routes which would help to restructure the economy are clearly important. So too is the development of feeder roads which bring peasant farmers into contact with outside markets. In general, in Tanzania, it has been felt recently that the transport programme has been too oriented towards trunk routes. In the early part of the First FYP, feeder roads took a large share of the budget. Gradually, however, trunk routes came to dominate, at the expense in both absolute and relative terms of the feeder road programme.

---

16 This same point is made by Hirschman (1970, 84).
17 It clearly would be oriented towards developing an integrated economy, and towards improving the communications of the poorest regions. There is, however, no *a priori* reason why a socialist transport policy would favour either trunk routes or feeder roads. The choice would depend upon the circumstances.

The Second FYP, as did the First, committed itself to a major expansion of the feeder road programme. No such expansion occurred in the early part of the plan. Again expenditure on trunk routes was greatest, but this time the trunk route programme was dominated by one road, the Dar-Tunduma highway. This highway, partially (70 per cent) financed by American and Swedish aid, is being built primarily to improve communication with Zambia. Originally it was thought that there would be a number of years when the road would take the copper traffic until the railway (Tazara, being built by the Chinese) was completed. The road has been delayed, while the railway is ahead of schedule. So the difference between the completion dates of the two projects will not be as great as originally thought. Nevertheless the road has aided the movement of goods into and out of Zambia. It is a clear sign of Tanzania's commitment to its opposition to white oppression in Africa.

Table 18 sets out the allocation of ministerial spending on transportation. Since this ministry is also in charge of the construction of certain government buildings, expenditure on these is included as well. In the early years, feeder roads were important, taking over 30 per cent of the budget. The development of trunk routes other than the Dar-Tunduma road then became important. These routes absorbed over 40 per cent of the budget in the middle years of the First FYP. Major construction on the Dar-Tunduma road started in 1968-9, and this project has dominated the budget of the ministry since then. In the Second FYP, the Dar-Tunduma road will account for over 50 per cent of this ministry's spending. Feeder roads have become important in the last two years of the Second FYP rising to about 20 per cent of the total expenditure. With the expenditure on the Dar-Tunduma highway drawing to a close, an opportunity now exists for the government to re-assess its continued heavy emphasis on this sector, and to develop an effective rural feeder road programme. It will be several years before it is clear whether Tanzania has taken this opportunity.

REGIONAL ALLOCATION

An important part of the Tanzanian commitment to socialism, as I have said several times before, is a strong commitment to equality. This commitment extends to an attempt to ensure equality between regions, and to eradicating some of inequalities fostered by colonial and neo-colonial development. Government expenditure has been regarded as a tool for redressing the balance. To what extent, then, has the pattern of government expenditure shifted to the poorer regions?

There is little evidence that there has been much shift in total expenditure. I have data on the regional impact of government expenditure, which cover all

TABLE 18

Allocation of transport spending (shs million)

	1964-5	65-6	66-7	67-8	68-9	FFYP	69-70	70-71	71-2	72-3	73-4	SFYP
Feeder roads	10.6	10.1	3.8	2.4	3.6	30.5	16.3	5.0	–	36.2	33.5	91.0
Trunk roads	10.2	13.9	61.0	43.1	147.9	276.1	116.3	154.4	128.6	82.9	59.3	542.0
Other roads	3.7	7.3	14.1	29.0	26.4	80.5	12.3	26.3	23.7	22.6	66.3	154.3
Aerodromes	2.4	0.9	11.1	9.4	4.3	28.1	32.4	37.1	20.5	11.0	10.9	111.9
Government houses, offices	0.4	0.5	0.9	3.7	3.0	8.5	5.1	5.3	2.5	3.8	6.6	23.3
Total	27.3	32.7	90.9	87.6	185.2	423.7	182.9	228.1	175.3	156.5	176.6	922.5
Feeder roads share (%)	39	31	4	3	2	7	9	2	–	23	19	10
Trunk roads share (%)	37	43	67	49	80	65	64	68	73	53	34	59
Of which Dar-Tunduma road (%)	–	–	10	12	62	38	84	97	98	80	88	91

projects which could be assigned regionally. Items like Defence, for which we have no data, are not included. Unfortunately my data are much better for the Second FYP than for the First. I have regional allocations for 74 per cent of Second FYP expenditure (given that Defence is 15 per cent of total expenditure, this figure is quite high), but have regional allocations for only 47 per cent of First FYP expenditure. Because of this difference in coverage, conclusions from this section must be treated very cautiously.

Regional spending will be compared with regional per capita income in order to measure the degree to which the government has tried to help the poorer regions. The best data available on regional incomes are those published in the Second FYP, which give monetary gross farm output per capita in 1967 for every region. There is no indication that the basic ranking of regions has altered since this census was done.

Table 19 presents the total expenditure per capita by region in the First and Second FYPs. The deviations are quite large in both Plans, but higher in the First than in the Second. In the First FYP the average deviation was 72 per cent of the average expenditure per region, and in the Second FYP it was 43 per cent. Statistically there is no significant relation between per capita income and per capita expenditure in the regions. If the data point to any conclusion, they would indicate a tendency towards a more positive relation in the Second FYP than in the First, but there is no strong evidence to support such a conclusion. The correlation coefficient between per capita income and per capita expenditure in the First FYP was 0.204, with a t-value of 0.806, insignificant at any level with 15 degrees of freedom. The correlation coefficient was 0.460 for the Second FYP but again this is statistically insignificant, with a t-value of 2.004 and 15 degrees of freedom. In the First FYP Dar es Salaam absorbed 12 per cent of total expenditure, and the Coast Region 29 per cent. In the Second FYP Dar es Salaam's share rose to 16 per cent, but the share of the Coast Region fell to 26 per cent. There would seem to have been little change in the concentration on the capital area.

It was thought that perhaps social services would be less correlated to income than total development expenditure. This appears to be true, but again the data are inconclusive.[18] In the First FYP such expenditure had a correlation coefficient of 0.049, insignificant at any level ($t = 0.188$). In the Second FYP it was 0.212, also insignificant ($t = 0.840$), but indicating a possible tendency to a greater positive correlation.

---

18 Our data are much better for social services, covering 88 per cent of health and education expenditure in the First FYP and 97 per cent in the Second.

TABLE 19

Per capita regional allocation of ministerial expenditure

	First Five Year Plan		Second Five Year Plan[1]		
	Total expenditure	Health and education	Total expenditure	Health and education	Monetary gross farm output per capita (shs)
Arusha	42.8	0.4	158.6	19.7	167.0
Coast	220.2	90.2*	401.8	94.3*	86.0
Dodoma	9.6	7.3	93.3	18.8	34.0
Iringa	12.7	8.4	202.2	33.6	105.0
Kigoma	13.5	2.5	99.4	18.3	35.0
Kilimanjaro	70.2	17.3	254.8	70.2	277.0
Mara	28.3	1.1	95.0	40.3	64.0
Mebeya	15.7	0.8	162.6	12.2	70.0
Morogoro	143.3	3.3	326.9	29.0	158.0
Mtwara and Lindi	85.3	0.7	87.2	65.5	67.0
Mwanza	33.3	5.5	106.4	55.0	101.0
Ruvuma	77.9	24.4	99.7	30.1	57.0
Shinyanga	31.9	8.1	59.3	8.0	97.0
Singida	18.3	16.5	69.7	20.6	28.0
Tabora	76.4	9.5	126.1	14.8	84.0
Tanga	43.1	23.1	154.6	14.2	212.0
W. Lake	20.3	6.9	133.3	12.5	75.0
Dar es Salaam	320.1	–	959.9	–	–
Average	56.1 (49.1 excl Dar es Salaam	13.0	173.6 (149.8 excl. Dar es Salaam	31.4	

*Includes Dar es Salaam
 1 Includes estimates for 1972-73 and 1973-74
SOURCE: Tanzania, 1969, vol. II, 33, 35.; Devplan Planning Information System

The decentralization which has occurred in government spending should make a difference. There was at least some attempt to make allocation to the regions for decentralized expenditure at least partially on a per capita basis, with poorer regions getting more per capita than rich (see Table 20). The correlation coefficient between regional allocation for the decentralized budget for 1973-4 and per capita income is negative (-0.267), but is still not statistically significant ($t = 1.072$, 15 degrees of freedom). This probably indicates an improvement on the previous performance of the total budget, and is as much as could be hoped for at the moment. Where there were good programmes available, resources were pushed into the poor regions.

TABLE 20

Regional allocation of 1973-4 decentralized budget[1]

	Regional allocation per capita	Per capita monetary gross farm output
Mtwara	24.5	67
Ruvuma	22.2	57
Mara	17.8	64
Singida	16.9	28
Kigoma	16.5	35
Arusha	16.4	167
Iringa	14.1	105
Tabora	13.2	84
Kilimanjaro	12.3	277
Lindi	12.0	NA
W. Lake	11.7	75
Tanga	11.6	212
Morogoro	11.4	158
Dodoma	10.9	34
Coast	10.4	86
Mbeya	10.4	70
Shinyanga	9.9	97
Mwanza	7.5	101

1 Based on estimates

EXPORT ORIENTATION

In chapter two I showed that the government's response to a lack of foreign finance was a policy of self-reliance. This policy did not imply a reduced emphasis on trade. Quite the contrary, a policy based upon a lesser reliance on foreign capital inflows probably implies even more emphasis on exports because of the need for foreign exchange. Nevertheless there has been much criticism in intellectual circles (see chapter eight) of Tanzania's continued dependence upon exports. It, therefore, seems worthwhile to analyze the extent to which public investment has been export oriented.

Table 21 shows the proportion of ministerial and regional spending which has gone towards export promotion in the period 1964-73. These proportions have been obtained by multiplying every project's expenditure by an export code indicating the orientation of the project towards exports. (For a fuller description see Appendix II). There would appear to have been a significant increase in the export orientation of ministerial spending. Part of this increase is explained by the construction of the Dar-Tunduma road. Most of the critics of an export

TABLE 21

Export orientation of ministerial spending

	1964-5	65-6	66-7	67-8	68-9	FFYP	69-70	70-71	71-2	72-3	73-4	SFYP
Ministries (%)	4	4	10	6	17	10	20	21	19	18	10	17
Regions (%)	–	–	–	–	–	–	–	–	–	2	4	3
Total (%)	4	4	10	6	17	10	20	21	19	15	8	16
Total without Dar-Tunduma road (%)	4	4	9	5	6	6	10	9	5	10	5	8

orientation would not criticize the corridor to Zambia even though it represents in economic terms a major thrust towards increasing foreign exchange earnings. If the road is excluded, then the rise in export orientation is much less. In the First FYP 6 per cent of ministerial spending was export oriented, versus 8 per cent in the Second FYP.

This is not the place to analyse the issue of dependency on exports. I will do so in later chapters. It does seem appropriate, nonetheless, to point out that the emphasis on exports in ministerial spending has never been very large. While many critics point to tea, coffee, and cotton programmes as a misplaced concentration on primary product exports, the fact remains that the overwhelming proportion of ministerial spending has gone to programmes with no particular export orientation. The trend also seems to be in this direction. Regional programmes have tended to concentrate on non-export products – an implicit goal is a degree of self-sufficiency in food for each region. As regional spending increases, the export orientation of over-all government spending will probably fall.

URBAN/RURAL DICHOTOMY

Concern over the possibility that the interests of the rural population will be sacrificed to promote rapid urban development and to improve the welfare of the present urban population has been a prominent element in the formation of economic strategy in Tanzania. Effort has been devoted to devising ways of measuring the emphasis on rural areas. One way has been to look at each individual programme, as I have done, and assess whether there has been a noticeable shift in direction. An attempt has also been to create statistics which would summarize the over-all urban bias of government spending. These statistics provide a convenient way of summarizing what has happened in a number of sectors. Three different measures[19] have been constructed. The first centres on location of government expenditure. It gives the amount of public investment which has gone to projects physically located in the cities. The second measure is a consumption index. For public investment which is not sold it gives the share which has gone to projects which serve the rural areas, urban areas, or the country as a whole (e.g., Defence). The third measure tries to incorporate both consumption benefits of a project as well as its developmental impact. Thus a project located in the urban areas and providing a service for urban residents may still have some positive impact on the rural areas (e.g., a livestock market in a town). Similarly rural projects can have positive externalities for urban development.

Tables 22-4 present each of these measures for the two Plan periods. Appendix III gives the same data on a yearly basis. All three measures confirm the impression gained from the sectoral analysis of ministerial spending. While there may have been progress in individual areas, in general the emphasis on the rural areas will be no greater in the Second FYP than in the First. The same share of ministerial spending (21 per cent) will be located in towns in both Plans. There has, however, been some movement away from concentrating this expenditure on only a few towns. In the First FYP, 86 per cent of ministerial expenditure located in towns was spent in Dar es Salaam, Tanga, Arusha, Moshi, and Mwanza. In the Second FYP, this share should drop to 80 per cent.

The indices for consumption and development expenditure confirm this picture of unchanged emphasis. In the First FYP, 66 per cent of ministerial spending (excluding spending benefiting the nation as a whole, or on projects whose output is sold), was on projects whose benefits were rural oriented. In the Second FYP, this share will probably fall marginally to 63 per cent. The development index shows no change, registering a 62 per cent share for the rural sector in each Plan (national projects excluded).

There is, however, a sign of hope. Both indices have registered a rising trend for the emphasis on rural areas since the nadir was reached in 1970-71 when both indices registered their lowest share for the rural sector (see Appendix III). The decentralization has also served to increase the rural emphasis of government spending. Regional spending in 1973-4 will be almost exclusively for rural projects. The consumption index registered 93 per cent rural for regional projects in 1973-4.[20] If the regions are able to continue to increase their share of the

19 These measures are incorporated in the Planning Information System described in Appendix II. The urban/rural code was first introduced in Tanzania, *Economic Survey*, 1970-71 (see pp. 00).

20 Data for 1972-73 and 1972-74 are based upon budget estimates rather than actual expenditures. The improvement for these years may, in fact, be less than is indicated.

TABLE 22

Ministerial spending in towns (%)

	Share of town spending	
	First FYP	Second FYP[1]
Dar es Salaam	59	57
Tanga	8	10
Arusha	6	3
Moshi	8	1
Mwanza	5	9
Sub-total	86	80
Other towns	14	20
Total	100	100
Town spending as share of regional and ministerial spending	21	21
Town spending as share of regional spending only	–	4

1 Includes estimates for 1972-73 and 1973-74

TABLE 23

Consumption benefits of ministerial and regional spending (%)

	First FYP	Second FYP[1]
Rural	46	40
Urban	24	23
National	26	36
Sold	4	1
% rural excluding national and sold	66	63

1 Includes estimates for 1972-73 and 1973-74

budget, then they will drag government spending along the direction of more emphasis on the rural sector.

OVERALL ASSESSMENT OF MINISTERIAL EXPENDITURE

The shift in emphasis in ministerial expenditure has not been as dramatic as one might have expected from the Arusha Declaration. Significant progress has been made in the social service field where all three ministries have made important

TABLE 24

Development and consumption benefits of ministerial
and regional spending (%)

	First FYP	Second FYP[1]
Rural	48	48
Urban	30	29
National	22	23
% rural excluding national	62	62

1 Includes estimates for 1972-73 and 1973-74

changes in their programmes. It is in the economic field, in the provision of
support services, or the development of infrastructure, that the change seems to
have been the least. No radical increase in the support given to economic development of the rural sector has occurred.

While this is an essentially pessimistic account of the progress which has been
made so far, there are important caveats which must be attached to any criticism. The first is that change takes time. It appears to take considerably more
time to develop an effective economic programme than it does to shift the
emphasis of the social service sector. In almost all cases, the trend appears to be
one of improvement. The immediate post-Arusha spending was, in the case of
many sectors, the worst in terms of urban bias.[21] Now the direction of government programmes does seem to have turned around. Decentralization seems to
have been one factor in this switch, but it is probably also true that there was a
time lag before an effective rural programme could be developed.

The second caveat which must be added to any criticism is that Tanzania
must not be judged only by its own standards, but by a comparison with other
countries. By the standard of many Third World countries Tanzania's performance has been good. It has made real progress in the provision of social services
to the rural areas while in many countries the trend has been towards increasing
concentration of services in the urban areas. While over-all its expenditure is not
more rural oriented, it is not less rural oriented either. Given that its urban
population has grown in relative terms throughout this period, this must be
viewed as at least a modest accomplishment. While it is probably right to expect
more, comparison of the Tanzanian experience with other countries should
always temper any criticism we might have.

21 In the next two chapters I shall look at the performance of the parastatal sector. Here
again we shall find that the immediate post-Arusha performance was one of moving
away from the Arusha goals, but that this has been followed by a shift to an increased
emphasis on developing rural socialism.

4

Investment by parastatals

INTRODUCTION

Purpose of chapter

This chapter will provide an overview of parastatal investment. After a short discussion of the data base used there will be a brief history of the development of the parastatal sector. It is important to have an understanding of the manner in which the sector developed. It was not created at one stroke. On the contrary, the colonial administration and the newly independent government created many of the institutions which were to form the basis of the parastatal sector. From these organizations a large number of new parastatals have developed over an extended period of time via both nationalizations and the creation of new firms. The result of this slow evolutionary development has been a parastatal sector which reflects the ideology of the government at many different stages. Since this ideology has changed significantly over time, the parastatal sector represents as much pre- as post-Arusha goals.

The chapter also tries to provide an overview of the performance of the parastatal sector. In many ways it is difficult to judge the parastatal sector from a macro viewpoint. A detailed sectoral analysis is necessary. This is provided in the next chapter. Here I will try to pull together the conclusions which can be drawn from a look at some broad indicators of performance. While the performance of the parastatals as a whole has been fairly good in a narrow economic sense, they do not seem to have responded to the shift in policy which occurred with the Arusha Declaration. In general, parastatals' investments since Arusha have not been directed towards developing the rural sector. Parastatals have concentrated on building enterprises which are often large, capital intensive, and outer directed, and which are not integrated in the rural economy. Far from mitigating the urban/rural dichotomy, they have exacerbated it.

There are signs of a change in the emphasis of the parastatal sector. The government appears to have been distressed by many of the investment choices made to date. Yet if a fundamental change is to occur, there will probably have to be a significant re-organization of the parastatal sector. A major push to create intermediate and small parastatals centred on rural development is needed at this time.

Data base

The Central Statistical Bureau produces two documents which provide detailed data on parastatals. The most important of these is the *Analysis of Accounts of Parastatals* (Tanzania, 1972). The other document is the *Survey of Industrial Production* (1966-70), a survey of all manufacturing firms (both private and public) with more than ten employees.

Much of the data used in the next two chapters come from these two sources. However, I have had to make extensive revisions to these data because they contained important errors. These errors and revisions are described in detail in Appendix IV. The most important change concerned the investment series for parastatals. I have obtained the balance sheets for virtually all parastatals, and from them have created a new investment series. The published figures are based upon a survey which is sent out in early February. Because firms often do not have audited balance sheets at that time, the data used by the Bureau are often only preliminary data, which do not agree with the figures as they appear in the final balance sheets. As well, the Bureau has committed a number of conceptual mistakes and has allocated investments incorrectly. The changes I have made have all been shown to the Bureau, which is currently engaged in an exercise to revise their series to incorporate my changes.

Data on parastatal firms are generally presented on a calendar year basis. In a few cases where the Planning Information System (see Appendix II) has been used to manipulate the data, the series will be on a fiscal year basis. Most of the data will be concerned with the period 1964 to 1971. No final figures are yet available on parastatals after 1971. The Planning Information System does contain projections on parastatal investment for the years after 1971, and these will be used where necessary. In general, however, I will concentrate on the period for which final data are available.

A parastatal is defined by the Central Statistical Bureau as one in which the government holds at least 50 per cent of the equity. There were, however, a number of firms in which the government did not do so, especially in earlier years. It is not clear, however, from a decision-making point of view, that 50 per cent is a critical number. The ways open to a government to influence decisions in a small, partially socialist economy like Tanzania's are many, and reliance on majority control is not essential. It is also likely that the motivation for investing is not related to majority control.[1] Thus in the early stages of development, when Tanzania sought to develop a number of industries already existing in Kenya, it did not always acquire majority control at the beginning. Portland Cement was only 20 per cent government owned. The Tiper Oil Refinery was 100 per cent private, with the government having the option to buy 50 per cent, an option finally exercised in 1968. For the purpose of this study, I will include all corporations in which the government has any equity holding. I will distinguish between majority parastatals (government holding 50 per cent or greater), and non-majority parastatals (government holding under 50 per cent) to give the reader a sense of the importance of these two different types. In terms of performance or structure there does not appear to be much difference between the two types. Non-majority parastatals are important, however, because they were a vehicle for a gradual extension of government control in the productive sector. By using such a vehicle, the government has created a parastatal sector which is not significantly different from the private sector.

For the most part I have excluded Tazara from the analysis of parastatals. This is consistent with the procedure adopted in Tanzania. Where appropriate I have included separately what data are available on Tazara. Since the project is not yet operational I have no data on its performance. Chapter six provides a detailed analysis on its financing (see section on Data).

THE CREATION OF THE PARASTATAL SECTOR

Early development of parastatals

During the colonial administration, and the early years after independence the government acquired a major stake in the economy. By 1964 the government had complete control of the electrical company, majority control of the most important mining company, of the meat packing plant, of several hotels and of a

1 In chapter six I will talk about the effect that the government acquisition of majority control in a number of firms in the immediate post-Arusha period had on the willingness of multinationals to invest in Tanzania. There I will argue that foreign firms have, in the past, invested in Tanzania usually after the government had indicated a desire to develop a certain industry, or some firm not in East Africa indicated a willingness to develop a project. If the multinational was to protect its retail market, or develop a market for capital goods it had to be prepared to build in Tanzania. Usually it entered into an agreement with the government to build a plant. In the post-Arusha period this entailed some government participation, but the motivation was essentially the same as in the pre-Arusha period.

major sisal and tea estate, and non-majority control in several manufacturing firms. As well, a number of institutions had been created which were to be the basis of later parastatal expansion. The National Housing Corporation (NHC) was established, as were a number of marketing boards – Lint and Seed Marketing Board (LSMB), National Agricultural Products Board (NAPB), Tanzania Coffee Board (TCB). The National Insurance Company (NIC) had been established in 1963 with the government holding 51 per cent of the shares, and the private insurance companies the other 49 per cent. At this stage the firm had virtually no assets, but its establishment meant that the government had a vehicle for the easy acquisition of the private insurance companies at a later date. The Tanganyika Agriculture Corporation (formed in 1954 by the British from the assets left after the groundnuts scheme failed), and the Tanganyika Development Corporation (established in 1962 to hold the government equity in Lake Manyara Hotel, Tanganyika Meerschaum Co., Tanganyika Development Finance Corporation, and Uplands Bacon) were merged in 1964 to form the National Development Corporation.

As well, a number of banking institutions have been created. In 1962, the Tanganyika Development Finance Co. was formed with the Tanganyika Government, the Commonwealth Development Corporation, and the Federal Republic of Germany holding equal shares. The Netherlands Overseas Finance Co. joined in sponsorship in 1965. TDFL was largely geared to encouraging local private investment by providing equity and loan capital, as well as managerial advice. In recent years, it has also started joint projects with government-owned enterprises, and now views its purpose as 'to supplement the efforts of the Government in bringing about socialistic economic development in Tanzania' (TDFL, 1970). Three rural-oriented credit institutions had been established: the National Co-operative Bank, National Co-operative Development Bank, and National Development Credit Agency. These banks were formed in 1964 to take over the work of the Agricultural Credit Agency, the Co-operative Revolving Loan Fund, and the African Productivity Loans Fund.

Thus by 1964 the government had acquired a significant amount of productive assets. Table 25 sets out the distribution of parastatal assets in 1964.[2] The amount of these assets, shs 610 million, greatly exceeds the amount of assets nationalized in 1967 after the Arusha Declaration. More importantly, many of

---

2 Figures for assets are the total fixed assets of the firm before depreciation. No allowance is made for the fact that the government's equity is different for different firms. If the government has any equity at all, then the full assets of the company are included. Thus, by this procedure, if the government increases its equity holding in parastatal firms, this does not affect the value of parastatal assets.

TABLE 25

Distribution of parastatal assets, 1964 (shs million)

	Majority	Non-majority	Total
Manufacturing	21	4	25
Mining	241	–	241
Construction	25	–	25
Electricity	231	–	231
Transport	–	–	–
Tourism	15	–	15
Commerce	13	–	13
Agriculture	56	–	56
Finance	4	–	4
Total	606	4	610

the institutions which were to play a critical role in the development of the parastatal sector, especially NDC, but also TANESCO, NIC, and Williamson Diamonds, had already been established at this early stage. I shall explore some of the implications of this later.

Growth of parastatal assets

Table 26 shows parastatal assets, broken down by sector from 1964 to 1971. In that period majority-owned parastatals' assets grew shs 2707 million to shs 3313 million (excluding Tazara). At the same time non-majority parastatals increased from shs 4 million in assets to shs 144 million, an increase of she 140 million. This growth resulted from three sources: (*a*) establishment of new parastatals; (*b*) acquisition by the government of shares in additional firms; (*c*) growth of already established firms. In order to get a better understanding of the development of the parastatal sector, I have attempted to assess empirically the importance of each of these sources of growth. Table 27 shows investment by new firms and Table 28 shows this investment as a share of total parastatal investment. Here I have estimated the investment by firms not previously established. Once the firm becomes operational at anywhere near normal capacity, then it is classified as established, and its investment is no longer counted as investment by a new firm (i.e. it moves from group (*a*) above to group (*c*)). Merely changing the ownership does not make a firm new. Thus Bora shoes, created out of BATA shoes, is classified established. I am trying to capture here the extent to which parastatal investment was breaking into a new field, developing a new organization, or merely allowing an existing organization to grow under a new umbrella.

TABLE 26

Parastatal assets 1964-71 (shs '000)

Sector	1964	1965	1966	1967	1968	1969	1970	1971
Manufacturing	21,191	22,862	43,033	277,181	416,994	551,971	759,200	971,206
Non-majority manufacturing	4094	51,240	68,182	69,517	110,061	138,405	123,961	107,762
Mining	240,404	244,889	250,808	255,800	259,971	265,951	276,423	299,787
Construction	25,015	32,030	43,302	45,691	51,918	61,426	72,593	109,194
Electricity	231,140	241,737	273,711	304,223	336,988	372,939	403,479	506,138
Finance	4126	6209	31,598	132,372	145,168	159,401	174,686	200,686
Non-majority finance	–	325	355	704	742	978	1299	2394
Transport	–	–	14,883	187,003	306,907	336,561	357,433	401,033
Tourism	15,061	37,843	38,944	41,054	49,189	76,027	110,796	127,951
Non-majority tourism	–	–	–	–	–	1246	8519	9674
Commerce	31,391	19,978	25,897	42,014	53,602	70,837	183,184	470,073
Non-majority commerce	–	1300	1300	1300	1300	7300	15,300	15,300
Agriculture	55,952	57,772	59,718	185,119	194,775	205,255	217,456	226,656
Non-majority agriculture	–	–	–	–	2713	4855	7411	8601
Total – majority	606,080	663,320	782,578	1,470,457	1,815,512	2,100,268	2,555,250	3,312,724
Total – including non-majority	610,174	716,185	852,415	1,541,978	1,930,328	2,253,044	2,711,740	3,456,455

TABLE 27

Investment by new firms (shs '000)

Sector	1964	1965	1966	1967	1968	1969	1970	1971	Total
Manufacturing	—	1399	17,866	45,786	27,681	33,371	149,023	123,424	398,550
Non-majority manufacturing	2094	34,648	15,572	36,856	37,831	23,103	—	—	150,104
Mining	—	—	—	—	—	—	—	—	—
Construction	—	—	—	—	—	—	—	—	—
Electricity	—	—	—	—	—	—	—	—	—
Finance	—	—	—	1576	9283	5356	—	—	16,215
Non-majority finance	—	—	—	—	—	—	—	—	—
Transport	—	—	16,074	157,292	114,392	—	—	—	287,758
Tourism	10,687	21,535	482	1531	7187	26,979	35,534	14,341	118,276
Non-majority tourism	—	—	—	—	—	1246	7298	1155	9699
Commerce	—	—	—	—	—	—	2049	—	2049
Non-majority commerce	—	—	—	—	—	5558	4712	—	10,270
Agriculture	—	—	—	—	—	3278	6905	—	10,183
Non-majority agriculture	—	—	—	—	—	2142	1778	—	3920
Total majority parastatals	10,687	22,934	34,422	206,185	158,543	68,984	193,511	137,765	833,031
Total non-majority parastatals	2094	34,648	15,572	36,856	37,831	32,049	13,788	1155	173,993
Total	12,781	57,582	49,994	243,041	196,374	101,033	207,299	138,920	1,007,024

TABLE 28

Share of new investment in total parastatal investment (per cent)

Sector	1964	1965	1966	1967	1968	1969	1970	1971	Total
Manufacturing	–	64	84	72	63	55	73	66	68
Non-majority manufacturing	100	100	91	96	98	77	–	–	90
Mining	–	–	–	–	–	–	–	–	–
Construction	–	–	–	–	–	–	–	–	–
Electricity	–	–	–	100	100	100	–	–	78
Transport	93	92	25	51	78	95	97	84	90
Tourism									
Non-majority tourism						100	100	100	100
Commerce							7		1
Non-majority commerce						100	100		18
Agriculture						30	37		26
Non-majority agriculture						44	54		24
Finance				35	65	36			20
Non-majority finance									–
Total – majority	19	34	33	70	61	35	48	29	45
Total non-majority	100	96	90	95	92	71	51	11	82
Total	22	56	41	73	66	41	48	28	48

TABLE 29

Distribution of new investment (per cent)

Sector	Majority	Non-majority	Total
Manufacturing	48	86	54
Mining	–	–	–
Construction	–	–	–
Electricity	–	–	–
Transport	35		29
Tourism	14	6	13
Commerce	–	6	1
Agriculture	1	2	1
Finance	2	–	2
Total	100	100	100

The most striking feature about Table 28 is the relative magnitude of new investment. Almost half (48 per cent) of parastatal investment in the period 1964-71 went towards the creation of new firms. The importance of new firms was not the same in each sector. In manufacturing, over 70 per cent of investment went towards the establishment of new firms. No parastatal investment was directed to the creation of new firms in mining, construction or electricity, and very little in finance, commerce and agriculture. In contrast 78 per cent of investment in transport was directed towards establishing the firms in that sector, and 90 per cent of the majority and 100 per cent of the non-majority investment in tourism has been directed to establishing new firms. Thus, the thrust of new investment has been into manufacturing, transport, and tourism. These three sectors have taken 96 per cent of new investment, with manufacturing by far the most important, making up 54 per cent, followed by transport with 29 per cent and tourism with 13 per cent (see Table 29).

The vehicle for the creation of these new firms was largely the National Development Corporation. From 1964 to 1969 NDC had control of most government assets in manufacturing (excluding the oil refinery), tourism, and food processing plants and agriculture (excluding the sisal estates). In 1969 the Tanzanian Tourist Corporation and the National Agriculture and Food Corporation were established. These organizations took the appropriate assets with them (hotels and tourist services in the one case, ranches, tea estates, and dairies in the other). In 1971 the Tanzania Wood Industries Corporation (TWICO) was set up, again with NDC assets (sawmill, chipboard factory, plywood factory). Finally in 1972 the State Mining Corporation was established, taking from NDC all its mining assets (Williamson Diamond Mines, Tanzania Gemstones and Portland Cement). Thus NDC has been the prime vehicle for the establishment of new parastatals.

TABLE 30

Acquisition of assets (shs million)

Sector	1964	1965	1966	1967	1968	1969	1970	1971	Total
Manufacturing				134	102	86	2	–	324
Mining									
Construction									
Electricity									
Transport									
Tourism				1					1
Commerce				11			86	250	347
Agriculture				120					120
Finance				96					96
Total				362	102	86	88	250	888

Its projects certainly account for over 50 per cent of parastatal investment in new firms. I shall look later at how successful the government has been in establishing these new enterprises.

The second major way the government has expanded the parastatal sector has been through nationalizations. Table 30 shows the amount of assets acquired in each year from 1964-71.[3] The most important period of nationalization was immediately after the Arusha Declaration. At that time the government acquired shs 362 million in assets: 37 per cent in industry, 33 per cent in agriculture, 27 per cent in finance, and 3 per cent in commerce. There was one acquisition not directly related to Arusha, the New Safari Hotel. In 1968 the Tiper oil refinery was acquired, as had been agreed when the company was originally established.

The next acquisition was Kilombero Sugar in 1969. In 1970 the government acquired 50 per cent equity in Shell/BP, Agip, and TANHIDE and in 1971 the Buildings Acquisition Act resulted in the purchasing of a large amount of property which can be roughly valued at shs 250 million. Thus, of a total of shs 888 million in assets acquired in the period 1964-71, 39 per cent were in commerce, 36 per cent in manufacturing, 14 per cent in agriculture, and 11 per cent in finance.

The government during this period also increased its holdings in a number of companies in order to acquire a majority control. In 1967 Portland Cement became majority government-owned as did Sikh Sawmills and Dar es Salaam

---

3 In Table 30 increases in the government holding are not included. Thus the acquisition of a majority share in Portland Cement in 1967 is not recorded. On the other hand the acquisition of a minority share in Tanganyika Extract Co. is recorded as this company's acquisition as a parastatal.

TABLE 31

Distribution of continuing investment 1964-71 (shs million)

	Majority (%)	Non-majority (%)	Total (%)
Manufacturing	185 (18)	26 (65)	211 (20)
Mining	70 (7)		70 (7)
Construction	137 (13)		137 (13)
Electricity	294 (28)		294 (27)
Transport	80 (8)		80 (7)
Tourism	13 (1)	–	13 (1)
Commerce	141 (14)	1 (2)	142 (13)
Agriculture	48 (5)	12 (30)	60 (6)
Finance	66 (6)	1 (2)	67 (6)
Total	1034	40	1074

Motor Transport in 1970, and Tanzania Bag Corporation and TANITA in 1971. Since the government previously held some equity in these companies this increase in ownership has not been treated as an acquisition.

The third way in which the parastatal sector grew was through the development of existing companies, either nationalized or started by the government but now operational. Total investment was shs 2081 million in the period 1964-71. Of this, about half (48 per cent) was new investment, and the other half was further continuing investment by established firms. Table 31 shows the distribution of continuing investment. TANESCO, the electricity parastatal, contributed 27 per cent of continuing investment, followed by manufacturing with 20 per cent. Despite the government's long involvement in mining, mining investment was not particularly large. Thus this sector has remained stagnant, contributing nothing to parastatal assets via nationalizations or new investment, and little even via continuing investment. Commerce and construction have both been important continuing investors, although both have not been important sources of new firms.

I can now present an over-all view of the parastatal sector. By 1971, as I have said, parastatal assets were shs 3456 million. The distribution of these assets is shown in Table 32. Manufacturing is the most important sector, contributing 31 per cent of the assets, followed by electricity with 15 per cent, commerce with 14 per cent, and transport with 12 per cent. Tourism and construction are not very important parastatal sectors, nor, in terms of assets, are agriculture, finance or mining. Each of the sectors has, however, grown in different ways, as I have mentioned when discussing the different methods by which the parastatal sector has grown.

TABLE 32

Parastatal assets in 1971 (shs million)

Sector	Majority (%)	Non-Majority (%)	Total (%)
Manufacturing	971 (29)	108 (76)	1079 (31)
Mining	300 (9)		300 (8)
Construction	109 (3)		109 (3)
Electricity	506 (16)		506 (15)
Transport	401 (12)		401 (12)
Tourism	128 (4)	10 (7)	138 (4)
Commerce	470 (14)	15 (10)	485 (14)
Agriculture	227 (7)	8 (6)	235 (7)
Finance	201 (6)	2 (1)	203 (6)
Total	3313 (96)	143 (4)	3456 (100)

TABLE 33

Growth of parastatal sector (shs million)

Sector	Assets in 1964	National-izations	New investments	Continued	Total
Manufacturing	25	324	549	211	1109
Mining	241	–	–	70	311
Construction	25	–	–	137	162
Electricity	231	–	–	294	525
Transport	–	–	288	80	368
Tourism	15	1	128	13	157
Commerce	13	347	12	142	514
Agriculture	56	120	14	60	250
Finance	4	96	16	67	183
Total	610	888	1007	1074	3579
Share (%)	17	25	28	30	100

Table 33 shows the size of parastatal assets in 1964 in each sector, the nationalizations which have taken place, the new investments in each sector, and the continuing investments. Most totals are slightly larger than the totals shown in Table 32 because not all investment increases the value of fixed assets. Some is needed to maintain them. The difference is not large in this case because of the relative newness of most parastatal firms. Manufacturing, almost non-existent in the parastatal sector in 1964, has grown primarily through the development of new firms, but also significantly through nationalizations. Mining and electricity were well established in 1964, and electricity, but not mining has grown rapidly.

Construction has increased in size through the expansion of National Housing Corporation. The commerce sector has grown almost predominately through nationalizations.

The parastatal transport sector has been created entirely by the government, which did not acquire an access to this sector, but developed new firms. The thrust of the government into the transport sector can only be understood in the context of UDI[4] by Rhodesia. UDI forced Tanzania, if it was to help Zambia, to develop over a very short period of time communication links with Zambia, links which did not really exist at that time. The importance of this event in the investment pattern of the country cannot be over-emphasized. I can give a rough estimate of its impact by looking at the five major projects it can be said to have initiated, as shown in Table 34.

TABLE 34

Investment in Zambian corridor

Tazama pipelines	shs 275 million
Zambia Tanzania road services	shs 75 million
Dar-Tunduma road	shs 550 million
Expansion DSM harbours	shs 100 million
Tazara[1]	shs 1400 million
Total	shs 2400 million

1 One-half cost of Tazara

UDI initiated a tremendous surge in investment in transportation, probably in the range of shs 2.4 billion in an economy where productive investment was usually only shs 1.0 billion, and total investment shs 2.0 billion a year. The parastatal sector has not, however, made a significant move into the internal Tanzania transport sector. This has largely been left to the East Africa Community, the cooperatives and the private sector.

Finance developed as a result of an initial nationalization, and continued growth of these firms. Agriculture also developed primarily through nationalizations, but there was an established parastatal sector in 1964, and these firms, especially TAC/NDC/Agriculture Department/NAFCO/NACO[5] have provided a real source of constant, if quite slow, growth.

4 Unilateral Declaration of Independence made by Rhodesia in 1964. This act declared that the colony was to be independent and implied a continued complete political domination by the colony's white population (5 per cent of the total population). Britain opposed the action but did nothing militarily to stop it.
5 Tanzania is noted for its changing organizational structure. Livestock farms have gone through each of these institutions since 1962.

TABLE 35

Non-majority parastatal investment (shs '000)

Sector	1964	1965	1966	1967	1968	1969	1970	1971	Total
Manufacturing	2094	34,648	17,156	38,372	38,469	30,200	7316	3526	171,781
Mining	—	—	—	—	—	—	—	—	—
Construction	—	—	—	—	—	—	—	—	—
Electricity	—	—	—	—	—	—	—	—	—
Transport	—	—	—	—	—	—	—	—	—
Tourism						1246	7298	1155	9699
Commerce	—	1300	—	—	—	5558	4712	—	11,570
Agriculture	—	—	—	—	2713	4855	7411	1190	16,169
Finance			44	359	42	243	207	200	1095
Total non-majority	2094	35,948	17,200	38,731	41,224	42,102	26,944	6071	210,314
Total investment (majority and non-majority)	59,271	102,851	121,069	331,809	299,561	239,383	433,849	493,820	2,081,613
Non-majority share (%)	4	35	14	12	14	18	6	2	10

Before turning to an over-all analysis of parastatals, I should discuss one more aspect of the development of the parastatal sector, the role of non-majority firms. Non-majority parastatals have played a significant role in the development of the parastatal sector, especially in earlier years. Although they held only 4 per cent of parastatal assets in 1971, they have since 1964 contributed 10 per cent of investment (see Table 35). This difference largely reflects the fact, mentioned earlier, that a number of parastatals were originally started with a minority government interest, and then later the government acquired majority control.

Another way of analyzing the degree of private involvement in the parastatal sector is to look at the average equity holding by the government. Table 36 shows parastatal investment weighted by the equity held by the government in the parastatal sector. (I have used the Planning Information System to compute these averages so the figures are on a fiscal year basis.) Up until the last two years of the Second Five Year Plan, the private share has been significant. The high government share for 1966-7 and 1967-8 reflects the building of the corridor to Zambia, and the Urafiki Textile Mill. There was no private participation in the Textile Mill, or the Road Service and only a small one in the pipeline.

Joint venture firms have tended to concentrate in the manufacturing sector. There are no joint ventures left in finance, construction, tourism, or commerce, and only small private equity holdings in transport and agriculture. In contrast, over 23 per cent of manufacturing investment in the period 1964-71 came from non-majority parastatals, and in 1971 two-thirds of parastatal manufacturing assets belonged to firms with at least some private equity holding.

A review of the development of the parastatal sector is important because it will help us to understand the performance of parastatal firms. The parastatal sector has involved the creation of a large number of new firms, and the extension of government involvement into sectors in which it was previously not involved. There has not, however, been a dramatic break with the past. There are several reasons for this. The first is that the prime institution used to create new enterprises was the National Development Corporation. It did not change its approach to investment in response to the changed ideology of the government. In the early years it was an institution whose role as far as project preparation was concerned was essentially passive. It viewed itself as an organization designed to attract foreign firms which had projects to build. There was little NDC participation in the actual design of the project. Often the area of investment chosen was in response to foreign initiatives, rather than the result of a NDC desire to penetrate a certain sector. NDC continued to operate in much the same way despite the change in government policy.

TABLE 36

Government equity in parastatal investment (shs million)

	64-5	65-6	66-7	67-8	68-9	FFYP	69-70	70-71	71-2	72-3	73-4	SFYP
(1) Total parastatal investment	81	112	236	314	266	1009	332	491	514	459	966	2762
(2) Investment weighted by equity	62	84	205	273	218	842	252	398	427	445	879	2401
(2) as % of (1)	77	75	87	87	82	83	76	81	83	97	91	87

The second reason for the failure to develop significantly different parastatal organizations was the role played by nationalizations. Despite the importance of new firms in the parastatal sector, many parastatal firms were previously privately owned. The parastatal assets acquired before 1964 were mostly private firms in which the government acquired equity control (all manufacturing and tourism firms, the mining firm and the electricity company). There were, as well, shs 888 million in assets acquired after 1964. Together these firms constitute 55 per cent of parastatals' assets not acquired through continued investment. These firms have not been significantly altered since their acquisition, and operate as essentially private firms under government ownership.

The use of nationalizations as a means of creating much of the parastatal sector was a two-edged sword. On the one hand, it allowed the government to move easily into the productive sector. By acquiring established firms the government minimized the degree of difficulty it would have operating the firms. On the other hand, the government acquired a large number of companies whose basic structure and orientation was that of private firms. If the Arusha Declaration was to mean the establishment of a radically different investment strategy, these companies would not be a good basis for such a change.

The creation of a parastatal sector through nationalizations meant that much of the scarce manpower available in Tanzania had to be devoted to managing these existing industries. This manpower could not be used in the development of new industries. While nationalized parastatals provided a good training ground for managers in some respects, in many other ways their effect was harmful. Tanzanians were trained to be good managers of large, capitalist firms, not to be socialist leaders. In this environment, the stereotype of a successful firm was Tanzania Breweries, or British American Tobacco – an efficiently-run, highly profitable enterprise. Yet these firms have many characteristics which are undesirable, and should not be imitated. I shall discuss these later in this chapter and in chapter five.[6] The nature of the development of the parastatal sector did not predetermine the type of firms which were established. A number of factors influenced the final performance of the parastatal sector. I shall discuss these in chapter seven, and I would now like to look at that performance in detail. Chapter five presents a sectoral analysis of parastatals. Only by looking at the performance of parastatals at this level can one hope to make an adequate assessment. Before doing that, however, I would like to provide an overview of the parastatal sector. This overview will give the reader an adequate understanding of the dimensions of the parastatals in order to assess parastatals on a sectoral basis. As well, it will give a brief summary of their over-all performance.

GENERAL PERFORMANCE OF PARASTATALS

The parastatal sector in 1971

In this section I will look at the distribution of parastatal investment and will assess the performance of the parastatal sector by looking at a number of measures. These are the capital/labour ratio, capital/value added ratio, rate of profitability, rate of return to fixed capital, import intensity, export orientation, average wage paid, value added per employee, and wages as a share in value added. I have, as well, classified all parastatals by the physical location of their fixed assets: whether in towns or not, and in what region. (See Appendix III for a full description of all these measures).

Table 37 presents some of the basic data on parastatals used to compute these ratios, and Table 38 presents the ratios themselves. There has been a wide range in the performance of different sectors. To some extent these differences reflect differences in the nature of the sector. It is not surprising that the capital/labour ratio of electricity is three times that of manufacturing or eleven times that of agriculture. In other cases, the high ratios reflect the manner in which the government entered the sector. The poor performance of tourist parastatals, for example, is the result of the type of firm the government chose to develop. Parastatal firms are much more capital-intensive and less profitable than are private firms in this sector. (See the next chapter for a detailed look at each sector).

6 I do not mean to imply here that I think Tanzania should not have nationalized these firms. It was wise to do so. I only want to point out that one of the effects of the use of nationalizations was that a conservative parastatal sector was created, and this probably discouraged radical innovation even in the design of new firms.

TABLE 37

Data on majority parastatals (shs million)

Sector	Assets 1970	Value added 1971	Employment 1971 (no. of persons)	Profits 1971	Return on capital 1971	Wages and salaries 1971	Export orientation (%)
Manufacturing	759	306	20,113	99	175	131	19
Mining	276	96	2683	54	68	28	99
Construction	73	24	3178	1	6	18	–
Electricity	403	71	3003	33	55	16	–
Finance	175	205[1]	4301	98[1]	153	52	–
Transport	357	103	2989	46	67	36	–
Tourism	111	12	2000	–7	1	11	100
Commerce[2]	183	200	6016	110	147	53	3
Agriculture	218	40	18,816	–	10	30	94
Total	2555	1057	63,099	434	682	375	29

1 Assigns imputed bank charges to value added, and profits
2 Excludes nationalized buildings

TABLE 38

Some basic ratios for majority parastatals

Sector	Capital/ value added	Capital/ labour (shs. '000)	Wages/ labour (shs. '000)	Wages/ value added (%)	Return to capital (%)	Profit rate (%)	Value added/ labour (shs. '000)
Manufacturing	2.5	38	6.5	43	23	13	15.2
Mining	2.9	103	10.4	29	25	20	35.8
Construction	3.0	23	5.7	75	8	1	7.6
Electricity	5.7	134	5.3	23	14	8	23.6
Finance	0.9	41	12.1	25	87	56	47.7
Transport	3.5	119	12.0	35	19	13	34.5
Tourism	9.3	56	5.5	92	1	-6	6.0
Commerce	0.9	30	8.8	27	80	60	33.2
Agriculture	5.5	12	1.6	75	5	–	2.1
Average	2.4	40	5.9	35	27	17	16.8

TABLE 39

Comparison of parastatals and monetary economy

Sector	Value added/labour		Wages/labour	
	Parastatals (shs '000)	Monetary economy (shs '000)	Parastatals (shs '000)	Monetary economy (shs '000)
Manufacturing	15.2	16.3	6.5	5.1
Mining	35.8	22.2	10.4	6.3
Construction	7.6	7.5	5.7	3.2
Electricity/ public utilities	23.6	8.7	5.3	5.4
Commerce/ tourism/ services[1]	26.4	24.6[1]	8.0	6.2[1]
Finance, real estate, insurance	47.7	56.3	12.0	10.0
Transport	34.4	20.0	12.0	6.5
Agriculture	2.1	NA	1.6	2.1
Average	16.8	NA	5.9	4.5[1]

SOURCE: Tanzania, *Annual Economic Survey*, 1971-2, 5, 39, 46
1 Excludes public administration

The parastatal sector is, in general, concentrated in the more capital-intensive areas of the economy. Table 39 compares the average wage and value added per worker in each parastatal sector to the economy as a whole. Parastatals consistently pay higher wages. This reflects both the policy of the government, and the more capital-intensive nature of the parastatal sector. This capital-intensive nature cannot be documented on a macro level, but is documented in the next chapter for those sectors where data are available. In most sectors, the parastatals have a higher value added per employee, again reflecting their tendency to be in the more capital-intensive ends of sectors. Where their value added per employee is less, this is generally a reflection of lower efficiency, not lower capital intensity as in the commerce/tourism/services sector (again see chapter five).

The profitability of parastatals is quite high. The profit rate is 17 per cent, and the return on capital 27 per cent.[7] Profits are, however, concentrated in a

7 The difference between these two measures is explained in Appendix II. The essential distinction is that profits are equal to return on capital minus interest payments on borrowed capital.

TABLE 40

Financing of parastatal spending (shs million)

	First FYP		Second FYP	
	Estimate	Actual	Estimate	Actual[1]
Own resources (%)	180	126	1003	770
	(18)	(12)	(41)	(28)
External (%)	587	665	973	1401
	(59)	(66)	(40)	(51)
Government local (%)	220	218	458	591
	(22)	(22)	(19)	(21)
Total (%)	987	1009	2434	2762
	(100)	(100)	(100)	(100)

SOURCE: Tanganyika, 1964, vol. I, 93, 95, 97; Tanzania, 1969, vol. II, 18
  1 Includes estimates for 1972-73 and 1973-74

few sectors. In 1972, finance and commerce accounted for 44 per cent of the return on capital and 48 per cent of the profits with 14 per cent of the fixed assets. In certain sectors – construction, tourism, and agriculture – the returns have been quite low.

Despite the apparent high profitability of parastatals, the parastatal sector as a whole has not financed as much of its programme as the government has wished. Table 40 presents the expected and actual financing of parastatals in each plan period. In the First FYP the government expected parastatals to finance 18 per cent of their programme through self-generated funds and local borrowing. Only 12 per cent of their programme was actually financed that way. In the Second FYP, 41 per cent of parastatal finance was to come through local borrowing or self-generated funds. Again there will be a short-fall. It is now expected that only 28 per cent will come from these sources. Part of the problem may have been caused by excessive optimism over the performance of parastatals. A more important explanation is the concentration of profitability in a few sectors. While the parastatals as a whole may have been profitable, these profits cannot always be used for investments in the desired area. Thus the government has been forced to rely upon its own resources and foreign borrowing more than it intended. (See chapter six for a fuller discussion of the problems in using parastatal surpluses.)

The parastatal sector is characterized by a heavy dominance of a few firms. The government has not created a sector composed of medium-size operations, but one in which a few firms own most of the assets, and most own very few. Table 41 presents the distribution of parastatal firms by sector. Eighteen firms (20 per cent of the total) own shs 2.0 billion in assets, or 80 per cent of

TABLE 41

Large firms[1] in the parastatal sector

	Assets		Number	
	shs million	percentage of parastatal total		percentage of parastatal total
Manufacturing	656	74	9	21
Mining	273	99	1	33
Construction	61	84	1	50
Electricity	403	100	1	100
Finance	60	33	1	8
Transport	343	96	2	50
Tourism	–	–	–	–
Commerce	60	33	1	6
Agriculture	182	83	2	22
Total	2038	80	18	20

1 Firms with fixed assets over shs 50 million.

parastatal fixed assets. In many sectors only a few firms dominate. In mining, construction, and electricity, one firm has over 80 per cent of the assets in each sector, and in agriculture and transport two firms have over eighty per cent of the assets in their respective sectors. Manufacturing is less concentrated, but is still dominated by a few firms. Nine manufacturing firms (21 per cent of the total) own 74 per cent of the assets in the sector. The firms listed in Table 41 (firms with assets over shs 50 million) have an average size of shs 113 million versus shs 6 million for firms with assets less than shs 50 million. These large firms which absorb most of the parastatal resources, bear the least relation to rural socialism. They represent an attempt by the government to develop and control the most modern sectors of the economy.

Parastatal investment over time

An assessment of the parastatal sector cannot, however, be made simply by looking at the sector at one point in time. It is necessary to look at the pattern of investment over time to see the direction in which the sector is evolving. Table 42 presents the average capital/labour (K/L) ratio, and capital/value added (K/VA) ratio of parastatal investments. Parastatal investments are more capital intensive, and have a much higher capital/value added ratio than does the parastatal sector as a whole. The difference reflects a difference between the firms which have been nationalized, and new firms or expansion projects of existing firms. Many of the firms nationalized were not very capital intensive (sisal estates, sugar estate, banks, insurance company, many of the manufacturing

TABLE 42

Capital intensity of parastatal investment

	64-5	65-6	66-7	67-8	68-9	FFYP	69-70	70-71	71-2	72-3	73-4	SFYP
K/L (shs '000)	91	90	90	88	78	86	91	100	83	72	67	80
K/L without Zambian corridor	91	89	76	71	68	76	90	99	81	72	67	79
K/VA	5.0	4.7	3.7	3.7	4.5	4.1	7.4	6.2	4.9	4.1	3.6	4.8

firms). The nationalized firms are often the most profitable and have the best capital/value added ratio. As a result they have improved the average for the parastatal sector as a whole.

In contrast, investment by parastatals has tended to increase the capital-intensive nature of parastatals. In the First FYP the average capital/labour ratio of parastatal investments was shs 86,000 and in the Second FYP shs 80,000. This apparent fall in capital intensity of parastatal investments is the result of the building of the corridor to Zambia in the First FYP. If the projects involved in the corridor are excluded, the trend is upwards from shs 76,000 in the First FYP to shs 79,000 in the Second FYP. The immediate post-Arusha period was one of rising capital intensity. A peak was reached in 1970-71 with the building of the fertilizer plant and the tire factory. Since then there appears to be an indication that the government is turning towards less capital-intensive investments (see chapter five, section on Manufacturing, for more detail on this shift). A similar pattern occurs with the capital/value added ratios.[8]

If parastatal investment does not show a marked improvement, the implications for the economy could be important. Parastatal investment has been growing rapidly, both in absolute terms and as a proportion of total investment. Increasingly the performance of the economy will depend on the performance of the parastatal sector. The economy cannot, however, sustain its present growth and certainly cannot improve it with the present type of parastatal investment. Investment by private firms and individuals and parastatals in the monetary economy has grown from shs 333 million in 1964 or 8.7 per cent of monetary GDP to shs 997 million or 15.8 per cent of monetary GDP. As I pointed out earlier in this chapter, total investment was 24.3 per cent of GDP in 1972 (or 19.7 per cent excluding Tazara). It is not likely that the share of total investment can be increased any further. If investment now grows only at the rate of the monetary economy, i.e., 6.4 per cent per year, then employment will in turn

8 Since I have only estimates for the last two years, a conclusion that there has been a real change must be tentative.

grow only at that rate provided that the average capital intensity of investment does not fall. Since the urban population is currently growing at 6.6 per cent a year, and will probably grow faster in the future, some attempt to get a lower capital/labour ratio, and thus a higher rate of employment generation will probably be necessary. Up to this point urban unemployment has been avoided largely bacause the ratio of investment to GDP has grown so quickly. It is not likely to do so in the future.

Similarly, it is clear that the performance of parastatals will have to be improved if the economy is to maintain its level of growth. If the capital/value added ratio for the monetary economy were 4.8 (the average for parastatals in the Second FYP), then investment, as a proportion of monetary GDP, would have to be 30.7 per cent instead of 21.7 per cent as it was in 1972 with Tazara excluded. To achieve a 10 per cent rate of growth in the monetary sector (equivalent to about a 5 per cent growth in per capita income), which many in Tanzania would like to see, 48 per cent of the monetary GDP would have to go towards investment – an impossible figure.[9]

This is not the place to have a discussion of the strategy of investment. I merely want to point out that parastatal investment, because of its growing importance, will increasingly determine the performance of the economy. Investment by parastatals has, up to this stage, been quite capital intensive. If parastatals are to be the leading investors this degree of capital intensity will have important repercussions for the economy as a whole.

Investment by parastatals has also been quite import intensive. Table 43 gives the percentage of parastatal investment which has gone each year into firms where more than twenty-five per cent of the raw materials used are imported. This table presents a similar picture to the one on capital intensity. If the Zambian corridor is ignored one gets a rising trend towards import-intensive industries culminating in a peak in 1969-70. There then is a downward trend which is arrested in the last year of the Second FYP when there is a return to some quite import-intensive investments. This is an important measure because it picks up the extent to which parastatals are exploiting local resources. The high

---

9 This is, of course, just a statistical argument. One could argue that the external economies of large, capital-intensive projects are so great as to offset the low direct returns of the projects. Given the increasing dominance of the parastatal sector, however, this will still have to be reflected in other more efficient parastatal projects and the average efficiency of the whole parastatal sector would be high. So far this has not been the case. If the whole parastatal sector consists of large projects, then one must rely upon a vibrant private sector to take advantage of these external economies, or be prepared for a long period of slow growth until the long-term effects eventually are felt, if indeed such a strategy produces these long-term effects.

TABLE 43

Import intensity of parastatal investments (per cent)

	64-5	65-6	66-7	67-8	68-9	FFYP	69-70	70-71	71-2	72-3	73-4	SFYP
Percentage share of firms with import intensity above 25 per cent	31	70	58	65	47	56	57	53	41	21	45	43
Share without corridor to Zambia	31	69	26	39	30	37	54	50	37	21	45	41

external orientation of much parastatal investment indicates that parastatals have failed to be 'self-reliant' and are developing the economy in a way which makes it quite externally dependent.

The extent to which the parastatal sector has been oriented towards exports has been an area of controversy in Tanzania. In particular, the effort spent developing the tourist industry has been questioned. The most important effort at export promotion has, however, often been overlooked. The corridor to Zambia already is an important source of foreign exchange to Tanzania, and will continue to increase in importance (see chapter five section on Transportation for a further discussion of this corridor). Table 44 shows the share of investment which has gone towards exports. (See Appendix III for a description of how these data are computed.) If we include Tazara (export orientation assumed to be 80 per cent), the pipeline, and the road service, 48 per cent of First FYP parastatal investment went towards exports and 43 per cent of Second FYP investment will do so. If we exclude these projects the share falls dramatically. In the First FYP 27 per cent of the investments were export oriented versus 22 per cent in the Second FYP. There does appear to be, then, a slight diminution in the export orientation of parastatal investment. Parastatals as a whole are not more export oriented than the economy as a whole except if one includes the corridor to Zambia (exports were 23 per cent of GDP in 1972).[10]

As we saw in chapter two, Nyerere advocated fairly early on the dispersal of productive investment. In particular, he felt that investment should not be

10 Given the long-run need for foreign exchange, Tanzania has probably not been excessively export oriented. I give these figures here only to show the degree of export
orientation of public investment, and because many critics of the government feel that
the policy has been too oriented towards export promotion. See chapters six and eight
for more discussion of this issue.

TABLE 44

Export orientation of parastatal investment (per cent)

	1965	65-6	66-7	67-8	68-9	FFYP	69-70	70-71	71-2	72-3	73-4	SFYP
Share to exports (%)	40	36	53	55	45	48	28	23	21	28	24	24
Including Tazara	40	36	53	55	45	48	28	39	44	51	34	43
Excluding corridor to Zambia	40	36	24	22	24	27	24	18	15	28	24	22

TABLE 45

Urban location of parastatal investment

	First FYP (shs million)	Percentage	Second FYP[1] (shs million)	Percentage
Dar es Salaam	350	58	603	35
Tanga	11	2	209	12
Arusha	5	1	80	5
Moshi	12	2	84	5
Mwanza	52	8	80	5
Sub-total	430	71	1056	62
Other towns	178	29	645	38
Total towns	608	100	1701	100
Towns as share of total		57		64

1 Includes estimates for 1972-73 and 1973-74

centred in Dar es Salaam. The policy of regional decentralization, and in particular a movement from Dar es Salaam, applied particularly to industry. In chapter five, I will discuss it more fully, and here I will summarize the effect of the policy. The Second FYP brought a major shift in parastatal investment away from Dar es Salaam, but the shift was to three other towns, Arusha, Moshi, and Tanga, rather than to the country as a whole, or out of towns and into the rural areas. In the First FYP, 57 per cent of parastatal investment was located in towns. Of this some 58 per cent was in Dar es Salaam, 8 per cent in Mwanza, and 5 per cent each in Arusha, Moshi, and Tanga (see table 45). In the Second FYP, 64 per cent of parastatal investment was located in towns. The share centred in Dar es Salaam fell significantly to only 35 per cent, but the share to the other four towns rose to 27 per cent. At present there is a move to decrease the importance of these three towns, but again the movement will be to another centre, Mwanza. There has been very little attempt given to locating parastatals in the rural areas, or in towns other than in the rich northern corridor bordering Kenya. The one-third of parastatal investment which is outside of towns is all investment which must be located there — hydro-electric schemes, the pipeline, the diamond mine. The failure to locate parastatals in the rural areas is related to the type of parastatals developed. A decision to start a large-scale, capital-intensive plant using imported raw materials is implicitly a decision to locate in an urban area, indeed in certain developed urban areas, where the infrastructure necessary to run such a plant is provided. It will be necessary to alter the orientation of the parastatal sector before there will be a significantly different urban policy.[11]

In this chapter I have tried to provide the reader with an overview of the parastatal sector, both of its development and performance. A real understanding can only come, however, by taking a detailed look at how parastatals have behaved in each of the different sectors which they have entered in the economy. This will be done in the next chapter.

11 Any urban policy will probably involve the development of several medium-size centres. It would not be wise to dissipate all of one's efforts on developing only rural industries. If there are to be developed economic and political counterweights to Dar es Salaam, there will need to be other centres of fairly substantial size. Thus it does not bother me that investment has gone to three or four towns. There are, however, two problems with the present policy. First, all these towns are in the northern corridor. Some effort should be made to develop the towns of the centre and the south. Secondly, almost no effort has been made to develop rural parastatals, especially rural industries. This is a critical gap in the present policy. (see chapter nine for further discussion of this point.)

5

Sectoral analysis of parastatal investment

INTRODUCTION

This chapter will provide a detailed analysis of parastatal investment, and is intended to confirm and strengthen the conclusions presented in chapter four. There is a strong tendency for parastatals to adopt the most advanced techniques, and build the most modern buildings. In manufacturing this tendency is exhibited as an inclination towards large-scale, capital-intensive, 'transformation' projects. In other sectors, like tourism, it results in the development of luxury hotels, almost all of which lose money.

There has been very little change in the orientation of the parastatal sector since the Arusha Declaration. Parastatals have largely ignored the rural sector. Credit by financial institutions to agricultural production has fallen in relative terms. On the other hand, credit to agricultural marketing institutions has increased dramatically, but this is probably the result of increasing problems with the distribution system. The manufacturing firms started in the immediate post-Arusha period were more dependent upon the use of imported materials than were previous parastatals. There has been no significant development of small-scale rural industries.

Most parastatals have adopted a very narrow definition of socialism. They act as if socialism meant only government control. There has been very little innovation on the part of parastatals in interpreting what the Arusha Declaration means for investment strategy. Thus the electricity parastatal continues to operate much as it did in pre-Arusha days. Its emphasis on providing power to large industries centred in a few major towns remains. The rest of the chapter is devoted to an analysis of each of the sectors in which parastatals operate.

MANUFACTURING

Role of parastatals in manufacturing

The manufacturing sector has been the focus of development for parastatals. Both in terms of nationalizations and the development of new firms, it has received the greatest priority by the government. Manufacturing investment was over a third of total parastatal investment in the period 1964-71, and is expected to continue to play as important a role in the near future. The emphasis by the government on manufacturing has resulted in a steady rise in the importance of parastatals in this sector. In 1964, manufacturing parastatals had a value added about shs 15 million (6 per cent of the value added in manufacturing), and employed about fifteen hundred workers (6 per cent of the workers in the sector).[1] By 1971, the value added by manufacturing parastatals had risen to shs 375 million or 56% of the total value added by manufacturing (excluding household and cottage industry). Employment by manufacturing parastatals was 25,600, or about 47 per cent of total wage employment in the sector.[2]

Parastatals have dominated investment in the manufacturing sector. Data on investment by sector are available only for the period 1966 to 1970. During that time, as Table 46 shows, parastatals have become steadily more important. In 1966 parastatals contributed only 24 per cent of total investment in manufacturing. By 1970, their share had risen to 66 per cent.

The declining importance of purely private initiatives in manufacturing should not lead one to conclude that the private sector has not played or will not continue to play an important role in the development of the sector. Private firms have been heavily involved in two ways. First, they have often gone into joint ventures with the government. In fact, the manufacturing sector is the parastatal sector where joint ventures have been most significant. In 1971 only about a third of the assets in the manufacturing sector belonged to firms owned completely by the government. While it is likely that this share will rise over time, the manufacturing parastatal sector will continue in the near future to be dominated by joint venture firms.

Secondly, private firms play an important role in this sector, even in those situations where the government owns the firm completely, because parastatals have relied in the past, and will probably continue to rely in the future, upon private firms, especially foreign firms, to develop industrial projects. There has

---

1 Only two manufacturing parastatals were operating in 1964, Tanganyika Packers and Tanzania Meerschaum Co., Portland Cement, Tegry Plastics, and Tanita were all under construction.
2 These figures include both majority and non-majority parastatals.

TABLE 46

Manufacturing investment (shs million)

	1966	1967	1968	1969	1970	1966-70
Purely private	121	94	123	87	111	536
Parastatals	38	102	82	90	213	525
Total manufacturing	159	196	205	177	324	1061
Parastatal as percentage of total	24	52	40	51	66	49

been no indigenous capacity to initiate and carry out many of the developments in the manufacturing sector. As a result many of the projects show few signs that they are owned by a parastatal as opposed to a private firm, because in fact their development was really the work of a private firm or firms.

Characteristics of parastatal firms

Size

What are the characteristics of the manufacturing parastatal sector? First, the sector is dominated by a few large firms. The average firm (in a statistical sense) in the manufacturing sector had about shs 20.0 million in assets[3] in 1970. Nevertheless, almost three quarters of the firms had assets less than this amount. These firms hold only 20 per cent of parastatal assets. On the other hand, the other 26 per cent of firms (twelve in number) hold the other 80 per cent of assets. Nine firms, had assets over shs 50 million. If we exclude National Milling from this list because it is really a number of firms (there were seven different firms nationalized and put under National Milling Corporation), we have eight firms with assets of shs 605 million in 1970, 68 per cent of the total.

It is worth looking at these large firms, and comparing them to the rest of the firms in the parastatal sector. In Tanzania, as in many countries, the large project which people hope will transform the economy, has a great attraction. Yet large firms in Tanzania are often much more capital intensive, less profitable, and have higher capital value added ratios than do smaller firms. They tend to create small groups of highly-paid workers in industries which are often quite inefficient (see Table 47).

The government has periodically announced attempts to develop a major programme of small, rural-based industries. Nothing has ever come of these announcements. The National Small Scale Industries Co. was established in 1965

---

3 Unless stated explicitly otherwise, data on parastatal assets refer to undepreciated assets.

TABLE 47

Comparison of large and small parastatal manufacturing firms[1]

	Large (shs 50 million and over)	Small (under shs 50 million)
K/L	60,500	18,579
K/VA	3.054	1.624
Profit rate	5.5%	20.5%
Return to capital	19.7%	35.9%
Import intensity	41%	53%
Export intensity	16%	26%
Average wage	8000	5239
VA/L	19,675	11,427
W/VA	40%	44%

1 K/L = Capital/labour; K/VA = Capital/value added; VA/L = value added/labour; W/VA = wages/value added. These data refer to 1971 data for value added, employment and wages and undepreciated assets for 1970.

as a subsidiary of NDC to develop such a programme. It has lacked both the staff and the financial resources to do anything meaningful.[4] By the end of 1971, the company's fixed assets stood at less than shs 1.5 million, about 1 per cent of the parastatal total in manufacturing.

Parastatals have tended to enter the sectors in which large firms dominate, and in turn to enter these sectors with quite large firms. As a result parastatals, on average, are much larger than private firms. Table 48 sets out the average size of firms in each sector, and the average size of parastatal firms. In almost every case the average size of the parastatal firm is higher than the average for all firms. It is also true that parastatals have tended to concentrate in those sectors with the largest firms.

These data do not show that parastatals tend to use larger firms to produce the same products as private firms. In general the two produce different products. What I am trying to show here, and will show in regard to other characteristics such as capital intensity, or reliance on imported raw materials, is that parastatals have tended to enter the areas of the economy where the plants are large, capital intensive, and oriented towards the use of imported raw materials. Moreover, I will argue that in many cases the difference in the products produced is not that significant. The parastatals, when faced with a product choice, generally opt for the more 'sophisticated' product, and thus implicitly a production process which has the above characteristics.

4 This lack of resources, of course, reflects a decision on priorities, not the unavailability of resources to carry out this type of programme.

Capital intensity
The manufacturing sector is also noted by its capital intensity. Parastatals, as Table 48 shows, are in areas – breweries, tobacco manufacture, textiles, oil refining, cement – which are more capital intensive than others. They have largely ignored such labour-intensive manufacturing sectors as oil milling, cotton ginning, repair shops, and furniture manufacture. Moreover, I will show by a number of examples later in the chapter that parastatals have tended to enter each sector in the most capital-intensive way possible. From the *Survey of Industrial Production* (Tanzania, 1966-70) I have been able to obtain data on depreciated assets of all industries. In 1969 all industries had a capital/labour ratio of shs 17,000. Parastatals had a ratio of shs 29,000 and non-parastatals a ratio of shs 4000, less than 15 per cent of the parastatal average.

Import intensive
Parastatal manufacturing firms also tend to be very import intensive. On the average, the import intensity of parastatal firms is 45 per cent. For non-parastatals (using assets as weights), the average is only 28 per cent.[5] This difference largely reflects the type of industries in which the parastatal sector is located, but it also reflects the particular approach used to develop the industry. Thus the fertilizer plant was not developed to use locally-available phosphates, but uses entirely imported raw materials. The tire factory uses only imported synthetic rubber despite the fact that Tanzania once grew rubber. The shoe factory uses imported plastics instead of local hides to make shoes, and the only local raw material used by the breweries is water.

Again, as with large firms, it can be shown that a number of characteristics of manufacturing firms seem to go together. Import-intensive firms tend to be more capital intensive, have a higher capital/value added ratio, and tend to be larger. Because they rely upon imported raw materials, such industries must be located on the coast, or in towns with good transportation connections. As a result, they tend to be located in the towns and regions which are already most developed. They are often industries developed by foreign firms, drawing heavily upon foreign personnel and dependent upon foreign technology. This dependence helps to explain their often excessive use of foreign raw materials.

Table 49 shows the different ratios for firms based upon local materials (import intensity less than 50 per cent), and firms based upon imported materials (import intensity over 50 per cent). The capital/labour ratio of import-oriented firms is more than three times that of local materials-based firms. The capital/value added ratio is, as well, 20 per cent higher, and the return on capital marginally lower. Only 0.2 per cent of the assets of imported materials-based

5 Based upon unpublished data from Tanzania, *Survey of Industrial Production,* 1970.

TABLE 48

Average size[1] of manufacturing firms in 1970

ISIC	Sector	All firms (shs '000 per firm)	Parastatals (shs '000)	Parastatal share of assets in sector (%)
207	Sugar factories	6222	33,965	72
208	Sugar confectionery	716	–	0
272	Paper products	552	–	0
360	Manufacturing and repair of machinery	1341	5704	71
3391/9294	Construction	315	2424	85
2091	Oil milling	67	–	0
209	Tea processing	2601	1445	9
2094	Coffee curing and roasting	2468	3840	31
2095/97	Cashewnut processing and miscellaneous food industries	2114	6096	86
213	Breweries	13,718	13,718	100
214	Soft drinks	558	–	0
220	Tobacco manufactured	8467	16,865	99
231	Cotton ginning	98	–	0
2312	Spinning and weaving of textiles	21,868	41,757	71
232	Knitting mills	544	–	0
233	Cordage ropes and twines	2102	1087	13
259	Wood products nec	108	400	12
291	Leather products	338	–	0
300	Rubber products	439	–	0
313	Paints	631	–	0
394/399	Misc. manufacturing industries	563	941	23
3190	Pharmaceutical and insecticides	474		0
311/21	Basic industries Chem. unedible oils; petroleum; soap; glycerine;	19,706	71,740	72
3193	Soap; glycerine; perfumes, etc.	1146		0
383/85	Motor vehicle assembly and mfg. of bicycle rims	545		0
384	Mfg. and repair of machinery	299		0
3194	Misc. chem. products	1513	2386	32
2510/11	Sawmill and plywood	385	2828	46
239	Kapok and coir processing	1800	8036	89

TABLE 48 cont'd.

ISIC	Sector	All firms (shs '000 per firm)	Parastatals (shs '000)	Parastatal share of assets in sector (%)
241	Footwear	958	3681	64
331/32/34	Bricks and tile; glass products and cement	12,922	35,100	45
342	Aluminum rolling metal products	2390	5500	20
280	Printing and publishing	534	2376	37
243/44	Wearing apparel and made-up textile goods	119		0
260	Furniture and fixtures	715		0
201/202	Meat canning and dairy products	1940	4327	95
205	Grain mill products	468	2181	29
206	Bakeries	336		0
	Total	2847	12,318	52

1 Depreciated assets.

firms are located outside of Dar es Salaam, Tanga, Arusha and Moshi, while 39 per cent of the assets of local materials-based firms are located outside these cities.

Export orientation
The parastatal sector has tended to be oriented toward import substitution. There are, however, a number of investments which have yielded some exports. Most of these exports are to other East Africa Community countries, and not all of them necessarily have a long-range future. Thus the oil refinery's exports to Zambia will end in the next two years, General Tyre's to Kenya depend upon continued troubles with the Firestone plant, and the fertilizer exports to Kenya depend upon the present world shortage of fertilizer. Altogether, about 19 per cent of the assets in the parastatal manufacturing sector are geared toward exports.[6]

Urban location
As I pointed out in chapter two the government has been concerned about the concentration of industries in Dar es Salaam. Tables 50 and 51 compare the

6 Obtained by multiplying the assets of each firm by the share of its output which is exported.

TABLE 49

Important ratios for parastatal manufacturing firms

	Capital/ value added	Capital/ labour (shs)	Average size of firm (shs. '000)	Wages/ labour (shs)	Wages/ value added (%)	Return to capital	Profit rate (%)	Value added/ labour (shs)
Local materials-based								
1 Agriculture	2.151	23,347	21,795	5116	47	25.4	15.2	10,852
2 Mining	3.236	65,272	27,167	7387	36	19.7	12.3	20,309
3 Forestry	1.521	15,228	8014	4267	43	37.7	11.2	10,009
Sub-total	2.210	25,030	20,295	5165	46	25.3	14.5	11,325
Imported materials-based								
4 Metals	2.841	32,204	7257	8655	76	8.3	0	11,332
5 Plastics/chemicals/ fuels	4.397	168,094	62,783	15,436	40	13.6	1.5	38,227
6 Food/fibre/ paper	1.288	39,904	13,214	7981	26	57.6	14.3	30,980
Sub-total	2.675	81,417	20,300	10,564	35	24.4	4.7	30,433
Total	2.379	34,908	20,297	6109	42	24.9	10.5	14,671

TABLE 50

Regional location of parastatals

	Dar es Salaam	Kili-manjaro	Arusha	Tanga	Mwanza	Other
Assets (shs million)						
(1970)	402	27	47	128	85	203
Per cent of total	45	3	5	14	10	25
Value added (shs million)						
(1971)	151	54	13	7	25	166
Per cent of total	41	1	4	2	7	45
Employment (1971)	12,506	238	840	430	1730	9840
Per cent of total	49	1	3	2	7	32

TABLE 51

Regional location of all industries, 1970

	Coast	Kili-manjaro	Arusha	Tanga	Mwanza	Other
Value added (shs million)	365	24	26	33	57	56
Per cent of total	65	4	5	6	10	10
Employment	22,016	2537	3020	4427	4964	11,735
Per cent of total	45	5	6	9	10	25
Population as per cent of total	7	6	5	6	9	67

SOURCE: Tanzania, *Survey of Industrial Production,* 1970, 72, unpublished data.

distribution of parastatal firms to the distribution of all industries. I have data on the value added and employment by firms in each region from *Survey of Industrial Production.* For parastatals, I present the figures for assets, value added, and employment. The parastatals are more evenly distributed in the country than private firms. Forty-five per cent of the value added of parastatal firms and 32 per cent of employment comes from firms located in other than Coast, Kilimanjaro, Arusha, Tanga, or Mwanza Regions. This compares to only 10 per cent and 25 per cent respectively for all industries in the country. In part this does reflect a political difference. Mostly, however, it reflects an inherited pattern of distribution, and says little about government policy which is only beginning to be felt along the lines described before. One interesting point emerges from this examination. Parastatal firms outside the five regions are more efficient than those within them. With only 25 per cent of the assets, these firms contribute 45 per cent of the value added and generate 32 per cent of the employment. This is really just another way of making the point I have made throughout this section. The large, import-intensive (and therefore located near the coast or transport lines), capital-intensive, non-rural-oriented firms seem, generally, to make less efficient use of capital.

The characteristics of the parastatal manufacturing sector reflect those of originally private firms. The use of nationalizations by the government as a means of building the parastatal sector has meant that the government acquired many firms which were large, located in Dar es Salaam, import oriented and capital intensive. This, in fact, is one of the ironies of a socialist strategy of nationalizing the commanding heights of the economy. By doing so, the policy thrusts the government-controlled institutions into the most modern sectors of the economy. But these firms often exhibit many of the characteristics which the government wants to avoid: capital intensity, location on the coast, import intensity, low export drive, etc. Thus the government finds itself saddled with institutions whose orientation is often in the wrong direction, and has used up its scarce managerial resources in managing these institutions, rather than creating new ones with a better orientation.

I do not mean to imply here that the government would not want to control these institutions, however bad their orientation. I merely want to point out one of the side-effects of nationalizing them. The parastatal sector was, in a sense, infected by the value system of the private firms. The tendency to opt for the sophisticated product, which I mentioned previously, was in part a result of the initial overwhelming dominance of previously private firms in the parastatal sector. The existence of a large number of successfully operating parastatals encouraged new ones to imitate the organization and investment orientation of these firms, and this encouraged the adoption of strategies which were not wholly consistent with the intentions of the Arusha Declaration.

Parastatal investment since Arusha

The bad[7] characteristics of the parastatal sector are not simply the result of the use of nationalizations. Investment since the Arusha Declaration has not altered the pattern. In fact in the immediate post-Arusha period parastatal firms tended to be larger, more capital intensive, less efficient, and more import oriented. It is only now, in the latter years of the Second Five Year Plan that the government seems to have shifted its direction somewhat.

Table 52 presents the data on parastatal manufacturing firms for three different periods: those established in the pre-Arusha period (pre 1967), those

---

7 Bad from the point of view of being inconsistent with what one would want if one developed a sector along the lines envisaged in the Arusha Declaration.

TABLE 52

Comparison of pre-Arusha, post-Arusha, and new projects

	K/L[1] (shs '000)	Import Intensity (%)	Av. size (shs million)	Export orientation (%)
Pre-Arusha firms	35	30	17	17
Post-Arusha firms	43	74	24	23
New projects	52	33	36	23

1 K/L = Capital/labour.

TABLE 53

Comparison of performance of pre-Arusha and post-Arusha firms[1]

	K/VA	Return to capital (%)	Profit rate (%)	Average wage (shs '000)	VA/L (shs '000)
Post-Arusha	5.161	11	−1	3.7	8.2
Pre-Arusha	1.887	32	16	7.0	17.0

1 K/VA = capital/value added; VA/L = value added/labour.

established after Arusha and up until the end of 1971, and those firms expected to be established after 1971, up until the end of the Second FYP.

The immediate post-Arusha Declaration firms were larger, more import intensive, and more capital intensive than the firms established before the Arusha Declaration. The capital/labour ratio of post-Arusha firms is shs 43,000 compared to shs 35,000 for pre-Arusha firms. The import intensity of post-Arusha firms averages a very high 74 per cent, compared to 30 per cent for pre-Arusha firms. Post-Arusha firms are 40 per cent larger, averaging shs 24 million in size versus shs 17 million for pre-Arusha firms.

Up to this point, post-Arusha firms have also performed much more poorly than pre-Arusha firms. As Table 53 shows, the rate of return of post-Arusha firms is about one-third pre-Arusha firms, and their capital/value added ratio is almost three times that of pre-Arusha firms. Post-Arusha firms as a whole are losing money compared to a positive rate of profit of 16 per cent for pre-Arusha firms.

The short life of these firms partly explains the poor performance in terms of the capital/value added ratio, profit rate, and return to capital. It does not explain the greater import and capital intensity. These characteristics reflect the orientation of the firm. Post-Arusha firms tend to have a poorer performance

because they have entered sectors of the economy which are more capital intensive, or more import intensive. Thus, if we look at Table 54 we see that post-
Arusha parastatals are more concentrated in import-intensive industries. Fifty-
seven per cent of post-Arusha firms' assets are in imported materials-based industries, while only 41 per cent of pre-Arusha firms are in those industries. As well,
post-Arusha firms are in the most capital-intensive sector – plastics/chemicals,
fuel, etc. Forty-seven per cent of their assets are in this sector, versus 28 per cent
for parastatals as a whole.

Post-Arusha firms have also tended, although not universally, to be more
capital and import intensive within each sector. Thus the capital/labour ratio for
post-Arusha firms in forestry-based industries is shs 39,000 versus the parastatal
average of shs 15,000. In metals based-industries, post-Arusha firms have a ratio
of shs 67,000 versus shs 32,000 for all parastatals, and in plastics, chemicals, and
fuels the differences are shs 217,000 versus shs 168,000. Only in the food/fibre/
paper, is the difference significantly the other way, shs 21,000 versus shs 40,000.
In agriculture, the two are almost the same, shs 22,000 versus shs 23,000.

Post-Arusha firms also tend to be more import intensive within sectors. Thus,
the average import intensity of local materials-based firms is 35 per cent for
post-Arusha firms, and 10 per cent for all parastatals. Within every sub-sector,
post-Arusha firms are as import intensive or more so than parastatals as a whole
(see Tables 54-5).

An industrial policy which complemented agricultural development could
have a number of components. One characteristic would be economic integration into the agricultural economy. There are a number of ways by which this
can be done. In the immediate post-Arusha period there was an attempt to
develop some of the backward linkages involved in agriculture. Industries such as
Ubungo Farm Implements or Tanzania Fertilizer represent attempts to develop a
form of integration between the rural and urban sectors different from what
previously existed. Table 56 shows the proportion of assets in the pre-Arusha
and post-Arusha periods involving forward and backward linkages with agriculture. In the pre-Arusha period 50 per cent of the assets belonged to firms
exploiting forward linkages, but there were no firms exploiting backward linkages. In the post-Arusha period, the industrial sector as a whole was much more
integrated. Over 80 per cent of the assets belonged to firms developing some
form of linkages with the agriculture sector. Over half of these were the assets of
the two firms developing the backward linkages.

In the *Annual Plan* for 1973-4 (12-13) the government announced a reversion
to the previous emphasis on developing the forward linkages in the economy.
Processing of agricultural products was to receive the highest priority. In part
this shift in policy reflected dissatisfaction with the current trend in parastatal

TABLE 54

Distribution of parastatals (per cent)

	Value added 1971		Employment		Assets	
	All parastatals	Post-Arusha parastatals	All parastatals	Post-Arusha parastatals	All parastatals	Post-Arusha parastatals
Local materials-based						
Agriculture	51	60	69	74	46	39
Mining	7		5		9	
Forestry	6	4	8	4	4	4
Sub-total	64	64	82	78	59	43
Imported materials-based						
Metals	2	1	3	4	3	6
Plastics/chemicals/ fuels	15	22	6	9	28	47
Food/fibre/paper	19	13	9	9	10	4
Sub-total	36	36	18	22	41	57
Total	100	100	100	100	100	100

TABLE 55

Parastatals formed since Arusha

	Capital/ Value added	Average size of firm (shs '000)	Capital/ labour (shs)	Wage/ labour (shs)	Wages/ value added (%)	Return to capital (%)	Profit rate (%)	Value added/ labour (shs)
Local materials-based								
Agriculture	3.321	22,636	22,350	3077	46	16	5	6733
Mining	—							
Forestry	6.150	5914	39,162	4288	67	5	−9	6367
Sub-total	3.470	17,858	23,296	3145	47	15	4	6713
Import materials-based								
Metals	23.319	8057	67,141	6587	229	−6	−15	2879
Plastic/chemicals/fuels	10.946	68,754	216,888	5875	30	6	−4	19,814
Food/fibre/paper	1.752	12,509	20,641	5410	46	31	15	11,780
Sub-total	8.147	33,226	112,250	5800	42	7	−6	13,778
Total	5.161	24,261	42,526	3719	45	11	−1	8240

TABLE 56

Comparison of agricultural integration of pre- and post-Arusha
manufacturing firms

	Share in total assets (%)	
	Pre-Arusha firms	Post-Arusha firms
Forward linkages	50	39
Backward linkages	–	42
Total – all linkages	50	81

manufacturing investment. The result of the shift in policy has been a significant
reduction in the import intensity of the new parastatal projects. The import
intensity of these projects is 33 per cent compared to the figure of 74 per cent
for the immediate post-Arusha firms. The new projects are, however, more
capital intensive and larger. The government has not confronted the issue of the
inability of the parastatal sector to develop small-scale projects. Thus among the
new projects is a major expansion of the existing shoe factory in Dar es Salaam.
No attempt to develop Ujamaa shoe shops has been made. Almost a quarter of
the investment in manufacturing over the next two years (1973-4 and 1974-5)
will go towards expansion of brewery capacity, in a country where well over 90
per cent of the population never drinks bottled beer. Sugar estates and refineries
will also absorb a significant share of the investment. Again the government has
ignored a smaller-scale, more labour-intensive alternative – jaggery (see section
on agriculture in this chapter).

The Small Scale Industries Corporation does not appear to have received any
noticeable increase in priority. Its budget has been increased to shs 3 million
from the miserable shs 1.3 million it received last year. Despite this unbelievably
low level of funding, there is even a question as to whether or not they can
implement all their projects, because they have so few staff!

Locational policy of the government seems to have been much more effective
than most other policies. The industries established since 1967 have not been
concentrated in Dar es Salaam, as Table 57 shows. Over 65 per cent of the assets
of parastatal manufacturing firms established before Arusha were located in Dar
es Salaam. In the period 1967-71, only 4 per cent of the assets of parastatal
manufacturing firms established then were located in Dar es Salaam.

The shift was not, however, out of Dar es Salaam into the countryside, or
even into towns in the west or south which had been neglected. Rather it was
primarily to four towns along the border with Kenya, towns which had always
been attractive, and were the centres of well-to-do regions – Tanga, Arusha,

TABLE 57

Location of parastatal manufacturing assets

	Dar es Salaam (%)	Tanga, Arusha, and Moshi (%)	Mwanza (%)	Other places (%)
Pre-Arusha firms	65	8	–	27
Post-Arusha firms	4	53	29	14
New projects	19	19	34	28
Share of urban population	47	19	6	28

Moshi, and Mwanza. The establishment of certain industries in Tanga (fertilizer, steel rolling mill) represented an attempt by the government to provide industries to a town which had been suffering a decline (Tanga is the centre of the sisal industry). The move to the other cities reflected a deeper problem. Parastatals tended to think of locating either in Dar es Salaam, or the four rich towns. As a result the share of assets located outside these five towns actually fell from 27 per cent for pre-Arusha to 14 per cent for post-Arusha firms. In the new projects Mwanza continues to be an area of great attraction, but Arusha, Moshi, and Tanga no longer dominate investment. The share of places other than Dar es Salaam and the four northern towns is back to its former level. To the extent that the policy was really one aimed only at shifting industry out of Dar es Salaam, it has been quite effective. However, it has not been effective in moving industry out of the cities, or even out of the most well-to-do centres.

Examples of parastatal manufacturing investments

Textiles
The failure of the post-Arusha companies to distinguish themselves significantly and favourably from the pre-Arusha companies points to one of the most important conclusions which can be made about the performance of the manufacturing parastatals, indeed about all parastatals. There has been, as yet, no developmental innovation on the part of parastatals to make themselves more consistent with the Tanzanian ideology. They have tended to want the most modern plants. Turn-key projects (i.e., in which one contractor manages the entire project), the most obvious example of failure to innovate, have not been uncommon. It is possible to illustrate the typical parastatal approach to investment by looking at

TABLE 58

Comparison of textile firms[1]

	K/VA	K/L (shs '000)	Firm size (shs million)	W/L (shs '000)	Return to capital (%)	Profit rate (%)	VA/L (shs '000)	Import In-tensity (%)	Sales (shs million)
Mwatex	2.9	41	71	5.6	21	12	14.3	47	55
Urafiki	1.0	12	39	4.2	61	55	11.4	34	68
Private (3 firms)	3.1	24	30	5.4	9	4	7.7	33	27

1 K/VA = capital/value added; K/L = capital/labour; W/L = wages/labour; VA/L = value added/labour.

parastatal investments in three areas — textiles, bakeries, and saw mills. Textiles provide a good contrast because of the large number of firms.

I will look at two examples of government-owned firms. The first is Mwatex, a project 40 per cent owned by NDC and built by a French firm. It is a 'typical' NDC project in that it has used a foreign company (from a capitalist country) to construct and manage it. The supplier took a 20 per cent equity in the firm, with the remainder held by the local co-operative. The other government-owned firm is Urafiki Textiles, a plant built by the Chinese. There was no real Tanzanian involvement in Urafiki. It was essentially a turn-key project, but one carried out by socialists. I will compare these firms to the average of the three private firms which are of comparable size. From the *Survey of Industrial Production* we can obtain data on these firms. A comparison is shown in Table 58. The data here are 1971 figures for all categories, including assets. Thus, the ratios are not lagged[8] as in previous cases. Assets are depreciated, and therefore the ratios are not comparable to those given for parastatals in the previous tables.

The most important thing to note in Table 58 is the very significant differences which are possible within an industry. In fact, if I showed the private firms individually, one would see even greater differences. Their capital/labour ratios range from shs 17,000 to shs 40,000 and their capital/value added ratios from 1.4 to 5.6. Thus, variation is possible if one innovates. Secondly, the superior performance in all respects of the Chinese project is worth noting. All the other plants use Western European technology. The Chinese use technology, which in western eyes, is twenty years old, but is also much more suited to Tanzania's

8 As explained in Appendix III, in general the ratios I use refer to 1970 undepreciated fixed assets and 1971 value added, labour, profits, or return on capital.

TABLE 59

Comparison of bakeries[1]

	K/VA	K/L (shs '000)	Firm size (shs million)	W/L (shs '000)	Return to capital (%)	Profit rate (%)	VA/L (shs '000)	Average sales (shs million)
NMC	7.1	282	24.000	4.7	12	11	39.7	17.169
Private	1.5	17	1.109	6.0	33	32	11.7	3.729

1 K/VA = capital/value added; K/L = capital/labour; W/L = wages/labour; VA/L = value added/labour.

factor proportions.[9] Finally, Mwatex, the government plant, is the most capital- and import-intensive firm in the country. Its capital/value added is similar to the private sector, although much greater than Urafiki's.

Bakeries

Another sector in which both private and public firms exist is bakeries. Until 1973, this field has been entirely private. The National Milling Corporation is in the process of completing, with the help of Canadian aid, a new bakery. It is possible to compare National Milling's project with existing plants. The figures for NMC are projections and bias our results heavily in favour of the government project. NMC's figures for costs have been depreciated over ten years with no additional investment in order to compare its total cost with the private firms for whom we have depreciated figures. I will look at bakeries with sales of over shs 2 million. There were four of these in the private sector (Table 59).

Here, the contrast is startling. The NMC bakery unit is more than sixteen times as capital intensive, it has a capital/value added ratio almost five times as great, and gets about one-third the return to capital. As with the textile firms, the government firm is much larger, more than twenty times the average private firm in our comparison. In fact, if we look at the industry as a whole the contrast is amazing. The average bakery in Tanzania has only shs 336,000 in fixed assets (see Table 48), whereas our bakery unit has shs 24 million in fixed

9 One could question whether the Chinese plant produces the same product as Mwatex. There are some differences. Mwatex textiles are generally of high 'quality,' having more variations in colour and more flexibility in designs. Implicitly I am assuming that the difference in quality is small and that the extra quality is not worth the price. Part of the challenge of socialist development is the need to develop an ideology which frees the country from imitation of the standards of developed countries, standards which the country cannot afford if it is to meet the needs of all the people.

assets (original cost shs 35 million, depreciated at rate specified by NMC for ten years). The government has chosen to enter a field which is characterized by small, labour-intensive firms, and to build a plant which dwarfs all others, and is more capital intensive than the oil refinery![10]

Sawmills

Another area where we see a similar pattern of parastatal intervention with large, modern plants is in sawmills. Again, like bakeries, this is a sector dominated by small, labour-intensive firms. The average sawmill has only shs 385,000 in fixed assets (see Table 48) and has a capital/labour ratio of shs 3000 *(Survey of Industrial Production)*. This is a sector which, I will argue later, should receive priority in parastatal investment, but not of the type which characterizes current plans. There are at present, three types of sawmills. There is already one parastatal, Sikh Sawmills. It is an Asian-run firm in which the government, since 1964, has gradually been increasing its equity holding. It is still essentially, in terms of source of entrepreneurship and management, a private firm, but it is a large one (hence the government's involvement). MECCO also has a number of sawmills, but it has not been possible to get a good breakdown of data for their mills. There are three District Development Corporations with sawmills. These are generally fairly small, but they represent an alternative form of socialist development of the sector. Finally, there are the numerous private firms (probably in the range of 140 (TWICO, 1972)), most small, some large. I will look at sawmills with sales over shs 1.0 million; I have data on five such mills.

It is into a sector characterized by largely small, labour-intensive firms that TWICO, the wood parastatal, is entering. It is starting to build a number of sawmills. The best prepared is one being built by the Swedes at Sao-Hill. As with the bakery unit, I will take their projections as data, biasing the results in their favour. The figures I take are from the feasibility study of the project *(ibid.)* They are projected figures for 1980, by which time the plant will have been operating for seven years, and the original total cost of the project will have depreciated from shs 8.6 million to shs 3.8 million. The comparison of this project with the other three types of sawmills is shown in Table 60.

The feasibility study predicts a rather remarkable performance for its mill, expecting it to get a return on capital of 115 per cent, and a profit rate of 77 per cent in its seventh year. It would be surprising if it does so well. On every other measure which is less open to optimism, Sao-Hill performs badly. Its capital

10 The oil refinery cost shs 102 million to build and employs 317 workers, giving a capital/ labour ratio of shs 322,000, while the bakery unit cost shs 35 million to build and employs 86 workers, for a capital/labour ratio of shs 407,000.

TABLE 60

Comparison of sawmills[1]

	K/VA	K/L (shs '000)	Average size (shs '000)	W/L (shs '000)	Return to capital (%)	Profit rate (%)	VA/L (shs '000)	Average sales (shs '000)
Sao-Hill[2]	0.7	18	3750	5.1	115	77	26.2	6450
Sikh Sawmills	0.9	6	2371	3.2	57	57	6.9	6266
DDC	0.5	2	548	2.3	80	80	2.2	548
Private	0.9	5	413	3.0	54	50	5.2	1255

1 K/VA = capital/value added; K/L = capital/labour; W/L = wages/labour; VA/L - value
added/labour.
2 TWICO, 1972, 8

labour ratio is three times that of Sikh Sawmills, and more than three times the
private mills. The District Development Corporations represent the most labour-
intensive form of sawmills, needing only shs 2000 to employ a worker. They also
employ less highly-paid workers, paying only shs 2300 a year, versus shs 3200
for Sikh Sawmills, and a very high shs 5100 for Sao-Hill. The value added per
worker is expected to be almost four times what it is in Sikh Sawmills. Thus, the
parastatal firm again enters the sector with the most modern equipment, creating
a small, highly-paid work force in a sector characterized by many, lowly-paid
workers.

Conclusion

The manufacturing sector was viewed as an area of priority by the government
for parastatal development. It has nationalized existing private firms and developed new firms in an effort to extend public control over the sector. Parastatals
now dominate manufacturing, and their importance will continue to rise.
Because parastatals will determine the development of this sector, and because
the country's attempt to industrialize will in part determine the success of its
over-all development strategy, parastatal performance in this sector is critical.

Efforts by parastatals to develop manufacturing firms have often resulted in
the development of firms which are in many ways inconsistent with the over-all
investment strategy. The firms originally established in the post-Arusha period
were often large, capital intensive, and based upon the use of imported raw
materials. Now the government seems determined to shift the direction back
towards firms using more local resources. Parastatals continue, however, to be
attracted by the large project versus the small one, and to have made no attempt
to develop rural industries.

By looking at three examples of firms developed by parastatals I tried to show that parastatals were not only attracted to areas characterized by large-scale, capital-intensive firms, but also tended to enter each sector in the large-scale, capital-intensive way. In chapter seven I will discuss why I think this is the case. Suffice it to say here that there are many pressures which cause parastatals to act in this way. Some of these, like a lack of ideological commitment to rural development, may be altered by political action. Others, like the lack of innovative ability, or shortage of entrepreneurs, may not be solved for a long time. As a result, a strategy for investment must take into account the limitations of a country. If it is considered desirable to have low capital/labour ratios[11], then these will have to be obtained by investing in sectors in which this ratio is low, rather than by investing in capital-intensive sectors but altering the factor proportions of the technology used.

TOURISM

The tourist sector was one of the original areas of focus for government investment. Originally it was dominated by private interests. As late as the end of 1968, the parastatal sector owned only four of the seventy-five operating hotels (Tanzania, *Report on Tourism Statistics*, 1968, 18). The public sector, defined to include the East Africa Railways and Harbors, Co-ops, and Workers Development Corporation, owned thirteen of the seventy-five. Despite the fact that this was an area left by the Arusha Declaration for private investment, the government felt it was one where government participation was worthwhile. This seems chiefly because of its potential as a major foreign exchange earner. It will be recalled from chapter four that there were almost no acquisitions in this sector. Only two hotels, the New Safari in Arusha, and the Fordhani Hotel in Dar es Salaam, were acquired, and both of these are quite small. Together they have less than 100 beds. The development of new hotels, first by NDC, then later by the Tanzania Tourist Corporation (TTC), was the method of developing the sector. Total investment in the period 1964-71 was shs 132 million. Most of this came in the last three years. Tourist parastatal investment reached a peak of shs 37 million in 1970. In 1968, parastatal beds were 514 (*ibid*, appendix III) out of a total 3150, or 16 per cent. By the end of 1970, they had risen to 1708 out of a total of 5459, or 31 per cent.

The thrust of parastatal investment has been into the luxury tourist class. In fact, the Tanzania Tourist Corporation has built only international class hotels, and has dominated the expansion of the field. In the period 1968 to 1970, the

11 I will argue that this is important for both political and economic reasons.

number of hotel beds increased by 2309 (*ibid.*, 1968, 1970). Parastatal beds, as we have said, increased by 1194, accounting for 52 per cent of the increase. International class hotel beds increased by 1639. The TTC (and NDC before it) accounted for 73 per cent of the increase in international class hotel beds. In 1968 parastatals accounted for 4 out of the 12 international hotels, and 41 per cent of the beds. By 1970, parastatals accounted for 10 out of the 23 international hotels, and 59 per cent of the beds.[12]

The public sector is somewhat larger than the parastatal sector. It consists, in addition to the TTC, of hotels run by the co-operatives, the Workers Development Corporation, and the East Africa Railways and Harbors. In addition, the two hotels in Zanzibar are often included in the public sector, but we will ignore them. In 1968, there were nine of these other public hotels, and they had 338 beds, or 11 per cent of the total. In 1970, their number had risen to 14, and they had 572 beds, about 10 per cent of the total. The orientation of these hotels is quite different from the parastatal hotels. They are usually smaller, and geared primarily for domestic travellers. Accommodation for tourists is a by-product of providing service for Tanzanians.

The economic benefits of parastatal investment in tourism have not yet been very great. By the end of 1970, assets in the hotel sector were shs 119 million. In 1971, this investment generated employment for 1731 people, with wages equal to shs 11 million, value added equal to shs 13 million, and a loss of about shs 8 million. Thus the capital/value added ratio for the sector was 9.2, capital/labour ratio shs 69,000, the return to capital less than 2 per cent, and the profit rate about -7 per cent. The import intensity of the sector has been roughly estimated by the Ministry of Natural Resources at 40 per cent.

The problems with the sector are threefold. First, there is a question of whether or not it is strategically a good sector to develop. In Tanzania there has been a great deal of criticism of the effort spent by the government in developing the tourist sector (see Shivji, 1973b). The debate has followed these lines. The government has argued that the sector offers an easy way of quickly making much-needed foreign exchange. The critics regard the strategy as another example of the government's 'outer-directed' orientation.[13] Tourism perpetuates the dependency relationship of the country. Its economic value is exaggerated and its social cost in terms of undermining the possibility of creating socialism (via the demonstration effect) is enormous.

12 The parastatal sector is actually slightly larger, although this is generally not noted. In acquiring 50 per cent ownership of Agip, they acquired 50 per cent ownership of the Motel Agip. As well, under the Buildings Acquisition Act the Hotel Skyway was acquired. Neither of these hotels is managed by TTC. They have 248 beds.
13 See chapter eight for the views of the critics of the government.

There are other problems with the sector. Tourism has not been the growth sector originally envisaged. In particular, tourists have tended to stay for shorter periods in Tanzania, and have spent less than originally thought. Kenya, by being the jumping-off point for tours of the northern game parks, has managed to capture many of the benefits of the industry. In general, the industry has been much more competitive than the Tanzanians originally thought.

There are also problems with the parastatal sector in particular. The government has built hotels which are extremely costly. It has become clear that the extra investment put into parastatal hotels cannot be recouped through higher prices. Thus the private sector, by building more economically, has been able to earn much better profits. Table 61 compares the cost per bed of parastatal and private hotels. In every category of hotel, the parastatal cost is much higher. Over-all, parastatals have spent more than two-and-one-half times more per bed than the private firms. Yet there is not a corresponding difference in the price they can charge. This shown in Table 62, which shows the potential revenue per shilling invested in each of the three major categories of tourist hotels. If both the private and parastatal hotels had 100 per cent capacity, the private hotels would earn shs 1.04 for every shilling invested and the parastatals only half that much, given the rates they actually were able to charge in 1971. Thus the parastatals would have to get much better occupancy rates than private hotels to do as well. In fact, the two groups get about the same rates. The parastatals do much better in the northern circuit because of their monopoly positions in the parks (see Table 63) but worse in the towns.

Around the hotels are a number of tourist facilities, like Tanzania Tours, Seafaris, Wildlife Safaris, etc. These tend to be more labour intensive, and help to lower the over-all capital/labour ratio of the industry. Many of these just started in 1971 so it is difficult to give firm statistics on them. Their assets amounted to shs 2.8 million in 1970, and their capital/labour ratio was about shs 28,000.

Finally there are the National Parks. There are no figures available on fixed assets. It is clear, however, that the parks are quite labour intensive. They employed 540 people in 1970, and contributed shs 2.5 million to the GDP. Although it would be desirable if National Parks paid their own way, their primary purpose is not to make money. Rather, they are to provide the attraction to draw the tourists. In 1971, they lost shs. 411,000.

Before concluding our brief review of the tourism sector, we should look at the future programme envisaged. To what extent does it deviate from the past pattern I described? Two major hotel construction projects are planned. A new hotel is to be built in Arusha to meet the expected, if not yet forthcoming, demand from the new airport. The hotel will cost about shs 35 million, and have 400 beds, for an average cost per bed of shs 87,500. This is still a very high ratio,

TABLE 61

Comparison of hotels

	Fixed assets 1972 (shs '000)	Beds	Assets per bed (shs '000)
Parastatal hotels			
Wildlife lodges			
L. Manyara	9083	200	45
Ngorongoro	11,681	150	78
Lobo	8279	150	55
Seronera	9429	150	63
Mikumi	9159	100	92
Sub-total	47,631	750	64
Town hotels			
New Africa	18,017	144	125
Kilimanjaro	35,998	400	90
Sub-total	54,015	544	99
Beach hotels			
Kunduchi	13,216	200	66
Mafia	6776	60	112
Bahari	8701	200	43
Sub-total	28,693	460	62
TOTAL PARASTATALS	130,339	1754	74
Private hotels			
Wildlife			
Tanzanite	2543	60	42
Tarangire	995	68	14
Sub-total	3538	128	28
Town hotels			
Delux Inn	1035	44	24
New Arusha	4224	142	30
Skyways	2392	140	17
Hotel Afrique	1392	60	23
Sub-total	9043	386	23
Beach hotels			
Silversands	913	90	10
Hotel Africana	13,525	370	37
Sub-total	14,438	480	30
TOTAL PRIVATE	27,019	994	27

SOURCE: Hallmark Hotels and Central Statistical Bureau

above even the current parastatal average, above the averages for both the parastatal wildlife and beach hotels, but below the town hotels. The other project is the expansion of the New Africa, a hotel with the highest cost per bed in the country, shs 125,000 per bed. The expansion will add 112 beds at a cost of between shs 19 million and shs 25 million. The original cost was shs 19 million,

TABLE 62

Comparison of hotels

	Potential revenue per shilling invested		Actual revenue per shilling invested	
	Private	Parastatal	Private	Parastatal
Wildlife lodges	1.22	0.51	0.41	0.22
Town hotels	1.17	0.46	0.72	0.22
Beach hotels	0.92	0.66	0.25	0.13
Total	1.04	0.52	0.43	0.20

SOURCE: Maliasili Paper 'Cost of Hotels,' mimeo

TABLE 63

Occupancy rates, 1971 (per cent)

	Private	Parastatal
Wildlife lodges	29	52
Town hotels	75	52
Beach hotels	26	28
Total	45	46

SOURCE: Tanzania (n.d.)

but the *Annual Plan* has budgeted shs 25 million. If we take the lower figure, the cost is shs 170,000 per bed. It is clear that there will not be a change in policy in the near future.

AGRICULTURE

When NDC was originally established, agriculture firms made up a considerable portion of its portfolio. It inherited the portfolio of the Tanganyika Agriculture Company, as well as the government holdings of Ralli Sisal Estates and Dindira and Bukoba Tea Estates. While initially the promotion of agriculture was held important by NDC, it became decreasingly so. Thus the development of new agricultural parastatals stagnated. The nationalizations of the sisal estates late in 1967 created a new parastatal agriculture sector, but not one new to the country. Agricultural productive capacity was not increased. In fact, the Tanzania Sisal Corporation had to oversee the running down of employment in the sisal estates. In 1969, the National Agriculture and Food Corporation (NAFCO) was established taking over the agricultural portfolio of NDC. This was part of a generalized re-organization of the parastatals which reduced parastatal activity so that they would report to only one sectoral ministry. This re-organization has provided the necessary institutional structure for a major increase in parastatal activity in this sector. Such an increase is only just beginning. Up to this point agriculture has been only a very small part of the parastatal sector, accounting for only 4 per cent of total investment in the period 1964-71.

Parastatals, then, at this point do not play a very large part in agricultural production. In 1971 they had a value added of only shs 39 million, 1 per cent of agricultural value added. They are more important in terms of investment, contributing 8 per cent of agricultural investment in the period 1966-70 if own account rural construction is excluded, and 4 per cent if it is included. Parastatal assets are concentrated in two sectors, sisal (81 per cent of parastatal assets in 1970) and livestock (8 per cent). In sisal, the Tanzania Sisal Corporation and Ralli Estates contributed about half the sisal production in the country.

Since the inception of NAFCO a number of projects have been started which extend the parastatal sector, in a small way, into different agricultural areas. A plantation has been started to produce beans and coffee, a fishing company was started, the Basuto Wheat Scheme was taken over from Kilimo, and a seed company was started to produce seeds. As well, both NACO and NAFCO have started a number of dairy projects. In general these projects represent attempts to use estate agriculture to produce locally consumed goods, especially where it is felt, as in dairying, that peasant agriculture cannot supply the market in sufficient quantity, or with the needed regularity. Often NAFCO has been moving to replace the Asian and European farmers who are selling or abandoning their farms. These farms provided supplies in certain critical products to urban areas.

In livestock, NACO, the livestock parastatal, has been gradually increasing its share of the production. A major effort is now under way to expand livestock production in the country, and the part played by parastatals is illustrative of the role agricultural parastatals are assigned. For several years a crisis in meat production has been developing in the country. Off-take rates have been falling, and shortages have developed in the urban areas. Despite the fact that Tanzania has the second largest cattle herd in Africa, it has not been able to develop a good export trade. In fact exports of meat have fallen.

The problems in the livestock industry are many. Prices have been kept low as a result of pressure from the urban areas, reducing the incentive to cattle owners to sell, and increasing the incentives to them to smuggle their cattle to Kenya or Uganda where prices are higher. The whole internal trading network has been deteriorating. As a result of government pressure local authorities have tried to squeeze the Arab and Asian businessmen out of the middleman role. These authorities were not given the resources, especially manpower, to do the job successfully, and the result has been a breakdown in meat distribution.

The shortage of meat in the major towns has put a great deal of pressure on the government, which has led it to promote the rapid development of parastatal ranches, in order to ensure a steady supply of meat to the urban areas. This tendency to fall back upon agricultural parastatals is further strengthened by the role played by aid donors like the World Bank who are suspicious of the Ujamaa programme and push heavily for a larger proportion of the funds earmarked for livestock development to go towards parastatal ranches rather than Ujamaa livestock schemes. I am not arguing here that parastatal ranches are a bad thing. They have a definite role to play in the development of the livestock sector. They can act as demonstration centres, and can give a steady source of output for products which cannot be produced satisfactorily by peasant production. The new emphasis on parastatal agriculture does represent an important shift in policy. Nevertheless, parastatals can represent a form of opting out, and when they are developed instead of tackling the real problem of peasant agriculture, i.e., its low productivity, they are diverting resources away from what should be the focus of attention.

Another area of thrust of the agricultural parastatals is into sugar production. This used to be an area held exclusively by private firms, especially Asian firms. The government first became involved in sugar when it took over Kilombero Sugar in 1968. In 1970 NAFCO concluded an agreement with the Madhvani Group to acquire 50 per cent ownership in Mtibwa Sugar Estates. The estate will be expanded from 2900 acres to 7200 acres, and a mill capable of processing 40,000 tons of sugar will be built (NAFCO, *Annual Report and Accounts,* 1969-70, 20). There are also plans to double the size of Kilombero, and to take over and expand Kagera Sugar. If all these plans are put into effect, NAFCO will control more than shs 600 million in assets devoted to sugar production, and three of the five sugar estates in the country.

The move into sugar production is in response to the rapid increase in consumption of sugar. Table 64 shows production and consumption of sugar from 1964 to 1972. The deficit has been growing continually as production has increased at an average of 4.7 per cent annually over the period while demand has increased 10.2 per cent. Self-sufficiency in food has become part of the interpretation of the meaning of self-reliance. For this reason this gap in production is regarded as unacceptable. While some members of the government are anxious to see this growth in estate agriculture, the official position is still one of opposition. Care has been taken, then, to ensure that a significant effort was made to develop outgrower production. In 1969, outgrowers supplied 9776 tons or 27 per cent of Kilombero's production of 26,041 tons of sugar. By 1971

TABLE 64

Sugar production and consumption

	Production (tons)	Consumption (tons)	Difference	Consumption per Capita (kilos)
1964	61,440	62,745	+1305	5.60
1968	82,429	82,912	+483	6.59
1969	92,043	88,740	−3303	6.86
1970	87,254	107,617	−20,363	8.11
1971	95,787	125,349	−29,562	9.19
1972	88,483	136,588	−48,105	9.76

SOURCE: Tanzania, *Hali Ya Uchumi*, 1972-3, 64

outgrowers were supplying 36 per cent of the production. The government has not, however, chosen to encourage through either its own parastatals or outgrowers increased production of jaggery, a much lower cost substitute for sugar. Jaggery tends to be grown in much smaller, less capital-intensive estates, or can be grown more easily by peasants. A sugar estate is as capital invensive as an average industry, about shs 34,000 per job, Jaggery estates vary widely in their capital intensity, but are generally only one-third to one-sixth as capital intensive (Tanzania, *Survey of Industrial Production*).

In summary, parastatal agriculture has been dominated by sisal and livestock, and now sugar. The production methods used are quite capital intensive in comparison with agriculture in general, but are generally less capital intensive than other parastatal sectors. In 1971, the capital/labour ratio of the sector as a whole was shs 11,000 (excludes sugar.) The sector as a whole has almost always lost money. The justification for continuing its expansion has been two-fold. In certain sectors it can have, through a demonstration effect and through the development of a market, an important positive effect on peasant agriculture. Secondly, the government has responded to shortages in certain agriculture goods, meat, dairy products, maize, sugar, by establishing parastatals as a way of ensuring adequate supplies. In many ways the growth of the parastatal agriculture sector reflects the failure of attempts to increase agriculture production. While an emphasis on agricultural parastatals probably represents a good trend at this stage in Tanzania's development, it would be a great deal more desirable if it were combined with a much greater effort at encouraging peasant production.

MINING

The parastatal mining sector has three operating firms, Williamson Diamonds Mines, Nyanza Salt Mines, and Gemstones Co. In 1970 there were only 11 firms

TABLE 65

Mineral sales (shs million)

	Diamonds	Gold	Salt	Gemstones	Other	Total
1960-62	105.4	25.9	5.5	0.5	11.5	148.8
1964	135.6	23.4	6.5	0.3	9.8	175.8
1965	142.3	22.8	7.8	1.0	12.0	185.9
1966	186.3	14.1	7.4	2.3	12.5	222.6
1967	232.7	4.7	7.2	3.0	10.5	258.1
1968	136.7	4.8	9.6	2.8	10.9	164.8
1969	141.6	4.7	7.9	2.8	7.6	164.6
1970	106.2	2.3	8.1	3.0	10.3	129.9
1971	128.0	0.0	8.6	0.7	5.1	144.4
1972	123.6	0.1	8.2	1.9	4.4	138.2

in the entire sector, and two parastatals (Gemstone was created in 1971). The two parastatals, however, employed about 70 per cent of the workers, accounted for 77 per cent of the value added, and contributed 35 per cent of the investment (Tanzania, *Survey of Industrial Production,* 1970; 1972a).

The sector as a whole has stagnated in terms of development since the discovery of diamonds. Until 1971, there were only the two parastatals both established before independence. Production by Williamson's reached a peak in 1967 (see Table 65). The mine is gradually being phased out, with an attempt to extend its life as long as possible. Salt production has increased only slowly, although there are plans to increase production substantially in the future. Gemstones was created in 1971 to encourage the mining of gemstones in Arusha region. It has about shs 1 million in fixed assets compared to about shs 290 million for mining parastatals as a whole.

In 1972 the State Mining Corporation was established taking over the firms controlled by NDC: Portland Cement (classified as manufacturing), Williamson Diamonds, Nyanza Salt, and Gemstones. This corporation is supposed to increase the exploitation of mineral resources in the country. The attractions of the sector are clear, especially in terms of saved or earned foreign exchange through import substitution or exports. Yet, the sector has clear drawbacks. It is highly capital intensive, with a capital/labour ratio of shs 103,000 in 1971. It often produces a group of workers where average wage is much above that of other workers, and considerably above the income earned by the rest of the population. In 1971, the average wage in mining and quarrying was shs 523 per month. This is three times the average wage in estate agriculture and 20 per cent above the average wage in manufacturing. It is exceeded only by wages in the transport and finance sectors. In fact, the parastatal average is considerably above the average for the mining sector as a whole because the private producers are much smaller and less capital intensive. The average wage for Nyanza Salt Mines and Williamson Diamonds was shs 1029 a month in 1971 (NDC *Annual Report and Accounts,* 1971, 25).

The mining sector remains an area with undeveloped potential. A critical decision will soon be made concerning whether or not to increase its priority. As a sector it does not fit well into a strategy that emphasizes rural development. On the other hand it is one in which the economic returns are often quite large. As I will show in chapter eight, it is also a sector whose development is seen as vital by many of Nyerere's critics if there is to be a transformation of the economy.

COMMERCE

The commerce sector has the second largest number of parastatal firms (17 in all) of the sectors under study. It is possible to divide this sector in four different groups: the export-oriented firms (mostly the marketing boards), import-oriented firms, firms oriented towards internal distribution of goods, and real estate firms. The trading firms do not all fit in easily into these categories, but one can look at the investment in each. STC has been classified as 70 per cent an importing firm, 20 per cent an exporting firm, and 10 per cent an internal distribution firm. This is approximately the share of imports, exports, and locally-produced goods in its turnover. National Agricultural Products Board (NAPB) has been classified as 50 per cent an exporting firm, and 50 per cent a firm for internal distribution. Shell/BP and Agip are classified as import firms because their main function is to improve the internal distribution of a good which is imported, and then processed. Natex (the firm controlling the distribution of textiles) is classified as 55 per cent internal distribution oriented, 40 per cent import oriented, and 5 per cent export oriented according to the goods distributed.

When the firms are classified in this way, 63 per cent of parastatal assets are devoted to distributing imports (oil classified as an import), 26 per cent are used to export locally-produced products, and only 11 per cent are oriented to distributing locally-produced goods internally. Thus the thrust of the parastatal effort is 'outer directed.'[14] The sector has been expanded through the nationalization of wholesale importing firms to form STC, and two oil companies whose main input is imports. The government now has a significant share of the export and import trades, but little control over internal distribution. Natex and NAPB are the only two institutions of any size set up to encourage better distribution

14 See in chapter eight for discussion of this term.

of locally-produced goods. This orientation reflects the structure of the economy, which is still quite outer-directed. It is also the result of the government's concern to control the most important sectors of the economy, and to move most decisively into those areas where foreign firms dominate. As in the case of manufacturing the result is a parastatal sector which has some of the worse characteristics of the previous private firms.

The other sector under commerce is real estate. Up until 1971, parastatal participation in this sector was minimal. In 1969, NDC in conjunction with Industrial Promotion Services (T) Ltd. (the Aga Khan group) built the IPS building. In 1971 this building was acquired under the Building Acquisition Act, and passed under the control of Registrar of Buildings. This Act turned the government into the major real estate owner in the country. In all, about shs 250 million in assets were acquired. The movement of the government into this sector can be regarded as a clear attempt to appease political pressure from the urban sector. As in most countries there was significant dissatisfaction with high rents. There was a rent control law, but it was not possible to enforce it. After acquiring the buildings the government ordered all rents to be held to the legal level. This meant a significant increase in the real income of those urban dwellers renting from the Registrar of Buildings.

The Building Acquisition Act also had important implications for the economy as a whole. It profoundly reduced the confidence of the Asian business class in their future in Tanzania. The buildings were largely Asian owned, and Asians had been turning to real estate as a way to hold their capital. There has, therefore, been a significant decline in the extent to which Asians are willing to risk their capital. This has hurt those sectors of the economy – small manufacturing, distribution, transport – which are still dependent upon private entrepreneurs for growth.

The commerce sector as a whole is highly profitable. In 1971, its return on fixed capital was 80 per cent, and it accounted for 25 per cent of parastatal profits. This is, of course, no indication of the over-all efficiency of the sector. Rather it reflects the pricing policy in Tanzania which allows the trading organizations to make very high profits.

TRANSPORTATION

I have already talked about the origin of parastatal transport in Chapter four. There are only four parastatal transport firms. The two parastatals directly connected with the corridor to Zambia — Tazama Pipelines and Zam-Tam Road Services — own 95 per cent of the sector's assets. There is, as well, the Tazara railway. Thus the parastatal transport sector is dominated by projects connected to the Zambian corridor. The benefits of these projects are two-fold. The foremost is political. There is little question that none would have been started had not Rhodesia illegally declared independence, and Zambia felt the need to dissociate itself economically from the racist regimes to the south.[15]

There are some important economic benefits. The corridor generates foreign exchange through the sale of transport services. Export earnings appear high in the sale of petroleum products, but these are offset by imports of crude to produce these products, and imports necessitated by the fact that Tanzania cannot meet its own oil needs. Zambia takes somewhat less than half the Tanzanian capacity and less than Tanzania imports in refined products (EAC, 1970). In 1974, oil exports will end as a result of the construction of the Zambian refinery. The loss to Tanzania will be minimal[16] because it will divert its production to its own use, and thus reduce its own imports of refined products. Thus it is really only the service charges gained from the corridor which are an economic gain. These have risen from shs 38 million in 1966 to shs 74 million in 1967 to shs 241 million in 1972 (Tanzania, *Annual Economic Surveys*). In the same period, total earnings on exports and services rose from shs 2134 to shs 3198 million, an increase of shs 1064 million. Thus freight services accounted for 19 per cent of the increase in foreign exchange earnings in the period 1966 to 1972.

There are few other benefits than these, since there are little spill-over effects. The transport system as it now stands simply moves goods through Tanzania. The railway has some potential to open up Mbeya and Iringa regions, but these types of benefits are not expected to be great. The road which is being built will probably have important externalities in Tanzania, but the trucking firm, Zam-Tam Road Services, has really no major impact. It simply moves goods in and out of Zambia. The employment effects of the two projects are quite small, 1530 employees, with fixed assets of shs 315 million, for a capital/labour ratio of shs 206,000.

The Tanzania China Shipping Line could also be described as partially a product of UDI by Rhodesia. It was initiated before it was determined that China would build the railway. It has operated fairly successfully, however, by taking advantage of the increased trade between Tanzania and China, trade which developed because of the building of the Tazara railway. Again its main benefit is

---

15 The wisdom of this move was proved in 1973 when Rhodesia tried to pressure Zambia into withdrawing its support for the guerillas by stopping the copper trains which pass through Rhodesia.
16 The only real loss will be the inefficiencies involved in serving the northern Tanzanian market from Dar es Salaam rather than Mombasa, Kenya.

foreign exchange. So far, one ship has been bought from China for the company. The ship cost shs 23.6 million to buy and equip. Total employment is 120, half Tanzanians, and half Chinese. The line is owned equally by both parties.

The only transport company directed to developing internal trade is the National Transport Company. Most of its assets were held by a subsidiary, Dar Motor Transport Co., a bus firm which supplies bus service to Dar es Salaam, as well as some bus service up country. The National Transportation Company (NTC) also owns a shipping company which runs the MS Mtwara from Dar es Salaam to Mtwara. Its role is critically important, because Mtwara is cut off from most of the country for large parts of the year because of rain. There are plans to secure a second ship. NTC plans to develop several companies to improve internal transportation. It has already established a subsidiary, the National Road Haulage Co., which will provide services along the Dar-Tunduma road (the road to Zambia). There is also a desire to start a hire-pool company to loan trucks to co-operatives for the peak season.

At the moment, however, the parastatal transport sector is essentially export oriented, with only a small part of the assets devoted to improving internal communications, and much of these centred in Dar es Salaam. This should not be taken to mean that the public sector has ignored transportation altogether. The East Africa Community and the co-operatives have always played an important role in this field. In part, it is their presence which has made the area of lower priority. Nevertheless, internal distribution is still highly dependent on the private sector.

ELECTRICITY

The electricity sector is one which both leads and follows growth in other sectors, particularly manufacturing. Tanzania, as I have shown in chapter four, has devoted a considerable proportion of its resources to developing its electricity capacity. The emphasis on electricity reflects the large-scale, capital-intensive bias noted in manufacturing. Thus, the priority on electricity development has been, and continues to be, the development of major electrical generating units to supply power to a few cities, and to large users within these cities. In 1963, Dar es Salaam, Arusha, Moshi, Mwanza and Tanga absorbed 93 per cent of electricity sales (Tanzania, *Statistical Abstract*, 1970, 123), while Dar es Salaam alone absorbed 36 per cent. By 1972, Dar es Salaam took 58 per cent of the total, while Arusha, Moshi, Mwanza, Tanga, and Dar es Salaam absorbed 93 per cent of electricity sales (Tanzania, *Hali Ya Uchumi*, 1972-3, 84). Thus, over the period there was no shift away from the major urban centres, and, in fact, Dar es Salaam's dominance was increased.

This same trend can be seen in other ways. Since 1966 they have classified sales by use – public lighting, domestic, commercial, light industrial, and industrial. Industrial is 'Any installation where the maximum demand exceeds 40 KVA and all demands in excess of 75 KVA' (Tanzania, *Annual Economic Survey*, 1971-2, 40). The split between electricity sold to light industrial versus industrial gives us an indication of service to small versus large industry. In 1966, 57 per cent of sales were to industrial, and 5 per cent to light industrial. By 1972, industrial sales were 65 per cent of the total, while light industrial had fallen to 4 per cent (Tanzania, *Hali Ya Uchumi*, 1972-3, 83).

Nor is there much sign of a change in policy. Almost all of TANESCO's budget, in fact much of the government's budget,[17] is going to build a huge hydro scheme called Kidatu to supply power to Dar es Salaam. Schemes to provide electricity to rural areas, or even smaller towns have been shelved for lack of funds.

CONSTRUCTION

There are three companies in the parastatal construction sector, Mwananchi Engineering and Construction Co. (MECCO), National Estates and Design Company (NEDCO) and National Housing Corporation (NHC). NHC is both a builder and a realtor, and as such should really be split between commerce and construction. The construction sector remains essentially in private hands in Tanzania. Of a value added of shs 501 million in 1972, only shs 20 million was contributed by the parastatal sector, about 4 per cent of the total (Tanzania, *Hali Ya Uchumi*, 1972-3, 5, 48).

NHC, as a builder of houses, is supposed to concentrate on low-cost housing. In 1971-2, it devoted 30 per cent of its budget to low-cost houses (average cost was shs 8800 per unit (Tanzania, *Annual Economic Survey*, 1971-2, 104). This is considerably above the cost of a house built privately using traditional means, and, as was pointed out by the government, such a house is quite out of reach of most urban workers (*ibid*). The average cost of a house built in 1971 by NHC was shs 21,000. Most of its other houses were in the shs 27,000 to shs 36,000 range, houses appropriate for middle- and upper-level civil servants (a middle-range civil servant would earn shs 14,000 a year before taxes).

Not all government housing is built by NHC. In fact, in 1971-2 a majority was not. Ministries and parastatals spent shs 50 million in that year building 947 units, at an average cost of shs 53,000. Thus government housing moves over

17 Nine per cent of local development resources, and more than 12 per cent of all development budget resources are devoted to the project.

quite a wide range from low cost units of shs 8800, to some parastatal housing in the range of shs 150,000. No ministry or parastatal was supposed to build a house costing more than shs 70,000, but this rule has been broken often. In 1973 the government reduced the limit to shs 40,000, and has said that NHC will be held responsible if it agrees to build a house for more. Given the very wide use of private contractors, it is not clear that the new rule will be enforced. Yet, there has been real pressure on the parastatals in particular to curb their extravagant practices, and some effect will probably be felt.

The real issue is whether or not the government ought to be significantly involved in constructing houses at all. So far it has meant the channelling of scarce resources into the construction of a relatively few units which can be afforded by only the top- or middle-range civil servant or manager. The scarcity of housing means that obtaining one becomes a real reward. The government now seems to be moving to shift its expenditure away from building houses per se, and more to providing sites for people to build their own houses. This seems a more rational use of resources, and one more in keeping with egalitarian principles.

FINANCE

Introduction

There is a wide variety of companies falling under the category of financial institutions. For the purpose of this study it is best to look at them in terms of three categories: development corporations, insurance companies, and banks. This distinction is made in order to facilitate the type of analysis I am undertaking. Finance companies are important not so much for the investments they undertake directly, but because of the way in which they influence other investments. In all other sectors I have looked at the fixed assets accumulated by each company. While these are not unimportant for finance companies (shs 201 million in 1971), the most important influence they have on the economy is in the allocation of the surpluses they control as loans to other companies. By shifting the allocation of these surpluses from one sector to another, financial institutions can redirect development priorities.

Development corporations

There are a number of development corporations, NDC, TTC, SMC, TWICO , NAFCO, and TDFL. The investments of all but the last of these development corporations have already been picked up in our analysis of the manufacturing,

TABLE 66

TDFL investments and commitments by
type of business (per cent)

Transport	0.4
Printing	2.3
Mining	2.6
Commercial hotels	4.5
Property	7.6
Agricultural	7.7
Food, beverages, and alcohol	15.2
Textiles	16.7
General industries	20.5
Tourist development	22.5
Total	100.0

SOURCE: TDFL, *Annual Reports and
Accounts*, 1970, 13

tourism, agricultural, and mining sectors. Any company in which these firms had equity has been included in that analysis and none of these development corporations are sources of solely loan finance. The only exception is Tanganyika Development Finance Ltd. (TDFL).

TDFL has both loaned and taken equity in many private firms. It has a policy of keeping its equity share below 30 per cent, and usually above 10 per cent. This has not been strictly true but is generally so. TDFL has tended to invest in manufacturing firms. Eighty per cent of the assets are in manufacturing, with the largest part in two textile mills, Tasini and Kiltex. Another 16 per cent is in tourism, Bahari Beach and New Arusha, and the remaining 4 per cent in agriculture, Mafia Coconuts. In terms of the number of projects, most are small, import-intensive manufacturing firms, but these firms make up only 16 per cent of the equity assets of TDFL firms. On the other hand, TDFL loans tend to be directed much more exclusively to small firms. Table 66 shows the distribution of TDFL loans and equity investments, including future commitments as of December 1970. Manufacturing and tourism dominate.

Insurance companies

There is only one insurance company in Tanzania. The National Insurance Co. (NIC) was started in October 1963 as a small company in which equity was held 51 per cent by the government and 49 per cent by the other insurance companies in Tanzania. Its total assets remained quite small until 1967. In February of that year it became the sole life insurance company in Tanzania, and on 1

TABLE 67

Distribution of NIC investments as of June 1971
(shs '000)

	Amount	Per cent
Government stock	44,276	43
Short-term deposits	30,825	30
Building projects	18,753	18
Loans on mortgages	2064	2
Loans on policies	1374	1
Other institutions	6244	6
Total	103,536	100

January 1968, the sole insurer. Its equity is now held entirely by the government. Its investments stood at only shs 2.9 million in June 1966. By June 1971, they were shs 103.5 million.

Table 67 shows the distribution of NIC investments at the end of June 1971. Since NIC started in 1963, one can assume that the balance at the end of June 1971 represents the increase from 1964 to 1971 and thus the investment by NIC over the period. The overwhelming majority of their surpluses were in long-term government stock (43 per cent) and short-term deposits (30 per cent), especially short-term government notes. Real estate took up most of the rest, shs 19 million or 18 per cent. Since the government uses NIC as a source of finance for the development budget, then NIC's surpluses are recorded in any analysis of government spending. The effect NIC has on shifting priorities in the economy, then, is minimal.

Banks

It is possible to conclude, therefore, that an analysis of development corporations or the insurance company does not affect any of our conclusions about public investment in Tanzania. This is not true of analysis of the banks. Through their control over credit, the banks can have a decisive influence on the allocation of resources in Tanzania. Here I would like to analyze the degree to which the banks have acted to encourage rural development. I have shown in chapter three that the quantitative emphasis on rural development as measured by ministerial spending has not increased. In chapter four I showed that parastatal investment in agriculture has been small. The main activity by parastatals up to this point has been the acquisition of the sisal estates. Little new development has occurred although there are signs that this is changing. Nevertheless, the possibility still exists that the government has shifted resources to the rural areas. Since the rural sector is still largely private, the most effective tool for rural development may be credit policy. Has the government used its control of the banking institutions to allocate an increasing proportion of the investible surplus for rural development?

There are two types of banks which lend money – commercial banks and investment/development banks. The two types are distinguished mainly by the nature of their loans. Commercial bank loans are short-term loans, and investment/development bank loans are usually long term. This distinction is not, however, perfect. The commercial banks have some long-term loans, and the Rural Development Bank gives short-term credits.

Commercial banks

I will outline briefly the credit policy of each of the banking institutions, and then provide a consolidated picture at the end of this section. The biggest lenders by far are the commercial banks. At the end of 1972 they had loans outstanding of over shs 1500 million, over 80 per cent of the loans by banking institutions. There are three such banks in Tanzania – the National Bank of Commerce, the National Co-operative Bank (now dissolved), and the People's Bank of Zanzibar. In the analysis so far I have tried to look only at mainland Tanzania. It is not possible, however, to get published data on commercial banks, which exclude the People's Bank of Zanzibar. From unpublished data, however, it is clear that its inclusion does not significantly offset our results. The National Bank of Commerce dominates lending by commercial banks, having provided 95 per cent of the loans in 1971.

Table 68 presents the data on commercial bank loans over the period 1964-72 broken down into four broad categories: agriculture, manufacturing/mining, trade/transport, and other. Using this classification it appears that agriculture has not done badly. It has received 46 per cent of the increase in credit over the period while its contribution to GDP has fallen from 50 per cent in 1964 to 40 per cent in 1972.

Table 69 provides a more detailed picture of the allocation of credit. From it one can see that the increase in credit has gone to marketing of agriculture, not production. Credit to agricultural production declined from shs 102.1 million in 1967 to shs 96.2 million in 1972. Credit to marketing, on the other hand, soared from shs 190.9 million to shs 531.5 million.

The emphasis given to the provision of credit to the marketing boards is certainly evidence of the government's desire to put emphasis on the rural sector. In fact, in the credit plan drawn up for NBC by Devplan, there are two sectors, the controlled sector and the restricted sector. Credit is not limited in the control sector. NBC is instructed to supply whatever credit is needed to that

TABLE 68

Lending by commercial banks using old categories (shs million)

	Agriculture	Manufacture/ mining	Trade/ transport	Other	Total
1964	194.3	55.2	167.7	192.7	609.4
1965	278.4	65.4	254.4	103.8	702.0
1966	317.5	100.2	312.6	117.9	848.2
1967	293.0	114.8	295.6	114.7	818.1
1968	292.5	142.0	353.2	110.9	898.6
1969	380.3	196.1	386.2	130.0	1092.6
1970	452.0	214.1	540.4	140.4	1347.1
1971	478.9	223.0	640.0	162.7	1504.6
1972	627.7	255.5	483.2	182.6	1549.0
Change 1964-72	433.3	200.3	316.0	−10.1	936.0
Distribution	46%	21%	34%	−1%	100%

sector. Three areas are covered: exports, marketing of primary products, and agricultural production. There is some internal control of this sector, especially over private agricultural estates to whom credit allocation has been falling, but the evidence is clear on the government's emphasis. It is another question whether this shift of credit into agricultural marketing necessarily means a shift of resources into the rural sector. It may be an indicator of the increasing inefficiency on the part of the marketing boards. Certainly, the conventional wisdom in Tanzania would support the belief that the efficiency of co-operatives and marketing boards leaves much to be desired.

Trade/transport is the next most important area of growth. Its share of credit rose from 27 per cent in 1964 to 34 per cent in 1972. Again, however, it is really one sub-sector which accounts for the growth. Credit to 'export of produce' actually fell from shs 148.4 million in 1967 to shs 115.0 million in 1972, and trade in capital goods has increased only slightly. The transport sector has grown quickly, but it is so small as to make only a small difference on totals. Its growth is largely the result of the need to increase overdraft facilities to East African Airways, which runs heavy losses. The growth sector has been 'all other trade.' Its credit has increased from shs 121.8 million in 1967 to shs 305.4 million in 1972. Credit to this sector is really credit to the State Trading Corporation. It accounts for most of the increases to this sector. In fact, NBC credit to the private trade sector has been falling. The problems with STC reached their peak in 1971, and as a result credit to 'All other trade' rose to shs 459.8 million, 31 per cent of the loans outstanding, versus only 15 per cent in 1967.

TABLE 69

Lending by commercial banks (shs million)

	Agriculture			Trade/transport					Mining/manu-facturing		Building and con-struc-tion	Public admin.	Tour-ism	Finan-cial Insti-tutions	Other	Total	Total
	Agric. Prod.	Market-ing	Total	Export of produce	Trade in capital goods	All other trade	Trans-port	Total	Other	Total							
1962			119.8					77.6		69.7						179.5	446.4
1963			189.0					79.8		55.7						120.2	444.7
1964			194.3					167.2		55.2						192.7	609.4
1965			278.4				6.1	254.4	8.9	65.4						103.8	702.0
1966			317.5				8.1	312.3	16.8	100.2						118.0	848.2
1967	102.1	190.9	293.0	148.4	15.0	121.8	10.4	295.6	25.2	114.8	4.0			9.0	76.5	114.7	818.1
1968	99.5	193.0	292.5	159.2	41.7	136.7	15.6	353.2	41.3	142.8	5.6			8.2	55.8	110.9	898.6
1969	109.6	270.7	380.3	141.2	42.2	184.3	18.5	386.2	40.8	196.1	3.3			21.3	64.6	130.0	1092.6
1970	171.6	280.4	452.0	139.8	53.1	303.2	54.3	550.4	35.6	214.1	2.8	24.8		31.7	45.7	140.6	1347.1
1971	81.3	397.6	478.9	107.2	32.7	459.8	40.3	640.0	27.9	223.0	2.4	8.8		74.7	48.9	162.7	1504.6
1972	96.2	531.5	627.7	115.0	21.2	305.4	41.6	483.2	31.1	255.5	1.9	13.7		68.2	67.7	182.6	1548.9

SOURCE: Bank of Tanzania, *Economic Bulletins*

If one looks at a trade sector as a whole, combining marketing of agriculture production with export of produce, trade in capital goods, and all other trade, one will see that the government has put increasing amounts of credit into this sector. Trade, defined in this way, has taken 68 per cent of the increase in credit since 1967, and now has 63 per cent of the loans outstanding, versus 58 per cent in 1967. It is likely that this increased emphasis reflects efficiency problems which accompanied the increased government control of the sector. There is some indication, and at least a lot of hope, that the worst of the problems are over. If our series had ended in 1971, instead of 1972, the picture would have looked worse. At the end of that year, trade had taken 71 per cent of the increase and accounted for 66 per cent of the loans outstanding.

The manufacturing and mining sectors have had a steady increase in the credit available to them. Since credit to mining is minimal, I will compare growth in the manufacturing GDP only to growth in credit in the sector. In 1964, manufacturing contributed shs 364 million to monetary GDP. This was equal to 8.2 per cent of GDP. By 1972, it had risen to shs 714 million, or 10.2 per cent of GDP (Tanzania, *Hali Ya Uchumi*, 1972-3, 5). Its share, then, increased 24 per cent. Manufacturing's share in commercial bank credit appears in two places. First, it appears under the heading mining and manufacturing. Here, as I have said, I am ignoring the mining part which is quite small. Secondly, credit to other financial institutions is almost exclusively credit to manufacturing. TIB is the main recipient of the credit (about 90 per cent) since it took over NBC's long-term portfolio. This portfolio was almost exclusively loans to manufacturing firms. Thus, one should add this credit to the credit direct to manufacturing. The absence of figures before 1967 need not worry us since TIB did not exist, and NDCA had very little investment in manufacturing. Credit to manufacturing, therefore, increased from 9.1 per cent of outstanding loans in 1964 to 20.9 per cent in 1972, an increase of 130 per cent. Thus, credit by commercial banks has significantly emphasized the growth of the manufacturing sector.

Table 70 sets out the credit allocation by the National Bank of Commerce for the period 1969-72. In that short period, one can see that significant changes have occurred in the allocation of credit, especially in the allocation between public and private enterprises. In every sector the government has used credit as a method to encourage the growth of parastatal enterprises and restrict the growth of private ones. Of course, this is not always such a conscious decision. Parastatals have more access to, and greater political weight with, the people who allocate credit. The result has been a massive shift in credit towards public enterprise. In 1969, private firms received shs 382 million in credit, some 48 per cent of the total. By 1972, this had fallen to shs 240 million, an absolute decline of shs 140 million, and a relative decline to only 19 per cent of total credit.

TABLE 70

Credit allocation by National Bank of Commerce

Summary by agency (shs million)		1969	1970	1971	1972
Public		414	542	989	1018
Private		382	424	309	240
Summary by area					
Controlled	Public	253	167	385	420
	Private	157	158	136	118
	Total	410	325	521	538
Restricted	Public	161	375	604	598
	Private	225	266	173	122
	Total	386	641	177	720

It is possible to conclude several things from this analysis of the credit policies of the commercial banks. First, while the government may not have acquired a large part of the fixed assets in commerce, and has left much of this sector in private hands, it has allocated a significant proportion of the loan capital of the country to government-owned trading organizations. In part this reflects a concern over rural development. There has been a significant rise in the credit allocated to the marketing boards, but it also reflects problems with the state-owned trading concerns. Injections of short-term credit have been used to prevent the State Trading Corporation's going bankrupt and to cover the inefficiency of the marketing boards. Secondly, it is possible to conclude that the government's emphasis on industrialization, which was obvious from our analysis of parastatal investments in fixed assets, is also clear from the analysis of credit policies of the banks. Finally, the commercial banking system has had a clear bias in favour of parastatals. It has thus been a tool in the government's drive to increase the role of public institutions in the economy by squeezing the credit allocated to private firms and granting credit liberally to parastatals.

Investment/development banks
The chief financial instrument for encouraging rural development has always been the rural credit banks, originally the National Development Credit Agency, and now its successor, the Rural Development Bank. The National Co-op Bank, the other bank under the umbrella of the National Co-operative and Development bank set up in 1964 and now dissolved, handled only short-term crop financing. Its loans have been picked up in the analysis of commercial banks. The importance of rural credit as part of the program of rural development has been stressed in Tanzania:

TABLE 71

Lending by NDCA/TRDB (shs million)

	Loans outstanding, March 31										Increase
	1950	1960	1962	1963	1965	1966	1967	1968	1969	1972	1964-72
Short term[1]	0.8	4.4	6.9	NA	NA	10.1	10.9	12.1	14.4	30.0	23.0
Med.-long term	3.5	20.3	27.3	NA	NA	44.1	41.3	38.9	58.9	46.2	18.2
IDA							8.8	13.1		27.0	27.0
Total	4.3	24.7	34.2	35.0	50.0	54.2	61.0	64.1	73.3	103.2	68.2

SOURCE: NCDB; TRDB, 1970-71; Tanzania, *Statistical Abstract,* 1970.

In Tanzania rural development receives top priority in national policies as most of the country's prosperity lies in the development of land and mobilization of the efforts and energies of rural people. The Tanzania Rural Development Bank was therefore instituted as a means of providing a comprehensive credit system for transforming the subsistence living into a modern cash economy, with its attendant increased employment opportunities and income distribution ... Thus the Bank is intended to be a dynamic institution for the promotion of rural development, which in Tanzania largely involves the sustained support of Ujamaa Village's development programme (TRDB, 1970-71, 5).

Table 71 presents the loans outstanding of the rural credit agencies from 1950 to 1972. In the period 1948-62, the agency was the Land Bank, after that the Agricultural Credit Agency (1962-4), then the National Development Credit Agency (1964-70), and finally the Tanzanian Rural Development Bank. Unfortunately data are not available for 1964, the one year for which I would like to have it. I will use the figures for 1963, which will build in a slight bias toward exaggerating the amount of rural credit made available. For 1963 I will assume that the split between short-term and long-term loans was approximately the same as in 1962. Thus, short-term loans were shs 7 million and long-term 28 million. Over the period 1964-72, total credit to the rural sector issued by these agencies increased shs 68.2 million. Most of this was the result of the development of IDA programs, which accounted for 40 per cent of the increase. Short-term loans accounted for 34 per cent of the increase, and medium- and long-term loans 26 per cent.

The insignificance of the increase in credit to the rural sector can be appreciated when this increase is compared to increases in credit by the commercial banks, or total investment in the economy. Thus commercial bank credit during

TABLE 72

TRDB loan distribution by region

	Loans outstanding[1] per capita (shs)	Monetary farm output per capita 1967[2] (shs)
Iringa	19.4	105
Tabora	11.2	84
Ruvuma	11.2	57
Arusha	8.2	167
Mbeya	8.0	70
W. Lake	7.3	75
Coast	5.9	86
Kilimanjaro	4.7	277
Tanga	4.7	212
Mwanza	3.8	101
Mara	2.3	64
Morogoro	2.1	158
Mtwara	1.2	67
Singida	1.0	28
Dodoma	0.3	34
Kigoma	0.1	35
Shinyanga	–	97

1 TRDB, 1970-71, 9
2 Tanzania, 1969, vol. III, 9

the same period grew by shs 940 million, more than thirteen times the increase in credit by rural development agencies. Medium- and long-term credit by TRDB was equivalent to 4.4 per cent of fixed monetary capital formation in 1961, but only 3.4 per cent in 1972.

TRDB's loans tend to be heavily concentrated in a few regions, generally the regions with export crops. Thus the regions growing tobacco – Iringa, Tabora, and Ruvuma – all received more than the shs 11 (per capita) in loans (see Table 72) in 1970 while other regions like Mtwara, Singida, Dodoma, Kigoma, and Shinyanga received less than shs 2 per capita in loans. Over half of TRDB's loans were for tea, tobacco, coffee, and cotton crop development (*ibid.*, 13).

Permanent Housing Finance Company was established on 3 January 1967, as a joint venture between the Commonwealth Development Corporation and the Tanzania Government, each holding 50 per cent equity. It only really began operations in 1968. Table 73 sets out its lending over the period 1968-72. All the lending has gone to housing and about half (41 per cent) to National Housing Corporation. Since investment in NHC is to build medium-cost houses sold to private owners, this investment is in addition to that recorded under NHC.

TABLE 73

Permanent Housing Finance Company of Tanzania Limited: statements of housing loans
outstanding at each year end since 1968

Year	NHC (shs)	Others (shs)	Total (shs)	NHC as per cent of total
1968	–	18,228,260	18,228,260	0
1969	2,324,088	21,737,353	24,061,441	10
1970	1,076,406	29,425,451	34,501,857	3
1971	16,556,836	34,037,588	50,594,424	33
1972	24,537,871	34,844,590	59,382,461	41
Change in loans outstanding				
1968	–	18,228,260 .	18,228,260	
1969	2,324,088	3,509,093	5,833,181	
1970	–1,247,430	4,112,137	20,092,567	
1971	15,480,430	4,612,137	20,092,567	
1972	7,981,035	807,002	8,788,037	

TABLE 74

Investments by TIB by sector

Sector	No. of loans[1]	Amount (shs '000)	Share (%)
Agriculture	5	3400	8
Tourism	1	3000	7
Transport	2	8015	19
Construction	–	–	–
Mining	2	4500	10
Industry	9	17,370	40
Others	1	7000	16
Total	20	43,285	100

1 Includes shs 1 million in equity investment

The Tanzania Investment Bank began operations on 16 November 1970,
taking over the long-term portfolio of the National Bank of Commerce. By 30
June 1972, TIB has lent shs 42 million and invested shs 1 million in projects.
Most of this (40 per cent) was in industry, but transport was also important (19
per cent). Table 74 shows the distribution of TIB investment by sector, and
Table 75 shows it by type of agency. Loans to non-parastatals have been very
small, only shs. 4 million. Thus TIB investments have almost been totally accounted for in our analysis of parastatal investment.

TABLE 75

Distribution of TIB loans by agency

Agency	No.	Amount (shs.'000)	Share (%)
Wholly public	8	20,195	48
More than 51 per cent public	5	9490	22
50 per cent public	2	8400	20
Less than 50 per cent public	–	–	–
Private	3	4000	10
Total	18	42,085	100

Investment/development corporations are not nearly so important in terms of credit allocation as commercial banks. They do, however, control the allocation of long-term credit, and their role as initiators and organizers of projects is probably growing. TRDB is the most important of these institutions, but its growth has been small when compared to the task it has been assigned. As one of the most important institutions for rural development, one might have expected it to receive top priority in terms of allocation of both manpower and capital. It has not been given such a priority. The Permanent Housing Corporation lends to primarily upper income urban dwellers. It is interesting to note that in the period 1964 to 1972, the increase in its loans were almost equal to the increase in loans by NDCA/TRDB (shs 59 million versus shs 68 million). Finally, the Tanzania Investment Bank has concentrated mainly on parastatal manufacturing and transport investments. These investments have all been analyzed in our study of parastatal investment and therefore do not affect our conclusions about sectoral allocation.

Summary of analysis

Table 76 provides a summary of the increase in credit provided by each of the financial institutions over the period 1964-72. Credit by TIB and TDFL to parastatals and by NIC to the banks or the government has been omitted. In total, the increase in credit was shs 1109 million, of which shs 987 million or 85 per cent was accounted for by the commercial banks, followed by shs 68 million (6 per cent) by NDCA/TRDB, shs 59 million (5 per cent) by PHFC, shs 28 million (3 per cent) by NIC, shs 13 million (1 per cent) by TDFL, and shs 4 million by TIB.

Table 77 shows the distribution of the increase in credit by sector, and Table 78 shows the loans outstanding in 1964 and 1972 classified by sector. There has been a major shift towards an increased allocation of credit to the rural sector.

TABLE 76

Increase in credit in the economy, 1964-72
(shs million)

Agency	Amount
Commercial banks	937
NIC	28
NDCA/TRDB	68
PHFC	59
TIB	4
TDFL	13
Total	1109

TABLE 77

Distribution of Increased credit

	Shs million	Share (%)
Agricultural production	59[1]	5
Agricultural marketing	448[1]	40
Manufacturing	285[2]	26
Construction, real estate	101[3]	9
Trade	281[4]	25
Others	−65	−6
Total	1109	100

1 Assumes credit to agricultural production in 1964 equal to credit
  in 1967 (see Table 69) and assigns short-term NDCA/TRDB credit
  to marketing of agriculture.
2 Credit by commercial banks to manufacturing and financial
  institutions, plus loans by TIB and TDFL
3 Credit by commercial banks to building and construction, plus
  NIC loans to real estate, plus PHFC loans.
4 Assumes transport credit in 1964 equal to credit in 1965
  (see Table 69)

This shift has come, however, in the form of support to agricultural marketing,
not to agricultural production. Agricultural marketing accounted for 15 per cent
of the loans outstanding in 1964. By 1972 its share had risen to 31 per cent.
Agricultural production's share, on the other hand, fell from 20 per cent to 11
per cent. One could wonder whether there needs to be more help for the peasant
producer, and perhaps less support for the parastatal distribution system.

The manufacturing sector, the priority sector in terms of parastatal investment, is also a very important area in terms of credit allocation by the banking

TABLE 78

Loans outstanding by sector (shs million)

	1964	Per cent	1972	Per cent
Agricultural production	130	20	189	11
Agricultural marketing	99	15	547	31
Manufacturing	55	9	340	20
Construction, real estate	9	1	110	6
Trade	161	25	442	25
Others	190	30	125	7
Total	644	100	1753	100

system. This sector absorbed 26 per cent of the increase in credit in the period 1964 to 1972 and increased its share of loans outstanding from 9 per cent in 1964 to 20 per cent in 1972.

Despite the emphasis of the banking system on trade, the financial institutions as a whole did not increase their allocation of credit to trade, excluding marketing of agriculture produce. Of course if marketing is included, the share of trade in total credit has risen significantly from 40 per cent in 1964 to 50 per cent in 1972.

Financial institutions have been used as an important instrument to increase the growth of the public sector. In 1969 parastatals took 40 per cent of the credit from financial institutions. By 1972 this had risen to a remarkable 71 per cent.[18] Given the relatively small size of the parastatal sector in the economy, this represents a major shift of resources towards public investment.

18 I take share of NBC credit going to parastatal sector and apply it to the commercial banks as a whole, and add PHFC loans to NHC and TIB loans.

6

Financing of public investment

Purpose of chapter

This chapter will provide an overview of the sources of funds for public investment. Although this study is primarily devoted to analysing the pattern of public investment, its financing is also relevant for several reasons. First, the desire for and necessity of shifting the emphasis on development funds away from foreign sources to local sources was an essential element in the Arusha Declaration. This shift in emphasis did show up clearly in the proposed financing of the Second Five Year Plan, as opposed to the expected financing of the First Five Year Plan. It has not, as I will show in this chapter, resulted in a significant shift in the actual financing of these plans. Public investment today remains about as heavily dependent on foreign funds as it did ten years ago. About one-half of public investment has been foreign financed. Nevertheless, there have been important shifts in the sources of foreign capital. Tanzania has been able to move significantly away from a reliance on high-cost credit suppliers to much lower-cost loans from foreign aid donors.

The financing of public investment is also an important area of study because the way in which resources are raised for investment affects the type of investment which can be made. This is true for both local and foreign capital. In chapter one I showed that most socialist scholars linked aid to a perpetuation of a dependency relationship. In chapter eight I will show that most of Nyerere's critics also centre on the distortive effects of reliance on foreign capital. It is worthwhile, then, to analyse the role of foreign capital in Tanzania in order to assess these arguments. I will conclude that use of aid finance has had distortive effects on development, but that in many cases it has had very positive results.

The negative effects are less in Tanzania than in most countries because Tanzania has attracted progressive donors, and because Tanzania's ideology prevents some of the worst abuses of aid. Clearer specification of the ideology would further reduce the problems with aid. Nevertheless, use of aid finance also reduces the flexibility of programmes, and in the long run self-reliance offers the only real hope for development.

I will also show that the concentration of parastatal surpluses in a few sectors, and in a few firms within those sectors reduces the flexibility of the government in setting investment priorities. Because of legal and institutional problems surpluses from profit-making parastatals are not freely available for distribution to other firms. As a result, there is a strong bias towards a perpetuation of the existing pattern of investment, and away from a radical reorientation of the parastatal sector.

Finally, in a brief note at the end of the chapter I look at the source of funds for public investment in terms of the distribution of the burden of raising those funds between urban and rural residents. I do this in case some readers may wonder whether a major shift in the way the government has raised revenue for the public sector has occurred, and whether this shift has significantly altered the burden on the urban areas. If such a change had occurred, and there had been a major increase in the urban burden, one could be less critical of the failure to increase spending on rural development. I will show, however, that despite major changes in the sources of finance for public investment the burden on urban residents has not altered significantly. Nor is it likely to do so in the near future. The very small size of the urban sector will make this impossible. As a result, any shift in emphasis towards rural development will have to come through shifts in public investment, rather than through the financing of that investment.

Data problems

Public investment for the purpose of this study has been defined to include only government ministerial development expenditure[1], parastatal investments, and investments by District Development Corporations. Investment by the East African Community and its enterprises, the co-operatives, and Ujamaa villages has been ignored except insofar as it was dealt with in chapter two. There have been significant revisions made to the published data on ministerial and parastatal expenditure. Some of these have been discussed in chapters three and four

---

1 The difference between development expenditure and investment is explained in chapter three.

respectively. Here I would like to briefly outline the revisions made to the data on sources of funds for this expenditure.

The major revision to the published data concerns foreign aid. Foreign aid flows to Tanzania in two ways. It can pass through the Treasury, and from the Treasury to the agency which is implementing the project. Aid received in this way is easily recorded. In general the aid donor agrees to reimburse the Treasury for approved expenditures. When the Treasury receives a bill from the implementing agency for an expenditure, it pays the bill, then passes the bill on to the aid donor who then pays the Treasury. In some cases, the aid donor will advance Treasury the money in order to reduce the time lag involved.

Aid can also go directly to a project. In this case, no money actually changes hands in Tanzania. A set of bulldozers, for example, is delivered by the Canadian government to the National Parks. If the aid is in the form of a loan, the value of the tractors may be agreed upon by the Treasury and the Canadian government. On the other hand, the value of the tractors may be lost in an agreement over a number of years on the total value of such direct aid, or, the tractors may come as a grant and therefore the value may never be determined. In general, the Treasury has had great difficulty in keeping track of such aid, and much has gone unrecorded in published documents showing total public investment.[2] A detailed presentation of the sources and amount of direct and total aid received by Tanzania is presented in Appendix V. Unrecorded direct aid amounted to about shs 0.9 billion from 1964-5 to 1973-4. This is equivalent to 20 per cent of the total aid received in this period.

Chinese aid is almost exclusively direct aid, and accounts for much of the direct aid not recorded. One project, Tazara, is particularly important in this respect. Because of the size of this project, its financing dominates the picture of financing of public investment over the last few years. It is therefore worthwhile to detail the financing of this particular project so that the reader can understand its impact.

The railway runs from Dar es Salaam to Kapiri Mposhi in Zambia. The cost of the project is being financed by a Chinese loan which is to be paid back by Tanzania and Zambia equally. To help offset the foreign exchange drain on China as a result of the local costs involved in the project, Tanzania and Zambia are supposed to buy Chinese commodities to sell in their own countries. The revenue from the sale of these commodities is put into a special account used to

2 Direct aid seems to get recorded as loans which must be repaid, but fails to be recorded as expenditure. This reflects the fact that aid donors keep track of how much they have lent Tanzania, and that is what is most important to them and Treasury, which has the typical accounting bias of finance ministries.

cover the local costs. The import costs come in the form of direct aid by the Chinese. The equipment is imported directly into Tanzania, and the Chinese give the Tanzanians estimates of its value.

There are two ways in which the value of the Tazara project can be estimated. Neither effect the total cost of the project, but the two differ on the timing of the expenditure. The Bank of Tanzania looks at the expenditure side of the project. It attempts to estimate the amount of investment carried on within Tanzania by judging from the progress of the railway the proportion of work conducted in Tanzania. In the last few years most work was done in Tanzania. In terms of assessing the immediate impact on the economy, the Bank of Tanzania's approach is the most meaningful (see expenditure approach in Table 79).

The budget division of the planning ministry has generally looked at the project from the financing perspective. The *Annual Plan* publishes figures which are based upon the balance sheets of Tazara, and assign fifty per cent of the cost of the project to Tanzania. These figures reflect Tanzania's liability for repayment. Table 79 sets out the two ways of evaluating of the cost of Tazara. For the purposes of this study, the financing approach has been used.

The other area where an attempt has been made to revise and add to the published data is the financing of parastatal investment. There are no accurate[3] data available on the source of funds for parastatal investment. In revising the data on parastatal investment (see chapter four and Appendix IV), I have tried to estimate the sources of finance. From the *Report of the Auditor-general* and the revision of the data on foreign aid, I have been able to determine the amount of investment which was financed by local government contribution or by foreign 'aid. The rest of the investment, then, was financed by self-generated funds, local borrowing or foreign borrowing. For the last three years fairly accurate data are available from the Devplan Planning Information System[4] on these sources of funds. For earlier years, I have had to make estimates. These estimates are based upon an examination of the balance sheets, and discussions with knowledgeable individuals. Investments which were partially or wholly foreign financed are well known, and the degree of foreign financing is usually clear from the balance sheets. I have, therefore, drawn up an estimate of foreign borrowing by parastatals for each of the years involved. Local borrowing and self-generated funds are the residual after local budget support, foreign aid and foreign borrowing are subtracted from total investment.

In order to use figures for the government budget, and for parastatal investment it has been necessary to synchronize the two series in terms of calander

---

3 The Central Statistical Bureau state that their data on this are not very reliable. See Tanzania (1972, 5).

4 For a description of the system, see chapter three and Appendix II.

TABLE 79

Costs of Tazara (shs million)

Expenditure approach	67	68	69	70	71	72	73-4+
Investment in Tanzania	–	–	–	273	617	662	500
Financing approach[1]	67-8	68-9	69-70	70-71	71-2	72-3	73-4
Local costs borne by Tanzania	0.7	5.5	8.0	1.5	5.0	6.3	11.0
Aid							
Local costs-commodity credit				71.1	145.0	193.0	200.0
Import costs				114.5	180.0	170.0	175.0
Total	0.7	5.5	8.0	187.1	330.0	369.3	386.0

SOURCE: Tanzania, *Annual Economic Surveys; Annual Plans; Reports of the Auditor-General*
1 One-half cost of Tazara is assigned to Tanzania, one-half is assigned to Zambia

and fiscal years. This problem was touched upon in chapter four. Parastatal investment, usually expressed on a calendar year basis, has been converted to a fiscal year basis. Wherever possible this has been done in a way which reflects the actual timing of the investment. If that timing was not known the conversion was simply on the basis of splitting the year in half.

SELF-RELIANCE

In chapter II I showed how disappointment with the amount of foreign capital available to Tanzania, and the political implications of accepting aid from certain countries gradually encouraged a shift in policy towards a view that Tanzania should not depend upon foreign financing for its development programme. This shift in policy was formally announced in the Arusha Declaration which called upon the country to become self-reliant.

This shift in policy shows up clearly in a comparison of the two five year plans. In the First FYP 74 per cent of the investment was to be foreign financed. In the Second FYP the expectation was that only 40 per cent of the finance would come from abroad. In actual performance the two plans do not differ significantly. If we exclude Tazara (the Plans had very incomplete figures for the expected financing of Tazara), the First FYP was actually financed 50 per cent by foreign capital and 50 per cent by local resources, and the Second FYP, 48 per cent by foreign capital and 52 per cent by local resources. If Tazara were included, the financing of the First FYP remains unaltered, but the Second FYP shows an increase in foreign financing. Including Tazara, 56 per cent of the Second FYP's investments will probably be financed abroad, up from the 50 per cent in the First FYP (see Table 80).

To fully understand why the shift in policy did not result in a shift in performance, one must have a detailed understanding of the flow of foreign capital, and the availability of local resources on a year to year basis, and broken down by type of implementing agency. Table 81 presents the financing of parastatal and ministerial expenditure on a year-to-year basis. Table 82 shows the year-to-year data for all public investment combined, and for public investment excluding Tazara.

In the initial years after independence aid flows did not increase notably. Aid passing through the Treasury was shs 70 million in 1964-65 and shs 83 million in 1967-8. It was this stagnation of aid which led to the belief that a policy of self-reliance was necessary. Nevertheless, it was wrong to assume that foreign capital could not be attracted to Tanzania. In fact during this period there was a significant inflow of capital, but it was private capital, not foreign aid. As Table 81 shows, parastatals were able to raise shs 516 million in private foreign loans in the First FYP. This was almost equivalent to the foreign aid which went to ministries in the period. What accounts for this inflow of private capital?

Tanzania, with its lack of resources and its position relative to Kenya, was not particularly attractive to foreign investors. If left free to choose, the multinational corporations would have continued to serve the Tanzanian market from abroad, or from Kenya. The independence government with increasingly aggressive policies altered the situation. It was determined to develop industries. Foreign suppliers were faced with a situation of losing a market, or investing. The result was an initial flurry of investments – cement, beer, cigarettes, and oil.

Market protection, however, only explains a small amount of the inflow of capital. The more important explanation is the increased role of the government in the productive sector of the economy. Conventional wisdom has always asserted that the way to attract foreign capital is to provide a proper 'investment climate.' Such a climate is usually characterized as involving little fear of nationalization and low direct government involvement in the economy. Tanzania shows the opposite to be true, in at least its own case. Foreign capital was attracted when the government initiated projects. International firms, anxious to sell equipment, were willing to have joint ventures, and provide suppliers credits to areas of the economy where they would have never gone without the security of government involvement and of government backed loans. When this government involvement also meant gaining control of a market (e.g., General Tyre), the attractions to the foreign supplier were great. Joint ventures with the government were often regarded as safer than purely private ventures because the terms on which the government could extend its control were often made explicit. Moreover, partial government participation reduced the likelihood that there would be dramatic changes in prices or taxes which would be detrimental to the company. The company, by being a parastatal, gained an effective lobby in the government.

TABLE 80

Expected and actual sources of funds (shs million)

	First FYP				Second FYP			
	Foreign		Local		Foreign		Local	
	Est.[1]	Actual	Est.[1]	Actual	Est.[2]	Actual[3]	Est.[2]	Actual[3]
Ministries	1217 (84%)	557 (39%)	230 (16%)	857 (61%)	1249 (41%)	1451 (45%)	1806 (59%)	1782 (55%)
Parastatals	587 (59%)	665 (66%)	400 (41%)	344 (34%)	973 (40%)	1401 (51%)	1461 (60%)	1361 (49%)
Total	1804 (74%)	1222 (50%)	630 (26%)	1201 (50%)	2222 (40%)	2852 (48%)	3267 (60%)	3143 (52%)
Total incl. Tazara	NA	1222 (50%)	NA	1207 (50%)	NA	4100 (56%)	NA	3175 (44%)

1 Tanganyika, 1964, vol. I, 97
2 Tanzania, 1969, vol. I, 213; vol. II, 18
3 Includes estimates for 1972-73 and 1973-74

TABLE 81

Government development programme – ministries and parastatals

	1964-5	1965-6	1966-7	1967-8	1968-9	1969-70	1970-71	1971-2	1972-3	1973-4	Total
Ministries[1]											
Recorded aid	70	78	116	83	117	139	206	211	226	453	1699
Direct aid			6	38	49	42	49	50	75	–	309
Total aid	70	78	122	121	166	181	255	261	301	453	2008
Local resources	98	103	175	213	268	322	379	288	335	458	2639
Total funds	168	181	297	334	434	503	634	549	636	911	4647
External as share (%)	42	43	50	36	38	36	40	48	47	50	44
Parastatals[2]											
Recorded aid	8	4	10	–	–	15	25	93	99	443	687
Direct aid	3	8	44	41	31	22	61	60	138	–	408
Sub-total aid	11	12	54	41	31	37	86	153	237	443	1095
Foreign private											
finance	34	43	149	180	110	151	166	92	14	32	971
Total external	45	55	203	221	141	188	252	245	251	465	2066
Local budget	36	45	21	51	65	115	170	71	93	142	809
Local raised by											
parastatals	–	12	12	42	60	29	69	198	115	359	896
Total local	36	57	33	93	125	144	239	269	208	501	1705
Total funds	81	112	236	314	266	332	491	514	459	966	3771
External as share (%)	56	49	86	70	53	57	51	48	55	48	55

1 Includes regions for 1972-3 and 1973-4
2 Excluding Tazara, including DDC's in 1973-4

TABLE 82

Government development programmes – ministries and parastatals combined

	1964-5	1965-6	1966-7	1967-8	1968-9	1969-70	1970-71	1971-2	1972-3	1973-4	Total
Recorded aid	78	82	126	83	117	154	231	304	325	886	2386
Direct aid	3	8	50	79	80	64	295	435	576	375	1965
Foreign private finance	34	43	149	180	110	151	166	92	14	32	971
Total foreign	115	133	325	342	307	369	692	831	915	1293	5322
Local budget funds	134	148	196	264	339	445	551	364	434	611	3486
Local resources raised[1] by parastatals	–	12	12	42	60	29	69	198	115	359	896
Total local	134	160	208	306	399	474	620	562	549	970	4382
Total all funds	249	293	533	648	706	843	1312	1393	1462	2241	9704
Share external (%)	46	49	61	53	43	44	53	60	63	57	55
Total foreign excl. Tazara	115	133	325	342	307	369	507	506	552	918	4074
Total local excl. Tazara	134	160	208	306	393	466	618	557	543	959	4344
Total all funds	249	293	533	648	700	835	1125	1063	1093	1855	8418
Share external excl. Tazara (%)	46	45	61	53	44	44	45	48	50	49	48

1 Taken as difference between total investment and government local contribution, direct and recorded aid and estimated foreign private borrowing.

Government intervention in the economy meant a raising of the level of investment, and the start of several projects which were unattractive to private investors. The most notable of these were those surrounding the corridor to Zambia – the pipeline, and the trucking firm. Both were financed by private capital from abroad, and the pipeline even had a small participation by a foreign firm (20 per cent). These projects alone attracted shs 310 million in foreign capital, 47 per cent of the private capital which came from abroad in the First FYP.

The Arusha Declaration and the subsequent nationalizations did not slow the inflow of foreign capital. In fact, if anything, they increased it by increasing the government's involvement in the economy. Table 83 shows the inflow of private capital by sector. The manufacturing sector, an area of significant nationalizations, continued to attract increasingly large amounts of foreign private capital up until 1970-1. The completion of the pipeline caused an initial drop in the inflow of foreign capital, but not a significant one.

After 1970-71 there is a noticeable decline in the amount of private foreign finance. This drop does not reflect an unwillingness by foreign firms to lend, but rather a reluctance on the part of Tanzania to continue to borrow at such hard terms. This shift in policy was made possible by the rapid growth in foreign aid which followed the Arusha Declaration, and a shift in the direction of foreign aid away from infrastructure towards directly productive projects. At present, it is almost impossible for parastatals to get permission from the Bank of Tanzania to borrow commercially abroad. Instead they are directed to get foreign aid loans, or to borrow from TIB or TRDB which are financed mostly through foreign aid.

The disputes with Britain and Germany and the uneasy relationship with the United States meant that Tanzania initially lost its traditional source of foreign aid, but did not acquire any new sources. The Arusha Declaration altered the situation. The doctrine of self-reliance and rural socialism was very attractive to many donors. The strategy behind the doctrine contrasted sharply with the elite-oriented Big Push strategies adopted by many countries. The socialist overtones, far from repelling western donors, attracted them. Tanzanian socialism was not so strong (at least at this stage) that it challenged the interests of western capitalism. What it meant to most donors was that the elite in Tanzania, because of the leadership code, would not enrich themselves on foreign aid, and would in fact strive to enact programmes to better the mass of the population. The Nordic countries, Canada, and the World Bank all found this a striking contrast to the situation in most of the Third World.

It was several years after the Arusha Declaration that the dramatic rise in foreign aid occurred. This slowness of response reflects difficulties in implementing projects and mobilizing aid. While some of these have been solved, it is

TABLE 83

Parastatal foreign financing

	1964-5	1965-6	1966-7	1967-8	1968-9	1969-70	1970-71	1971-2	1972-3	1973-4
TANESCO			14,920		2500			7000		8100
Tourism	16,031	10,710								
Mfg.	18,050	24,282	28,349	42,422	41,431	128,307	135,218	18,886	14,239	24,260
Transport		8037	106,026	135,943	63,440	19,447	30,708	35,878		
Agriculture								29,902		
Total	34,091	43,029	149,295	179,721	110,084	150,814	165,926	91,666	14,239	32,360

nevertheless true that even today there is probably more aid available (for specific types of programmes, especially rural-oriented ones) than can be utilized. The rise in the inflow of aid has, despite these problems, been impressive. In 1964-5 foreign aid was shs 97 million. In 1973-4 it is expected to total shs 886 million excluding Tazara, and shs 1261 million including it.

Foreign aid initially was a source of funds reserved essentially for ministries. In the First FYP, 80 per cent of foreign aid went to ministries. Over time, however, this concentration on social and economic infrastructural projects has lessened and aid donors have been willing to finance directly productive activities. The development of state-owned enterprises made this possible. It became clear that the initiation of economic activity was the real problem in Tanzania, and aid donors were politically better able to support projects along these lines if they were government owned, not private. The development of investment banks also was important. These institutions gave donors an easy mechanism by which to inject large amounts of funds into the productive sector. In increasing numbers of cases, these funds have been given without ties as to their use. In this way aid donors avoid the problems of having to choose projects.

In the Second FYP, then, aid has replaced much of foreign private capital as a source of finance for parastatals. Parastatals will receive 39 per cent of the aid given in the Second FYP (compared to 20 per cent in the First FYP), and foreign private finance will make up only 31 per cent of the foreign capital used by parastatals as opposed to 78 per cent in the First FYP. The amount of foreign financing will not be less. In fact, in absolute terms it will have doubled. In relative terms it will remain virtually unchanged. If the pipeline, the road-service and railway to Zambia are excluded, 51 per cent of parastatal investment was foreign financed in the First FYP versus an expected 48 per cent in the Second FYP. If the Zambian projects are included in both plans, the degree of foreign financing is still constant in relative terms (66 per cent in the First FYP versus 66 per cent in the Second FYP), but the amount of foreign financing will have quadrupled.

The relative constancy of the share of foreign financing reflects not only the growing inflow of foreign capital, but the increasing ability of the economy to generate local resources. One could well have expected the doctrine of self-reliance to have been so self-nullifying (in the sense that it made Tanzania attractive to both private and public foreign capital) that the degree of foreign financing would have actually increased in the post-Arusha period. This did not happen because the doctrine of self-reliance and the Arusha Declaration had implications for the availability of local resources. Domestic sources of funds climbed rapidly after the nationalizations (at an annual rate of 30 per cent per year from 1965-6 to 1970-71) when the government gained control of the banking system. The stopping of the foreign drain on savings which characterized foreign ownership of the banks, and the ability to use central bank financing of government spending allowed government resources to grow almost as quickly as foreign resources.

After 1970-71 there is a significant fall in government local resources. Much of the initial surplus funds in the banking system had been used up, and the foreign exchange problems of the country made the government cautious about excessive money supply creation. By 1973-4 the world-wide commodity price boom, and the heavy inflow of foreign aid to Tanzania had so improved the foreign exchange position of the country that the government was prepared to once again play an expansionary role.

In recent years the newly-created parastatal sector has also become an important source of finance. In the First FYP, parastatals contributed only 12 per cent of the finance for their investments. In the Second FYP this figure is expected to more than double to 28 per cent. While the performance of parastatals has not been as impressive as originally hoped (see chapter four), their creation has given the public sector an inportant new source of finance. Resources available for re-investment (profits plus depreciation allowance) rose from shs 118 million in 1966 to shs 553 million in 1971. These resources are not, however, spread evenly among all parastatals, and cannot always be used in the way the government would prefer. There are then, restraints imposed by the type of finance on the type of investment which can be initiated. Let us look at these in more detail.

EFFECT OF TYPE OF FINANCE ON TYPE OF INVESTMENT

Local resources

The rise in resources generated by the parastatal sector has not increased the ability of the government to initiate new projects as much as had been hoped. Not all parastatal funds are available to the government. There are both legal and political limitations on the use that can be made of these funds.

The parastatal sector has, as I showed in chapter four, evolved gradually. As a result, the organization of the sector tends to reflect pre-Arusha goals, rather than the goals of a country firmly committed to socialism. Parastatals are quite autonomous institutions. Control by their parent ministries is often slight. No established mechanism exists for the government to gain control over their surpluses other than by taxation, or dividend payments. Moreover supervision of their investment plans, and their operating expenditure, is haphazard.

The central planning ministry has attempted to rectify this situation by insisting that all investment plans be approved by it, and that surpluses be theoretically regarded as available for disposition anywhere in the economy. These attempts at greater central control have been partially thwarted by a number of factors.

First, the existence of a large number of firms which are jointly owned by the government and private enterprise imposes legal restrictions on the use of surpluses generated by these parastatals. The government is simply unable to demand the entire surplus of this type of company.[5] There are a significant number of these types of firms, especially in the manufacturing sector, and their contribution to parastatal surplus generation is important.

Secondly, there are real institutional problems involved in trying to control parastatals even if they are 100 per cent government owned. As I have said, the parastatals currently enjoy a great deal of autonomy. The central planning ministry does not have the manpower to effectively scrutinize parastatal operations. This lack of manpower causes the ministry then, to concentrate its attention on parastatals which are doing badly rather than on those which are doing well. It therefore becomes difficult to tell a parastatal which is earning large profits and can finance projects on its own not to go ahead with a scheme. The parastatal seems successful, and the planning ministry has usually not had time to fully research the project. Surplus-generating parastatals are largely left alone. As a result their surpluses are not tapped significantly, and bad projects (e.g., the bakery by NMC, see chapter five) can be initiated by them.

These problems associated with the current organization of parastatals are made worse by the concentration of surpluses in a few sectors, and a few companies. Table 84 shows the amount of surplus available for investment in each sector. Agriculture has only 1 per cent of the parastatal surplus, and must rely upon the government and foreign aid for its finance. In contrast, the commerce sector generates a great deal of surplus, far more than the government would probably want to invest in that sector.

---

5 A short anecdote may serve to illustrate this point. Tanzania Breweries has been planning to build a new brewery in Mwanza for several years. One day when the president was visiting his village he was interviewed by a *Daily News* reporter. The president was quoted as saying that he thought it absurd to be building a new brewery when most people drank pombe, and the country could not even afford to give them decent water. Taking this cue Devplan told NDC to stop plans for the brewery and give the funds to be used to Devplan for use in other areas. After a small fight NDC won when it became clear that the government would be entitled to only a small share of the funds generated by the brewery. Legally the government owned only 50 per cent of the profits of the company. The other 50 per cent plus the depreciation allowances could not be taken away from the company without a change in the law, a change which would affect all joint enterprises. Because of Tanzania's heavy reliance on this form of organization, the government was not ready at this stage to move to a whole new type of organization of parastatal sector.

TABLE 84

Parastatal surplus generation

Sector	Profits 1971 (shs million)	Depreciation allowance (shs million)	Total 1971 (shs million)	Share in total (%)
Agriculture	0.1	7.1	7.2	1
Mining	53.9	13.9	67.8	12
Manufacturing	99.3	45.6	144.9	26
Construction	1.4	4.1	5.5	1
Electricity	32.7	14.7	47.4	9
Commerce	105.4	13.3	118.7	21
Transport	46.3	11.9	58.2	11
Finance	97.6	8.2	105.8	19
Total	436.7	118.8	555.5	100

The sectoral concentration of surplus is exacerbated by the dominance of a few firms in each sector. The manufacturing sector generates only 26 per cent of parastatal surplus, significantly less than the priority this sector holds in the government's strategy. Even this surplus is not available, however, to use to develop new industries. Three firms earn 73 per cent of the profits in the manufacturing sector, and generate 60 per cent of the surplus. Two of these, T. Breweries and British-American Tobacco are only partially government owned. They generate 50 per cent of the manufacturing surplus. Similarly, one firm earns 95 per cent of the surplus in mining, and two marketing boards generate 30 per cent of the surplus in commerce. The finance sector is essentially made up of three firms — the central bank, the commercial bank, and the insurance company.

The solution to these problems may appear obvious — end all joint ventures and institute a system whereby all surpluses are automatically centralized, and then re-allocated. The Tanzanians have not implemented this solution for several reasons. They continue to regard joint ventures as necessary in order to obtain foreign technology and manpower. Partial ownership by the foreign partner supposedly gives him greater incentive to make the company work. Centralization of funds has been rejected because of a deep-felt belief by many Tanzanians that decentralized organizations work better. Such central control would destroy the ability of the corporation to act innovatively. Moreover, there is simply not the skilled manpower yet in Tanzania to run a centralized planning system. Significant centralization at this stage would probably have an important efficiency cost.

There are, however, measures which can be taken to improve the present system. At present the local portion of the development budget can grow only as quickly as the money supply plus the small increase which takes place in the surplus available from financial institutions. The share of the surplus taken from these savings institutions by the government cannot grow much larger. This limit on the growth of the local resources available to the government limits the flexibility of public investment. It is important to create a mechanism which would give the local development budget a more dynamic source of growth. Such a mechanism might be a special tax on corporations specifically ear-marked for the development budget. This would draw off some of surplus of the profit-earning corporations, but at the same time would not involve complete central-ization of the budget.

Control over surplus-earning corporations could also be improved without a great increase in manpower. If the investment strategy were made more explicit, and crude indicators of adherence to this strategy adopted, then fewer bad projects would result. This would occur because the parastatals would have a better idea of what projects were desirable, and the central planning ministry would have easy measures by which to judge projects. I will develop these ideas further in chapter nine.

Foreign finance

There has always been a great deal of criticism on the left of the distortive effects of foreign finance, both private finance and foreign aid. These criticisms, we shall see in chapter eight, are echoed by many people in Tanzania. It is worthwhile, then, to detail, as much as possible, the impact of foreign financing on Tanzanian development. Let us first review the general criticisms made of this type of finance.

Foreign finance can distort investment choices in capitalist countries because foreign firms may choose to develop the wrong types of products, e.g., high-income consumption goods, and may pre-empt the long-term development of local industries. In a country like Tanzania these distortive effects are minimized by public ownership. Foreign investors do not enter the economy without the agreement and encouragement of the government. Nevertheless, foreign firms do encourage projects in only certain specific areas. Parastatals are constantly being offered deals with international suppliers. Because these suppliers tend to pro-duce products geared to developed capitalist economies, these suppliers encour-age the development of industries which may not be appropriate for Tanzania's stage of development. A certain asymmetry tends to result. A parastatal can take an offer of a relatively easily-implemented project in a less desirable area or try to work up one of its own. Because of the shortage of manpower, there is a strong tendency to choose the project which can be most easily implemented.

Thus, when NDC is faced with a choice of either trying to develop small-scale industries, or build a detergent factory, it has traditionally chosen to push the detergent factory. Why? The management is anxious to show success. Lever Brothers will come and erect a detergent factory in a year (as they have done in Kenya and Zambia). Despite the poor economics of such a project from a developmental point of view, NDC appears more successful than if it had spent the year trying to organize Ujamaa village work shops.

Foreign finance has also been regarded as involving a distortion of factor choice. Because most finance comes from developed nations, and involves the importation of capital equipment, the technology employed corresponds to the factor proportions of the developed nation, not the poor nation. Recently, however, this view has come under increasing attack. The ILO study of Kenya found that within a given industry multinational firms were less capital intensive than local firms. Their explanation was that the multinational had better management, and could handle the manpower problems involved in using labour-intensive methods (ILO, 1972, 185). Other factors probably also help to make a multinational more labour intensive than local firms. Multinationals often have access to second-hand equipment (their own) which local entrepreneurs do not. They have a broader knowledge of the technology available in the world, whereas local entrepreneurs often know only a few suppliers.

Multinationals are, however, more capital intensive because they concentrate on more capital-intensive sectors. They can, then, have a distorting effect, as mentioned before, on factor proportions by drawing investment into capital-intensive sectors.[6] Foreign aid can act much the same way. Given that most aid is tied (even World Bank aid is tied to member countries), it works in the same way as private foreign loans. There is, however, one difference. Foreign aid can, in many cases, be much cheaper than suppliers' credits. In fact aid from rich countries may be less capital intensive than aid from poorer countries because of this difference in cost.

Canadian loans, for example, are given at a zero rate of interest with 10 years grace and 50 years to repay. Suppose the Canadians gave Tanzania a shs 40 million loan. The present value of such a loan, discounted at 10 per cent, would be about shs 3.8 million. Now if the Tanzanians borrowed from the Indians or the Soviets, the loan would be usually on terms of no years grace, 7 years to

6 Multinationals can distort factor choices by distorting the whole environment in which choice is made. By raising the level of the quality of the goods available, and by increasing the emphasis on product differentiation, multinationals force all industries to imitate western standards, standards not appropriate to very poor countries such as Tanzania.

repay, and 7 per cent interest. On these terms, the total cost of the Indian or Soviet project would have to be shs 4.3 million, about 10 per cent of the Canadian loan, to give an equivalent present value. Thus the capital intensity of a Canadian project, in terms of the cost of capital, may be much less than more 'labour-intensive' Indian project.

This argument must be modified to take into account the other costs involved in a project. Capital-intensive projects often involve higher local costs absorbed by the Tanzanians. Thus, in the case of the bakery unit (see chapter five), the Canadian loan was for only shs 25 million, the equipment proportion of the project. The equipment necessitated the construction of a shs 10 million build-ing, an extraordinarily expensive building for Tanzania. Even if the terms of the Canadian loan are taken into account, the depreciated value of the project is about shs 8.5 million (undepreciated value shs 12.4 million) giving a capital/labour ratio of shs 100,000 (using depreciated assets[7]) which is almost six times the average for private bakeries. Also capital-intensive projects often involve more import-intensive operating costs which decrease their value to the economy.

The lack of people able to develop good projects, and the availability of foreign finance and technology in a single package encourages the development of large-scale, capital-intensive projects. In many respects the role of inter-national finance, both private and public, has been to allow Tanzania to carry out projects which it simply never could have done otherwise, not so much because of lack of capital, but because of lack of expertise to develop or run the project. In my view, therefore, some of the projects should not have been carried out. Those which require a turn-key approach are the very projects which use the least Tanzanian resources, and employ the most advanced techniques, and develop the most elite type of labour force. They are the exact opposite of projects which should come out of a philosophy of self-reliance.[8]

---

7 The undepreciated capital/labour ratio is shs 146,000, more than Portland Cement.

8 Several examples of this type of distortion can be given in order to illustrate the point. In chapter nine I will outline three projects often advocated by those who would like to 'transform' the Tanzanian economy. They are: an iron/steel complex, an electricity/ aluminum complex, and a petroleum/chemical complex. All of these projects are beyond the current capacities of Tanzanians to develop. They involve the importation, on a long-term basis, of large numbers of expatriate personnel. No one in Tanzania, in fact, has the ability to adequately evaluate these projects, or supervise their develop-ment. Foreign consultants will be used for this. These types of projects do not develop the Tanzanian ability to initiate and develop other projects. The Tanzanians remain observers of the whole process. The purely economic returns of such projects should be extraordinary before they are initiated.

Foreign aid probably has a distortive effect on ministries' programmes as well. Because foreign aid usually involves the importation of a large number of technical personnel, the country is swamped with people who are generally, in the case of capitalist aid, suspicious of socialism. Aid donors are often skeptical of the Ujamaa village programme,[9] and try to undermine it. Aid also has an important demonstration effect. The presence of highly-paid western-oriented technical personnel makes it difficult for a value shift in the urban elite to occur.

Aid also has the potential to distort investment by drawing off local resources in areas not considered to be the main priorities. Aid donors do not usually provide 100 per cent of the cost of programmes. Usually they give two-thirds of the cost, although many now pay three-quarters or even eighty per cent of the cost. The Tanzanians are put in the position that one shilling allocated to an area selected by the donor can yield three shillings worth of investment, while the shilling put in an area not desired by the donor yields only a shilling's worth of investment. If local funds are scarce, and aid donors' preferences do not correspond to those of the recipient country's preferences, then there can be a distortion of priorities.[10]

In Tanzania, aid donors have distorted the choices in this way but to only a limited extent. The very large presence of aid from Nordic countries, some of the more progressive donors in the world, and the clear Tanzania ideology, which has attracted progressive elements in aid donors not noted for their generally progressive attitudes, i.e., World Bank, US, and Canada, has produced an aid programme which is mixed in its effect. Thus, in general, aid has not been urban oriented. We saw how it was aid which provided the impetus to the shift in the water and health programmes. As the country's policies on these programmes began to change, aid provided an important mechanism to speed up the shift. Thus in the First FYP aid was concentrated initially in urban water, not rural. With the Arusha Declaration and the beginning of significant Swedish aid the shift to rural water was made (see Table 85). Similarly aid tended to concentrate on urban health programmes until recently. Aid's effect was basically negative, reinforcing an indigenous tendency to stress high-cost quality care. Foreign personnel were, however, prominent in the fight to switch the policy of the ministry to a more rural oriented programme, and foreign aid, by backing the change with resources, was instrumental in making the switch possible.

9 Many aid donors were attracted by Tanzania's emphasis on rural development, but are sceptical of basing such development on socialist villages.
10 Aid should release local funds for other areas. This may or may not be the case. The attraction of aid is such that a country may end up spending more in terms of even local funds in the area of the aid donor's priority than it originally intended.

TABLE 85

Aid to water (shs)

	1964-5	1965-6	1966-7	1967-8	1968-9	1969-70	1970-71	1971-2	1972-3	1973-4
Rural water	NA	2	1	3	20	16	22	26	30	47
Urban water	NA	11	2	13	–	–	–	–	5	76

Foreign aid has played a less positive role in education. Aid to primary education has been non-existent. Donors have, instead, concentrated on secondary, technical, and university education. They have continued to encourage the development of very elitist, high-cost schools. Only in the last few years has some shift in aid occurred. Sweden now contributes to the adult literacy campaign, and the World Bank is considering an adult education programme. Nevertheless, aid still goes overwhelmingly to post-primary education.

Foreign aid has also tended to reinforce the Tanzanian emphasis on large infrastructural projects. In early years the Chinese were the only major supporters of directly productive activities. Aid from other sources concentrated on roads and aerodromes, electricity and education. In 1969-70, with the building of the road to Zambia, this tendency reached its peak. In that year only 6 per cent of aid went to directly productive projects, none went to health, and 10 per cent went to rural water. In contrast, 72 per cent went to roads, aerodromes, and electricity. Since that time, aid has become less concentrated. By 1973-4, 25 per cent of aid will go to directly productive projects, 5 per cent to health, and 5 per cent to rural water, while 26 per cent will go to roads, aerodromes, and electricity.

The Tanzanians have, of course, been very sensitive to the issue of foreign aid. Nyerere has tended to view the problem as one of maintaining the country's foreign political stance as neutral, rather than worrying about the more subtle distortive effects of any type of aid. There has been, therefore, an effort made to diversify the sources of aid. This has been quite successful, although there has been no significant shift away from a reliance on capitalist nations. Table 86 shows the source of aid for the two plan periods. At independence almost all aid came from Britain. By the beginning of the First FYP British aid was less than twenty per cent of the total, and by 1968-9 had ceased altogether. Now Tanzania draws its aid from a host of countries and is not at the mercy of any one donor.

Tanzania continues, however, to remain dependent on western capitalist countries for its aid. The East European socialist countries have contributed no

TABLE 86

Source of aid (direct and recorded) (shs million)

	1964-5	1965-6	1966-7	1967-8	1968-9	Total/Share 1964-8	1969-70	1970-71	1971-2	1972-3	1973-4	Total/Share 1969-73	Total/Share 1964-73
Britain	19	14	7	8	–	48 (7)	–	–	–	–	–	–	48 (1)
United States	20	30	22	23	61	158 (22)	16	41	55	24	75	211 (6)	369 (9)
IDA/IBRD	13	19	43	36	56	167 (24)	58	82	86	194	84	504 (14)	671 (15)
Canada	–	–	1	9	2	12 (2)	4	6	14	40	138	202 (6)	214 (5)
Nordic	11	13	14	20	29	87 (12)	58	83	94	179	373	787 (21)	874 (20)
Germany	14	8	8	1	19	50 (7)	35	35	40	31	85	226 (6)	276 (6)
Israel	8	2	–	–	–	10 (1)	–	–	–	–	–	–	10 (–)
USSR and others	–	–	1	–	–	1 (–)	5	3	3	10	7	28 (1)	29 (1)
China	6	–	20	43	8	77 (11)	–	185	325	363	381	1254 (34)	1331 (31)
Others	6	22	29	22	20	99 (14)	42	91	122	60	118	433 (12)	532 (12)
Total	97	108	145	162	197	709	218	526	739	901	1261	3645	4354

significant aid to Tanzania. Even if personnel were counted, their aid would be insignificant. Chinese aid is dominated by Tazara. Initially the Chinese started a cattle ranch, which they still run, and an irrigation scheme. They have built the Urafiki Textile Mill (shs 60 million) and the Ubungo Farm Implements Factory (shs 5 million) and are now building a pharmaceutical factory (Chinese contribution about shs 6 million). They had also a number of smaller projects involving personnel, especially in health. These projects account for shs 77 million of Chinese aid up to the end of 1972/73. The rest of the aid went to Tazara.

There have been major shifts in the source of aid from the capitalist world. These shifts reflect a move primarily from the central capitalist powers, to more peripheral ones which have stronger social democratic traditions. The most important of these are the Nordic countries. In the Second FYP, they will have contributed 28 per cent of non-Tazara aid. In contrast the share of the United States dropped from 22 to 9 per cent.

Foreign financing, then, has had both good and bad effects on Tanzanian development. In general the negative effects have tended to be rather subtle ones, rather than the result of crude attempts to distort preferences. The type of financing available, both local and foreign, does go part way towards explaining the pattern of public investment which has emerged in Tanzania. In the next chapter I will try to trace out the other factors affecting the pattern.

DISTRIBUTIONAL ASPECTS OF FINANCING

There are essentially five sources of funds for public investment: local government budget, foreign aid, foreign borrowing by parastatals, parastatal self-generated funds, and local borrowing. As I said earlier I have no breakdown of parastatal self-generated funds and local borrowing.[11] Table 87 shows the breakdown of these sources of funds in each of the plan periods.

In this section I would like to analyse these sources of funds in terms of the distribution of the burden of investment between the rural and urban areas. A rigorous analysis of this issue would involve a major study. My attempt here is simply to provide a rough estimate of the distribution of the burden over time. I do this essentially so that I can argue that the source of finance, for distributional purposes, can be ignored. The shifts in sources of finance, in terms of the distributional issue, have not been so significant that any of the conclusions drawn from an analysis of public investment alone is invalidated. Moreover, the

11 Until recent years, the CSB figures indicated that about one-third of these funds were borrowed and two-thirds self-generated. In the last two years CSB shows a dramatic increase in borrowing. Since this rise is probably the result of STC's use of overdraft to finance inventory, it should probably be discounted. See Tanzania (1972a, 6).

TABLE 87

Sources of funds for public investment (%)

	First FYP	Second FYP		Both plans[1]	
		Incl. Tazara	Excl. Tazara	Incl. Tazara	Excl. Tazara
Government contribution of local funds	44	33	40	36	41
Foreign aid	30	50	40	45	37
Foreign borrowing parastatals	21	6	7	10	11
Local resources raised by parastatals	5	11	13	9	11
Total	100	100	100	100	100

1 Includes estimates for 1972-73 and 1973-74

bulk of the burden of public investment falls on the rural areas. This fact reflects the overwhelming importance of the rural sector in the economy. It will be a long time before the urban areas will be developed to the point where they finance the development of the rural areas. The current burden on the urban areas in Tanzania probably cannot be markedly increased. One can, then, focus attention on investment strategy as the critical element in development strategy and assume that the financing of that strategy, in distributional terms, is not important. The reader who wishes to accept this conclusion can probably skip this section and go to the next chapter. What follows is a detailed analysis of the distributional implications of each source of finance.

Foreign aid and foreign borrowing by parastatals can be grouped together for the purpose of discussing the distributional aspects of the financing of investment. Both are essentially loans, and depend upon the ability of the country to generate foreign exchange in the future. Recently an increasing proportion of foreign aid has come in grant form, but the overwhelming share is still loans. The relative dependence on foreign borrowing has not altered significantly over time.

The burden of these loans falls on the country as a whole. If one was to try to assign a distribution to this burden, the overwhelming proportion would be on the rural areas, those which generate most of the foreign exchange. Nevertheless their share would not be any more than their share in the population, and probably somewhat less.[12] It seems fair to say that there is no important

12 Services and diamond exports, both non-rural activities, are major foreign exchange earners.

distributional implication of foreign borrowing other than the fact that the burden is distributed according to the population.

The second major source of funds is the government's contribution of local resources. This share has been falling slowly over time as local resources raised by parastatals has increased. Table 88 sets out the financing of the local resources of the government development budget.

The local portion of the government development budget is financed mainly by borrowing, and only to a limited extent by taxation. Although tax revenue has been very buoyant, growing from 11.9 per cent of GDP in 1962 to 22.2 per cent in 1972-3 (Tanzania, *Hali Ya Uchumi,* 1973-4, 5, 34), recurrent expenditures have also grown quite quickly, at an annual rate of about 13 per cent. The amount of resources left over to finance the development budget has, therefore, remained constant in absolute terms, and fallen in relative terms as the development budget has grown.

It may be argued that this division between recurrent revenue and development revenue is artificial, and it is therefore important to have an understanding of the impact of taxation, even if only a small share of this tax revenue goes toward development. There has been only a little work done on the distributional impact of taxation in Tanzania, but it points to the conclusion that significant advances have been made towards increasing the burden of taxation on the urban well-to-do versus the urban poor.[13]

---

13 See Loxley, 'The Finance of Government Spending in Tanzania Since Independence' (TIB n.d.), and M.A. Bienefeld, 'Planning People' (Uchumi Editorial Board, 1972). In that article, Bienefeld concludes: 'Thus by the middle of 1968 the Government had come to grips with the problem of income distribution. Though more remained to be done, it had done more than any other modern Government, bar some where old structures had been smashed by violent revolution. As a result of these actions salary differentials have been reduced dramatically. In terms of gross salaries, before tax, the ratio of the highest salary in the country to that of the starting labourer is now 22:1, while a more reasonable comparison of the starting point of the highest scale with the starting point of the lowest scale produces a ratio of 14:1. When one takes into account the graduated income tax these two ratios fall to 14:1 and 9:1 respectively. Inclusion of fringe benefits would widen them slightly.

In addition there have been other measures which by general agreement have further narrowed real differentials. Chief among these have been various indirect tax measures that have contributed substantially to the steep rise of prices for luxury and non-essential goods. Since the prices of goods consumed by the upper income group have increased faster than average, their real incomes have fallen relative to the real incomes of the other groups.'

See also I.M. Kaduma and I.R. Modi, 'Tax Reform Planning in the United Republic of Tanzania,' quoted in TIB (n.d., 24).

TABLE 88

Financing of the local resources of the government development budget

	First FYP (%)	Second FYP (%)	Both plans (%)
Taxation	26	13	17
Bank borrowing	} 54	49 } 81	72
Non-bank borrowing		32	
Other	20	6	11
Total	100	100	100

TABLE 89

Estimate of percentage of incomes paid in tax

	Direct	Indirect	Other	Total
Rural incomes	2.0	8.5	1.6	12.1
Urban incomes total	11.0	21.0	3.5	35.1
Of which incomes over				
shs 12,000 p.a.	17.5	18.6	5.0	41.1
Shs 3600-12,000 p.a.	5.0	25.1	2.0	32.1
Shs 1800-3600 p.a.	1.0	22.2	0.8	24.0
Below shs 1800	–	17.0	0.5	17.5
National average	6.0	14.0	2.5	22.5

SOURCE: Kaduma I.M. and I.R. Modi, 'Tax Reform Planning in the United Republic of Tanzania,' 1970 + (quoted in TIB, n.d., 24)

There is less evidence on the impact of taxation on rural incomes versus urban incomes. In 1969, I.M. Kaduma and I.R. Modi did a study estimating the percentage of incomes going to taxes for different groups. Their results are shown in Table 89. They found that urban workers paid almost three times the proportion of their incomes in taxes as rural inhabitants. If their figures are correct, taxes probably come in absolute terms about equally from the urban areas as from rural areas.[14] There is, however, no indication of the trend over time of this distribution. Since the main source of tax revenue from the rural areas is indirect taxes, a proxy of their relative tax burden would probably be the importance of indirect taxes in total revenue. The share has remained virtually constant since

14 Calculated by applying the rate of tax of urban workers (35.1 per cent) to the urban wage bill in 1971 yielding a revenue of shs 507 million, and the rate of rural workers (12.1 per cent) to the rural wage bill, yielding a revenue of shs 461 million. The rural wage bill was estimated at shs 3.8 billion, or the economically-active population in the rural areas, times the average rural income (shs 730), plus the wage bill of agriculture estates.

independence[15] indicating no trend to increase the use of urban-biased taxes to raise revenue. Nevertheless, the tax burden is disproportionately borne by the urban areas, and this fact must be noted in assessing the over-all impact of public spending.

The absolute and relative increase in the share of government development revenue coming from borrowing is explained by several factors. First, the nationalizations stopped the outflow of capital via the banks and the insurance companies, and insured that savings would be devoted to investments in Tanzania. Secondly, government control of the savings institutions has increased the share of the loans by these institutions which have gone to public institutions, and to government in particular. Thirdly, the development of a national central bank has allowed the government to use money supply creation as a method of raising revenue.

According to neo-classical welfare theory, borrowing is voluntary and rewarded by interest payments. We do not have to be as concerned about the distributional aspects of such investment. This approach is rejected by many development economists. Savings diverted from one region or area to finance development in another, even if these savings are rewarded by interest payments, may be a form of exploitation. The decision to invest the savings in the other region may not be economically beneficial in the long-run, but may rather reflect short-run considerations or rigidities in the investment decision-making institutions. Development economists generally do want to consider the issue of the source of savings lent by financial institutions.

Non-bank savings are essentially urban savings. I estimate that about 88 per cent of these savings come from the urban areas.[16] Bank lending comes from two sources. About half of the bank loans to the government have come from the

15 See various issues of Tanzania, *Annual Economic Surveys*. Direct taxes have always made up about 25 per cent of total tax revenue.

16 The most important source is the provident funds. These contributed 62 per cent of non-bank lending to the government in the period 1969-70 to 1971-2, and are supposed to contribute 68 per cent in 1973-4. These are essentially urban savings. Sinking funds of the government are the second largest non-bank lender, contributing 18 per cent of the funds in the period 1969-70 to 1971-2. These funds are surplus taxes, and therefore can be regarded as having the same distributional characteristics as taxes. The next largest source is the insurance company, NIC, which should contribute 10 per cent in these years, and represents an urban savings source. The East African Community, the post office savings bank, and private individuals are the other sources. The Community can be treated the same as taxes, the post office bank probably gets about half its savings from the rural areas, and private individuals are probably exclusively urban. The urban share, then, represents the sum of the provident fund (62 per cent), half the sinking funds (9 per cent), the insurance company (10 per cent), half the Community (35 per cent), half the post office bank (2 per cent) and all of individual savings (1 per cent).

Bank of Tanzania.[17] This reflects money supply creation, and involves no burden on any particular group. The distribution of the burden of inflation depends upon which type of goods rises fastest in price. I will assume that the burden is distributed according to incomes, which means about 60 per cent falls on the rural and 40 per cent on the urban areas. Commercial bank lending represents essentially urban-generated savings. I have estimated that about 68 per cent of their deposits are from urban savings.[18]

The only other source of funds for the development budget are internal grants by domestic charitable organizations. In fact, many are really foreign institutions established in Tanzania. Their grants entail no burden on a particular group.

It is possible to summarize this discussion on the financing of the government budget in the following way. The share of taxes in government development revenue has been relatively small, and falling. In the First FYP it was 26 per cent of government revenue, and in the Second FYP only 13 per cent. Over-all, the sources of these taxes has probably not changed over time in terms of urban/ rural distribution, but the burden on the urban well-to-do has increased. About half the tax revenue comes from the urban areas, and half from the rural areas. Most government revenue has come from borrowing. If we assume savers are adequately rewarded by interest payments, then we can ignore borrowing. If we assume this is not true, then we must assign most of this burden to the urban areas, excluding only the share borrowed from the Bank of Tanzania of which only 40 per cent falls on the urban areas. Over-all, then, the urban areas absorbed about 13 per cent of the burden of government development revenues (compared to their share of 6 per cent of the population) if voluntary borrowing is assigned according to source of savings. The increased reliance on borrowing (essentially a reliance on urban savings) has increased the burden of government finance on urban areas over time.

17 This is based upon a comparison in the increase of government assets of the Bank of Tanzania and the commercial bank. See Bank of Tanzania, *Economic and Operations Report* (Dec. 1972, Tables 1, 16).

18 The source of commercial bank deposits, and the origin of the savings as I have assigned them are as follows: central government, 20 per cent of savings, and 50 per cent urban as in taxes; local government, 2 per cent of savings and 50 per cent urban; East African Community, 6 per cent of savings and 50 per cent urban; foreign deposits, 3 per cent of savings and 6 per cent urban according to share in population; public enterprises, 17 per cent of savings, and 15 per cent rural according to share of agriculture enterprises and marketing boards in parastatal profits; and private deposits, 52 per cent of deposits, and 75 per cent urban, equal to share of non-agriculture sector in monetary economy. See Bank of Tanzania, *Economic and Operations Report* (Dec. 1971, Table 15).

The other two sources of funds for public investment are local borrowing by parastatals, and self-generated parastatal funds. Parastatal borrowing is mainly from the banking system, and can be assigned an urban bias equal to the share of non-agircultural parastatal assets in total parastatal assets (91 per cent). Over the two Plans, self-generated funds contributed somewhat more than borrowing (see n. 18). In the First FYP local borrowing was probably more important, and in the Second, self-generated funds more important.

What, then, can be said in total about the burden of financing public investment? Over-all the urban sector has contributed disproportionately to public investment. This share, however, has not altered significantly over time. If we assume that savings taken from the urban sector represent a burden, then the urban sector contributed 30 per cent of the funds in the First FYP, and 31 per cent in Second FYP, including Tazara, and 35 per cent excluding it. (Table 90 shows the urban share using the different criteria.) If we assign borrowing a national burden, then there has been a slight increase in the urban burden, but the share is much less. The urban burden was 13 per cent in the First FYP and 16 per cent in the Second FYP (18 per cent excluding Tazara).

Now one must be careful about the conclusion that one draws from this type of analysis. There is no reason to assume that investment ought to be distributed according to the burden of raising the funds. In fact one of the chief advantages of public ownership is that it increases the ability of the government to shift the allocation of funds from one sector to another. Nevertheless, it is important to have an idea of the source of investment funds in assessing the over-all impact of a government programme. Knowledge of the burden of finance gives us a basis to judge the distribution of the benefits of public investment. Over-all, the disproportionate share of the investment has gone to encourage urban development. If we use the over-all urban/rural index described in chapters three and four as a proxy, then 45 per cent of public investment has gone towards urban development in the period 1964-73 (excluding Tazara). Thus the urban areas have received an allocation of investment considerably above the burden in raising these funds. They have received about half the investment, while having only 6 per cent of the population and contributing 34 per cent of the funds.

In chapters three, four, and five, I showed that the investment programme has shifted to the rural regions only in selected areas. Over-all, in fact, the trend has been toward an increased urban bias. The urban/rural index showed an allocation of 36 per cent of investment to urban development in the First FYP, versus 49 per cent in the Second FYP. If this shift had been accompanied by a dramatic shift in the burden of finance from the rural areas to the urban areas, one would be less disturbed than when one notes that no significant shift has occurred.

TABLE 90

Urban contribution to public investment funds (%)

	First FYP	Second FYP[1]		Both plans[1]	
		Incl. Tazara	Excl. Tazara	Incl. Tazara	Excl. Tazara
Taxation only a burden	13	16	18	15	16
Borrowing and taxation a burden	30	31	35	31	34

1 Includes estimates for 1972-73 and 1973-74

This lack of shift in the burden of finance is not really surprising. The urban sector in Tanzania is not large enough yet to finance its own expansion. Indeed any development programme for the country will probably involve some transfer of surplus from the rural areas to the urban. The real question, and the one we will pursue in chapters eight and nine is how great a discrepancy between the burden and benefits of investment is wise both politically and economically.

7

Explanations for pattern of investment

INTRODUCTION

We are now in a position where we can provide an overview of what has happened in Tanzania in the last ten years, and to deal more explicitly with why it has occurred. We saw in chapter two that the president's early commitment to equality was gradually translated into a more explicit ideology which could be summarized as self-reliant, rural socialism. Rural development and more particularly agricultural development centered on Ujamaa villages was to be the basis of growth. Urban areas and investment in industry were to receive lower priority. While foreign finance was not to be rejected, it should not be depended upon, or regarded as essential to development. The people must use their own resources, specifically the land and their labour, to improve their welfare.

Chapter three reviewed the pattern of ministerial development expenditure. I showed that there was a qualitative shift in spending in the rural areas away from an emphasis on capital-intensive settlement schemes to an emphasis on the Ujamaa village programme, but that the quantitative emphasis on rural development had not increased. In fact, spending on economic support programmes for rural areas was actually less, in relative terms, in the Second FYP, than in the First. In contrast, spending on rural social services and infrastructure rose significantly. Spending on primary education and literacy programmes rose from 9 per cent of the education budget to 29 per cent and on rural water from 19 per cent to 45 per cent. In health, the change has come much more slowly but in the last two years an important shift seems to have occurred. Spending on rural health centres and dispensaries will absorb 49 per cent of the health budget in 1973-4 compared to an average of 30 per cent in the First FYP. Thus the government was more effective in responding to the need to shift services, than to developing economic programmes for the rural areas.

In chapters four and five, I looked at the parastatal sector. In general I found only a few indications of adherence to the Arusha ideology and a few signs of the beginnings of a shift in policy. In manufacturing, the post-Arusha firms were characterized by large size, high capital intensity, extreme import intensity, and concentration in a few towns. The tourist sector consisted mainly of a number of expensive, loss-making luxury hotels. Most of the support sectors, especially commerce and electricity, continued to emphasize the urban areas. The financial sector decreased its emphasis on agricultural production, but did increase its support of marketing of agricultural products.

In chapter six, I showed that the proportion of foreign finance has not changed much, although its nature, source and direction has. In the First FYP 50 per cent of the development effort of ministries and parastatals was foreign financed. In the Second FYP 47 per cent will be foreign financed, if Tazara is excluded, and 56 per cent if it is included. The doctrine of self-reliance was self-nullifying in the sense that it made Tanzania more attractive for both private and public foreign capital. There has, then, been no major change in the degree of self-reliance in Tanzania.

The ideological switch to self-reliant rural socialism in Tanzania has resulted in only a partial switch in actual performance. In general, the switch has occurred least decisively in terms of economic development. Where it is necessary to switch the basic orientation of growth, the switch has not occurred. Why is this so? One could well turn around the question, and ask why a switch to socialism in Tanzania occurred at all. In many African countries there was, in the period after independence, an initial commitment to socialism. In almost all cases this commitment has meant very little in terms of actual performance. Yet this is not true for Tanzania. However disappointed one may be with the progress Tanzania has made towards reaching its goals, it has gone much further towards building socialism than most countries in Africa, and certainly further than any country in sub-Sahara Africa.

A good explanation of why Tanzania moved so far along toward socialism has not yet been written. When it is, a major factor explaining the post-independence developments in Tanzania will be the vacuum of political power which existed at the time of independence. In chapter two I tried to outline some of the dimensions of this vacuum, which I shall summarize here. Tanzania's lack of resources and less attractive climate discouraged heavy foreign involvement in the economy. Settlers were fewer than in neighbouring Kenya, and European businesses established there were often only subsidiaries of Kenyan branches. The stake of western imperialist forces, and especially of Britain, was therefore small. This relative lack of interest by Britain and its growing weariness of colonies meant that Britain gave Tanzania its independence almost without a struggle, and long before a strong political movement had developed in the colony.

The type of economic development which occurred in the colonial period did not produce strong political forces in the African population. Africans were largely excluded from the urban middle class because of the presence of the large Asian community. The slow growth of the urban sector meant that there was only a very small urban working force. Thus the African population committed to urban development, either as a middle class or a working class, was relatively small. Moreover, the use of migrant labour by the agricultural estates resulted in a rural work force which was not completely proletarized, but remained integrated into the rural subsistence economy.

The small elite which gained power at independence did not face, as a result of these factors, strong interest groups which effectively constrained their actions. They had in their choice of actions a much greater degree of freedom than did the elites in other countries. What also clearly distinguishes Tanzania from other countries is the use of that freedom by the elite. For whatever reasons, and I do not want to delve into them here, the elite chose to push Tanzania along a path of development quite different from that followed by its neighbours, one which would deny them many of the benefits which can accompany such power. It is important to understand that Tanzanian socialism in its initial stages was not a mass movement. It was a programme devised and implemented by the elite. It is only now that the elite has moved to build the commitment and involvement of the people in building socialism.

CLASS STRUCTURE

A familiarity with the historical context in which Tanzania became committed to socialism makes an understanding of the problems in implementing that commitment easier. What is clear in Tanzania is that the conversion to socialism occurred essentially at the top, indeed at the very top, and has not yet permeated the whole society. As a result there remain many anti-socialist forces in the society. Tanzania inherited and continues to function with a traditional British bureaucracy, with its emphasis on rules, formal qualifications, and hierarchical relations, which acts to impede any radical change. Moreover, the Tanzanians who man the bureaucracy were raised in a colonial system, and acquired colonial ideas. It would be surprising to expect them to lead a revolution.

It is precisely this point which several writers have made concerning the formation of health policy in Tanzania.[1] The top-level bureaucrats in the health

---

1 See Segall (Uchumi Editorial Board, 1972, 159) and Gish (1973a, 402), quoted in Chapter three, p. 000.

ministry for a long time thwarted attempts to switch policy. They did so for several reasons. First, their colonial education made them feel that 'good medicine' and sophisticated western medicine were equivalent. Thus attempts to reduce standards (and thus expand coverage) were resisted. Moreover, if Tanzania were to develop, this meant development of first-class facilities, equivalent to the best in the world, the opportunity cost of which is the failure to provide care of any type to the masses of the people. This same type of problem is evident in all sectors. Thus managers of parastatals often sought the most 'advanced' techniques in developing an industry. Using the labour-intensive techniques employed by local Asian entrepreneurs, or buying used equipment[2] which carries with it a technology now regarded as obsolete, does not seem to be moving ahead to those with traditional values.

The second reason for opposing change is self-interest. In the case of health policy the issue was quite clear cut. A major shift to a rural-oriented, preventive programme meant a drastic reduction in the health care of the elite. This is no trivial loss. To consciously deprive yourself of a standard of health care to which you are accustomed involves endangering your own life, and those of your family. This is a very difficult thing to do. Moreover, it is clear that the position of an educated Tanzanian would be maximized by rapid urban development. A truly rural-oriented development strategy would probably involve the diminution of many of the positions held by the elite. It is clear that such national parastatals as NDC, TTC, NAFCO, or NMC would cease to grow. The sense of power, or feelings of prestige which are derived from managing a rural industrialization programme (e.g., starting small shoe shops in Ujamaa villages) does not match that of being the general manager of NDC, for someone socialized in capitalist values. Is it then surprising that NDC, when given a choice, always opted for the large-scale urban-centred plant rather than rural-oriented programme?

The importance of the urban elite in derailing attempts at radical change has been emphasized by many writers, but most forceably by John Saul:

And it must be affirmed that, by and large, the elite has yet to engage itself *fully and effectively* in the task of socialist construction; its continuing lack of a realized capacity for *socialist creativity* remains a major constraint in Tanzania (Saul and Arrighi, 1973, 287-8, emphasis in original).

The ideological bent of much of the elite is particularly patent, a clear triumph for colonialism (and neocolonialism) in the cultural sphere, and crystalizes around such truisms as the 'necessity' of aid, the (unequivocal and

2 There are, however, very real problems with taking over old technologies from advanced countries, and we will discuss some of these later in the chapter.

neutral) 'superiority' of Western technology and management systems, the priority of 'efficiency,' narrowly and technocratically conceived, over radical risk and that release of human energies referred to as a possibility above (*ibid.*, 289-90).

... their [the elite's] role in the concrete articulation of Tanzania's socialism is, at least in the short run, absolutely crucial (*ibid.*, 287).

... the so-called vacuum is already partly filled by the brand of self-interest and cultural set which continues to mark many of Tanzania's own indigenous decision-makers and implementers even in the post-Arusha period. Since these attributes ... tend to be inimical to socialism, it remains a fact that the members of Tanzania's ruling petty bourgeoisie too often act as saboteurs (whether conscious or unconscious) of socialist effort at precisely the point where the task of socialist development presents its most subtle and intricate challenges (*ibid.*, 288).

It would be wrong, however, to centre only on the top part of the bureaucratic elite as the source of the problem. In some sense, this is the problem most easily solved. Already, it is clear that the president is gradually placing more ideologically committed people in top posts. The lack of socialist commitment extends throughout the government bureaucracy and society. Because of the lack of a revolution, there is no social force to drive the average person to give up personal gain for public good. Moreover, the failure to define more explicitly the ideology (a point to which I shall soon turn) leaves a vacuum in which rhetorical commitment to socialism can suffice. The education system has been slow to change, and appears to be moving slowest at the highest levels. Thus graduates from the university come through a system which reinforces a traditional self-centred view of the world. Moreover, little has been done to alter their values, to de-emphasize urban living and white-collar jobs as ultimate signs of success.

In analyzing Tanzania many writers point to the cuts in salaries and restrictions on imports as signs of elite commitment to socialism. There is no question that Tanzania stands out among countries of the world in the willingness of its leaders to forego some of the normal fruits of political power. But the sacrifice of the elite must be put into perspective if the political situation is to be fully understood. The reduction of privileges has meant only a reduction in privileges of positions, not in the welfare of individuals. Because of the rapid replacement of expatriates by Tanzanians, especially in government posts,[3] many Tanzanians have experienced very rapid promotion. Thus, from the individual's perspective,

3 In 1962, only 39 per cent of senior and middle-grade civil servants were citizens; by 1971, 91 per cent were citizens (Tanzania, Annual Economic Survey, 1971-2, 133).

although he may be moving to a position which no longer carries all the benefits held by its former expatriate holder, he is still improving his own welfare dramatically. We can get a sense of this movement by looking at the employment statistics. In 1966 there were 2960 male citizens in the public sector earning over shs 1000 a month. By 1969, this number had risen to 4082. In the private sector the increase was from 3095 in 1966 to 5525 in 1969. Thus, the size of the urban elite increased by more than 50 per cent between 1966 and 1969, an increase of 3552 positions. Many members of the urban elite are new to their privileges, and the fact that these privileges are reduced is not so significant.

The position of the incoming graduates from the universities is much different. They are entering a bureaucratic structure in which the period of very rapid mobility is almost over. Improvements in their welfare will have to come as much through increased benefits to the positions they hold, as from promotions. They do not enjoy the opportunity to exercise power and influence. Their lack of commitment to a real revolution, and their dissatisfaction with the rewards they are receiving pose a real threat to continued change. In some sense, the opposition of the elite was bought off through rapid promotions.[4] This is no longer possible with the new generation.[5] The next ten years may then be a very critical period. If the political forces pushing for adherence to the ideology expressed in the Arusha Declaration are weak, then this middle-level group, discontent with its position, will triumph. The result will not be a move away from socialism, in the sense of government ownership, but a move to a type of bureaucratic socialism with more significant income differentials, and an increased emphasis on urban areas.

Finally, a third group should not be ignored. Although Tanzania has, by comparison with many other Third World countries, a small urban work force, such a force does exist and is extremely powerful politically. In 1969 (the year for which we have the best breakdown of the data) there were 368,000 persons in wage employment of which 252,000 were in non-agricultural sectors. Of this latter group, some 9000 earned more than shs 1000 per month. These 9000 constitute the middle and upper echelons of the bureaucratic elite. The remaining 243,000 workers constitute the urban working force, the largest group of whom earned between shs 150 to shs 199 per month (Tanzania, *Statistical Abstract*, 1970, 180-81).

4 This view is exactly counter to the typical view expressed in Tanzania, that the elite has sacrificed.
5 Nyerere is not unaware of this problem, and he has made two moves to solve it. The age of retirement for government employees has been lowered from sixty-five to fifty-five, and voluntary retirement is now possible at forty-five. As well, the decentralization has opened up a whole new set of high-level positions to be filled.

TABLE 91

Growth of wages 1965-71 (%)

	All employed	Non-agricultural
All	63	52
Productive sector	78	65
Public sector	44	47

TABLE 92

Wage and productivity changes in certain sectors 1965-71 (%)

	Change in productivity	Change in wages	Parastatal rate of profit
Mining	24	120	20
Electricity	−11	75	8
Manufacturing	+11	66	13
Transport	37	44	13
Construction[1]	4	6	1

1 Because of the difficulty of including Tazara in 1970 and 1971, an average was taken for 1965-9 and extrapolated to 1971

These workers cannot be ignored. Economic policies have had to be distorted to appease them. Thus, the minimum wage has, like wages generally, risen rapidly. In the period 1965-71 (earlier data appear unreliable) the average wage rose 63 per cent, 78 per cent in the enterprise sector, and 44 per cent in the public sector (the enterprise sector includes parastatals). Because of the declining importance of agriculture, and the slower growth in agricultural wages, non-agricultural wages, i.e., the wages of the urban work force, on an average grew somewhat more slowly, 52 per cent in the period. Non-agricultural enterprise wages grew 47 per cent. These figures are presented in Table 91. Total GDP per capita in this period grew 35 per cent, and monetary GDP per capita grew 41 per cent. Thus, the urban work force has taken a larger share of total output.

In general, urban wages have risen much faster than productivity. Table 92 presents the data on productivity and wages in five key urban sectors. In every one, wage increases have out-stripped productivity, often by as much as five or six times. In general, wages have risen fastest in the most profitable sectors. We have tried to show this by giving the figures for rate of profit for parastatal firms, the only data available. In a purely socialist society, wages and productivity would not be related on a sectoral basis. If the society chooses to develop a capital-intensive industry, the workers, doing similar types of work in terms of difficulty as workers in labour-intensive industries, would not receive higher pay.

This is not true in Tanzania. Wages vary with the capital intensity (and thus productivity) and profitability of a firm. The average wage in Mwatex (as I showed in chapter five, section on textiles) is shs 5600 per year versus shs 4200 in Urafiki. Workers driving trucks for Urafiki earn less than drivers for Tanzania Breweries, a much more profitable enterprise. The average wage in Tanzanian Breweries is more than 40 per cent higher than the average wage in Kilimanjaro Breweries, which is much less capital intensive.

The urban work force has demonstrated its ability to gleen for itself the benefits of urban investment. This calls into question any strategy which advocates urban investment with the surplus creamed off for further investment, or for provision of rural social services. Capital-intensive investments serve to increase income inequalities, and to strengthen the political power of the urban work force by making it both larger and more critical. In doing so it must undermine any strategy based on rural development.

Finally, any analysis of the ideological base of socialism in Tanzania, and the role of classes, must not ignore the peasantry. The peasantry in Tanzania is neither socialist, nor yet politically very mobilized to defend its own interests. Thus while Tanzania has gone far, compared to many countries, in building a mass-based party, it is clear that there is much work to do. The rural sector appears yet to have no decisive voice in political events. Instead, it must rely upon the beneficence of a leader who feels strongly about the need to develop the rural areas. Yet this is clearly not sufficient to ensure a major switch in emphasis. A mobilized and influential peasantry is an important missing counterweight to the urban working force.

POLICY VACUUM

An explanation which centres only on class interests is not complete. The commitment to a redirection of the development effort was, and continues to be, made in Tanzania. While it is clear that Tanzania is not a China or a Cuba, there is also clear evidence that it is not a Kenya or a Nigeria. Its leaders have given up much. Many of the decision-makers are sincere in their efforts. Yet the progress is not all that one might have hoped. There seem to me to be a number of other forces which act to thwart a switch in priorities. These should be examined.

An equally important cause of the failure to implement a shift in policy is the gaps which exist in policy enunciation. The Arusha Declaration involved a high-level commitment to socialist ideals. The concrete interpretation of these ideals remained vague. Subsequent documents went only part way toward removing this ambiguity. Thus the 'Socialism and Rural Development' paper (see chapter two, p. 46) set out an explicit programme for agricultural development. Development should centre around non-capital-intensive Ujamaa villages. In general, this shift in policy has occurred. The paper 'Education for Self-Reliance' (see chapter two, p. 45) called for a specific change in the course content of primary education, and an increased emphasis on this line of education. While it is difficult to know how much the schools have actually changed, we do know that the emphasis on primary education has increased dramatically. Thus, in some instances where specific policy papers have been written, change has come.

I have shown throughout this study that the policy shifts have occurred more readily in the areas of social services than in the economic sphere. This tendency reflects the policy gap which exists in Tanzania. In the left, there is widespread agreement on the need to equalize the provision of government services. Thus, a failure to state explicitly that health and water facilities should be provided to the rural areas did not prevent the eventual shift in policy. The shift in health was certainly delayed because the top-level political commitment to rural health was absent, but progressive forces in the government eventually triumphed. No one could seriously dispute that a socialist society was committed to equalizing access to health facilities.

In the economic sphere, there is no universal agreement among socialists as to the correct strategy for development. In the next chapter I will look at the alternative paths advocated by different people, all socialists, for Tanzania. The divergence in view is rather immense. I will show that Nyerere's particular approach is a bit out of the mainstream of conventional socialist thinking. Thus, there was a greater need than ever to be explicit in the type of economic approach being advocated.

Rather than being explicit, policy statements on such issues as an industrial strategy have vacillated, and have generally ended up by stressing the need for such a strategy. In chapter two, I showed that Nyerere's writings seem to point to an industrial strategy which would have the following characteristics: low capital intensity, locational dispersal, high linkages to the rural areas, and generally a lower priority in terms of call on resources than agriculture. But Nyerere has not always been consistent. In introducing the Second Five Year Plan, Nyerere seems to argue for an approach which would involve a higher priority on industrialization, and an increased willingness to accept urban-oriented capital-intensive industries. 'We shall continue to expand simple manufacturing, the processing of primary commodities, and the provision of basic construction materials ... it is comparatively easy to produce your own textiles, cement and similar goods; beginning to produce your own capital goods, and goods which are used only in the production of other things, is a more complex operation and demands a more sophisticated degree of economic planning. Yet such a move is essential for long-term growth' (Tanzania, 1969, vol. I, xiii).

The Second Five Year Plan, despite its over-all emphasis on the rural sector, takes off from its introduction, and advocates a more traditional socialist approach to industrialization, one emphasizing the need to develop certain basic industries. 'Therefore, the process of simple consumer and construction goods import substitution having been completed, capital goods and intermediate goods used as inputs by the new industries will be limited in supply because they must be purchased abroad and therefore, depend upon export potential and aid possibilities. Thus if a high growth rate is to be sustained the strategy of industrial planning should be gradually changed. The development of basic intermediate and capital goods industries should receive an increasing priority' (*ibid.*, 62).

The industrial programme outlined in the Second FYP involved heavy investments in capital-intensive sectors. Over-all, the Plan called for a programme with a capital/labour ratio, on average, of shs 51,000, an export orientation of 40 per cent, and an import intensity of 50 per cent.[6] In fact, the programme has turned out to be more capital intensive (capital/labour ratio of shs 80,000), about as import intensive (import intensity of 43 per cent), and quite a bit less export oriented (export orientation of 24 per cent). In the absence of any explicit change in approach, and in fact with official documents still advocating an emphasis on capital-intensive industrialization, decision-makers implemented projects which did not differ significantly from those implemented in neighbouring capitalist societies. Kenya was going to get a fertilizer plant and a tire factory, so Tanzania built them too. Uganda had a steel rolling mill, so Tanzania acquired one. In fact, several of the more important industrial projects actually implemented in the post-Arusha phase were part of the industrial programme advanced in the First FYP written over three years before Arusha![7]

In other economic spheres, electricity, commerce, and transport, little attempt has been made to work out what the Arusha Declaration implied for strategies in these areas. As a result agencies, especially the parastatals, have carried on as if nothing has occurred. Although the rhetoric of these institutions often contains many phrases about socialism, the emphasis is on public ownership, rather than on concrete ways in which public ownership will affect investment patterns. The vacuum in policy allows the class interests of the urban elite to dominate, and produce a programme which bears little relation to the Arusha Declaration.

Again, John Saul makes a similar argument.

And yet, in Tanzania it is the relative absence of a comprehensive design, of a strategy for forward movement, that continues to confront us in the economic sphere. Much too often, in fact, the rhetoric of self-reliance has been substituted

6 Estimated
7 Both the fertilizer plant and the tire factory were First FYP projects.

for the concrete goal of a self-centered economic system and for a specification of the steps which must be taken, in the context of day-to-day planning, for its realization (Arrighi and Saul, 1973, 275).

... Writing in 1967, in the immediate aftermath of the Arusha Declaration and the issuing of other related policy documents concerning education and rural development, Arrighi and I argued that 'it will be easier to assess the direction of [Tanzania's] course if and when a presidential paper is issued which concerns itself with policies for industrialization.' Today, five years later, this gap has not been closed; economic strategy narrowly ('industrial strategy') or broadly (as above) conceived, is without doubt the crucial missing term in Tanzania's socialist equation (*ibid.*, 276).[8]

NATIONALISM

The lack of an explicit socialist investment strategy and the existence of powerful urban forces have allowed an ideology of nationalism to triumph. The long period of domination by foreign powers has engendered in Tanzanians (as in most Africans) a strong desire to assert their independence and to prove their worth relative to other countries in the world. This desire is natural, and a necessary step towards development. Yet nationalism is a dangerous force which can be used by the elites to justify self-serving programmes. It is often nationalism which is used to encourage the development of large-scale transformation projects whose cost is borne by the mass of the population but whose benefits are concentrated on the few.

ECONOMIC AND MANPOWER CONSTRAINTS

Other factors also work to divert performance away from the direction in which the ideology would take it. Throughout the study I have continually emphasized the capital intensity of investment choices. There are several reasons why parastatals will tend to choose capital-intensive technologies. In Tanzania, it is probably safe to say that capital is not the most scarce resource. Rather, both entrepreneurs, people with the ability to initiate projects, and managers, people with the ability to operate them, are in short supply. In Tanzania, on the basis of only casual impression, I would argue that it is the first that is most lacking. There is a tendency to have large projects because there are not enough people

8 Work has now begun on an industrial strategy, and should be included in the Third Five Year Plan. When this strategy is made public we shall know better which direction Tanzanian development will take.

to initiate many small ones. The opportunity cost of initiating the fertilizer plant employing 400 workers may in fact be a smaller project, in terms of capital, which would still employ only 400 workers, not two or three smaller projects employing 1000 workers. If the absolute value added of the larger plant is greater than the small, and the cost of capital can be covered by the larger plant, then it may be economically rational to build the larger plant, assuming the supply of capital is elastic.

The view that entrepreneurial talent is the binding constraint should not be taken to mean that the supply of capital in Tanzania is perfectly elastic. Constraints are binding in specific situations. Thus, it is clear that a movement in Tanzania toward numerous labour-intensive projects would run into an entrepreneur constraint long before it reaches a capital constraint. In other societies (e.g., India) this may not be the case. On the other hand, significantly capital-intensive programmes would quickly press against a capital constraint. While Tanzania is popular among aid donors, it is popular for its rural aid programme. It is not clear that donors would be willing to finance a major programme of heavy industrialization.

While the lack of entrepreneurs drives the country towards capital-intensive projects, the difficulty in getting labour-intensive capital goods has also played an important part. Western firms offer quick, reliable delivery of capital goods. To buy from countries like China takes time, and involves a degree of uncertainty. A country which is impatient to develop does not want to wait three years for a Chinese textile mill, if it can have a western one next year. In many cases the impatience may seem irrational, but often it is not. Many times the real problem is to get things going. Delaying projects to get mythically better ones may mean no progress at all.

The effect of the heavy reliance on foreign aid has been, as I mentioned in chapter six, to strengthen the tendency towards adoption of large-scale, capital-intensive projects. Since most aid is tied, and most aid donors are not interested in small projects, capital becomes elastic in supply only for large-scale, capital-intensive projects. It is difficult to develop a good aid programme for small-scale industry.[9]

LOW LEVEL ABILITY FOR INNOVATION

Finally, a problem in Tanzania which is difficult to define, but is nonetheless important, is the lack of socialist innovation. This is a difficult area to discuss,

9 To try to solve this problem the Tanzanians have recently tried to turn to such Third World countries as India and Mexico for help.

one which is often charged with emotion, but which is essential nevertheless. The colonial experience is a scarring one. It is not conducive to developing the innovative characteristics of people; on the contrary, it suppresses them and often causes a significant retrogression in the development of a society.

At this stage in its development Tanzania is shy of people who can take foreign technologies and adapt them to local needs. There is neither the cultural setting nor the availability of manpower, which seems to have existed in some countries (e.g., Japan), which would allow the society to absorb only the most useful parts of western technology. Nor has there yet been developed economic programmes which reflect the new ideology. Heavy reliance continues to be placed on foreign experts. The rural programmes are not so very different from those of ten years ago. Developing new economic strategies is more difficult than simply saying that money will be spent on rural water rather than on urban. Because Tanzania has not yet managed to overcome those difficulties, the economic pattern of investment changes only slightly. Unless a country can find a way of unlocking the creative energies of its people, then there are many aspects of its development pattern it will not be able to change. Perhaps this is simply another cost of imperialism.

Yet it is not sufficient to state simply that Tanzanians appear, at this stage, to be less innovative than the people of some other societies: Tanzanians are no less intelligent or creative than other people. The question which must be answered is which institutions can best develop the abilities of the people. Any strategy of development which hopes to create an economy which has a long-run potential for growth must be built around a strategy for the development of the people.

In this chapter I have tried to look at the various factors that have caused the pattern of investment to deviate from what one might have expected given Nyerere's ideology. The lack of commitment by the urban elite, the presence of a strong urban working force, the shortage of entrepreneurs, the availability of western technology and cheap capital, all work towards shifting the country from a rural-oriented strategy. These influences become dominant in the vacuum created by the failure to define more explicitly what a socialist strategy means for Tanzania. Many writers recognize this need, and have begun the effort needed to fill it by advocating certain strategies. I turn to these in the next chapter.

8

Criticisms and alternative strategies

INTRODUCTION

The pattern of public investment which has emerged in Tanzania over the last ten years has not gone uncriticized. Although this study represents the first attempt to pull together all the relevant data in order to make a systematic comparison of policy and practice, other writers have criticized both specific programs and the broad approach of the government and parastatals. Within the government the criticism has been rather narrow. In general the ideals of the Arusha Declaration are accepted, and criticism centres on the failure to live up to these ideals. Outside the government, especially at the university, the criticism is much broader. There, a few writers have attacked the philosophy of the Arusha Declaration. The charge is made that Nyerere's strategy is inadequate for transforming the economy and building socialism. This chapter will be devoted to summarizing the criticisms of these writers,[1] and outlining the alternative approaches they advocate.

Nyerere's critics differ on many details. They have, however, a common theme, and write from a common perspective. In Chapter one, I talked about the strong tradition among socialist scholars to centre on the relations of Third World countries with imperialist nations as the critical element in their pattern of development. Socialist scholars have argued that the failure of poor capitalist nations to develop springs essentially from their dependency relationship with international capitalism. This dependency relationship is fostered by trade, aid, and foreign investment. The solution to underdevelopment lies, according to some members of this school of thought, in breaking down this dependency

1 While there has been some muted criticism of Nyerere from the right, most criticism has come from the left. In this chapter I will be concerned only with criticisms made by socialists.

relationship. A socialist strategy of development involves undoing the distortive effects of early peripheral capitalist development and in avoiding the pattern of growth fostered by capitalist development.

Most of Nyerere's critics are writing in this radical tradition. They often begin their work by a quick theoretical recitation of the radical objection to the various forms of dependency. They proceed from there to argue that a strategy of investment in Tanzania must have as its central focus the removal of this dependency. This approach thus brings them into conflict with much of Nyerere's approach and leads them to propose an investment strategy much different from one based on the Arusha Declaration.

EXTERNAL DEPENDENCE

One further piece of background should be supplied before I present the views of these critics in detail. Up to this point only partial data have been available on what has actually been happening in Tanzania. These data have tended to create the impression that there has been a sharp increase in external dependence in Tanzania. This impression is a false one and has led to an inaccurate presentation of what has happened in Tanzania. External dependence today is certainly no more but probably somewhat less in Tanzania than it was in the First FYP.

In order to show that external dependence has not increased, I have looked at three measures – degree of foreign finance, export orientation of investment, and dependency on trade. Because of problems with obtaining other data, most people have looked at the development budget or at ministerial spending alone to see the degree of dependence on foreign aid. Foreign aid to ministries has been rising as a share of total funds, especially if ministries such as Defense and Home Affairs are excluded. As well, aid passing through the development budget to parastatals has also risen dramatically. In the First FYP aid recorded as passing through the development budget was only 6 per cent of government transfers to parastatals, but in the Second FYP aid was 62 per cent of budget transfers. From these data an impression of rapidly rising external dependence is easily obtained.

As I showed in chapter six, a more accurate view of external dependence can be obtained only by looking at all forms of foreign borrowing, including borrowing from private institutions. Since this form of borrowing has fallen in recent years, it partially offsets the rise in foreign aid. Much of the rise in foreign aid is related to projects connected to the corridor to Zambia. Since most of Nyerere's critics are sympathetic to aiding Zambia, it seems appropriate to exclude the projects involved in the corridor – the pipeline, the road company, the shipping firm developed with China, the road, and the railway. When these investments are excluded, the picture becomes different (see Table 93). The over-all change

TABLE 93

Dependence on foreign finance (Zambian Corridor projects excluded)

	First FYP		Second FYP[1]	
	Foreign (shs. million)	Local (shs. million)	Foreign (shs. million)	Local (shs. million)
Ministries	485 (37%)	836 (63%)	1106 (40%)	1634 (60%)
Parastatals	355 (51%)	344 (48%)	1315 (48%)	1361 (52%)
Total	840 (42%)	1180 (58%)	2421 (45%)	2995 (55%)

1 Includes estimates for 1972-73 and 1973-74

TABLE 94

Export orientation of public investment excluding
Zambian Corridor (%)

	First FYP	Second FYP[1]
Ministries	6	8
Parastatals	27	22
Total	15	15

1 Includes estimates for 1972-73 and 1973-74

in external dependence has been slight. Ministries are marginally more dependent, parastatals marginally less dependent, and the total program slightly more dependent because of the increased importance of parastatals in the Second FYP compared to the First (parastatals are more dependent than ministries, and their higher weight pulls the average up).

Again with export orientation of investment it is best to look at the data excluding the corridor to Zambia. Table 94 presents the data in this way. Ministerial spending appears to be slightly more export oriented, and parastatal spending less export oriented. The export orientation of all government spending is unchanged. About 15 per cent of public investment in both plans went toward projects which encouraged or produced exports. Given the present structure of the economy, this figure does not appear to be unduly high.

The ratio of trade to GDP, another measure of external dependence, fell steadily, but slowly, from 1962, when it was 55 per cent, to 1969, when it was 46 per cent. The building of Tazara has caused it to rise again to 54 per cent in 1971 and 53 per cent in 1972. If, however, Tazara is excluded, the ratio of trade to GDP would have been a constant 46 per cent since 1969.

Any discussion of external dependence should not ignore the important structural changes which have occurred in the economy. While one can make many criticisms about the parastatal sector, the creation of that sector signifies a major increase in the degree to which Tanzanians now control their own economy. As I showed in chapter two, the importance of parastatal investment has been rising rapidly. Moreover, the degree of government involvement in the parastatal sector has been increasing. As I showed in chapter four, the importance of non-majority parastatal investment has fallen, and the average government equity holding in parastatals has been increasing.

Nevertheless, Tanzania still remains very dependent upon the rest of the world and, specifically, the capitalist world. The Arusha Declaration and the subsequent behaviour of the government and its parastatals has not brought a very rapid decrease in dependence. To someone who views dependency as the critical variable in the development of socialism, this slow change is a cause of concern.

It is impossible to present the views of everyone who has criticized Nyerere's strategy. It would also serve little purpose to do so. What I would like to set forth here are a few examples of the type of criticism which is often made, especially among intellectual circles, of the Nyerere approach. As I said in chapter seven, one of the critical factors explaining a lack of dramatic change in Tanzania has been the lack of specification of a socialist investment strategy. I will attempt in the next chapter to go part way toward specifying such a strategy. Many people who have criticized Nyerere have also begun the work of making more explicit the type of strategy they see as essential if socialist development is to take place. Since many of these people have played and will continue to play an important role in the devleopment of Tanzania, their views are of particular importance. I will begin my review of Nyerere's critics by presenting the ideas of three Tanzanians; A.N. Babu, a politician; J.F. Rweyemamu, a professor of economics; and I.G. Shivji, a student at the University of Dar es Salaam.

A.N. BABU

Abdulrahman N. Babu was until 1971 the Minister for Economic Affairs and Developing Planning.[2] From his position in the cabinet, he criticized as much as

2 Despite his rather prominent position and his obvious influence in intellectual circles, Babu did not have a powerful political base in Tanzania. In fact, he was from Zanzibar and soon found himself in jail on mainland Tanzania, suspected of being part of the assassination plot against Karume. His views are important, however, because of their influence on other writers and because he represents one political faction within Tanzania.

was politically possible the direction Tanzania was taking.[3] Babu approaches the problem of underdevelopment from the viewpoint that its underlying cause lies with the distortive effects of colonial development. Moreover, underdevelopment can be eradicated only by ending that integration. Babu argues for an 'inward-looking' approach which will transform the economy from being externally responsive to being internally responsive.[4]

3 Babu first set out his views in a paper entitled 'A New Strategy for Development.' A short version of this paper was printed in the *London Financial Times* (9 Dec. 1971). Babu has written a postscript to Rodney (1972), which presents most of his views.
4 In the postscript to Rodney (1972, 312-14), Babu says: 'It is clear, especially after reading Rodney's exposition, that throughout the last decade we have been posing the wrong questions regarding economic backwardness. We did not "look into the past to know the present." We were told, and accepted, that our poverty was caused by our poverty in the now famous theory of the "vicious circle of poverty" and we went round in circles seeking ways and means of breaking that circle. Had we asked the fundamental questions which Dr Rodney raises in this work we would not have exposed our economies to the ruthless plunder brought about by "foreign investments" which the exponents of the vicious circle theory urged us to do. For, it is clear, foreign investment is the cause, and not a solution, to our economic backwardness.
    'Are we not underdeveloped now because we have been colonised in the past? There is no other explanation to the fact that practically the whole of the underdeveloped world has been colonised either directly or indirectly by the western powers. And what is colonialism if it is not a system of "foreign investments" by the metropolitan powers? If it has contributed to our underdevelopment in the past is it not likely to contribute to our underdevelopment now, even if the political reins are in our hands? Put in this way the question of underdevelopment is immediately rendered more intelligible, even to the uninitiated. And this is how Dr Rodney is directing us to pose our questions.
    'The inevitable conclusion is that foreign investment does not only help to undermine our economies by extracting enormous profits, etc., but it does more serious damage to the economies by distorting them into lopsidedness and if the process is not arrested in time, the distortion could be permanent. As long as we continue, as we have done for centuries, to produce for the so-called "world market" which was founded on the hard rock of slavery and colonialism, our economies will remain colonial. Any development will be entirely incidental, leaving the vast majority of the population wholly uninvolved in the economic activity. The more we invest in export branches in order to capture the "world market" the more we divert away from investing for people's development and, consequently, the least effective our development effort.
    'Almost without exception, all the ex-colonial countries have ignored the cardinal development demand: namely, that, to be really effective, the development process must begin by transforming the economy from its colonial, externally-responsive structure, to one which is internally-responsive. Where we went wrong is when we followed blindly the assumptions handed down to us by our exploiters. These assumptions can be stated briefly as follows: Growth in underdeveloped countries is hampered by inadequate growth in exports and inadequate financial resources and is made worse by "population explosion" in these countries. And the solution is prescribed as follows: Step up exports, increase aid and loans from the developed countries and arrest growth in population.

Babu regards Korea and Albania as excellent examples of countries which have transformed their economies. The type of industries Babu would develop are clear – high technology, capital goods industries. If trade has to be carried on, it should be with socialist countries and be on the basis of long-term barter agreements such as those Cuba concluded with the Soviet Union and the east European socialist governments. Aid should be accepted only from socialist countries, and joint projects with international capitalist firms should be ended. Agriculture should be restructured so that the emphasis is on food production, not export crops. Most importantly, Tanzania must seek to develop the industrial and scientific base to become technologically independent.

J.F. RWEYEMAMU

Justinian Rweyemamu, one of two Tanzanians with a PhD in economics, formerly Dean of the Faculty of Arts and Sciences at the University of Dar es Salaam, Principal Secretary in Devplan and now economic advisor to the President is also part of the radical group critical of some aspects of Tanzania's present path of development. He is not as critical as some writers on Tanzania, but he does have a position on strategy which is fundamentally opposed to many of the present policies of the government. His importance in the urban elite undoubtedly explains his reserved behaviour. On the other hand, his position makes it important to discern the direction of his ideas.

Dr Rweyemamu's thesis, written at Harvard University and now published by Oxford University Press, entitled *Underdevelopment and Industrialization in*

'Throughout the last decade our efforts have been to follow religiously the above prescription, and even if our own experience continues to disapprove it, we still adhere to it even more fanatically! The greatest need appears to be a process of mental decolonisation, since neither common sense nor sound economics, not even our own experience is with us in this.

'Experiences of other countries that have chosen a different path, a path of economic reconstruction, is most instructive here. Take North Korea or Albania. Both these countries were underdeveloped as late as the fifties. The reason why they have been able to register most oustanding economic progress is that they have decided to opt out of production for the so-called world market and diverted their resources towards the development of material and technological base internally.'

5 See also Rweyemamu (1969); his article, 'Planning, Socialism and Industrialization: The Economic Challenge' in Uchumi Editorial Board (1972); his article 'Industrial Development in Tanzania and the Next Plan," in TIB (1973); and his article 'The Silent Class Struggle in Retrospect," in Shivji (1973a).

Tanzania (Rweyamamu, 1973)[5] is essentially an historical study of the development of Tanzania up to the time of the Arusha Declaration. Its essential argument is that colonial development in Tanzania led to its integration into the world capitalist system. This integration led to perverse[6] capital development, a type of development not conducive to the long-term growth and transformation of the economy. The argument is summarized below:

The characteristics of underdevelopment alluded to above are the *dependency* relationships created by a colonial division of labour — dependency on foreign markets for the sale of their output and the provision of basic inputs, technological dependency on the advanced countries and dependency on foreign [private] entrepreneurs — which work in such a way as to produce *perverse* capitalist industrial growth. Such growth is characterized by the establishment of a productive structure that (a) is biased against the capital goods industries, thus limiting industries contributing to the production of farm equipment and transport facilities, (b) utilizes relatively more capital-intensive techniques of production, thus compounding the problem of urban unemployment and the widening of urban-rural differentials, (c) has limited linkage effects, especially with respect to the traditional sector, (d) fosters lopsided development both in terms of geographical location within the country, and sectoral distribution of consumer goods output favouring luxuries, and (e) sets up uncompetitive oligopolistic structures.

It is thus obvious that the system that will be adopted in order to overcome underdevelopment must be capable of liquidating the depencency relationship (Uchumi Editorial Board, 1972, 31; emphasis in original).

The solution lies, as the last sentence in quote states, in liquidating the dependency relationship. In concrete terms, what does this mean?

The most important dependency relations are: *technological* dependency; *market* dependency and *managerial* and *entrepreneurial* dependency. These dependency relationships are reproduced and deepened by a productive structure inherited from colonization but perpetuated by a neo-colonial investment pattern which reveals a lack of symmetry between the structure of production and the structure of consumption. This basic structural feature has many implications for industrial policy to which we shall return in due course (TIB, 1973, 7).

---

6 For origins of this term, see Sach (1960).

Rweyemamu rejects the 'inward looking' approach of Babu. Trade will continue to be essential to Tanzania's development. The structure of that trade must be altered. Here the influence on Rweyemamu's thinking of Hirschman, under whom he did his thesis, and Brewster and Thomas, whom I will discuss later in this chapter, is clear:

The present pattern of Tanzania exports is such as to continue fragmenting the national economy thus widening the gap between the structure of production and the structure of consumption. Almost all exportables have no home base; they are not an extension of the internal market. They are rather specifically produced for the external market. This is no doubt the major cause of *unequal exchange* and its manifestation viz. worsening terms of trade, violent fluctuations of export prices, etc. In order to rectify this pattern we must endeavour to have exports that are an *extension* of the domestic market as much as possible in the future. The policy with regards to exports therefore is not one of reducing total exports in total product, nor that of 'inward looking.' The proper policy will have to look at the nature of the exports themselves. With respect to existing exports we should try to find as much *domestic use* as is technologically possible. A commodity by commodity study will reveal that there are many such possibilities that have not been exploited largely because our concern has been directed to the traditional export-oriented markets (*ibid.*, emphasis in original).

His industrial policy, then, becomes:

It can safely be asserted, for example, that production should be geared to producing *basic goods,* basic in the sense that they are used in the production, directly or indirectly of all the other goods. These basic goods consist essentially of *wage goods* and the *means of production* that establishes the foundation of a self-sustaining economy, and a fortiori guarantees that reproduction of wage goods. It is the first category of basic goods that has often been given attention, even though wage goods have sometimes been confused with consumption goods. The former do not include luxuries *ex definitione*. Wage goods can be subdivided into primarily *private* consumption wage goods and *collective* consumption wage goods although this latter distinction is not unambiguous.

    The means of production necessary for guaranteeing the reproduction and expansion of the basic goods, have often been given scant attention in our development plans. But these are the only goods that can transform our economy from a dependency relationship to one of economic independence. They include machines and machine tools to make textile machinery, construction materials, hospital equipment, buses, water pipes, tractors, etc. (Uchumi Editorial Board, 1972, 37-8).

The development of machine tool industries is the key to Rweyemamu's strategy. These are the industries which maximize forward and backward linkages in a developed economy.[7] Rweyemamu believes that the development of machine tool industries has historically speeded the development of a skilled, disciplined work force. He thinks that this teaching characteristic of machine tools is probably their most important attribute.[8] He rejects the traditional arguments against the development of capital goods industries which state that such industries are too capital intensive and will suffer from lack of demand. Rweyemamu argues that many capital goods industries are not capital intensive and that the demand problem can be solved by regional integration.[9]

Rweyemamu feels strongly that his program cannot be introduced piecemeal. He therefore accepts the views of the supporters of the Big Push. Tanzania

7 But not necessarily, as I will argue later, in an underdeveloped economy.

8 Moreover, there is an important learning process involved in machinery production and a high degree of specialisation which is conducive not only to an effective learning process but to an effective application of that which is learned. This highly developed facility in the design and production of specialised machinery is perhaps the most important single characteristic of a well-developed capital goods industry and constitutes an external economy of enormous significance to the rest of the economy' (Editorial Board, 1972, 38).

9 The major argument against capital goods industries in the underdeveloped countries such as Tanzania is the lack of economic capacity to do so; in particular the failure to take advantage of economies of scale that are assumed to characterise modern industrial production. It is thus appropriate to review, though briefly, the nature and significance of this argument.

'In the first place, a fair proportion of capital goods industries (metal working industries) is small scale and relatively labour intensive. Metal work industries do not, therefore, by and large take advantage of economies of scale. The major problem of introducing capital goods industries therefore is not one of acquiring economies of scale; but one of having sufficient demand to absorb the very *specialized* output that the industry produces. And as to the existence of adequate demand, I can see no demonstrable reason why regional integration *among* developing countries cannot solve this problem.

'The economies of scale argument must therefore be made to refer to the basic raw materials of industry, i.e., iron and steel, chemicals, etc. Here the major source of purely physical unit cost savings as output is increased derive from the phenomenon of "cubic dimensions," and the ability to avoid "short runs." Yet these factors are often neutralized by other pecuniary factors which do not vary inversely with output such as factor prices, external economies or diseconomies, exchange rate, etc. Hence, evidence of monetary economies of scale do not necessarily establish the case for attaining a certain minimum level of output that can be regarded as optimal' (Uchumi Editorial Board, 1972, 38).

should immediately allocate a major proportion of its investment to the development of industries to produce both capital goods and wage goods. Rweyemamu suggests allocating 30-40 per cent of investment to capital goods alone.[10] In a country where manufacturing investment as a whole has absorbed only 17 per cent of investment, this program represents a major alteration of the present pattern.

Rweyemamu is generally hopeful that the changes which he feels are necessary in government policy will be made. He regards the urban elite as having many members who are willing to pursue policies which will destroy their elite position.[11] He is sceptical of the revolutionary potential of the peasantry and the workers.[12] Because the masses have grown up in a non-socialist environment, and because the development of Tanzania did not produce a real proletariat class, or a group of landless exploited peasants, most people in Tanzania remain conservative. Rweyemamu sees, then, the driving force toward socialism as continuing to come from the top. The urban elite must, however, strive to maintain close contacts with the people in order to sense their aspirations and to monitor the effectiveness of government policies.

10 'To build up such industries implies starting almost from scratch. The technologies chosen must therefore bear this constraint in mind. By a combination of imaginative improvisation and adaption, the absorption of scientific knowledge from abroad, an emphasis on technical education, tolerance of initial imperfections by the customers, and accumulated experience and confidence coming from self-achievement, Tanzania should be able to establish a strong and healthy technology producing sector over a period of fifteen to twenty years. The Soviet Union, Japan and China have demonstrated in this century that the transition from a largely imitative to an innovatory role can be accomplished in this way. This implies that at least 30-40 per cent of investment spending must be concentrated in this sector or at least the proportion to be invested in this sector must be large enough to overcome the "threshold" below which gradual changes dissipate without tangible results to give emergence to a new qualitative situation where economic development becomes a self-feeding process' (Uchumi Editorial Board, 1972, 40).
11 'Finally it should be pointed out that so long as part of the elite continues to reject the temptations of becoming more bourgeois, and identifies itself with the interests of the workers, the elite can be expected to play an effective liberating role. To some this means that the elite must "commit suicide" in order not to betray the revolution. But this is by no means peculiar to the elite substratum. For the proletariat does not fulfill its tasks either until it suppresses itself ... ' (Shivji, 1973a, 136).
12 'And the existing reality is that the working class of an underdeveloped society is unable to liberate itself without the assistance of an enlightened intelligentsia. This is partly because a necessary element of the liberating process requires knowledge and understanding for operating the acquired means of production, which is at the present time largely possessed by the elite' (Shivji, 1973a, 136).

I.G. SHIVJI

Issa G. Shivji, a recent graduate of the University of Dar es Salaam, produced an article in Cheche, a TANU Youth League magazine at the university which typifies the thinking of many of the radical university students.[13] He is much more sceptical about the role played by the urban elite. Shivji sees a situation of emerging bureaucratic capitalism with the bureaucratic elite aligned with international capitalism to perpetuate Tanzania's dependent relation:

Nationalisation was a step forward insofar as it is a prerequisite for building socialism. But by nationalisation, as we shall try to show, the country did not cease to be a neo-colony. Neither did it become a workers' state. Nor does state ownership alone mean socialism ...

At the same time the post-Arusha nationalisations have set the pace for the rise of an economic bureaucracy. The 'new stratum' of managers, sub-managers, directors and administrators of parastatals already constitute a formidable bureaucratic layer.

Rather, Tanzania appears to be in a situation of flux − a situation of latent but definite class struggle. *On the one hand, there is the economic and political bureaucracy (objectively backed by the international bourgeoisie, the country being still in the neo-colonial framework), and on the other are the most vocal and conscious elements − largely small groups of intelligentsia, including a few enlightened leaders.* The economic bureaucracy does not have a definite upperhand as would be the case under bureaucratic capitalism. But the fact that the economic bureaucracy is a powerful force can be gleaned from the attitudes of the parastatal management generally towards what may be called 'socialist measures.' This attitude has facilitated the perpetuating of neo-colonial interests. 'Services industry − tourism, hotel building, running entertainment houses, breweries, etc. − has loomed large in NDC investment policy. By the end of 1968, for example, roughly one-third of NDC's investments was concentrated in luxury items: breweries, cigarette production, hotels, and tourism while only one-tenth per cent was invested in subsidiaries and associated companies producing consumer necessities. This accords well with the investment policies of the international corporations, which are fighting desperately to maintain their hold on the Tanzanian economy, in order to ensure that it remains within the neo-colonial web.

13 'The Silent Class Struggle,' printed in Shivji (1973a), also in Cliffe and Saul (1973, vol. 2).

This may be done in various ways. Of late, many foreign monopoly corporations have entered into partnerships with NDC in various projects; they also manage and operate many projects on behalf of NDC; they supply management and consultants and act as technical advisers. They even undertake the so-called feasibility surveys, making huge profits on all these activities (Cliffe and Saul, 1973, vol. 2, 313-14; emphasis in original).

His attack is centred on the National Development Corporation's investment policies, which he looks at in detail:

This means that NDC investments are hardly helping the country to construct an integrated economy and a strong industrial sector which is a sine qua non if the country is really to develop. The large portion of the surplus generated by the hard toil of the masses finds its way to the metropolis through these foreign partners. What remains with NDC is partly eaten up by the petty bourgeois and the bureaucratic stratum and partly invested. But as the economic structure is as described above, this investment is done mainly in export-oriented activities — whose basic character is 'commercial.' Thus there is dominance of commercial capital which is not 'transformed' into industrial capital (*ibid.*, 318).

Shivji lays the bulk of the blame for Tanzania's failure to transform its economy on Tanzania's continued integration in the capitalist world. International capitalists recruit a dependent bourgeoisie in the neo-colony. Together they thwart attempts at structural change.[14]

The solution to this problem is the development of TANU as a vanguard party and the disengagement of the economy from international capitalism. Shivji is convinced that the bourgeois tendencies of the bureaucratic elite are linked to their relations with international capitalism. Sever these links, and the tendencies

---

14 'Capitalist development and neo-colonial underdevelopment are the two necessary halves which constitute the whole — international monopoly capitalism.
    '*Consequently, the class struggle, too, is on the international plane.* Hence, when one talks about class struggle in Tanzania, one cannot but analyze the international scene. The fundamental *and antagonistic contradiction*, let it be emphasized, is between *imperialism* and the *people*, which form the dialectical opposites of the international capitalist system. However, the international bourgeoisie administers its interests in individual countries through varied means ... whether it is the petty bourgeoisie of the neo-colony *par excellence*, or the national bourgeoisie of State Capitalism; or the economic bureaucracy of bureaucratic capitalism — they serve to a greater or lesser extent as on-the-scene agents of the international bourgeoisie (Cliffe and Saul, 1973, vol. 2, 319; emphasis in original).

will disappear. Economically, this means industrialization and the building of an integrated economy. Despite his mention of industrializing Ujamaa villages, Shivji's program is basically one of developing heavy industry and withdrawing from the world economy. In agriculture, he pushes for a more capital-intensive approach.[15]

J.S. SAUL

There has been a number of non-Tanzanian writers who have written about Tanzania. In fact, a measure of the long-lasting effects of colonialism is the dominance of expatriates in most collections of writings on Tanzania.[16] I will not attempt to survey everything which has been written on Tanzania's economic strategy by non-Tanzanians, but will try to isolate some of the most important work and that which typifies much of the thinking done in the area.

John Saul, until recently a lecturer at the University of Dar es Salaam, stands out as one of the most important analysts of Tanzania. His long stay in the country (seven years), as well as his solid radical political credentials, has made him a dominant figure intellectually. He is a political scientist, and therefore his writings often lack the specificity in terms of economic strategy that is desirable from our perspective. Nevertheless, through his writings (Arrighi and Saul, 1973; Uchumi Editorial Board, 1972), a common approach is clear and can be discussed.

Saul, like the previous writers, sees integration in the capitalist world as leading to perverse development, i.e., development which in the long run is not self-sustaining. He differs from many writers in his willingness to take into

---

15 'The outcome of the struggle described will very much decide whether Tanzania truly becomes a Socialist State or willy-nilly slips into the neo-colonial state of the type described as "bureaucratic capitalism" with the features mentioned therein. The task of building an integrated socialist economy, too, will depend on how the above struggle is resolved. This cannot be done in "co-operation" with the international monopoly corporations. If planned integrated economies could be built in partnership with the international monopoly corporations, then socialism can be built in partnership with imperialism.

'Tanzania, in order to disengage from the imperialist economy and make a break with its underdevelopment, must industrialise. Even the success of "Ujamaa Villages" will decisively depend on whether the productivity and the standards of living of the peasants in the Ujamaa Villages are higher than those of individual peasants. Mechanisation and the provision of essential social infrastructure... are sine qua non if the Ujamaa policy is not to fall into discredit with the peasantry.

'Maybe the Great Uhuru Railway is a historical opportunity for Tanzaniz to make a breakthrough in the industrial sphere—especially to lay a base for an iron-steel complex' (Cliffe and Saul, 1973, vol. 2, 321; emphasis in original).

16 See for example Cliffe and Saul (1973), or Uchumi Editorial Board (1972).

account the very real difficultues in disengagement from the capitalist world, in the attention he pays to the importance of the rural sector, and in his focus on the internal political developments of the country versus external influences. Let us look at each of these differences.

While recognizing the importance of the negative contributions of international capitalism, Saul perceives, as few writers do, that the role of international capitalism is not the most critical at this stage in Tanzania's development. International capitalism allows and supports a type of development.[17] For Saul, socialist development is not possible within the confines of integration in international capitalism. Yet, disengagement from international capitalism does not solve the basic problem, which is the internal political structure of most countries:

The foregoing discussion suggests the advisability of a policy of self-reliance vis-a-vis international capitalism for two main reasons:

(1) because of the drain on the surplus which, sooner or later, is engendered by dependence on foreign capital; and (2) because of the impact of foreign investment (with respect to choice of techniques and to its sectoral distribution) upon the structure of the tropical African economies. It does not follow, however, that the disengagement from international capitalism is a *sufficient* condition for development. As we have seen, the emergence of a labor aristocracy, with considerable political power, was brought about not only by the pattern of foreign investment but also by the acceptance of a colonial salary structure on the part of independent African governments. The labor aristocracy will therefore continue to use its power in a state-controlled modern sector in order to appropriate a considerable share of the surplus in the form of increasing discretionary consumption. Under these conditions, 'perverse growth' would continue notwithstanding state ownership of the means of production. In order to achieve 'real' long-term development, disengagement from international capitalism will have to be accompanied by a change in the power base of African governments (Arrighi and Saul, 1973, 21).

Thus Saul rejects Shivji's view as inadequate:

But even if the class interests of the Tanzanian 'petty bourgeoisie' were more clearly defined in this way, one might still wonder whether Shivji has expressed

17 While historically the role of international capitalism has been critical in Tanzania's development, now the most important impediment to socialist development is, and will increasingly be, the internal class structure.

his argument about Tanzania's class structure in the most effective way. For by placing the base of this class outside Tanzania (in 'the international bourgeoisie') he is tempted to underestimate its deep roots in Tanzania itself. This limitation may arise, in turn, from the author's failure to attach sufficient importance to the role of the neo-colonial state in the production process. Regis Debray has written of the Latin American 'petty bourgeoisie' that 'it does not possess an infrastructure of economic power before it wins political power. Hence it transforms the state not only into an instrument of political domination, but also into a source of economic power. The state, culmination of social relations of exploitation in capitalist Europe, becomes in a certain sense the instrument of their installation in these countries.' It could be argued that a similar trend has been apparent in Africa, and this gives locally privileged elements a solidity that must not be defined away (Cliffe and Saul, 1973, vol. 2, 355-6).

Saul is also concerned about the lack of analysis of the rural sector. It is worth noting that almost all other writers who propose a strategy of development for Tanzania ignore the rural sector. Saul worries about the rural sector for two reasons. First, he is concerned about the signs of the development of a rural capitalist class in the relatively classless rural areas of much of Tanzania. A socialist strategy must be a strategy which is based upon a rural socialist sector. Secondly, Saul is also sensitive to the issue that every African government must confront – the problems of low productivity in the rural areas. Saul is not so doctrinaire that he is willing to dismiss the notion that some capitalist growth may be necessary to break through the technological backwardness of the rural areas.[18] Nor is total disengagement from international capitalism possible in view of the current dependence of rural areas on world markets. Thus the rural sector severely constrains a socialist strategy and necessitates a more flexible and creative response:

Yet even the re-allocation of surplus from the discretionary consumption of the 'labor aristocracy' to productive investment, though a necessary condition, is not sufficient for steady long-term growth. Productive investment in the modern sector must be directed toward the creation of development stimuli in the traditional sector; that is, it must be directed to the expansion of those industries producing the capital and the consumer goods most suited to the requirements of the traditional sector. Failing this, as the history of socialist development in nonindustrial environments has so often demonstrated, the growing demand for labor and produce following upon industrialization would merely lead to

18 It is clear Saul prefers a solution based upon collective production.

unfavorable terms of trade for the traditional sector, restraining the exploitation of its surplus productive capacity.

The problem of creating incentives to exploit surplus productive capacity in the traditional sector is crucial because there still exist, among the peasants of tropical Africa, surplus land and surplus labor-time. The second problem involved in raising the productivity of African peasants (see above) is that of ensuring the productive absorption of the surplus produced in the traditional sector. Here the question of rural transformation is more starkly posed, even if difficult to answer at the theoretical level. It will involve some calculations as to whether the transformation of traditional economies is best attained through the formation of an agrarian capitalist class or the gradual absorption of the individual peasant families into larger units (cooperatives, collectives, communes): whether through the utilization or superseding of traditional forms of work cooperation, or through reliance upon central marketing boards of traders for the collection of produce from, and distribution of manufactured goods to, the traditional producer (Arrighi and Saul, 1973, 21-2).

Saul's policy response is mainly political. The answer lies in the development of a strong socialist party. The approach is two-pronged. The party must be strengthened, and it must be reformed. A strengthened party is necessary if the power of the bureaucratic elite is to be controlled. There is little point in strengthening the party unless this is done in a way which increases its socialist content. Such a party needs a mass base and a source of support and ideas. The Ujamaa program is critical in this respect. The party needs the support of 'a genuinely conscious and socialist peasantry (Uchumi Editorial Board, 1972, 25). The economic program which supports this political one is the development of labour-intensive, capital goods industries centred on providing inputs to the rural areas, and the development of low-cost consumer goods industries. Because Saul believes that international capitalism is uninterested in such industries, he feels that there would no longer be the type of turn-key projects or joint enterprises which have characterized parastatal investment to this stage. Investment geared exclusively to the export market would be down-played and the economy redirected toward internal growth as quickly as possible.

C. THOMAS

A second example of non-Tanzanian writing on Tanzania is the work of Clive Thomas. Thomas is a West Indian economist who was briefly in Tanzania in 1972 and wrote an article on economic strategy in Tanzania. In 1974, he produced a book on investment strategy (Thomas, 1974a). His approach to Tanzania is similar to that used in his book written with Havelock Brewster. *The Dynamics of West India Economic Integration* (1967). The central concept behind Brewster's and Thomas' approach is that an economy can achieve self-sustaining growth only if it is integrated. Integrated is here defined as a correspondence between demand and production. Thus an economy which produces many goods which it does not consume is not integrated, e.g., sisal, coffee, tea, etc. An integrated economy can still be an export economy, if the export is a spillover from domestic consumption.

Brewster's and Thomas' approach draws heavily on Hirschman. In effect, they argue that development can occur only by maximizing linkage effects. Hirschman drew on the input-output empirical studies of Chenery and Watanabe to show that in many countries such basic industries as steel, chemicals, textiles, and rubber have the highest linkage effects. Brewster and Thomas argue that it is these industries which must be developed, and developed simultaneously. Again they draw on Hirschman's conclusion that the linkage effects are maximized and the risks minimized by simultaneous development of basic industries.[19]

Thomas applies this approach basically unchanged to Tanzania. The essential element in a strategy of development, according to Thomas, is to know where you want to go. This can be determined by looking at the structure of developed countries. This reveals, as we have said, the 'basicness' of certain industries: iron and steel, textiles, paper, plastics, rubber, glass, leather, cement, wood, fuel, and industrial chemicals. What is needed is a 'period of transition' in which these industries are created. This period should be as short as possible. Once it is over, many of the problems of dependence analyzed by other writers will be solved. Agriculture's role is confined to producing the food to feed the growing urban work force, and needed raw materials. It must be redirected away from purely export crops.

Thomas scoffs at the faint-hearted who believe that the problems involved in the transition may be severe, or who feel that many small economies cannot economically rationally support a fully integrated industrial economy. He attacks Sweezy's and Huberman's analysis of the problems of Cuba's attempt to industrialize as betraying 'the uncritical acceptance of the market notion of

19 Brewster and Thomas draw heavily on Hirschman. This does not imply that Hirschman necessarily agrees with their strategy. Hirschman's essential contribution was the notion that we must look at obstacles to decision-making. In some circumstances, i.e., Latin America, he felt that the implementation of certain capital-intensive projects would help to solve this decision-making bottleneck. It is wrong to jump from that conclusion to the conclusion that capital-intensive projects are appropriate everywhere, and Hirschman is careful to avoid doing this.

demand as a constraint on output ... [representing] common and unsupported prejudices about the real "variety" of modern industry and the impact of size in determining the social costs of establishing it (Thomas, 1974a, 191). Cuba's failure was not excessive industrialization. Quite the contrary in Thomas' views. It failed to put sufficient emphasis on industrialization and failed to undertake a programme of industrialization oriented towards the structural transformation which Thomas' sees as necessary for development.

CONTRAST TO NYERERE'S VIEWS

It is now possible to bring together what these writers say and contrast it with the philosophy of Nyerere, as outlined in Chapter two. Almost all critics are unanimous in condemning Tanzania's direct links to international capitalism via aid, foreign investment, and international firms. It is these links which perpetuate the structural dependence of the economy and the lack of an independent technological base. Nyerere, in contrast, while maintaining that the primary emphasis must be on self-help, rejects the notion that Tanzania should or could develop without help. Stated in the most favourable way, Nyerere's view is that Tanzania should not end the Swedish rural water program just because Sweden is a member of the international capitalist community. Nyerere is interested in making immediate improvements to the lives of the people living in the rural areas, and if foreign aid will speed this process, then he will accept it. Nor is Nyerere convinced that Tanzania has the indigenous manpower to go it alone. Building steel mills and cement factories requires technologies which Tanzania does not yet have. If these are not obtained from multinational firms, then they must be obtained exclusively from socialist countries. Nyerere is unwilling to commit himself totally to the socialist camp. He is convinced that a policy of non-alignment is essential to Tanzania's survival. Receiving aid from virtually every aid-giving country in the world is a way of maintaining that position. Nor does Nyerere believe that the socialist countries regard Tanzania as so important in terms of strategic political terms that they are willing to match western aid. Non-socialist aid to Tanzania will exceed $100 million (US) in 1973-4. Almost all of this will be on IDA terms or better. Both Cuba and Korea were terribly important politically to the socialist camp, in a way in which Tanzania is not.

The second major difference between Nyerere and his critics is the role they assign to agriculture. They accuse Nyerere of ignoring, in his writings, the need to 'walk on two legs.' On the other hand, their concern centres on only one leg-industry. As I mentioned earlier, the rural sector is basically ignored in most writings on development strategy for Tanzania. Saul and Cliffe are exceptions to this statement. Their concern is, however, with the type of rural development.

The engine of growth in the economy is seen by almost all radicals in Tanzania as industrialization. It is for this reason that almost all discussions of strategies for growth in Tanzania always focus almost exclusively on industrial strategy, even though industry currently contributes less than 10 per cent of GDP.

Moreover, the type of industry generally regarded as central to the strategy is industry unrelated to the rural areas or related only in the sense that it depends on the rural areas as a source of demand. Thus, discussions do not center on rural industrialization, or small scale industries, or decentralization of industries. Almost all the industries which are the focal point of attention are urban based or are set apart from the rural economy. Even Rweyemamu, who stresses small engineering firms, or capital goods industries, sees a large steel complex as part of the strategy and is more interested in industries producing machine tools for urban factories than in Ujamaa tractor repair and maintenance shops.

Thirdly, the effect of economic strategy on class formation in Tanzania is not fully explored by most radical critics. While Nyerere's writings generally ignore the class implications of his strategy, their own analysis ignores Nyerere's penetrating insight, that the strategy chosen must not be one which leads 'to the position where the real exploitation in Tanzania is that of the town dwellers exploiting the peasants' (1968b). Nyerere is extremely concerned about inequality and the urban/rural dichotomy. Neither of these issues is the focal point of that analysis for most of his critics. As I mentioned earlier, their writings often completely ignore the rural sector or assign it a subsidiary role. Inequality is discussed mainly in terms of the growth of a capitalist rural class or in terms of privileges gained by the very top of the bureaucratic elite. In contrast, Nyerere is worried as well about other types of equality such as inequality between sectors of the economy. He is unwilling to promote rapid industrialization if that means that one small group of people will have high incomes and live in a very modernized society while most people will have been left far behind.

In the next chapter I will try to present my own views on investment strategy. In doing so, I will criticize in more detail what has gone on so far in Tanzania and criticize the strategies proposed by Nyerere's critics. I will also try to pull together the conclusions one can reach about devising a socialist investment strategy from a study of the pattern of public investment in Tanzania over the last ten years.

9

Conclusion: a strategy and an approach for investment

LESSONS OF THE TANZANIAN EXPERIENCE

The essential notion behind this study is that a detailed analysis of the attempt by one country to develop socialism can give some guidance to the problems of developing a strategy for development, and in particular a strategy for socialist economic development. What then do we have to learn from the Tanzanian experience in the last ten years? The first lesson, and one not surprising to any student of history, is the very narrow range for manoeuver which leaders in Tanzania had.[1] They were, in many ways, effectively constrained by the historical setting in Tanzania, and by international events beyond their control. The pattern of investment in Tanzania, then, can be viewed as determined less by the political events in the country, than by other phenomena. The Arusha Declaration, in short, was only one of many factors determining the pattern of investment.

Throughout the study, and particularly in chapter seven, I talked of these other factors. The heritage – in political, social, and economic terms – of colonialism is obviously a dominant influence. The emphases on infrastructure and on post-primary education in the First FYP were, for example, direct responses to the neglect of the colonial government. In broader terms, the continued emphasis of government programmes on a few export crops in a few regions reflects the economic reality that the country is dependent upon the foreign exchange earnings of such crops. It takes time to shift the basic structure of the economy.

---

1 This does not contradict the early statement that Tanzanian leaders had more freedom to develop a socialist strategy of development than the elites in other newly independent countries.

Outside political events forced Tanzania to make investment decisions which it would probably not have taken otherwise. The most notable example is UDI, by Rhodesia. As we have mentioned, this called forth shs 2.4 billion in investment, almost a quarter of the government's development programme. This is not, of course, to imply that the investment decision does not also reflect the ideological commitment of the country. No other country has responded to Zambia's needs in any where near the extent that Tanzania has. Nevertheless, the initiating force behind this investment decision was an outside political event.

Thirdly, the pattern of investment in Tanzania can be said to have been determined by the international setting in which it finds itself. Its continued integration into international capitalism has encouraged technological dependence, and constrained the choice of types of development it has tried. It is true that it has been a political choice on the part of Tanzania to maintain this integration, and in that sense it has been a political choice to accept the constraints on the pattern of investment. Nevertheless, it is unlikely that the socialist countries would be willing to finance a Cuba-style break with international capitalism for Tanzania. When the costs of such a break are contrasted with the apparent short-run benefits offered by integration – aid, quick access to technology, personnel – it is not surprising that Tanzania has remained integrated. This integration has affected the pattern of investment.

Finally, the pattern of investment reflected the emerging class structure of Tanzania. The urban class was not as strong in Tanzania as in other newly-independent countries. The independence party was very rurally based. These two factors allowed the Tanzanian leadership, which was unusually progressive, to formulate a strategy of development and investment which emphasized rural as opposed to urban development, and equality versus favoritism to strong interest groups. Yet the position of the urban forces – the elite, the middle ranks of the bureaucracies, and the working class – was not so weak in Tanzania that they could not effectively resist the actual implementation of this strategy. Indeed they have done so, and in many ways strengthened their position. For the fight over the strategy of development is not just a fight over short-run gains. It is a fight over the long-run development of the society. An urban-oriented strategy, involving the creation of a larger and more critical urban interest group, makes a more egalitarian, rural-oriented strategy even less politically viable in the future. Because of their critical position in the decision-making process, the urban classes have pushed for programmes which differ little from those of neighbouring countries. Often the emotive appeal of nationalism, self-reliance, and socialism are invoked to support these investment decisions, but the ultimate result is a programme which bears only some resemblance to the 'official' strategy.

The constraints on an investment strategy are not, however, so overwhelming that the strategy is predetermined. The political situation, in particular, is still extremely fluid, and is as much a product of the investment strategy as a determinant of that strategy. At present, there still exists a leadership firmly committed to the Arusha strategy, and committed to developing the political and bureaucratic power of the rural areas. The fight has just begun, and will continue for some time. The investment strategy which emerges from this fight will be a major factor in determining the ultimate victor.

Non-political constraints on the investment strategy are again not binding. Yet it is important to take these constraints into account, for they do impose severe restrictions on the strategy. They do not, however, rule out a rural-oriented strategy, but simply make such a strategy less than ideal.

One conclusion which may be drawn from this study is that the focus for socialist development must centre on the economic sphere. While it is important to worry about the development of socialist social policies, these policies are relatively easily defined, more easy to implement, and force less political opposition than do economic ones. For it is the economic development of the country which strikes at the root of the political system, and challenges the political base of many leaders. In poor countries, such as Tanzania, where the commitment to economic growth is so great, social and economic policies cannot diverge in the long run (as I pointed out in the case of water) and economic policies will, in the end, determine the pattern of investment. Therefore an approach to socialist development must be one which fully accepts the central importance of the economy.

There must be detailed specification of the strategy. This applies to all spheres, but most importantly to the economic sphere because of its central role in any over-all strategy, and because the lack of consensus among socialists as to a proper economic strategy. In Tanzania, the reverse of this approach has been true. Specification of policy has been achieved more in social fields than in economic ones, in part because of this lack of consensus, in part because of a failure to recognize the centrality of the economic sector, and in part because specification of an economic strategy would force the commitment to socialism to be taken to a higher level.

It is also important, as I stressed in chapter one, to realize that any investment strategy must be embedded in a political strategy. I agree with the call of people like Shivji and Saul for a renewed emphasis on the Party as an instrument of development. The Party must become an effective instrument of socialist transformation. It must be the key which releases the creative energies of the rural population, and directs those energies towards collective efforts to improve their own welfare.[2]

2 On the other hand Rweyemamu is probably correct that a select part of the elite will continue for some time to be the main driving force behind the drive to socialism. If, however, socialism is to have a long-run future in Tanzania it must have a mass base.

NYERERE'S CRITICS

The essential element of a socialist strategy of development is that it is a strategy which is designed to achieve a number of objectives. I talked about those objectives in chapter one. The critical objective in the Tanzanian context is equality. In chapter two I showed how a stress on equality was at the basis of all of Nyerere's thinking on strategy, and of his commitment to socialism. An investment strategy for Tanzania must have as its goal: *growth with equality.*

It is important to review the strategies proposed by the critics of Nyerere in this light. While it may appear to simplify their positions, the position of Nyerere's critics can be summarized as follows: despite the overwhelming rural nature of the Tanzanian economy, the future lies with industrialization, not with agriculture. The technological backwardness of Tanzanian agriculture, and the conservative nature of the peasant means that transformation of agriculture is difficult, if not impossible. Change will occur only by massive infusions of capital. This requires investment in industries supplying inputs to the rural sector (fertilizer, tractors, etc) and continued emphasis on parastatal ranches and estates. Meanwhile, a socialist strategy of development is distinguished from the one followed by most capitalist countries by its emphasis on the long-term development of the society. This long-term emphasis implies two things. First, such a strategy must concentrate on the transformation of the labour force. Historically such a transformation has been achieved by the development of machine tool industries. Only in this way is it possible to create an economy which is technologically independent, with innovation which is generated internally. Secondly, the long-run future of agricultural exports is bleak, and the shortage of foreign exchange can be solved only by opting out of the present role of supplier of raw materials, and buyer of intermediate and capital goods. This does not imply a reduction in emphasis on exports, but a shift in the type of exports towards those based on domestic demand, and whose long-run price performance will be good.

The approach of Nyerere's critics contains much that is valid. As I said in chapter eight, the approach grows out of a response to the proposition that Third World countries ought to emphasize solely primary product exports. Justinian Rweyemamu's first article (1969) was essentially an attack on this proposition. In the long run it is clear that Tanzania must industrialize, and cease to be solely a primary product exporter. In addition, the stress that Nyerere's critics have placed on devising a strategy which will effect the long-run transformation of the economy is important. The emphasis they place on producing a skilled work force able to understand and adapt modern technology is justified.

Nyerere's critics, nevertheless, fail to adapt their strategy to the particular stage, both economic and political, in which Tanzania finds itself. While many would not disagree with their approach as a basic strategy for Third World nations, there is a real question as to whether Tanzania must not advance through several earlier stages before it can embark on such a strategy. To adopt such a strategy now would be unwise for several reasons.

First, Nyerere's critics do not pay sufficient attention to the distributional effects of their strategy. In a society which has undergone a revolution, and has a revolutionary party firmly in power, it may be possible to dissolve the relationship between productivity and wages. I showed earlier in chapter eight that such a relationship continues to exist in Tanzania, and remains quite strong. Nyerere's critics would favour the rapid development of an industrial sector, and the development of some of the most capital-intensive industries[3] within that sector. The result of such a strategy would be a significant widening of income differentials in Tanzania.

These differentials would increase in terms of both intersectoral and intrasectoral differences. In the course of development, income inequalities may have to widen as highly capital-intensive industries are started. The degree of inequality, however, which results from starting these industries will depend on the level of development attained before they are started. At present most of Tanzania's economically active population is engaged in non-estate agriculture, or related activities (forestry, fishing, hunting). The average family income of this population is shs 1128 per year (in 1969, average worker earned shs 730). The rest of the population is engaged in activities where the average annual income for workers ranged from shs 1944 in 1969 for estate agriculture to more than shs 10,000 for mining, chemical, and metal industries.

The average wage of an adult male citizen in the non-agricultural sector was shs 4573, or 4.1 times the average family income in peasant agriculture. The average wage of a worker in the manufacturing sector was shs 4212, below the average for the whole non-agricultural sector. Thus the problem of income inequalities does not lie with manufacturing per se, but with the type of manufacturing. An emphasis on infrastructure or on capital-intensive types of manufacturing will increase over-all inequality.

The strategy of Nyerere's critics concentrates on developing basic industries. The result would be an increase in the number of people at the top, but at the cost of leaving most of the society unaltered. The average wage of the non-agricultural sector of the society would increase. A programme of allocating 40 per cent of investment to manufacturing, and half of that to basic industries, would significantly widen the urban/rural dichotomy in the society. A programme, on the other hand, which developed labour-intensive low wage industries or which

---

3 To produce an 'integrated' economy almost all of Nyerere's critics favour the development of steel and chemical industries.

allocated significant resources to the rural sector would reduce the urban/ rural gap.

Secondly, the strategy of Nyerere's critics ignores the political implications of such investment. Because many of the writers centre their analysis on the external relations of the country, they ignore the internal political developments which would flow from their approach. The revolution has not yet been secured in Tanzania. It is clear that the balance of power between the urban elite, and the urban work force on the one hand and the rural sector on the other is a very delicate one. At this stage, it is probably only the president who stands in the way of that balance being tipped decisively in favour of the urban areas, as it has been in almost all less-developed countries. Of prime importance in this stage in choosing a strategy is to ensure that it reinforces the political forces which will preserve and strengthen the shift to rural socialism.

There are at present, three main projects which are being considered in Tanzania, and lie at the heart of the 'integrated industrial sector' strategy. The first project is the development of an iron and steel complex around the coal and iron deposits in Mbeya. These deposits appear to be only marginally economical to develop, but the complex is favoured by many for the externalities of the project. Such a complex would cost at least shs 1.0 billion (at a minimum scale), and produce employment for about 5000 people.

The second project is the Stigler's Gorge hydro/aluminum development. This is a joint electricity/manufacturing project. The power potential of the dam so exceeds the projected demand in Tanzania that consultants have suggested developing an aluminum industry around the dam. The aluminum industry would use all imported materials, export most of its product, and probably involve a partnership with one of the large multinational aluminum companies because of their control of the market and the sources of supply of raw material. The dam, aluminum plant, and aluminum rolling industries would cost about shs 2.3 billion and employ about 5500 people.

The third project would be a petroleum complex with a new refinery, chemical plants and fertilizer factory. Total investment for these industries would be shs 1.3 billion, and employment 2700. Again, the basis of the industry would be imported materials, and the industry would have to draw heavily on foreign technology and manpower.

What would be the effect of going ahead with any of these projects at this stage in Tanzanian's development? The economic result is the establishment of a group of industries whose immediate links, although wide with other urban industries, are slight with the rural areas. At best, they can provide inputs to the rural areas. In general they fail to use local resources, but instead are very outer directed. The industries remain apart, often both physically and economically, from the rest of the economy.

TABLE 95

Development of basic industries

	No. of Firms	Assets (shs million)	Employment (no. of persons)	Capital/labour (shs '000)	Wages/labour (shs)
Current situation					
Transport	44	360	3000	120	12,000
Electricity	1	400	3000	130	5300
Mining	1	270	2000	135	12,500
Manufacturing	2	260	1100	236	15,500
Total of dominant parastatals	8	1290	9100	142	10,730
Share of all parastatals	10%	50%	14%		
Average of all parastatals				40	6200
Addition of iron/steel complex					
Total of dominant parastatals	11	2290	14,000	166	11,800[1]
Share of all parastatals	13%	60%	20%		
Average of all parastatals				52	6800
Addition of hydro/aluminium complex					
Total of dominant parastatals	11	2590	14,600	177	12,500[2]
Share of all parastatals	13%	53%	21%		
Average of all parastatals				71	6900
Addition of petroleum/chemical complex					
Total of dominant parastatals	11	2590	11,800	219	11,800
Share of all parastatals	13%	67%	18%		
Average of all parastatals				58	6600

1 Assumes average wage of shs 12,000 p.a. for new industries, as in mining today.
2 Assumes average wage of shs 15,500 p.a. for new industries, as in fertilizer and oil refinery today.

This economic dualism is also mirrored in the work force. These industries create a small group of highly-paid workers. Already in Tanzania a few firms, and their workers, dominate the economy. Table 95 shows this dominance. Eight parastatal firms employing 14 per cent of parastatal workers hold 50 per cent of parastatal assets. These workers earn more than 70 per cent above the earnings of the average parastatal worker, and about 120 per cent above the average non-agricultural worker. The capital/labour ratio of these firms is more than three times the parastatal average. Implementation of any of the proposed projects would only worsen the situation. The petroleum/chemical complex, based as it is on imported materials, is probably the worse project. It would result in a situation where 11 parastatal firms held 67 per cent of parastatal assets. The capital/labour ratio of these firms would be more than five times the current parastatal average, and the average wage almost 90 per cent above it. The iron/steel complex is the best project, but its social and political implications are severe. Some 12,000 workers in 11 firms would be controlling 60 per cent of parastatal assets. These workers would enjoy the high wages which are the result of the enormous capital with which they work (shs 166,000 versus shs 40,000 for parastatals today). In fact, 70 per cent of rural households in the country have a cash income of less than 10 per cent of the average wage paid to these workers (Tanzania, 1972a, 37).

The political implications of this type of labour force development, ignoring the obvious distributional effects, would be dangerous. Already in Tanzania a very few workers have the ability to control a very large share of the productive assets. Giving such a small group such control, setting them apart in terms of location, wages and productivity would risk tipping the political balance decisively in favour of the urban sector. There are numerous examples in the less-developed world of such small groups distorting the development path of the country. Unless the political power of the rural sector has been secured, a strategy of this type appears disastrous.

The third problem with the strategy of Nyerere's critics is that it is not based upon a realistic assessment of the economic viability of such a strategy. Tanzania is a very poor country, with an extremely small market, and a very limited amount of resources available to invest. In the near future Tanzania, no matter what strategy it adopts, will continue to be poor. Table 96 sets out projections for the Tanzanian economy. In ten years, if the Tanzanian economy continues to grow at its present rate, Tanzania will be approaching the position of Kenya today. Its GDP per capita will still be less, shs 905 versus shs 1072, but its GDP will be larger, shs 16,600 million versus shs 12,937 million (or $2.4 billion versus $1.8 billion).

In twenty years, Tanzania would, if its growth rates do not change, still be a very poor rural country by today's standards. Its GDP would be shs 27,115

TABLE 96

Projections of Tanzania's economic future

	1972	1982 (current growth)[1]	1982 (high growth)[2]	1992 (current growth)	1992 (high growth)
Total GDP (shs million)	9850	16,625	21,583	27,115	47,293
Monetary GDP (shs million)	6975	12,664	15,324	21,963	38,307
GDP per capita (shs)	699	904	1139	1129	1855
Monetary GDP per capita	495	688	811	915	1502
Population (millions)	14.1	18.4	18.9	24.0	25.5
Urban population (million)	0.835	1.582	2.166	2.998	5.6
Urban pop. as share of total popl (%)	6	9	11	12	22
Agriculture GDP (shs million)	3950	5403	7014	6779	11,823
Share agric. GDP (%)	40	32.5	32.5	25.0	25.0
Investment (shs million)	2397	4156	5396	6779	11,823

1 Assumes GDP per capita grows at 2.6 per cent per year, population grows at 2.7 per cent per year, urban population grows at 6.6 per cent, subsistence sector's share of GDP declines at 0.5 per cent per year, share of agriculture sector declines at 0.75 per cent per year, investment is 25 per cent of GDP.

2 Assumes GDP per capita grows at 5.0 per cent per year, population grows at 3.0 per cent per year, urban population grows at 10.0 per cent per year, subsistence sector's share of GDP declines at 0.5 per cent per year, share of agriculture sector declines at 0.75 per cent per year, investment is 25 per cent of GDP.

million or $3.9 billion dollars, and its per capita income shs 915 or $131. Eighty-eight per cent of its population would be rural. In terms of total effective demand, the position of Tanzania would still be weak. With a population greater than Canada's present population (27.1 million versus 21.8 million), it would have a monetary GDP of only $3.1 billion dollars, 2.5 per cent of Canada's current GDP. Its investible surplus would be about $0.8 billion dollars (assuming 25 per cent of the GDP is invested), again about 2.5 per cent of Canada's current gross capital formation.

Now it is possible to assume that the adoption of a 'Big Push' strategy would radically accelerate growth, and significantly alter the structure of the economy. Again, however, even the most wildly optimistic growth rates will not alter the basic character of the Tanzanian economy in twenty years. I assume for the projections in Table 96 a growth rate for per capita GDP of 5.0 per cent per year, almost twice the current rate. Total population will grow at 3.0 per cent per year (versus the current 2.7 per cent per year), and urban population will grow at 10 per cent per year (versus 6.6 per cent now). In twenty years, the total GDP would be shs 47.7 billion, or still only $6.8 billion dollars. The population would be 25.5 million, but still predominantly rural (78 per cent would live in the rural areas). GDP per capita would be shs 1855 or $265.00. Its investible surplus would be shs 11.8 billion or $1.7 billion.

These projections are helpful because they help to make clear the very narrow range of Tanzania's options. Because of the extremely rural nature of the society today it will be at least twenty to thirty years before the country is significantly altered in this respect. For this reason a strategy which ignores the rural sector ignores most of the population.

More importantly, these projections raise some very real questions about the viability of industries which require large markets. While it is true that Tanzania could, and probably should start machine tool industries, or elaborate repair facilities in some sectors (railways, tractors, etc.), a general strategy of building capital goods industries quickly runs up against a demand constraint. Rweyemamu, as I pointed out in chapter 8, recognizes this. His answer is to rely upon the East African community, and to expand the degree of integration with other African countries. There is some possibility of doing this. In twenty years time, the total GDP of Kenya, Uganda, and Tanzania will probably be about shs 108.5 billion, or $15.5 billion.[4] A GDP of this size would allow some capital

4 Assumes Kenya's GDP per capita continues to grow at 3.7 per cent per year, and population grows at 3.3 per cent per year. Also assumes Uganda's GDP per capita grows at 2.5 per cent per year and its population at 3 per cent per year. Assumes current growth rates for Tanzania. High growth rates for Tanzania would give a total GDP for the community of $18.2 billion.

goods industries to exist. Nevertheless, the past performance of the EAC has not been good. Trade within the community, as I showed in chapter two, has stagnated. Attempts by one country to develop an industry has initiated attempts by the others to start the same industry. If the response of the Kenya and Uganda governments to a Tanzanian initiative to develop a capital goods sector followed this pattern, then the whole strategy would be called into question.[5]

A strategy which calls for the rapid development of certain basic industries would do so at a high opportunity cost in terms of the development of the rest of the economy. Rweyemamu suggested that 30-40 per cent of investment must be allocated to the development of capital and intermediate goods industries. About 10 per cent of total investment in recent years has gone into consumer goods industries.[6] One can assume that Rweyemamu would want these industries to continue to receive about this share in total investment. Thus Rweyemamu is, in effect, arguing for an allocation of between 40 and 50 per cent of investment to manufacturing.

The effect of such a strategy would be to reduce significantly the relative share of investment going to social services and agriculture. Table 97 sets out the past allocation, and the effect of the proposed strategy. Investment in agriculture would probably fall from 18 per cent of the total in the period 1966-70 to 12 per cent. If this occurred, the investment per capita in the rural areas would fall from shs 32.5 invested today to shs 29.7 in 1982, if the present growth rates prevailed, or rise only marginally to shs 38.7 if high growth rates prevailed.[7] Similarly investment in services (government administration, construction, commerce and other services) would probably fall from 21 per cent of investment to 13 per cent implying a decline from an investment of shs 35.7 per capita on services to shs 29.4 per capita (current growth rates) or a small increase to shs 37.1 per capita (high growth rates). The strategy of Nyerere's critics would involve a stagnation of investment in these sectors.

Moreover, the strategy would involve shifting resources away from investments in processing industries geared primarily towards exports (e.g., cashew nuts,

5 Since the time of writing relations between Tanzania and Kenya have soured considerably. In late 1974, the two countries closed their borders to each other and by 1977 the EAC seemed on the verge of collapse. It seems a risky strategy to depend upon the EAC as a whole as a source of demand for industries.

6 In the period 1966-70 parastatal consumer goods investment was 4 per cent of total investment in the economy. Since private investment has been more consumer goods-oriented, then total consumer goods industries investment in the economy has been at least 8 per cent of investment in the economy, but possibly closer to 10 per cent. Total manufacturing investment in the economy was 17 per cent of total investment in the period 1966-70.

7 Obtained by dividing investment in agriculture in 1982 by rural population in 1982.

TABLE 97

Allocation of investment with basic industries strategy

	Allocation 1966-70 %	Share %	Available investment (shs billion) over 10 year period
Peasant agriculture	12	8	3.4
Estate agriculture	6	4	1.7
Service sector	21	13	5.6
Infrastructure	44	35	15.1
General manufacturing	11	10	4.3
Basic and intermediate industries manufacturing	6	30	12.9
Total	100	100	43.1

pyretheum, hides, sisal rope, tea processing, meat packing) towards inter-mediate and capital goods industries. The result would again be a stagnation in investment in processing industries, in order to build up this integrated industrial sector.

Stagnation of the agriculture and processing sectors would post serious diffi-culties for the economy. Already food shortages are a major problem in Tan-zania. A strategy which would quicken the growth of the urban sector while at the same time decreasing investment in agriculture would bring the problem to a crisis point. Moreover, development of these other sectors is essential for two reasons. First, an inner directed strategy assumes growing internal demand. Stag-nation of the rural sector means stagnation of demand for mass-produced con-sumer goods. Secondly, the import needs of the economy will remain high for some time. The economy as a whole will be dependent for the next twenty to thirty years on the export earnings of the rural areas. Stagnation in this sector would threaten the growth of the whole economy.

The opportunity cost of such a strategy could be lessened if the adoption of the strategy meant an increase in aid flowing to Tanzania. Resources would not have to be shifted out of agriculture, services, and small-scale manufacturing to finance the programme. There may be some validity in this reasoning. Tazara, as I showed in chapter two, raised the level of investment from 17.3 per cent in 1969 to a peak of 29.2 per cent in 1971. Tazara, however, had unique political implications. It is not clear that foreign aid donors could be attracted to such a degree for an industrial programme, or that the aid could be organized for such a programme. Tazara was able to raise investment rapidly because it was only one project run by an essentially foreign enterprise.

In fact, there is a strong reason to believe that a turning away from a rural-oriented strategy would reduce the level of aid available. As I showed in chapter six Nordic aid has become increasingly important to Tanzania (20 per cent of total aid in 1972-3, 33 per cent of aid excluding Tazara). This aid, like much of World Bank/IDA aid, has been attracted by Tanzania's current strategy. A shift in strategy might affect the inflow of that aid. If such a fall occurred, even at high growth rates the investment per capita on services and agriculture would have to be less ten years from now than it is today in order to finance the industrial strategy.[8]

The projections can be misleading because they show the position after twenty years growth. They do not show how to get there. In twenty years Tanzania will be approaching the position of Egypt, and in thirty years the position of North Korea today.[9] This fact does not justify Tanzania's developing the industries Egypt or North Korea are developing today or even those that they developed twenty years ago. One must establish the best strategy for getting to that stage. North Korea was the industrialized part of Korea before partition, having over four-fifths of its heavy industry, and three-quarters of its hydro potential (Economist Intelligence Unit, 1973). It had a large skilled industrial work force. Korea was simply exploiting its natural advantage, and developing its historical economic base when it developed its capital and heavy goods industries.

Other socialist countries will have to exploit other sectors of the economy as a means of attaining economic development. The sector chosen will depend upon the historical development and the material base of the economy. Cuba, as I pointed out in chapter one, has decided that it must develop its agriculture. It has made this decision despite the widespread belief among Cuban socialists that its historical dependence on sugar was bad. Nevertheless the sugar industry exists, and provides an effective sector to use as a base for further development. Again Tanzanians should not decide that they must develop their sugar industry

8 If investment were 20 per cent of GDP, still a very high figure, then investment per capita on agriculture would be shs 31.0 in 1982 assuming high growth rates, and on services would be shs 29.7. These figures compare to the current rate of shs 32.5 and shs 35.7 respectively.

9 In 1971 Egypt's per capita GDP was $206 compared to an expected value of $161 for Tanzania at current rate of growth or $265 at high rates. Data on the Democratic Republic of Korea are difficult to obtain. Its per capita income was probably close to (if not higher than) that of the Republic of Korea which was $277 in 1972. If Tanzania's economy grew at its current rate it would take 41 years. i.e., until the year 2013, to reach this per capita income. Thus it will take Tanzania probably somewhere between twenty and forty years to reach South Korea's current position.

because Cuba did. That is no more logical than looking at Korea and deciding a strategy emphasizing capital goods is best. The strategy chosen must reflect the Tanzanian situation.

A similar point can be made with respect to the transformation of the work force. A disciplined and skilled work force has been created in many different ways in countries. In only some has the creation of a large industrial base been the mechanism. In China, the war and revolution began the process of bringing such a transformation. Now the commune, based essentially on agriculture, but including industries, is used for this purpose. Tanzania too must find its own way, and cannot simply duplicate the experience of other countries. It is clear that one cannot speak of a strategy which transforms the labour force in Tanzania and which is not firmly embedded in the rural sector. That is where the labour force is, and where it will continue to be in the near future.

A STRATEGY

A strategy which will suit the Tanzanian environment must, as I have said, be based upon developing the rural areas. In defining in more explicit terms an investment strategy for Tanzania I will build essentially on Nyerere's over-all development strategy. Nyerere has understood the constraints on Tanzanian development, and outlined a strategy which offers the best hope of building socialism in that environment. He has failed to be sufficiently explicit in setting forth the investment implications of such a strategy. Let us try to do that here.

Agriculture

Tanzania must increase its emphasis on agriculture. As difficult as it may be to devise programmes to transform the agricultural sector, any abandonment of an attempt to do so implies denial of the goal of equality. The emphasis on agriculture must continue to be linked with Ujamaa villages. By bringing people together, such villages offer the best hope of transforming the mode of production.

The important contribution of Nyerere's critics has been to again point out the danger of a continued emphasis on primary product exports, especially products whose long-term price will not continue to rise. The government has, however, belatedly realized this, and is beginning to diversify its emphasis on agriculture in two ways. First, a greater emphasis must be placed on the production of domestically consumed agricultural products. Tanzania still imports major amounts of wheat, maize, sugar, and dairy products. It has the ability to produce all these economically.

Secondly, Tanzania is able to produce products such as meat, pyretheum, cashew nuts, and cotton whose long-term price looks good. Only recently has the government directed its attention in any serious way to improving the production of the first three of these commodities. Exports of meat were only 3300 tons in 1972 compared to a peak of 8100 tons in 1966. This drop was in spite of an 80 per cent rise in the unit price of meat exports. Thus the country with the second largest herd of cattle in Africa (and a herd larger than that of Texas) suffers internal meat shortages, and only exports shs 42 million ($6.0 million) worth of meat exports.

Non-agricultural development

A mistake often made is to equate rural development with agricultural development. Success in transforming the Tanzanian economy without developing an urban elite lies with developing non-agricultural rural activities. At present both primary activities – forestry, fishing – and secondary activities – processing, small-scale manufacturing – are neglected. The result is an exacerbation of the urban/rural dualism. There has not been the development of activities which raise the skill and productivity levels of the population marginally. A peasant moves dramatically from a sector where output per worker is shs 600 to sectors where the output per worker ranges from a low of shs 4500 in services to shs 12,200 in trade, and averages shs 7685 (Tanzania, 1972a, 27). What is essential is an intermediate stage.

This lack of an intermediate stage is reflected in the gap in development of socialist institutions. The Ujamaa villages, almost exclusively agricultural, are the vehicle for socialist expansion in the rural areas. Parastatals, concentrating as I have shown on large-scale non-agricultural enterprises, are the tool of the government for socialist development in the modern sector. There is no intermediate socialist institution, designed to develop enterprises which employ only a few workers (50 or less), and to operate with only a little capital (less than shs 1.0 million in fixed capital). It is this area where private enterprise, and particularly the Asians, still clearly dominate.

The District Development Corporations, as I pointed out in chapter two, have been established to fill this void. They have not been given any significant support either in terms of manpower or money. Nor has the other institution, the National Small Scale Industries Corporation, which was designed to fill this void, been given significant support. Its programme, as I pointed out in chapter five, has been thwarted through lack of resources. Only by dramatically increasing the role of these institutions can the government hope to encourage rural socialist development. This strategy implies a shift in the role of regional administrators away from their current emphasis on social services and economic infrastructure, towards a role where development of directly productive enterprises is as important as this service function.

Manufacturing

The strategy proposed here would not involve a diminution in the emphasis on manufacturing. It stresses, however, that at this stage Tanzania must develop an industrial structure which links urban and rural areas. Industries based upon imported raw materials (and thus invariably centred in the towns near the ports) should not be started. Their development can come in ten or fifteen years time when the rural population is stronger both politically and economically. Rather, industries based upon increasing the value added of local raw materials should be started. There are still many obvious linkages which Tanzania has only begun to exploit — sisal rope, sisal carpets, hides, shoes, cashew nuts, meat products. Instead Tanzania has a shoe factory which makes plastic shoes, or a tire factory using imported synthetic rubber.

Industries should be small in size and as a consequence distributed widely throughout the country. The one or two large projects 'which will transform the economy' must be avoided.[10] If equality is to be promoted, then, the country will have to be willing to pay the short-run economic cost of locating industries in every region. It is not clear that this cost will be great. There are many projects in supposedly undeveloped regions (e.g., fish-processing plants, sawmills, boat-building industries in Kigoma) which go unexploited. At present Tanzania is sacrificing these opportunities to build steel rolling mills, tire factories, elaborate bakeries, and fertilizer plants of dubious economic value in the large centres.

Industries should be labour intensive. Labour intensity is important for two reasons. Resources are not unlimited in Tanzania, and therefore there is some opportunity cost to capital-intensive industries. Secondly, capital-intensive industries encourage the development of a small part of the labour force whose productivity greatly exceeds that of the surrounding population. If the strategy is built around the notion of integrating the rural and urban economies, it is important that the industries located in the rural areas can be integrated. The Williamson diamond mine, despite its rural location, is not integrated into the surrounding area. Peasants must be able to move from farming to working in the industry without great difficulty.[11]

The characteristics of the industrial strategy I have outlined — use of local raw materials, regional dispersal, rural location, small size, labour intensity — are not contradictory. In fact, one of the noteworthy features of the industrial structure which currently exists in Tanzania is this very dichotomy between

10 It is likely that such projects will not transform the economy, but rather lead to economic stagnation.
11 In northern Canada, the industries established there, especially forestry, served this very process of gradually urbanizing the labour force.

industries. Some industries have the characteristics described above; others have virtually opposite characteristics. The dichotomy is, of course, not always clear cut, and exceptions do exist. More importantly, often industries which could be small are made large. Those that could be labour intensive, are capital intensive, and those that could be rurally located, have been located in urban areas.

The point I would like to make here, however, is that a decision to exploit industries with any of these characteristics will naturally lead to pressure to conform to the other characteristics. A sawmill (based upon local products), in order to be economically viable should be based in the rural areas. There are very real limits to how capital intensive a sawmill can be. Despite the capital intensity of the Sao-Hill Sawmill, one could still build twelve such mills for the cost of the oil refinery, employing more than seven times the workers, and even adding 1.7 times as much value added.[12] The mill itself is small, less than shs 10 million in assets, and its process easily understood by all. In fact, because it uses local raw materials it has a significant impact on the local area. The skill levels required to work there are easily learned, and movement from agriculture to industry is facilitated. The oil refinery has no such externalities.

Economic infrastructure

In the empirical chapters I showed how economic infrastructure has absorbed a significant share of public investment, and how the thrust of this investment had been towards large-scale transformation projects. It is difficult to assess the wisdom of some of these decisions. The corridor to Zambia was politically very important. The lack of routes at independence necessitated some expenditure on developing the over-all transportation grid. The low-level electricity production of the country, despite its obvious hydro potential, naturally attracted investment.

The time has been reached, however, for a shift in direction. This shift has two aspects. First, there should be some diminution in the over-all emphasis on infrastructural investment. As I showed earlier in this chapter, investment on transport and utilities has absorbed 44 per cent of total investment in the economy in the period 1966 to 1970. With the building of Tazara, the share of this sector has not been less in recent years. There is in Tanzania, as there appears to

12 Obviously the benefits would be greater if socialist institutions could learn to duplicate some of the Asians' parsimonious behaviour. One could build 19 Sikh sawmills for the price of the oil refinery, employing 22 times the workers, and generating almost 8 times the value added. In fact, if the resources spent on the refinery had been used to develop the wood industry, employment in manufacturing in 1971 would have been more than 10 per cent higher today.

be in many countries, a great attraction in infrastructural projects. Yet it is not clear that such projects meet the real need — to develop productive enterprises which will improve the productivity of the labour force. If I may borrow a page from Hirschman (1970, chap. 5).[13] I would argue that the roads will get built soon enough if there is something to move on them. The need is to produce the goods to move. Indeed, my experience in Tanzania would lead me to believe that the goods will get out virtually without roads if they are produced, and there is an incentive to export them from the region!

The second type of shift is one in the nature of infrastructure developed. Despite the emphasis on transport and utilities, the developmental impact of this expenditure has been slight. As I showed in chapters two, four and five, the public sector has virtually ignored transportation. Public investment has largely gone into the Zambian corridor, or into trunk roads or aerodromes. Yet the critical need in the future in Tanzania is to replace the local Asian or Arab entrepreneur who runs a truck or two from the rural areas to the small towns, or from the small towns to the large. This gap parallels the gap in manufacturing. There has been no emphasis on the intermediate level, the level most firmly in capitalist hands, and the level where deterioration is greatest because of the uncertainty over the role of private investment, and more specifically the future of the Asians. Thus for both ideological and economic reasons, the government must soon move decisively to fill this gap.

The government must also move to put more emphasis on lower-level infra-structure. By and large this is what it seems to be doing. The increased stress on feeder roads is part of this change in emphasis. Nevertheless, there still remains a tendency to join with an aid donor in building the large trunk highway or the modern urban road. The electricity parastatal still thinks primarily in terms of massive hydro developments designed to serve large industries in a few industrial centres. There has been little attempt to study the power needs of an industrial strategy emphasizing decentralized small-scale industries.

Social services
The policy of the government on social services has increasingly moved in the desired direction. Today the emphasis on raising the educational level of the

---

13 Hirschman argues that one should concentrate one's attention on saving investment decisions. The real blockage to development is the failure to get things going. One should therefore concentrate one's effort on doing projects which force other decisions to be made, and projects to be started. Building a road does not force the development of an industry, but building an industry does force the development of a road. Therefore, one should build industries.

mass of the population, through adult and primary education, is much greater than it was ten years ago. Similarly the health programme is much better than it used to be, although it still needs improvement. The stress on preventive medicine versus curative, rural health versus urban, low-cost widespread coverage versus high-cost intensive care must be increased. Finally, the government has recognized the importance in both social and economic terms of water in the rural areas. The rural water programme must continue to be a major priority of the government.

It is important to make two points about social services. The first is their importance in terms of any strategy of rural development. It is not possible to stop urban migration, to prevent the best sections of the rural population from going to cities, without a comprehensive programme to make the rural areas an attractive place to live. If the urban areas are centres of social services, they will become centres of attraction as well. Moreover, a strategy of rural development based as it is on a commitment to equality is a fraud if it does not imply equal provision of social services.

The second point about social services is their relation to other programmes. Here I am merely re-emphasizing a point I have made several times. It is impossible to have a social programme based on equality and rural development, yet have an economic strategy built around a 'Big Push' for industry. Contradictions will necessarily emerge, and the pull of the economic strategy will eventually force a change in social policy: resources will have to be drawn from rural water programmes to provide water for the new industries; schools will have to be built to train the required technicians, while the primary school programme will be slowed down in order to prevent the development of a large class of primary school leavers facing unemployment because of the lack of development of labour-intensive low technology industries; the new highly-paid urban work forces will demand good health services and the cost to the country of shutting these industries down will force the government to accede to their demands. Thus the government must choose its strategy, and this strategy must be consistent in all sectors.

Dangers of the strategy

It will be objected that the strategy risks certain dangers. An emphasis on the rural sector is an emphasis on the one sector where socialist institutions are the weakest. Do we not risk creating a kulak class, a class of economically progressive peasants who ride on the backs of the general expansion of the rural sector and establish a rural capitalist class? The weakness of the Ujamaa programme in the regions which are at present most developed (see chapter two) means that it is a real possibility that agriculture will remain in private hands in the foreseeable future.

There are really two arguments against this fear of rural capitalism. The first is that there are things which can be done to prevent it. The Ujamaa programme is the vehicle for emphasizing rural development, so it is through the development of socialist institutions that one expects to see the rural sector transformed. While an emphasis on rural development will undoubtedly help all farmers, it will be directed towards simultaneously creating socialist institutions. It is also important to remember that rural development and agricultural development are not the same thing. While it may be difficult to decisively alter the pattern of ownership in agriculture, it is not impossible to do so in non-agricultural rural activities. Again, I am emphasizing the critical role of intermediate socialist institutions. If private agriculture was surrounded by socialist institutions in all other fields — transport, trade, local manufacturing — then the dangers of a small group of capitalist farmers[14] would be minimized.

Secondly, the alternative to my strategy seems even worse. Ignoring the rural sector, as most of Nyerere's critics do, is surely no answer. The problem of capitalist development in the rural areas can only be solved by a vigorous programme of socialist development in this sector, not by building socialism in the urban centres. A large, capitalist rural sector which stagnates economically poses just as explosive a political threat as does an economically viable one.

Moreover, Nyerere's critics seem to me to have a misplaced dislike of peasant capitalists. While it may be heresy on the Left to say this, I do find it amazing to hear socialists advocating the creation of an elite group of laborers earning shs 10,000 a year, and of managers earning shs 35,000 a year in order to prevent the possible development of a large number of peasants earning shs 2000 to shs. 5000 a year. Now I recognize that the two groups may be in a quite different class — one is an employer and one an employee — but the fact remains that in terms of distribution of income and in terms of thwarting socialist development, the urban-based group can be just as much a danger as the rural group. It seems to me a real question how far one ought to go in order to prevent the development of a rural capitalist class — is the stagnation of the rural sector, or the development of a system of bureaucratic capitalism (à la Soviet Union) really preferable?

The other danger in such a strategy is that it risks continued dependency for Tanzania. It is clear that the strategy implies a continued emphasis on exports, and a continued reliance on foreign technology. Will not Tanzania find itself ten years from now just farther behind the rest of the world, still dependent on the industrialized world?

The experience of other countries has taught us that the problem of dependency is not always best solved by a direct attack on the problem, an attack

14 Farmers employing labour, and accumulating significant amounts of investible surplus.

which relies upon the country leaping many stages in development, Cuba had a much higher income than Tanzania, and more importantly, had a large skilled work force at the time of its attempt to industrialize rapidly. Nevertheless, this attempt resulted in more rather than less dependency because it led to economic stagnation and balance of payments problems.

The most effective way to achieve independence is to build a strong viable economy based upon local resources, and on an indigenous labour force where skills are constantly being upgraded. The economy must be structurally transformed as quickly as possible, but not in a way which leaves large sections of the society behind. Thus the emphasis should be on a frontal approach of raising the level of productivity across the whole working population. There must be no slackening in the determination to transform the economy, but this determination should not lead to a programme of advancing rapidly in only a few sectors. Such a 'Big Push' approach may become viable at a later stage of development when the resulting cultural, economic, and political gap which such a concentrated effort produces will not be so serious.

It is important to distinguish my strategy from the one advocated for most capitalist Third World countries. The critical aspect of this strategy is that development occurs through socialist institutions. In a capitalist country the economy can be trapped at different stages because it ceases to be in the interest of the property-owning classes to allow a transformation. Thus industrialization was delayed in Latin America because of the power of the landowning classes and imperialism. Backward integration, the development of certain types of exports, or the creation of indigenous research capacity may be slowed in Third World countries today because it is not in the interests of multinationals to allow such developments to occur.[15] In Tanzania the most important owner of the means of production is the state. The state, then, can shift resources from an emphasis on labour-intensive, small-scale enterprises to more capital-intensive, technologically-advanced enterprises, or from processing industries to capital goods industries when such shifts seem economically appropriate. It is clearly naive to believe that there are no interest groups in socialist societies or that these interest groups will not resist change. Because the Tanzanian economy has not been fully socialized, some of these interest groups are also owners of property. Nevertheless, the ability of the Tanzanian government to allocate the

15 No conspiracy theory is needed for such a statement. In Canada, as in many countries, the multinationals prefer to locate their research facilities in the centre (usually the United States). Since 65 per cent of Canadian manufacturing is foreign owned, the result of this individual preference is a lack of research centres in Canada, and a failure by Canada to generate its own technologies.

investible surplus to new areas, and thereby to alter the structure of the economy, is fairly large, and certainly significantly larger than most governments.[16] Moreover, the commitment of a socialist government to full employment, and to a social welfare programme, lessens the costs to any interest group of a shift in emphasis. There is not a need in a socialist country, as there very well might be in a capitalist country, to skip stages simply to avoid creating certain interest groups who are likely to block further change.

Nor should the strategy I have outlined be misconstrued as a strategy of depending upon primary product exports. The strategy does involve a continued reliance on such exports. To advocate Tanzania's abandoning its current source of foreign exchange is to advocate a policy of non-development. The programme I have outlined has stressed the need to raise the level of productivity of the work force by improved methods and the influsion of capital in agriculture and by greatly increasing the value added by non-agricultural rural activities – the manufacture of low-income consumer goods, repair shops, processing activities, etc. This is a programme of structural transformation, but one which accepts the very early stage of development in which Tanzania finds itself, and seeks to move the society to the next stage.

Finally, one could argue that my strategy may be desirable, but it is not practical. It could be argued that Tanzania does not have the capacity to initiate a programme involving the gradual development of the entire agricultural sector, and the initiation of many small rural industries. Large-scale transformation projects are attractive to the Tanzanians just because they are easily implemented.

To argue that Tanzania must accept a Big Push strategy because it is the only viable alternative seems to me too pessimistic. The Tanzanians show an increasing ability to mobilize their people. To abandon that attempt is to abandon any effort to create a mass-based socialism. Moreover, my strategy should not be portrayed in its extreme. I do not advocate the end to the development of intermediate-size industries, nor the end to any use of foreign firms to develop industries. I am simply arguing that the shift must be away from the large-scale, capital-intensive project to a smaller-scale project based upon simpler technologies, and on local resources. This means that Tanzania would press ahead with its plans for textile mills, meat packing plants, tanneries, and cement plants. These are all quite large undertakings, based on local resources and fairly simple

16 By 1971, public investment was 57 per cent of productive investment in the monetary economy, excluding Tazara, and 73 per cent including it. Public investment was 54 per cent of total investment in the whole economy, excluding Tazara, and 64 per cent including it.

technology. It should, however, postpone attempts to develop an iron and steel complex, or chemical industry, and use these resources to develop its wood industry, shoe factories in Ujamaa villages, repair shops, or fishing exports. Tanzania has the capacity to make this type of shift, and in doing so will be preparing for the time when the long-run transformation of the economy can be successfully completed.

IMPLEMENTATION OF THE STRATEGY

It is not enough to outline a strategy. One must set forth how to implement it. The most important lesson one learns from the study of development is that a strategy is meaningless unless it is institutionalized. To anyone other than a student of neo-classical economics, it would be obvious to say that the development of the proper type of institutions is an essential part of any approach to socialist development. But economists have essentially stopped reading sociology since Max Weber, and still approach the problem of planning as one of developing rational policies to be carried out by a Weber-like rational command-responsive bureaucracy.

The thrust of most studies of bureaucracy since Weber has been that the actions of bureaucracies are much more complicated. Crozier (1964), for example, has shown that bureaucracies respond to pressures, but these pressures may not be the ones formally conceived as dominant. Thus it is important to go beyond the organizational chart to study what pressures exist on the bureaucracy, and which will dominate in which instance. In Tanzania, parastatals are formally under the control of the central planning ministry, but their responsiveness to its demands are often slight. In fact, organizations like NDC, TANESCO, NBC, and NMC are frequently worried more about their reputations with international organizations than with fulfilling the pressures exerted by the central planning ministry. Their contact with representatives of these organizations was often greater (NDC with managers of its subsidiaries, NBC with personnel from its associate banks), and their work identity with them was greater than with what were regarded as rather naive central planners. Even more important, the isolation of parastatal executives made them relatively immune from the pressures of the poverty of Tanzania and the overwhelming dominance of the rural sector. Housed atop sparkling new buildings, in the capital city, conferring almost exclusively with international firms (consultants and suppliers), the parastatal executive was removed from any direct pressure to relate to the reality of Tanzanian development. One could also argue that many academics isolated in a campus set apart from the city fall into the same category. Thus it is not surprising that such institutions failed to be centres of socialist innovation. TANESCO executives felt more pressure to meet the demands of the World Bank than of the Tanzanian government. Officials in NDC or NBC always talked about the maintenance of their international reputations as sound financial institutions, and would compare their balance sheets to those of private Kenya firms to see if they were successful.

Having chosen a strategy for development, then, one must devise the institutions which can carry out that strategy, and form them in such a way as to exert the proper pressure on them to perform the desired function. One problem in Tanzania was that many of the institutions which carried out the socialist exercise were, as I showed in chapter four, formed in the pre-1967 period, and reflect non-socialist goals in their structure. Perhaps the most important of these institutions is the National Development Corporation, whose goal, as I showed earlier, was initially to encourage private enterprise. Although this purpose was later abandoned, the organization remained unchanged, as did many of its personnel. NDC tended to think of socialist investment as entailing its taking 80 per cent or 100 per cent equity rather than 50 per cent or 40 per cent. The projects it implemented, as I have shown, were many of those left over from the First FYP, or stemmed from ideas obtained by looking at the import-substituting programmes launched by neighbouring countries.

Now in forming institutions which will aid the development of a socialist strategy, several things should be borne in mind. It seems useful to define the goals and activities of an organization rather narrowly. One way of creating a certain type of development is to create institutions which can only carry out that type of development. Tanzania has increasingly moved in that direction. It has dismantled NDC, and created specific companies to carry out development in tourism, agriculture, and mining. NDC now is really a manufacturing development firm, emphasizing import substitution, and later forms of processing. In this way the central planning bureau can more easily shift its emphasis by shifting an allocation of investible surplus between these institutions. Moreover, one can more easily see whether investment activity is moving in the right direction by the relative activities of each institution.

Narrowly defining the role of institutions becomes particularly important in a political situation such as exists in Tanzania, where large numbers of the people are unsympathetic to socialism. One has to devise ways which will force these people to act in the desired manner. The decentralization which occurred in 1972 can be understood as an attempt to do exactly this. As I have shown, the emphasis on rural development did not increase in relative quantitative terms after the Arusha Declaration. In general, people tended to want to plan fertilizer plants, or sisal pulp mills, rather than chicken hatcheries. The decentralization exercise, however, put a large number of bureaucrats, and some of the best bureaucrats, in the position where their advancement meant developing programmes which benefitted the rural areas. As I said in chapter two, the activities which were decentralized were rural activities. Moreover, the economic realities of the situation prevent the regional director of a backward region like Kigoma conceiving of building a steel mill. His efforts are directed towards developing saw mills or fish-processing plants.

Moreover, in the total complex of the government, eighteen new pressure groups (there are 18 regions) were created to push for rural development. This produces a bureaucratic counterweight to the central institutions, ministries, and especially parastatals which tend to be urban-oriented. The effect of decentralization was immediate. The activities under their jurisdiction received more than twice the allocation that they received when they were under ministerial control. The urban/rural code, as I pointed out in chapter three, registered a dramatic shift in rural emphasis.

The explanation for the rural-oriented nature of decentralized administrations does not lie simply in their formal structure, although this is important. Decentralized bureaucrats face the immediate pressure of the rural population. While the reality of democratic control envisaged in the decentralization exercise (see chapter two) has probably not been achieved, there is little question that decision-making at the regional and district levels is less immune from the will of the people. This points to another lesson of the Tanzanian experience. Socialist literature quite rightly has stressed the need for institutions to be controlled democratically. Government structures must be fashioned so as to involve people in their decision-making activities. While this is desirable in its own right, what Tanzania shows is its importance in terms of achieving socialist goals.

It is not possible to create socialism from the top. This is true for several reasons. First, because, as I have argued, there is no *a priori* socialist strategy, the development of correct policies must take into account the experience in actually implementing policies. Thus a leadership must not remain immune from the results of its policies. Moreover, the chief challenge in development is to use creatively the resources available. This can be done only by tapping the knowledge and imagination of the people. Secondly, no socialist revolution successfully purges all those who oppose socialist measures. Indeed, people change over time, and it is easy for someone who was at the vanguard of the revolution to tire of the hardships socialism inevitably imposes on the elite. Thus the decision-makers must always be subject to the pressure of the people. Socialism usually abolishes the market place as an effective disciplinary mechanism. However poor this mechanism is, it does serve to provide a degree of check on the actions of bureaucrats. By abolishing competition, without replacing it with democratic forms of control, socialist countries can run the risk of creating bureaucracies totally immune from the needs of the people.

Having devised a strategy, and developed a set of institutions, one must create a set of mechanisms to ensure that the strategy is carried out. To do so involves abandoning much of the intellectual baggage of the traditional economist's approach to project selection. Neo-classical economics teaches an approach which depends upon the marginality of the decision. In development economics, most government decisions are not marginal. Moreover, if they are to come to grips with the reality of the situation they must look beyond the short-time horizon assumed in neo-classical economics. The problem in development economics is the structural transformation of the economy. Any approach whose validity presupposes an unchanged structure, then, has little use.

The alternative is to begin with a broader view and work downward. Basically, one must pose the question: where can Tanzania reasonably expect to be twenty years from now? The asking of this simple, obvious question seems to mean to go a long way towards eliminating many of the strategies currently proposed. Moreover, by asking the question one confronts the hard issue of the kind of society which Tanzania wants to build. Working down from that level of generality, one can begin to specify what this vision means in terms of each sector, and each sub-sector. As well, allocations between sectors become clearer.

Flowing from this greater degree of specification should come an idea of the type of project which fits into the over-all strategy. Naturally there should be a mix of projects, but some notion of the mix should have been developed. Now what is critical for a country just beginning the road to socialism is that it abandon the notion of examining every project on its merits, but rather devise crude measures which force decisions along certain lines. In fact, emerging socialist countries must be prepared to overcompensate in order to break the grip of the inherited structure. What does this mean in more concrete terms? Basically, it means in the case of a country like Tanzania that it must specify limits on the share of credit which can go to non-agricultural sectors, or government spending in the urban areas. It should prohibit projects with capital/labour ratios above certain limits, or import intensity ratios which are too high. Targets must be set on the amount of resources going to the regions, and limits specified on the amount of investment in any one region.

Now it will be argued that such an approach will involve misallocating resources. There are good capital-intensive projects. One must have balanced growth. Opportunities in rich regions should not go unexploited. These arguments miss the vital lesson of the Tanzanian experience. Change is difficult to enact. It is constrained by outside forces, and often opposed by people who will lose by it. To get change one must force the pace, decisively break with the past. This must be done in a way which permanently establishes institutions which will preserve the change. Once the power of the perverse structure has been broken, one can talk of balanced growth, and surveying the investment horizons. Before that occurs, however, one must create the political conditions which will ensure that the balance of political forces is such as to ensure long-run growth. In countries, like Tanzania, which have undergone a process of underdevelopment, this may mean temporarily distorting the growth in the opposite direction to achieve a proper balance.

Crude rules prevent opposers of the policy from thwarting it by claiming ambiguity. They also serve the function of specifying, in ways everyone can understand, the national objectives. What does rural socialism mean? It means, for example, spending over 60 per cent of ministerial development expenditure on rural development, or 150 per cent as much per capita on the poorest 5 regions as on the other regions. It means prohibiting the development of industries with capital/labour ratios over shs 50,000 or import intensity ratios over 25 per cent. It means decentralizing at least half the development budget, and transferring at least 25 per cent of the investible surplus allocated to productive investments to the regions. Crude guidelines such as these force people to confront more clearly the issue of allocation of resources. In Tanzania one still finds a separation between the rhetorical commitment to a programme, and the idea that such a commitment involves allocating the necessary resources to carry out the commitment. Despite Nyerere's pronouncement that 'to plan is to choose' Tanzanians, as of course do most people, try to avoid choosing. Insisting on crude guidelines forces such choice.

Tanzania is approaching a critical stage in its development. While the period since independence has not been easy, Tanzania has not suffered from great internal conflict. Many of the advances – the nationalizations, the leadership code, the better distribution of social services – could be made without making very many people worse off, or at least without making many Africans worse off. This is no longer true. In future Tanzania may develop a truly socialist society in which the rural sectors play a meaningful and active role, and equality with growth continues to be the major goal. On the other hand the possibility of a bureaucratic socialism backed by the force of the army is very real. There will be no repudiation of the past commitment to socialism. In fact, if anything, the rhetoric will grow louder and more extreme, but the society will be controlled by a small urban elite which will direct development in a way which serves its interests, not the interests of the people. The pattern of investment over the next ten years will, in part, determine what the future for Tanzania will be. For this reason a critical examination of what is the best strategy is needed, and commitment made in concrete terms to implementing that strategy must be made.

CONCLUSION

Anyone writing about Tanzania must find themselves in an awkward position. It is easy to write only about the good aspects of Tanzanian development, for there are many. There are few people who visit Tanzania who do not become 'Tanzophiles.' Tanzania provides a stark contrast to the type of unequal growth which is so common in most parts of the world. The Tanzanians, despite their poverty, have not sacrificed their principles for short-run gains either on international or domestic issues. One does not have to look very closely at public leaders in other countries to see how unique is the Tanzanian leadership.

Yet it is not enough to write how well Tanzania compares relatively. There are real problems in Tanzania. The danger still lurks that the initial experiment at fostering a different type of development will be derailed by internal and external forces. It is not a favour to Tanzania to hide criticisms, or to keep quiet one's doubts about certain programmes. In fact it is my faith in the Tanzanians that has made this study seem worthwhile. I am confident that they will accept that which is appropriate and reject what is irrelevant or misguided in my criticism.

Let me conclude by emphasizing the difficulty any person has in knowing how to build socialism. The task is a long and difficult one. It is for this reason that it seems to me necessary to involve the people in decision-making as much as possible, for no other strategy offers any more hope of leading to the right conclusions. The test of intellectuals is to present the issues and facts as clearly as possible. I hope this study helps to do that.

APPENDIX I

Data on the economy since independence

TABLE A1

Gross domestic product at factor cost by industrial origin (at current prices) (shs million)

Industry	1964	1965	1966	1967	1968	1969	1970	1971	1972[1]
1 Agriculture, hunting, forestry, and fishing	2790	2596	2952	2855	2973	3074	3378	3497	3956
2 Mining and quarrying	134	139	192	198	134	172	108	121	124
3 Manufacturing and handcrafts	371	429	525	594	647	724	794	893	973
4 Electricity and water supply	42	46	62	64	69	74	83	91	107
5 Construction	168	184	222	309	325	316	387	481	501
6 Wholesale and retail trade and restaurants and hotels	661	704	825	862	974	1000	1107	1170	1280
7 Transport, storage, and communications	349	386	482	536	621	668	713	788	867
8 Finance, insurance, real estate, and business services	516	586	618	729	759	804	844	921	1052
9 Public administration and other services	592	647	689	746	788	814	919	1018	1142
10 Less imputed bank service charges	29	46	49	101	85	92	111	131	152
11 GDP at factor cost	5594	5671	6518	6792	7205	7554	8222	8846	9850
Subsistence production									
12 Agriculture, hunting, forestry, and fishing	1342	1361	1550	1574	1646	1630	1731	1905	2122
13 Construction	43	47	51	53	57	59	63	67	75
14 Owner-occupied dwellings	385	418	453	477	511	530	559	601	678
15 Total subsistence production	1770	1826	2054	2104	2214	2219	2353	2573	2875
16 Total production in the monetary economy	3824	3845	4464	4688	4991	5335	5869	6273	6975
Total	5594	5671	6518	6792	7205	7554	8222	8846	9850

SOURCE: *Hali Ya Uchumi*, 1973-4, 5   1 Estimate

TABLE A2

Gross domestic product at factor cost by industrial origin (at 1966 prices) (shs million)

Industry	1964	1965	1966	1967	1968	1969	1970	1971	1972[1]
1 Agriculture, hunting, forestry and fishing	2623	2575	2952	2954	3062	3080	3189	3162	3366
2 Mining and quarrying	141	163	192	183	137	148	138	155	137
3 Manufacturing and handcrafts	394	446	525	584	627	687	729	784	832
4 Electricity and water supply	51	53	62	66	72	82	91	100	112
5 Construction	190	198	222	299	315	293	322	375	367
6 Wholesale and retail trade and restaurants and hotels	670	710	825	853	950	973	1051	1050	1118
7 Transport, storage, and communications	387	400	482	536	618	644	730	814	845
8 Finance, insurance, real estate, and business services	575	618	618	707	709	745	763	796	831
9 Public administration and other services	620	658	689	741	764	771	865	956	1020
10 Less imputed bank service charges	32	48	49	98	80	85	99	113	124
11 GDP at factor cost	5619	5773	6518	6825	7174	7338	7779	8079	8504
Subsistence production									
12 Agriculture, hunting, forestry and fishing	1377	1381	1550	1608	1660	1588	1615	1662	1752
13 Construction	48	50	51	52	53	55	57	58	60
14 Owner-occupied dwellings	429	441	453	466	479	492	506	521	536
15 Total subsistence production	1854	1872	2054	2126	2192	2135	2178	2241	2348
16 Total production in the monetary economy	3765	3901	4464	4699	4982	5203	5601	5838	6156
17 Total	5619	5773	6518	6825	7174	7338	7779	8079	8504

SOURCE: *Hali Ya Uchumi*, 1972-3, 7   1 Estimate

TABLE A3

Growth of GDP in 1966 prices

	1965	1966	1967	1968	1969	1970	1971	1972	Average 1965-72
Total GDP	2.7	12.9	4.7	5.1	2.7	6.0	3.9	5.3	5.4
Monetary GDP	3.6	14.4	5.3	6.0	4.4	7.6	4.2	5.4	6.4
Per capita GDP	–	9.9	1.9	2.3	–	3.2	1.2	2.5	2.6
Per capita monetary GDP	0.9	11.4	2.5	3.2	17.0	4.8	1.5	2.6	3.6

TABLE A4

Growth of GDP in current prices

	1965	1966	1967	1968	1969	1970	1971	1972	Average 1965-72
Total GDP	1.4	14.9	4.2	6.1	4.8	8.8	7.6	11.3	7.4
Monetary GDP	0.5	16.1	5.0	6.5	6.9	10.0	6.9	11.2	7.9

SOURCE: *Hali Ya Uchumi*, 1972-3, 5, 7

TABLE A5

Rate of inflation (GDP deflator)

	1965	1966	1967	1968	1969	1970	1971	1972	Average 1965-72
Total GDP	−1.3	1.8	−0.5	1.0	2.0	2.6	3.6	5.7	1.9
Monetary GDP	−3.0	1.5	−0.3	0.5	2.4	2.2	2.6	5.5	1.4

SOURCE: *Hali Ya Uchumi*, 1972-3, 5, 7

TABLE A6

Retail price indices

Year	Minimum wage earners (1961 = 100)		Middle-grade civil servants (1963 = 100)
	All items	Food	All items
1963	94	95	100
1964	96	95	107
1965	102	101	115
1966	102	101	119
1967	110	108	125
1968	114	110	128
1969	115	108	130
1970	119	112	132
1971	123	117	136
1972	135	129	143

SOURCE: *Hali Ya Uchumi*, 1972-3, 45

TABLE A7

Capital formation by public and private sector (at current prices) (shs million)

	1964	1965	1966	1967	1968	1969	1970	1971	1972[2]
Central government	118	148	182	215	276	356	408	408	402
Local authorities and East African Community	39	43	38	48	50	29	45	30	34
EAC enterprises	36	28	78	119	78	62	83	127	106
Parastatal enterprises[3]	41	34	102	260	279	153	629[4]	1096[4]	1122[4]
Total public sector	234	253	400	642	683	601	1165	1661	1664
Private-monetary[1]	292	383	441	455	465	456	480	521	436
Fixed capital formation monetary	527	635	841	1097	1148	1057	1645	2182	2100
Increase in stocks	47	58	79	28	51	66	171	198	75
Capital formation-monetary	574	693	920	1125	1198	1123	1816	2380	2175
Non-monetary									
Private fixed capital formation	147	154	150	174	171	160	170	177	198
Increase in stocks (cattle)	46	49	32	52	43	24	18	23	24
Total non-monetary capital formation	193	203	182	226	214	184	188	200	222
Total capital formation (monetary and non-monetary)	767	896	1102	1351	1412	1307	2004	2580	2397

1 Includes co-operative and residual unidentified
2 Estimate
3 CSB figures; for my revisions, see chapter four and Appendix IV
4 Includes Tazara. Parastatal figures without Tazara would be 356, 470, 460, respectively

TABLE A8

Volume of domestic[1] exports

Commodities	Unit	1962	1965	1966	1967	1968	1969	1970	1971	1972	Average annual percentage change
Coffee	000 tons	26.1	28.2	50.6	44.4	49.2	49.5	44.8	35.5	54.7	9
Cotton	000 tons	33.1	56.2	86.2	60.8	56.7	56.7	60.7	54.0	64.5	7
Diamonds	000 grams	129.5	165.7	181.1	197.5	136.5	156.0	143.9	161.6	125.0	—
Sisal	000 tons	223.0	213.6	198.9	204.4	189.1	171.9	217.2	160.8	153.1	−3
Cloves	000 tons	7.8	8.6	14.4	17.3	12.2	7.3	4.8	9.0	11.8	+4
Cashewnuts	000 tons	59.9	64.6	72.2	70.9	79.7	82.2	77.4	95.9	112.9	7
Tea	000 tons	4.0	4.3	6.3	6.1	6.7	7.6	6.9	8.3	9.2	9
Meat	000 tons	7.0	5.7	8.1	6.5	5.0	5.8	3.9	3.3	3.3	−7
Tobacco	000 tons	0.4	2.1	2.3	4.1	5.0	4.5	6.0	4.7	5.6	30
Petroleum	000 litres	—	—	53.7	411.8	658.1	631.5	707.3	799.9	944.8	∞

SOURCE: *Hali Ya Uchumi*, 1972-3, 29
1 Exports outside EAC, includes exports from Zanzibar

TABLE A9

Export price index (1966 = 100)

Commodity	1966	1967	1968	1969	1970	1971	1972
Cotton	100.0	101.9	110.8	101.7	100.3	110.0	128.4
Coffee	100.0	88.9	91.1	87.7	117.6	108.3	188.2
Sisal	100.0	83.4	71.2	78.7	69.8	70.6	80.2
Cashewnuts	100.0	94.0	92.2	104.6	107.4	90.1	96.2
Tea	100.0	100.1	94.2	89.3	85.4	82.7	82.2
Meat	100.0	105.4	122.5	116.0	126.4	162.3	181.9
Diamonds	100.0	133.6	99.8	114.5	112.6	130.1	99.5
Tobacco	100.0	120.7	116.3	115.4	110.4	134.3	129.7
Petroleum	100.0	347.3	264.5	178.5	168.8	192.5	245.2
Cloves	100.0	101.2	99.0	402.9	446.4	385.5	297.6

SOURCE: *Hali Ya Uchumi*, 1972-3, 28

TABLE A10

Value of domestic[1] exports (shs million)

Principal commodities	1962	1966	1967	1968	1969	1970	1971	1972
Coffee	132	301	237	265	257	312	224	383
Cotton	148	350	251	283	235	247	245	336
Sisal	315	235	201	159	160	179	134	145
Diamonds	109	186	223	135	178	161	209	124
Cashewnuts	47	100	92	107	119	115	120	150
Petroleum products	–	5	133	162	105	111	143	215
Cloves	42	74	90	60	152	109	179	240
Tobacco	2	16	34	40	35	45	43	49
Tea	32	45	43	45	48	42	49	54
Meat and meat preparation	46	57	48	43	47	35	38	42
Hides and skins	30	43	29	31	36	27	27	42
Oil seeds, nuts, and kernel	46	53	45	45	45	36	37	36
Other commodities	127	203	219	210	250	270	284	247
Total	1076	1668	1645	1585	1667	1689	1735	2063

SOURCE: *Hali Ya Uchumi*, 1972-3, 20
1 Includes exports from Zanzibar

TABLE A11

Composition of imports (shs million)

	Consumer goods[1]	Intermediate goods[2]		Capital goods		
		Building and construction materials	Other	Transport equipment	Other equipment	Total
1966	800	103	464	125	199	1691
1967	578	224	438	135	250	1625
1968	731	142	540	151	270	1834
1969	642	141	554	116	257	1710
1970	682	210	709	185	488	2274
1971	690	318	881	245	591	2725
1972[3]	880	365	954	194	536	2929

SOURCE: *Hali Ya Uchumi*, 1972-3, 15
1 Includes a portion of passenger cars
2 Includes spare parts
3 Estimated

TABLE A12

Sources of net imports (shs million)

Area/year	1962	1966	1967	1968	1969	1970	1971	1972[1]
United Kingdom	296	412	382	424	378	411	487	461
India	61	70	43	54	48	55	51	42
Hong Kong	17	36	26	43	34	28	21	20
Other sterling area	75	31	45	61	58	73	88	119
European Economic Community	126	292	344	374	317	466	485	607
North America	58	96	137	95	88	173	130	182
Japan	111	93	69	120	130	143	151	162
CMEA countries	11	39	45	47	34	37	47	53
China	–	80	72	86	79	265	601	508
Other	130	210	182	228	253	288	353	444

SOURCE: *Hali Ya Uchumi*, 1972-3, 25
1 Estimated

TABLE A13

Destination of domestic exports (shs million)

Area/year	1962	1966	1967	1968	1969	1970	1971	1972[1]
United Kingdom	373	486	473	385	429	371	424	360
India	85	129	108	115	132	122	144	171
Hong Kong	78	141	113	126	103	127	132	130
Other sterling area	73	61	193	237	227	308	259	282
European Economic Community	239	224	250	216	209	240	199	281
North America	113	169	117	93	144	185	155	163
Japan	43	97	67	108	82	96	46	76
CMEA countries	3	36	56	27	45	55	33	39
China	–	69	59	55	78	59	84	135
Other	69	256	209	223	218	126	259	426
Total	1076	1668	1645	1585	1667	1689	1735	2063

SOURCE: *Hali Ya Uchumi*, 1972-3, 26
1 Estimated

TABLE A14

Value of Tanzanian inter-East African trade (shs million)

	Kenya			Uganda			Total			
	Imports from	Exports to	Trade balance	Imports from	Exports to	Trade balance	Exports	Imports	Trade balance	Volume of trade
1962	207	56	-151	35	9	-26	65	242	-177	307
1965	285	94	-191	52	27	-25	121	337	-216	458
1966	269	81	-188	63	17	-46	98	332	-234	430
1967	231	68	-163	49	15	-34	83	280	-197	363
1968	261	74	-187	41	17	-24	91	302	-211	393
1969	257	80	-177	34	24	-10	104	291	-187	395
1970	295	119	-176	40	29	-11	148	335	-187	483
1971	295	159	-136	16	38	+22	197	311	-114	508
1972	326	118	-208	6	15	+9	133	332	-199	465

SOURCE: *Hali Ya Uchumi*, 1972-3, 24

Planning information system

In the central planning ministry (Devplan), there is a planning information system (see Clark, 1972; Spence, 1972) which keeps track of all development projects, i.e., projects by ministries, regions, DDCs and parastatals. This system was started in 1971. It is a computerized system with all data on projects stored on computer tapes. Each project is classified in a number of ways: by International Standard Industrial Classification (ISIC) number, by export orientation, by regional and town location, by the sectoral classification used in the Second Five Year Plan, by implementing agency, and by an urban/rural code. There are, as well, a number of codes applicable only to parastatals. I will describe these shortly. The ISIC number is the United Nations system for classifying activities according to which sector in the economy they contribute. For export orientation, I assign a percentage which indicates the proportion of the item exported. Thus a tea programme would have an export orientation of 100 per cent, while a maize programme would be 0 per cent. All infrastructure projects, unless specifically geared towards exports, have an orientation of 0 per cent. Thus secondary schools, trunk roads, rural feeder roads all have an export value of 0 per cent. On the other hand, tobacco feeder roads have a value of 100 per cent. Products which are partially exported, e.g., livestock, get assigned a value equal to share of output exported, unless the project is specifically geared to exports.

Projects are located physically, by regions and by towns. If a project has no definite physical location, or if this location is not determinable, then it is not located. Many projects are multi-regional, i.e., feeder road programmes. Where possible, expenditure has been allocated by region, but this has not always been possible. (See Table A15). There are fifteen towns in Tanzania (as designated by the Central Statistical Bureau). Projects are classified as in a town, partially in a town, or not in a town. If in a town, the town is specified (see Table A16).

The Second Five Year Plan gave a sectoral breakdown of all projects. It is similar to the ISIC code, but differs in some respects. Its most important use is

TABLE A15

Code for Regions and Districts

Code	Region
20	All multiregional projects
21	Unspecified
19	All projects outside mainland Tanzania (includes Zanzibar)

Projects within specific region or district in mainland Tanzania

01	Arusha
02	Coast
03	Dodoma
04	Irings
05	Kigoma
06	Kilimanjaro
07	Lindi
08	Mara
09	Mbeya
10	Morogoro
11	Mtwara
12	Mwanza
13	Ruvuma
14	Shinyanga
15	Singida
16	Tabora
17	Tanga
18	West Lake

that it classifies expenditure into directly and non-directly productive activities. I also classify projects according to their implementing agency. These have changed significantly over time. I use the agency classification as it stood in 1972-3. Thus all labour projects, once under the Ministry of Transport, Communication and Labour, are now under the Ministry of Labour and Social Welfare. I do this because the later classifications tend to be more sectorally specific, and thus more meaningful. I do not do this type of reclassification in one case – changes in the type of implementing agency. Thus, in the early period, a number of sawmills were started by the government, and then handed over to TWICO, the wood parastatal. Because I want to keep a clear distinction on the amount of parastatal and government expenditure, these projects are classified under the Ministry of Natural Resources until their transfer to TWICO. (See Table A17 for ministry classification.)

TABLE A16

Code for urban centres

01	Not in an urban centre
02	Dar es Salaam
03	Tanga
04	Mwanza
05	Arusha
06	Moshi
07	Morogoro
08	Dodoma
09	Iringa
10	Ujiji/Kigoma
11	Tabora
12	Mtwara/Mikindani
13	Musoma
14	Lindi
15	Mbeya
16	Bukoba
99	In more than one town
98	Some projects are in an urban centre; some are not

I also have urban/rural codes. These are codes which were designed by Devplan to capture the urban orientation of the development programme. The first urban/rural code was introduced in the Economic Survey of 1970-1 (see Tanzania, *Annual Economic Survey*, 1970-71, 52-3.). Subsequently, there have been attempts to refine the code. The impact of a project has several dimensions. The first type of impact is the effect on demand for locally produced goods or imports of the development expenditure of a project. Secondly, a project can continue to generate demand through its operating costs. Projects bring consumption benefits, which are sold if the project is a parastatal one, or are usually given away or sold at far below cost if it is a ministerial one. Finally, projects can have externalities encouraging the development of one type of growth or another. The urban/rural impact of a project can be assessed in terms of these dimensions. In 1972, the urban/rural code, then, was extended to include five different classifications: the over-all one, the percentage of development costs going to urban factors, or imports, the percentage of consumption benefits, if given away, going to urban dwellers, and the developmental impact of the project, whether it encouraged rural or urban development. A project like a rural health centre may have little impact on the rural areas in terms of development and operating expenditure but a significant effect in terms of consumption benefits. Almost all parastatal projects sold their output, and therefore had no consumption benefits. Ministerial projects were treated as having only

TABLE A17

Item number classification

Item number	Sector
	10 Directly productive
11	Mining
12	Manufacturing and processing
13	Agriculture – food
14	Agriculture – commercial crops
15	Agriculture – livestock
16	Tourism
17	Others
18	Trade, distribution
19	Banking, insurance
	20 Research, surveys, and investigations
21	Agriculture research
22	Other research
23	Surveys and investigations
	30 Power, water, and sanitary services
31	Electricity
32	Rural water and sanitary services
33	Urban water and sanitary services
34	Others
	40 Other economic infrastructure
41	Roads and Aerodromes
42	Communications and Broadcasting
43	Technical Education and Training
44	Agricultural Improvement – crops
45	Agricultural Improvement – livestock and fishery
46	Agricultural Improvement – forestry
47	Drainage and Irrigation
48	Storage
49	Others
	50 Social Infrastructure
51	Primary Education
52	National Service
53	Housing
54	Health
55	Culture and Welfare
56	Others
	60 Administration and Security
61	Defence
62	Police
63	Prisons
64	Others
	70 Non-Classified

consumption benefits, since the impact of their externalities were generally the same as their consumption benefits.

For parastatals I have also computed a number of measures applicable only to them. These are: capital/labour ratio, capital/value added ratio, rate of profitability, rate of return to fixed capital, import intensity, average wage paid, value added per employee, and wages as a share in value added. I will describe how each of these ratios has been calculated. Our measure of capital/labour ratio, unless otherwise noted, is fixed capital at original cost divided by average number of employees per year. I have used undepreciated capital for two reasons. First, I avoid difficulties about differences in the rate of depreciation. Secondly, rising prices produce a bias towards higher capital/labour ratios over time. This bias is offset by the use of fixed capital undepreciated which includes much capital whose true worth is much below original, or replacement cost. I ignore in all our calculations current assets. This is unfortunate because firms do differ in their efficiency in the use of liquid capital. Unfortunately, these data are difficult to get, and not reliable. I have tried to use measures which are fairly clear, and reliable. These characteristics are particularly true of the capital/labour ratio as I have defined it.

The capital/value added ratio is also quite well known. Its use is perhaps controversial, and I shall argue that in terms of development strategy it is of quite limited use. The ratio I have calculated is one which uses market prices. The distortions in this measure are well known and need not be documented. To try to calculate a capital/social value added ratio would involve doing a cost/benefit analysis of every firm in the parastatal sector. This simply was not possible. It would have involved delving into the whole area of what prices are applicable to the Tanzanian context. This I did not want to do.

We can look at the next two ratios together. The rate of profitability is trading profit before taxation, after charging directors' fees, audit fees, depreciation, and interest charges over fixed capital. The second measure is the return to fixed capital. It is calculated by subtracting from value added wages and salaries. This measure tries to capture the return to capital. It differs from the first because it includes interest and rent payments. Ideally I would exclude rent and interest paid on current capital. In this way I would get a better measure of the return on fixed investment. If I used the profitability measure, a firm financed by equity capital would appear to have a higher return on fixed capital than one financed by loan capital. The problem with rent and interest paid on current capital is not serious since firms do not differ radically on this item. They do differ, however, on their method of financing fixed capital.

The import intensity of a firm I define to mean the share of raw materials which are imported. I have obtained these data from the *Survey of Industrial*

TABLE A18

Ministries

State House
Central Establishment
Foreign Affairs
Prime Minister's Office/Regional Development
Defence
National Service
Agriculture
Development Planning
Education
Commerce and Industry
Transport and Communication
Urban Affairs
Treasury
Home Affairs
Health
Information and Broadcasting
Natural Resources and Tourism
Water and Power Development
Labour and Social Welfare

Production (Tanzania, 1966-70). The import intensity of a firm is not a measure of its total reliance on imports. A firm's use of fuel which is indirectly imported, will increase its use of imports. Because of the difficulty in measuring these types of indirect imports I have excluded them. Rather, our measure centres on the degree to which the basic material inputs into the production process are imported, or locally based. The measure is fortunately quite unambiguous. Most firms are either quite import intensive, or quite local materials based.

The average wage per employee is simply the total wage bill per year divided by the average number of workers per year. Value added per employee and wages as a proportion of value added are both measures of the labour intensity of an operation. To compute all these measures I have used 1971 data on employment, wages, value added, and profits, and 1970 data on fixed assets, unless I state otherwise. I have tried to give our ratios an appropriate but not large lag. The 1970 data on fixed assets give the value of assets as of 31 December, 1970. Thus I am relating, let us say, average employment in 1971 to fixed capital at the end of 1970.

Urban / rural impact of ministerial spending

TABLE A19
Over-all index

	1964-5	65-6	66-7	67-8	68-9	First FYP	69-70	70-71	71-2	72-3	73-4	Second FYP
% Rural	53	55	42	42	53	48	49	45	41	53	52	48
% Urban	36	32	29	28	29	30	36	36	28	22	25	29
% National	11	13	29	30	18	22	15	19	31	25	23	23
% Rural excluding national	60	63	59	60	74	62	58	56	59	71	68	62

TABLE A20
Consumption benefits

	1964-5	65-6	66-7	67-8	68-9	First FYP	69-70	70-71	71-2	72-3	73-4	Second FYP
% Rural	50	54	43	44	47	46	35	32	30	54	46	40
% Urban	38	36	25	22	13	24	27	26	20	21	23	23
% National	7	9	29	30	37	26	36	41	49	23	28	36
% Sold	5	1	3	4	3	4	2	1	1	2	3	1
% Rural excluding national and sold	57	60	55	66	78	66	56	55	60	72	67	63

TABLE A21

Ministerial and regional spending in urban centres (shs million)

	1964-5	65-6	66-7	67-8	68-9	First FYP	1969-70	70-71	71-2	72-3	73-4	Second FYP
Dar es Salaam	33	18	26	33	13	123	60	63	30	58	160	371
Tanga	–	4	1	4	7	16	–	21	25	4	14	64
Arusha	2	1	2	5	3	13	4	7	2	3	5	21
Moshi	–	–	6	5	5	16	–	1	1	1	3	6
Mwanza	–	1	3	3	4	11	17	14	11	6	9	57
Sub-total	35	24	38	50	32	179	81	106	69	72	191	519
Other cities	1	5	6	12	5	29	20	33	17	26	37	133
Total allocated	36	29	44	62	37	208	101	139	86	98	228	652
Unallocated urban	5	14	17	24	27	87	3	5	1	2	15	26
Total urban	41	43	61	86	64	295	104	144	87	100	243	678
Total urban as % of ministerial	24	24	21	26	15	21	21	23	16	19	34	23

Parastatal data

The Central Statistical Bureau has a publication called *Analysis of Accounts of Parastatals* (Tanzania 1972). The latest takes in the period 1966-71. Data are obtained for this document by the means of a questionnaire sent to parastatals in late January or early February of each year. The data received through the questionnaire form the basis for the investment series established, although some adjustments are made if the data appear to have inconsistencies.

There are several problems with these data. The first is that the part of the questionnaire dealing with investment has changed over the years. From 1966 to 1968, the questionnaire asked the firms to specify the total value of their fixed assets undepreciated for the previous year and for the year under study. Net investment was taken as the difference between these two. From 1969 onwards, it asked the firms to specify their total expenditure on fixed assets less any sales of fixed assets. These two methods would produce the same answer only if there were no sale of fixed assets or if the sale of fixed assets was valued at original cost rather than the value for which they are sold. The problem with the series thus formed, however, besides this inconsistency, is that firms should value the sale of fixed assets not at original cost but at the value they receive for them. Thus, if all firms by accident did decide to value their sales at original cost (how to value the sales was not specified) then there would be a consistent series but one which would have a downward bias in investment. In fact, firms differ on the value they assign to sales — some use original cost, others depreciated book value, and still others the sale value.

The procedure I have used to obtain an investment series is to analyse the balance sheets of the firms involved. Most of these are published documents. Investment in any year is equal to the value of depreciated assets at the end of that year, less the value of depreciated assets at the end of the previous year, plus depreciation during the current year, plus any loss on the sale of fixed assets, minus any profit on the sale of fixed assets. I will give an example of how this procedure works and compare it to the CSB method(s).

Suppose I have a firm which at the end of year one has fixed assets at original cost equal to shs 10 million with cumulative depreciation equal to shs 2.0 million, giving the assets a depreciated book value of shs 8.0 million. In year two the firm buys a piece of machinery worth shs 1 million and sells off a piece of machinery whose original book value was shs 0.5 million, but whose depreciated value is now shs 0.3 million. It receives shs 0.4 million for this piece of machinery. How much has it invested? The correct answer I have assumed to be shs 0.6 million, i.e., 1.0 minus 0.4. I can show how the method outlined above will give this answer. Suppose I assume a depreciation rate of 10 per cent on assets. The depreciation charged for the year will be 0.1 x 10.0 plus 0.1 x 1.0 equal to 1.1 million shs. Thus depreciated assets will equal shs 8.0 minus 1.1 plus 1.0 minus 0.3, equal to shs 7.6.

DA[1] (year 2)	7.6
DA (year 1)	8.0
Difference	0.4
Depreciation	1.1
Sub-total	0.7
Less profit on sale	0.1
Investment	0.6

1 DA = Depreciated value of assets

Now the method CSB was using prior to 1969 would give the answer shs 0.5 million. The original cost value to fixed assets in year two will be 10.0 plus 1.0 minus 0.5. Its method is:

UDA[1] (year 2)	10.5
UDA (year 1)	10.0
Investment	0.5

2 UDA = undepreciated value of assets

From 1969 onwards the answer could be shs 0.5, 0.7 (valuing the sale at depreciated book value), or 0.6 million, depending on which value of the item sold was chosen.

The second major problem with the CSB data is that CSB occasionally puts the investment in the year in which a new plant becomes operational, rather than when the investment actually occurs. This tends to produce a rather lumpy investment series. The Friendship Textile Mill is the most obvious example of

TABLE A22

Comparison of CSB parastatal investment and author's figures for parastatal investment 1966-71 (shs million)

	1966	1967	1968	1969	1970	1971
CSB figures	102	261	279	153	356	397
Author's figures	104	293	258	197	407	488
Difference	−2	−32	+19	−42	−51	−91

this. The plant construction started in July 1966 and was completed by July 1968. CSB records all the investment as occurring in 1968. I have adjusted this figure by assuming that 20 per cent of the investment occurred in 1966, 60 per cent in 1967, and 20 per cent in 1968.

The third type of error is the failure to revise the data from past years when adjustments are made. The data are obtained annually and only a few attempts have been made to incorporate any corrections to the past data. This also leads to serious errors.

The CSB definition of a parastatal is a firm in which the government owns at least 50 per cent equity. It is included in the series only when it adheres to this definition. A number of firms have been included in 1966 which were parastatals by this definition only in 1967. They are: BAT, Kilimanjaro Breweries, Metal Box, Portland Cement, and Tanzania Shoe. The result of excluding these firms is to greatly reduce parastatal investment in 1966. The CSB series shows a decrease in parastatal investment in manufacturing from 1966 to 1967. There was actually an increase. This is more logical given the large number of nationalizations in this sector in 1967.

Finally, there are two other general reasons why the CSB data disagree with my own. The first is that their figures are often based on preliminary data. When the questionnaire is filled out, final audited accounts for firms are often not ready. Thus, by taking final audited figures I get more accurate data. Secondly, their figures rely on a questionnaire. Questionnaires inevitably involve some errors. There is no way to control the quality of the data. By using published audited figures, this type of error is reduced. All my figures have been shown to the Bureau, and they are in the process of revising their series. Their series has yet to come out. In general their series has improved over time. There are almost no differences in the two series after 1971, except for the tourism sector, in which they continue to underestimate investment.

CSB in the revised *National Accounts* (Tanzania, 1972a) figures also presented data for parastatal investment in 1964 and 1965. These figures are shown in Table A23 with my estimates for these years.

TABLE A23

Comparison of parastatal investment 1964-5
(shs million)

	1964	1965
CSB figures	41	34
Author's figures	57	67
Difference	−16	−33

Thus, total investment by majority-owned parastatals from 1964-71 was, according to CSB, shs 1623 million. If my figures are correct, the total was some 15 per cent higher, or shs 1871 million. The question arises as to the effect of this change on the national accounts. Total investment in the economy is measured by the CSB in the following way. From trade figures it obtains total imports of equipment and machinery. This forms the basis of its estimate of investment in this area. From the parastatal questionnaire, and samples of the private sector, it obtains estimates of parastatal investment on equipment, and construction, and private investment on construction. It also obtains separately figures on central and local government investment and investment by the EAC. From these figures it can obtain total investment and the share between private, parastatal, government, and EAC. The effect of changing a figure for parastatal investment will depend on whether (a) the change results simply from a reclassification of the data (e.g., Tiper is classified in 1968 as private by CSB, parastatal by me), (b) the change affects the figure for equipment or construction. If the classification is the same, but the whole change is in equipment investment, total investment remains unaltered, but the share between private and public changes. This is because CSB obtains estimates of equipment investment from the import figures and uses the parastatal data only to estimate the split between private and parastatal. On the other hand, if the figure for construction changes, then the figure for over-all investment in the economy must change since the parastatal data are the only data used to estimate parastatal construction.

I have attempted to estimate the effect of the changes on investment figures. The methodology has been the following: where the problem is one of classification, the effect is simply to alter the ratio of private versus parastatal investment. Where the change is a distinct one in which the ratio of equipment to construction investment is known, then the appropriate adjustment is made. In all other cases, I have assumed a certain proportion in construction. The proportion varies depending on the sector. For example, I have assumed that only 20 per cent of investment in electricity is construction. Thus any change in the parastatal figures will have only a small impact on over-all investment in the electricity. For commerce, I have assumed that 60 per cent of investment is in construction.

TABLE A24

National accounts – parastatal investment 1964-71 (shs '000)

Sector	1964	1965	1966	1967	1968	1969	1970	1971
Manufacturing			34,100	26,900	89,500	41,200	195,100	136,900
Mining			4900	5000	4100	6100	16,200	25,600
Construction			3800	6100	6000	8500	24,700	31,800
Electricity			33,700	31,400	32,800	41,200	27,600	79,300
Transport			15,000	157,400	116,400	4800	17,600	43,600
Finance			-600	4300	12,800	13,200	9600	26,000
Trade			4200	21,300	13,400	17,400	59,500	42,500
Agriculture			5400	6000	2400	9700	11,300	9200
Services			1200	2100	2000	10,800	600	2100
Total	41,000	34,000	101,700	260,500	279,100	152,900	356,100	397,000

TABLE A25

Majority-owned parastatal investment 1964-71 (shs '000) (author's distribution and figures)

Sector	1964	1965	1966	1967	1968	1969	1970	1971	Total
Manufacturing of which	—	2178	21,292	63,326	43,618	60,185	205,340	192,281	588,220
agriculturally based manufacturing						1702	8169	49,014	58,886
Mining	9086	4705	4775	4954	4390	6264	12,609	23,364	70,147
Construction	8751	12,828	10,919	8458	11,286	15,811	32,137	36,601	136,791
Electricity	24,713	11,266	32,966	31,131	34,077	25,226	31,592	102,659	293,630
Transport			16,074	157,292	114,392	13,352	23,743	43,600	368,453
Tourism	11,487	23,393	1931	3019	9205	28,450	36,741	17,155	131,381
Commerce	2339	7107	8493	14,770	20,536	22,317	30,409	36,889	142,860
Agriculture	534	1194	5474	5660	6563	10,989	18,489	9200	58,103
Finance	267	4232	1945	4468	14,270	14,687	15,845	26,000	81,714
Total	57,177	66,903	103,869	293,078	258,337	197,281	406,905	487,749	1,871,299

TABLE A26

Investment in the economy (shs million) (author's data)

Author's data	1966	1967	1968	1969	1970	1966-70
Services, tourism	105	115	118	150	165	652
Manufacturing	159	196	205	177	324	1061
Commerce	18	26	27	29	48	149
Agriculture/Rural Own-Account	229	247	246	250	274	1245
Transport	330	493	505	392	798	2518
Construction	32	39	26	35	48	180
Electricity	56	77	90	104	111	438
Mining	16	16	10	18	30	90
Govt. admin.	55	70	86	84	138	433
Total	1000	1279	1313	1239	1936	6767
CSB *data*						
Total	991	1271	1318	1217	1947	6744

TABLE A27

Productive investment in the economy (shs million)

	1964	1965	1966	1967	1968	1969	1970	1971	1964-71
CSB *data*									
Private	292	383	441	455	465	452	486	521	3499
EAC	36	28	78	119	78	62	83	127	611
Parastatal	41	34	102	261	279	153	356	397	1623
Total	369	445	621	835	822	671	925	1045	5733
Private as percentage of total	79	86	71	54	56	67	52	50	61
Author's *data*									
Private	280	360	448	433	481	434	424	457	3117
EAC	36	28	78	119	78	62	83	127	611
Parastatal	57	67	104	293	258	197	407	488	1871
Total	373	455	630	843	817	693	914	1072	5799
Private as percentage of total	75	79	71	51	59	63	45	43	57

SOURCE: Tanzania, 1972a; *Hali Ya Uchumi*, 1972-3

For 1964 and 1965, CSB does not give us a breakdown of either parastatal or over-all investment on a sectoral basis. I have therefore assumed that average investment is 30 per cent construction and adjusted their total investment series accordingly. For 1971, I have no sectoral breakdown of total investment, so can only show the effect on total investment. Table A26 shows the sector breakdown of investment using my figures for the period 1966-70. Table A27 shows productive investment in the economy from 1964 to 1971. Total productive investment in the economy over this period was shs 5799 million, only 1 per cent higher than the figure presented by CSB. The share of the private sector is noticeably smaller. Over-all it contributed 57 per cent of productive investment (compared to CSB's figure of 61 per cent). Its share drops dramatically in 1967 from 71 per cent to 51 per cent, rises again to 63 per cent in 1969, and then drops to 45 per cent in 1970 and 43 per cent in 1971. Thus the over-all effect of my revisions is to alter the share of investment which can be assigned to the private sector, but not to alter significantly the total amount of investment which has gone on in the economy.

CSB's classification of firms appears to me to be erroneous in some cases and to obscure data in others. They classify TTA under trade. Most of its assets should be under agriculture and manufacturing. As well, more than just NAFCO headquarters is included under finance. All its subsidiaries should be in either manufacturing or agriculture. Tourism is partly classified under trade and partly under services. I have removed services entirely and put it in commerce and substituted a tourism sector. As a result of this the importance of tourism as a sector is made clear. Finally, I separate out from manufacturing those firms whose investments ought really to be divided between the two sectors. Industries such as Mtibwa Sugar or Kenaf Estates are partly manufacturing and partly agriculture enterprises. Where possible, I have divided their investments between the two sectors.

Sources of finance

There are several ways in which a development project can be foreign financed. First, aid can come to the development budget via the Treasury from an aid donor. Secondly, aid can go directly to a project. Thirdly, an aid donor can give money via the Treasury to one of the investment banks to loan to firms or individuals carrying out projects. Fourthly, private 'charitable' organizations can raise money abroad to build schools, hospitals, etc. Finally, parastatals can go abroad and borrow in the conventional private market getting suppliers' credits, or commercial bank loans.

In the past there has been inconsistent treatment of aid going directly to projects. In the estimate books some of this aid was shown separately with an asterisk beside it. This began in 1966-7. In the period before that direct aid was not shown at all. In the *Reports of the Auditor-general* direct aid is not recorded until 1971-2. In that year a new procedure was adopted. Any direct aid going to a project which appeared in the estimates book was recorded, because Treasury would make a payment to the agency involved in the amount of the value of the direct aid, and then the agency would return the money; in this way direct aid got on to the books. In general this procedure has worked well, although it seems that there are still a few problems in evaluating the amount of the aid, and in getting the procedure followed in all cases.

The real problem with direct aid is that most of it is not recorded anywhere, even in the estimates book, prior to 1971-2. Several institutions received substantial amounts of direct aid. These are: TANESCO, NHC, NDCA, NDC, Tazara, National Parks, Health, Education, and Defence. For TANESCO, NHC, and NDCA, the figures are as accurate as possible, having been obtained from the accountants of each institution. For NDC, the figures are from the Swedish International Development Agency, and should be accurate. I have assumed that estimates of direct aid equal actual aid received for National Parks and Defence. This is

TABLE A29

Parastatal projects receiving private foreign finance

Manufacturing	Agriculture	Transport	Tourism
Coastal Dairies	Mtibwa Sugar	Tazama Pipelines	Mt Meru
Northern Dairies		Z-T Road Service	Mwanza Hotel
Mwatex			T. Tours
Tasini/Kiltex			Serengeti Safari
T. Fertilizer			
New Brewery Mwanza			
T. Distilleries			
Mtwara Cashew			
Instant Coffee			
Tob. Processing			
Tegry Plastics			
TANITA			
T. Blanket			
T. Bag			
Kenaf Estates			
General Tyre			
Steel Rolling			
Tembo Chipboards			
Tabora Msitu			
Tiper			
Imara Plywood			

probably not a bad guess for National Parks. For Defence, it is simply impossible to know. It certainly underestimates aid to Defence in recent years because aid to Defence is no longer shown in the estimates. For Education and Health, I have taken estimates from their planning office.

Table A28 shows direct aid for each agency for the period 1966-7 to 1972-3. For the years before that no breakdown by agency is possible. For 1973-4 direct aid is no longer distinguished from aid passing through the Treasury.

Foreign private loans are difficult to measure. The East Africa Community has some data on this, but their figures seem incomplete. It is possible to get a good estimate from our parastatal figures of the size of private capital inflow. From the balance sheets of the firm one can usually tell the amount of foreign borrowing. Where this has not been possible, I have questioned people who knew the project to determine if it was foreign financed. If it was, I have assigned the equipment cost as the part foreign financed. Table A29 gives the names of firms whose initial development, or a major expansion programme was privately foreign financed. These estimates are rough, but I think are generally accurate. They correspond reasonably well with figures obtainable from the Bank of Tanzania for recent years.

Foreign private borrowing by parastatals reflects two factors, the availability of alternative foreign financing, and the type of projects undertaken. In the years up to 1971-2 alternative foreign financing was not available so that the series reflects the nature of the projects. Large, capital-intensive projects necessitate heavy foreign borrowing because the country's ability to generate foreign exchange is not such as to allow alternative ways of financing such projects. Thus the building of the corridor to Zambia-Tazama pipelines – Zam-Tam Road Service – in 1966 and 1967 shows up clearly. Again the building of the fertilizer plant and the tire factory produce a bulge in 1970 and 1971. It is also interesting to note that private foreign borrowing is concentrated in two sectors, and is usually tied to some external equity participation, as was the case with the pipeline, and is the case with most NDC large projects. In contrast, TANESCO, 100 per cent government owned, has relied almost exclusively on foreign aid, especially IBRD.

TABLE A28

Summary of direct to project aid by agency (shs '000)[1]

Agency	66-7		67-8		68-9		69-70		70-71		71-2		72-3
	E	A	E	A	E	A	E	A	E	A	E	A	E
Kilimo	1898	1898	3979	3209	15,779	15,557	5505	2935	9614	9614	11,733	10,052	20,318
Ardhi	1320	1320	–	6600	–	2400			2200	1777	2200	2200	5652
Maliasili	1278	2481	3334	3334	2864	3098	2414	2414	1000	1000	1868	1156	7699
TANESCO	1839	1839	5156	5156	12,300	12,300	–	14,184	19,429	33,785	58,220	39,750	76,119
Parks	5114	5114	3234	3234	6429	6429	–	5138			5800	6300	2840
NHC	1963	1963	35,520	1217	3500	1494	–	8430	4800	4800			
TRDB	13,094	13,094	6318	6318	1286	3976	–	1608	7700	7231	–	3679	
Defence			25,000	25,000	22,000	22,000							
PMO					300	300							
Maji					6000	6000			2477	2477	5017	394	10,300
Elimu							6021	6021	5224	3256	8160	8160	10,515
Afya							3400	30,400		28,070		18,000	828
Maelezo											3300	778	3625
Kazi							171	171	3536	2467	3221	3221	4290
Natl. Dairy Board									8100	8100			
Mincom											2106	2106	9437
Comworks											4000	4000	1400

TABLE A28 cont'd

Agency	66-7 E	66-7 A	67-8 E	67-8 A	68-9 E	68-9 A	69-70 E	69-70 A	70-71 E	70-71 A	71-2 E	71-2 A	72-3 E
NAFCO											2684	2684	11,613
State mining											5000	3789	1216
TWICO											1512	1512	1512
Natl. Service													4000
Uchumi													1100
NMC													10,000
NDC								1267		6627		2097	7000
Mecco													4000
TIB													17,380
TTC													6380
Friendship Textile Mill		22,000	22,000	25,000		7000							
Ministry total	4496	5699	32,313	38,143	46,943	49,335	17,481	41,941	24,051	48,661	41,605	50,067	79,164
Parastatal total	22,010	44,010	50,228	40,925	23,515	31,199	–	22,197	40,029	60,543	73,216	59,811	138,600
Tazara	–	–	–	–	–	–	–	–	–	185,600	–	180,000	170,000
Total	26,506	53,709	82,541	79,068	70,458	80,554	17,481	64,138	64,080	294,804	114,821	289,878	387,224

1 E = estimated; A = actual

Bibliography

Alpers, E.A. *The East African Slave Trade*. Nairobi, East African Publishing House for Historical Association of Tanzania 1967

Arrighi, G. and J.S. Saul *Essays on the Political Economy of Africa*. New York, Monthly Review Press 1973

Baer, W. and M.E.A. Herve 'Employment and Industrialization in Developing Countries' *Quarterly Journal of Economics* LXX, no. 1, Feb. 1966

Balassa, B. *et al. The Structure of Protection in Developing Countries*. Baltimore, John Hopkins Press 1971.

Bank of Tanzania *Economic and Operations Report*. Dar es Salaam, Bank of Tanzania, all years

— *Economic Bulletin*. Dar es Salaam, Bank of Tanzania, all years

Baran, P. *The Political Economy of Growth*. New York, Monthly Review 1957

Barkin, D.P. and N.R. Manitzas, eds. *Cuba: The Logic of the Revolution*. Andover, Mass. Warner Modular Publications Inc. 1973

Bowles, S. 'Class Power and Mass Education.' Mimeo 1971

— 'Cuban Education and Revolutionary Ideology.' *Harvard Educational Review*, Nov. 1971a

— 'Unequal Education and the Reproduction of the Social Division of Labor.' *Review of Radical Political Economics* III, no. 3, fall 1971b

Brewster, H. and C.Y. Thomas *The Dynamics of West Indian Economic Integration*. Jamaica, Institute of Social and Economic Research, University of the West Indies 1967

Caves, R.E. *Trade and Economic Structure*. Cambridge, Mass., Harvard University Press 1960

Chenery, H.B. 'Comparative Advantage and Development Policy.' *American Economic Review* LI, no. 1, March 1961

Clark, W.E. *Planning Information System: A User's Manual.* University of Toronto Tanzania Project, unpublished, Aug. 1972

Cliffe, L. *One Party Democracy, The 1965 Tanzania General Elections.* Nairobi, East African Publishing House 1967

– and J.S. Saul *Socialism in Tanzania. Vol. 1: Politics.* Dar es Salaam, East African Publishing House 1973

– *Socialism in Tanzania. Vol. 2: Policies.* Dar es Salaam, East African Publishing House 1973

Cline, W.K. *Potential Effects of Income Redistribution on Economic Growth.* New York, Praeger Publishers 1972

Coupland, R. *East Africa and Its Invaders.* London, Oxford University Press at Clarendon Press 1939

Crozier, M. *The Bureaucratic Phenomenon.* Chicago, University of Chicago Press 1964

Deutscher, I. *Stalin: A Political Biography.* New York, Vintage 1960

Dumont, R. *Tanzanian Agriculture after Arusha.* Dar es Salaam, Government Printer 1969

East African Community (EAC) Trade Statistics, 1970

Economist Intelligence Unit *Quarterly Economic Review. Annual Supplement.* London 1973

Edwards, R., M. Reich, and T. Weisskopf (eds) *The Capitalist System.* New Jersey, Prentice-Hall 1972

Falcon, W.P. 'Farmer Response to Price in an Underdeveloped Area.' *American Economic Review*, May 1964

Frank, A.G. *Capitalism and Underdevelopment in Latin America.* New York, Monthly Review Press 1969

– 'The Development of Underdevelopment.' in Rhodes (1970)

– *Lumpenbourgeoisie and Lumpendevelopment: Dependency, Class and Politics in Latin America.* New York, Monthly Review 1973

Frank Jr., C.R. 'Urban Unemployment and Economic Growth in Africa.' *Oxford Economic Papers* XX, no. 2, July 1968

Fuggles-Couchman, N.R. *Agricultural Change in Tanganyika 1945-60.* Stanford, Stanford Food Research Institute 1964

Ghai, D.P. 'Territorial Distribution of the Benefits and Costs of the East African Common Market.' *East African Economic Review*, June 1964

– ed. *Portrait of a Minority: Asians in East Africa.* London, Oxford University Press 1965

Gish, O. 'Resource Allocation, Equality of Access, and Health.' *International Journal of Health Sciences* III, no. 3, 1973a

– 'Doctor Auxiliaries in Tanzania.' *The Lancet*, Dec. 1973b

Gotsch, C.H. 'Technical Change and the Distribution of Income in Rural Areas.' Economic Development Report no. 205 DAS. Cambridge, Mass., Harvard University

Gurley, J. 'Capitalist and Maoist Economic Development.' *Bulletin of Concerned Asian Scholars*, April-July 1970

Haq, Mahbul ul 'Employment in the 1970's: A New Perspective.' *International Development Review* XIII, no. 4, 1971

Harbison, F. 'The Generation of Employment in Newly Developing Countries.' In S.R. Sheffield, ed., *Education, Employment and Rural Development*. Nairobi, East African Publishing House 1967

Hatch, S. *Tanzania: A Profile*. New York, Praeger 1972

Hawkins, H.C.C. *Wholesale and Retail Trade in Tanganyika: A Study of Distribution in East Africa*. New York, Praeger 1965

Hayter, T. *Aid as Imperialism*. Harmondsworth, England, Penguin 1971

Hazlewood, A. 'The East African Common Market: Importance and Effects.' *Bulletin of the Oxford University Institute of Economics and Statistics*, Feb. 1966

Heckscher, E. 'The Effects of Foreign Trade on the Distribution of Income.' American Economic Association, *Readings in the Theory of International Trade*, London, Allen and Unwin 1950

Helleiner, G.K. *Agricultural Planning in East Africa*. Nairobi, East African Publishing House 1968

Hirschman, A.O. 'The Political Economy of Import-Substituting Industrialization in Latin America.' *Quarterly Journal of Economics* LXXXII, no. 1, Feb. 1968

– *The Strategy of Economic Development*. New Haven, Yale University Press 1970

– *A Bias for Hope*. New Haven, Yale University Press 1971

Huberman, L. and P.M. Sweezy *Cuba: Anatomy of A Revolution*. New York, Monthly Review 1961

– *Socialism in Cuba*. New York, Monthly Review 1969

Hyden, G. *Political Development in Rural Tanzania*. Nairobi, East African Publishing House 1969

Iliffe, J. *Tanzania under German Rule*. London, Cambridge University Press 1969

– 'Agricultural Change in Modern Tanganyika: An Outline History.' Paper presented at Universities of East Africa Social Science Conference, Dar es Salaam, 27-31 Dec. 1970

Ingham, K. *A History of East Africa*. New York, Praeger 1967

Ingle, C.R. *From Village to State in Tanzania: The Politics of Rural Development.* Ithaca, Cornell University Press 1972

International Bank for Reconstruction and Development (IBRD). *The Economic Development of Tanganyika.* Baltimore, Johns Hopkins Press 1961

International Labour Office (ILO) *Towards Full Employment: A Programme for Columbia, prepared by an interagency team organized by the ILO* Geneva 1970

– *Employment, Incomes and Equality: A Strategy for Increasing Productive Employment in Kenya.* Report of an Inter-Agency Team financed by the United Nations Development Programme and Organized by the International Labour Office. Geneva, ILO 1972

– *Matching Employment Opportunities and Expectations: A Programme of Action for Ceylon.* Geneva 1971

Kamarck, A.M. *The Economics of African Development.* New York, Praeger 1971

Kenya *Economic Survey 1967-8*

– *Economic Survey 1973.* Nairobi, Central Bureau of Statistics 1973

– *Statistical Abstract 1964*

– *Statistical Abstract 1972.* Nairobi, Central Bureau of Statistics 1973

Kessel, D. 'Effective Protection in Tanzania.' *East African Economic Review,* June 1968

Kimambo, I. and A. Temu, eds. *A History of Tanzania.* Nairobi, East African Publishing House 1970

Kuznets, S. *Modern Economic Growth.* New Haven, Yale University Press 1966

Leibenstein, H. 'Technical Progress, the Production Function, and Development.' W.W. Rostow, ed., *The Economics of Take-Off into Sustained Growth.* London, MacMillan Press 1963

Lenin, V.I. *Imperialism.* New York, International Publishers 1939

Lewis, W.R. 'Economic Development with Unlimited Supplies of Labor.' Manchester School, May 1954

Lint and Seed Marketing Board *Annual Report and Accounts.* Dar es Salaam, LSMB, all years

Little, I., T. Scitovsky, and M. Scott, *Industry and Trade in Some Developing Countries.* London, Oxford University Press 1970

Lofchie, M. *Zanzibar, Background to Revolution.* Princeton, NJ, Princeton University Press 1967

MacEwan, A. 'On the Transition to Socialism: A Review.' *Monthly Review,* March 1974

- 'Incentives, Equality and Power in Revolutionary Cuba.' *Socialist Revolution,* forthcoming
Magdoff, H. *The Age of Imperialism.* New York, Monthly Review 1969
Mangat, J.S. *A History of Asians in East Africa circa 1886-1945.* London, Oxford University Press 1969
Marx, Karl and Friedrich Engels. *The German Ideology.* New York, International Publishers 1939
Mellor, J.W. 'The Process of Agricultural Development in Low Income Countries.' *Journal of Farm Economics* XLIV, no. 3, Aug. 1962
- and B.F. Johnston 'Role of Agriculture in Economic Development.' *American Economic Review,* Sept. 1961
Moffet, J.P. *Handbook of Tanganyika.* Dar es Salaam, Government Printer 1958
Morris, H.S. *The Indians in Uganda.* London, Weidenfeld and Nicolson 1968
Mulokozi, E.A. 'Planning in a System of Decentralized Development Management: The Case of Tanzania.' In TIB (1973)
Mundell, R.A. 'International Trade and Factor Mobility.' *American Economic Review,* June 1957
Myrdal, G. *Economic Theory and Underdeveloped Regions.* London, Duckworth 1957
- 'Development and Underdevelopment.' Extract reprinted in G. Meier, *Leading Issues in Economic Development.* London, Oxford University Press 1970
National Agricultural and Food Corporation (NAFCO) *Annual Reports and Accounts.* Dar es Salaam, NAFCO 1969-70, 1970-71
National Agricultural Products Board (NAPB) *Annual Report and Accounts.* Dar es Salaam, NAPB, all years
National Co-operative and Development Bank Group (NCDBG) *Chairman's Report and Accounts.* Dar es Salaam, NCDBG 1966-7, 1967-8
- *Final Report and Accounts.* Dar es Salaam, NCDBG 1969-70, 1970-71
National Development Corporation (NDC) *Annual Report and Accounts.* Dar es Salaam, NDC, all years
National Housing Corporation (NHC) *Annual Report and Accounts.* Dar es Salaam, NHC, all years
National Milling Corporation (NMC) *Annual Report and Accounts.* Dar es Salaam, NMC, all years
Nurkse, R. *Problems of Capital Formation in Underdeveloped Countries.* New York, Oxford University Press 1961
Nyerere, J.K. *Freedom and Unity.* London, Oxford University Press 1966
- *Freedom and Socialism.* London, Oxford University Press 1968a
- *Ujamaa: Essays on Socialism.* Dar es Salaam, Oxford University Press 1968b
- *Decentralization.* Dar es Salaam, Government Printer 1972a

— *The Rational Choice.* Dar es Salaam, Government Printer 1972b

Ohlin, B. *Interregional and International Trade.* Cambridge, Mass., Harvard University Press 1933

Oliver, R. and G. Mathew, eds. *History of East Africa.* London, Oxford University Press at Clarendon Press 1963

Parkhurst, R.P. *Kenya: The History of Two Nations.* London, Independent Publishing Co. 1954

Papanek, G.F. *Pakistan's Development: Social Goals, and Private Incentives.* Cambridge, Mass., Harvard University Press 1967

— 'The Effect of Aid and Other Resource Transfers on Savings and Growth in Less Development Countries.' *Economic Journal,* Sept. 1972

— 'Aid, Foreign Private Investment, Savings and Growth in Less Developed Countries.' *Journal of Political Economy,* Jan. 1973

Pearson, D.S. *Industrial Development in East Africa.* Nairobi, Oxford University Press 1969

Prebisch, R. *Towards a New Trade Policy for Development.* Report of the Secretary-General of UNCTAD, United Nations 1964

Resnick, I.N. *Tanzanian Revolution by Education.* Arusha, Longmans 1968

Riskin, C. 'Marxism and Motivation: Work Incentives in China.' *Bulletin of Concerned Asian Scholars,* July 1973

Rhodes, R.I., ed. *Imperialism and Underdevelopment: A Reader.* New York, Monthly Review Press 1970

Roberts, A. *Tanzania Before 1900.* Nairobi, East African Publishing House 1968

Rodney, W. *How Europe Underdeveloped Africa.* Dar es Salaam, Tanzania Publishing House 1972

Roemer, M. 'The Neoclassical Employment Model Applied to Ghanaian Manufacturing.' Economic Development Report no. 225 DAS. Cambridge, Mass., Nov. 1972

Rosenstein-Rodan, P.N. 'Problems of Industrialization of Eastern and Southern Eastern Europe.' *Economic Journal,* June-Sept. 1948

— 'Notes on the Theory of the Big Push.' In H. Ellis, ed., *Economic Development for Latin America.* New York, St. Martin's Press 1962

Ruthenberg, H. *Agricultural Development in Tanganyika.* New York, Springer-Verlag 1964

Rutman, G.L. *The Economy of Tanganyika.* New York, Praeger 1968

Rweyemanu, A., ed. *Nation-Building in Tanzania; Problems and Issues.* Nairobi, East African Publishing House 1970

— and B.U. Mwansasu, eds. *Planning in Tanzania, Background to Decentralisation.* Dar es Salaam, East African Literature Bureau 1971

Rweyemamu, J.F. 'International Trade and Developing Countries.' *Journal of Modern African Studies* VII, no. 2, July 1969
— *Underdevelopment and Industrialization in Tanzania.* London, Oxford University Press 1973
Sach, Ignaly 'On Growth Potential, Proportional Growth, and Perverse Growth.' *Czechoslovak Econ. Papers* 1960
Samuelson P.A. 'International Trade and Equalisation of Factor Prices.' *Economic Journal* LVIII, June 1948
— 'International Factor-Price Equalisation Once Again.' *Economic Journal* LIX, June 1949
Schultz, T.W. *Transforming Traditional Agriculture.* New Haven, Yale University Press 1964
Scitovsky, T. 'Two Concepts of External Economics.' *Journal of Political Economy,* April 1954
Seers, D. 'The Meaning of Development.' *International Development Review* I, no. 4, Dec. 1969
Seidman, A.W. 'Comparative Industrial Strategies in East Africa' Dar es Salaam, Economic Research Bureau, University College 1969
— and R. Green *Unity or Poverty?* Harmondsworth, Penguin Press 1968
Shivji, I.G., ed. *The Silent Class Struggle.* Dar es Salaam, Tanzania Publishing House 1973a
— *Tourism and Socialist Development.* Dar es Salaam, Tanzania Publishing House 1973b
Silverman, B., ed. *Man and Socialism in Cuba: The Great Debate.* New York, McClelland and Stewart 1971
Singer, H. 'The Distribution of Gains between Investing and Borrowing Countries.' *American Economic Review,* May 1950
Spence, W.R. *Design and Implementation of a Development Project System in Tanzania.* University of Toronto, unpublished PHD dissertation 1972.
State Trading Corporation (STC) *Annual Report and Accounts.* STC, Dar es Salaam, 1970, 1971
Stephens, H.W. *The Political Transformation of Tanganyika 1920-1967.* New York, Praeger 1968
Streeten, P. *The Frontiers of Development Studies.* New York, John Wiley and Sons 1972
Svendsen, K.E. and M. Teisen, *Self-Reliant Tanzania.* Dar es Salaam, Tanzania Publishing House 1969
Sweezy, P.M. *The Theory of Capitalist Development.* New York, Monthly Review Press 1968

- 'Toward A Program of Studies of the Transition to Socialism.' *Monthly Review* XXIII , no. 9, Feb. 1972
Szentes, T. *The Political Economy of Underdevelopment.* Budapest, Centre for Afro-Asian Research of the Hungarian Academy of Sciences 1970
Tanganyika *Development Plan for Tanganyika 1961-2, 1963-4.* Dar es Salaam, Government Printer 1961
- *Five-Year Plan for Economic and Social Development 1964-1969.* Vols. I and II. Dar es Salaam, Government Printer 1964
Tanganyika African National Union (TANU) *TANU Guidelines 1971.* Dar es Salaam, Government Printer 1971
Tanganyika Development Finance Co. Ltd. (TFDL) *Annual Report and Accounts.* Dar es Salaam, TFDL, all years
Tanganyika Electric Supply Co. (TANESCO) *Annual Report and Accounts.* Dar es Salaam, TANESCO all years
Tanzania *Statistical Abstract.* 1938-51, 1938-52, 1958, 1963, 1964, 1965. 1970
- *Budget Survey.* Dar es Salaam, Government Printer 1959-60, 1960-61, 1961-2, 1962-3, 1963-4, 1964-5, 1965-6
- *Survey of Employment and Earnings.* Dar es Salaam, Central Statistical Bureau 1962, 1963, 1964, 1966, 1968, 1969, 1970
- *Report of the Auditor-General.* Dar es Salaam, Government Printer 1964-5, 1965-6, 1966-7, 1967-8, 1968-9, 1969-70, 1970-71, 1971-2
- *Census of Industrial Production in Tanganyika 1961.* Dar es Salaam, Central Statistical Bureau 1964
- *Background to the Budget 1966-67.* Dar es Salaam, Government Printer, 1966
- *Annual Economic Survey.* Dar es Salaam, Government Printer 1966-7, 1967-8, 1968-9, 1969-70, 1970-71, 1971-2, 1972-3
- *Survey of Industrial Production.* Dar es Salaam, Central Statistical Bureau 1966, 1967, 1968, 1969, 1970
- *A Mid-Term Appraisal of the Achievements Under The Five Year Plan July 1964-June 1969.* Dar es Salaam, Ministry of Economic Affairs and Development Planning, April 1967a
- *Survey of Industries 1965.* Dar es Salaam, Central Statistical Bureau, 1967b
- *Report on Tourism Statistics in Tanzania.* Dar es Salaam, Central Statistical Bureau 1968, 1969, 1970
- *Second Five-Year Plan for Economic and Social Development 1969-74.* Vols. I, II, III, and IV. Dar es Salaam, Government Printer, 1969
- *Annual Plan.* Dar es Salaam, Government Printer 1970-1, 1971-2, 1972-3, 1973-4
- *Survey of Distributive Trade Dar es Salaam – 1970.* Dar es Salaam, Central Statistical Bureau

– *National Accounts of Tanzania 1966 to 1968, Sources and Methods.* Dar es Salaam, Bureau of Statistics, March 1971
– *Analysis of Accounts of Parastatals 1966-1971.* Dar es Salaam, Bureau of Statistics 1972
– *National Accounts of Tanzania 1964-70.* Dar es Salaam, Bureau of Statistics, Feb. 1972a
– *Directory of Industries 1971.* Dar es Salaam, Bureau of Statistics 1972b
– 'The Co-Operative Development Plans 1964-74, a Performance Analysis.' Office of the Prime Minister and Second Vice-President, mimeo 1972c
– *Hali Ya Uchumi,* 1972-3, 1973-4[18]
– Ministry of Industry and Tourism, 'Cost of Hotels.' Mimeo, w.d.
Tanzania Investment Bank (TIB) *Rasilimali.* Dar es Salaam, TIB 1973
Tanzania Rural Development Bank (TRDB) *Annual Report and Accounts.* Dar es Salaam, TRDB 1970-71, 1971-2
Thomas, C. *Dependence and Transformation.* New York, Monthly Review 1974a
Thomas P.A., ed. *Private Enterprise and the East African Company.* Dar es Salaam, Tanzania Publishing House 1969
Todaro, M.P. 'A Model of Labor Migration and Urban Unemployment in Less Developed Countries.' *American Economic Review.* LIX, no. 1, March 1969
Tordoff, W. *Government and Politics in Tanzania.* Nairobi, East African Publishing House 1967
Turnham, D., assisted by I. Jarger *The Employment Problem in Less Developed Countries.* Paris OECD 1971
TWICO 'Feasibility Study for Sao-Hill.' 1972
Uchumi Editorial Board. *Towards Socialist Planning.* Dar es Salaam, Tanzania Publishing House 1972
Ward, A. *The Groundnut Affair.* London 1950
Wheelwright, E.L. and B. McFarlane *The Chinese Road to Socialism.* New York, Monthly Review 1970
Weisskopf, T. 'The Impact of Foreign Capital Inflow on Domestic Savings in Underdeveloped Countries.' *Journal of International Economics,* Feb. 1972
Wright, F.C. *African Consumers in Nyasaland and Tanganyika.* London, Her Majesty's Stationary Office 1955
Yaffey, M.J.H. *Balance of Payments Problems of a Developing Country: Tanzania.* Munich, Weltform Publishing House 1970

Glossary of abbreviations for ministries and parastatals

MINISTRY/PARASTATAL:	ABBREVATION USED IN THE TEXT
President's Office	CABINET
Central Establishment Division	ESTABS
Institute of Development Management	IDM
Ministry of Foreign Affairs	FOREIGN
Prime Minister's Office	PRIMEMINISTER
Ministry of Agriculture, Food and Co-operatives	KILIMO
National Agricultural Products Board	NAPB
Tanzania Sisal Board	TSB
Tanzania Tobacco Board	TTB
Tanzania Pyrethrum Board	TPB
Tanzania Coffee Board	TCB
Tanzania Sisal Corporation	TSC
Tanzania Tea Authority	TTA
National Milling Corporation	NMC
National Dairy Board	NDB
National Sugar Board	NSB
National Agricultural and Food Corporation	NAFCO
Lint and Seed Marketing Board	LSMB
Ministry of Economic Affairs and Development Planning	Devplan
National Scientific Research Council	NSRC
Ministry of National Education	EDUCATION
Ministry of Communication and Transport	COMWORKS
National Transport Corporation	NTC

Mwananchi Engineering and Construction Company Ltd.	MECCO
National Estates and Designing Company	NEDCO
Ministry of Commerce and Industries	MINCOM
National Development Corporation	NDC
State Trading Corporation	STC
National Distributors Ltd.	NDL
National Small Industries Corporation	NSIC
Tanzania Italian Petroleum Refinery Company	TIPER
Tanzania Petroleum Development Company	TPDC
Ministry of Lands, Housing and Urban Development	LANDSURVEY
National Housing Corporation	NHC
Ministry of Home Affairs	HOME AFFAIRS
Ministry of Health	HEALTH
Ministry of Information and Broadcasting	MAELEZO
Ministry of Finance	Treasury
Bank of Tanzania	BT
National Bank of Commerce	NBC
National Insurance Corporation	NIC
National Computer Corporation	NCC
Tanzania Audit Corporation	TAC
Tanzania Rural Development Bank	TRDB
Tanzania Investment Bank	TIB
Permanent Housing Finance Company of Tanzania Limited	PHFC
Tanzania Development Finance Company	TDFL
Institute of Finance Management	IFM
Ministry of Natural Resources and Tourism	Maliasili
National Parks	PARKS
Tanzania Wood Industries Corporation	TWICO
Tanzania Tourist Corporation	TTC
Ministry of Water Development and Power	MAJI
Tanzania Electricity Supply Company Ltd.	TANESCO
Ministry of Labour and Social Welfare	KAZI
Workers' Development Corporation	WDC
National Provident Fund	NPF

MULTI-NATIONAL PARASTATALS:

Directorate of Civil Aviation	DCA
East African Airways Corporation	EAAC

East African Community   EAC
East African Development Bank   EADB
East African Harbours Corporation   EAHC
East African National Shipping Line   EANSL
East African Posts and Telecommunication EAP & T
East African Railways Corporation   EARC
Tanzania-Zambia Railway Authority   Tazara
Tanzania-Zambia Pipeline   TAZAMA
Zambia-Tanzania Road Services   ZTRS

INTERNATIONAL ORGANIZATIONS:

African Development Bank   ADB
Commonwealth Development Corporation   CDC
Economic Commission for Africa   ECA
European Economic Community   EEC
International Bank for Reconstruction and Development
  (World Bank)   IBRD
International Monetary Fund   IMF
Swedish International Development Agency   SIDA
International Development Association   IDA
United Nations Conference on Trade and Development UNCTAD
United Nations Development Programme (Special Fund) UNDP (SF)
United Nations Educational, Scientific and Cultural
  Organization   UNESCO
United Nations Food and Agricultural Organization UNFAO
United States Agency for International Development USAID
World Health Organization   WHO

Index